T0360550

Organization as Time

The bulk of Management and Organization Studies deals with time as organization. Time is performed, organized, enacted, and as such is a locus of power. In this edited book, we stress the importance of organization as time. Time is an organizing force. The happening and becoming of collective activity, its technologies, its images, keep empowering, dominating or (more rarely) emancipating the fragile and ephemeral subjectivities of our world. The turn to digitality in all aspects of contemporary life has made the organizing power of time more pervasive than ever. How to describe organization as time? How to explore the relationship between becoming, duration, images, events, non-events or historicity and their relationships with power and emancipation? These are the rich and varied challenges seized by this book by a team of leading scholars interested in time and temporality in the context of management and organization.

François-Xavier de Vaujany is Professor of Organization Studies at Université Paris Dauphine-PSL (DRM). His research deals with the relationship between new ways of organizing work and societal transformations, particularly its time and space dimensions. His latest publications are *Apocalypse managériale* (Belles Lettres) and the co-edited *Oxford Handbook of Phenomenologies and Organization Studies* (Oxford University Press).

Robin Holt is Professor of Strategy and Aesthetics at the University of Bristol Business School and a visiting professor at Copenhagen Business School. He studies the nature of organizational form, with a specific interest in the aesthetic process of its creation (entrepreneurship) and shaping (strategy).

Albane Grandazzi has been Assistant Professor at Grenoble École de Management (GEM) since 2020. Her research is based on an ethnographic and critical approach to organization and management studies. She is interested in the role of the body in new work practices, building on the work of the philosopher Merleau-Ponty to this end. Her last publication, *The Oxford Handbook of Phenomenologies and Organization Studies* (Oxford University Press) is related to the role of gestures in this process.

Organization as Time

Technology, Power and Politics

Edited by

François-Xavier de Vaujany
Université Paris Dauphine-PSL

Robin Holt
University of Bristol Business School

Albane Grandazzi
Grenoble École de Management

CAMBRIDGE
UNIVERSITY PRESS

Shaftesbury Road, Cambridge CB2 8EA, United Kingdom

One Liberty Plaza, 20th Floor, New York, NY 10006, USA

477 Williamstown Road, Port Melbourne, VIC 3207, Australia

314–321, 3rd Floor, Plot 3, Splendor Forum, Jasola District Centre,
New Delhi – 110025, India

103 Penang Road, #05–06/07, Visioncrest Commercial, Singapore 238467

Cambridge University Press is part of Cambridge University Press & Assessment,
a department of the University of Cambridge.

We share the University's mission to contribute to society through the pursuit of
education, learning and research at the highest international levels of excellence.

www.cambridge.org
Information on this title: www.cambridge.org/9781009297257

DOI: 10.1017/9781009297288

© Cambridge University Press & Assessment 2023

This publication is in copyright. Subject to statutory exception and to the provisions
of relevant collective licensing agreements, no reproduction of any part may take
place without the written permission of Cambridge University Press & Assessment.

First published 2023

A catalogue record for this publication is available from the British Library.

*A Cataloging-in-Publication data record for this book is available from the Library of
Congress*

ISBN 978-1-009-29725-7 Hardback

Cambridge University Press & Assessment has no responsibility for the persistence
or accuracy of URLs for external or third-party internet websites referred to in this
publication and does not guarantee that any content on such websites is, or will
remain, accurate or appropriate.

Contents

Contents

Figures

Tables

Contributors

TIMOTHY BARKER, University of Glasgow

AMÉLIE BOUTINOT, EM Strasbourg Business School

ANDRÉ CARLOS BUSANELLI DE AQUINO, University of São Paolo

SYLVAIN COLOMBERO, Grenoble École de Management

RÉMY CONCHE, Université Paris Dauphine-PSL

GABRIEL J.COSTELLO, Galway-Mayo Institute of Technology

RENATA CHERÉM DE ARAÚJO PEREIRA, USP

FRANÇOIS-XAVIER DE VAUJANY, Université Paris Dauphine-PSL

HÉLÈNE DELACOUR, IAE Nancy School of Management

CLAIRE ESTAGNASIÉ, Université du Québec à Montréal & Université Côte d'Azur

JONATHAN FEDDERSEN, Copenhagen Business School

MIRIAM FEULS, Copenhagen Business School

WILLIAM M. FOSTER, University of Alberta

CHRISTIAN GARMANN JOHNSEN, Copenhagen Business School

SILVIA GHERARDI, University of Trento

ALBANE GRANDAZZI, Grenoble École de Management

TOR HERNES, Copenhagen Business School

ROBIN HOLT, University of Bristol

SAM HORNER, University of Liverpool

GAZI ISLAM, Grenoble École de Management

JOCHEN KOCH, European University Viadrina

HANNES KRÄMER, University of Duisburg-Essen

AURÉLIE LECLERCQ-VANDELANNOITTE, Centre National de la Recherche Scientifique, LEM and IESEG School of Management, University of Lille

CHRISTINA LÜTHY, Copenhagen Business School

DAMIAN O'DOHERTY, University of Liverpool

ANDREAS RECKWITZ, Humboldt University

ELEN RIOT, Université de Reims Champagne Ardenne

SILVIYA SVEJENOVA, Copenhagen Business School

DENIZ TUNÇALP, Istanbul Technical University

MARCO VELICOGNA, Institute of Legal Informatics and Judicial Systems of the National Research Council of Italy

MATTHIAS WENZEL, University of Lüneburg

MIKE ZUNDEL, University of Liverpool

Organization as Time
Power and Emancipation in the Happening of Management

François-Xavier de Vaujany, Robin Holt and Albane Grandazzi

Introduction

As Virginia Woolf put it, clocks are machines that strike time. To strike is to hit, but also to found or yield, and in periodically referring to the bell Big Ben marking the hours in her novel *Mrs Dalloway*, Woolf attends to this intimacy between organization, sound and time passing. As the quarter hours are struck the civic, commercial, ritual and domestic rhythms of London unfold with a distinct yet mutually accommodating order:

Shredding and slicing, dividing and subdividing, the clocks of Harley Street nibbled at the June day, counselled submission, held authority, and pointed out in chorus the supreme advantages of a sense of proportion, until the mound of time was so far diminished that a commercial clock, suspended above a shop in Oxford Street, announced genially and fraternally, as if it were a pleasure to Messrs. Rigby and Lowndes, to give the information gratis, that it was half-past one. (Woolf, 1925, 154–5)

It is as if the city is nothing other than a meshwork of temporalities evoking and organizing the localized activity: Harley Street for doctors, Oxford Street for the retail trade, and so on. These are most obviously clock based, such as timetables, delivery times, deadlines and most markedly, the bell ('[F]irst a warning, musical; then the hour, irrevocable') (Woolf, 1925, p. 5). Yet into the structure provided by these materializations of time Woolf introduces the 'inner' time of recollection and expectation. The clocks and bells are not just spatial and aural marks: their appearance resonates with sonorities, with fate and with uncertainty. The boundaries between inner experience and outward structures are porous, which is what lends the novel its peculiarly atmospheric quality. Immediate emotional disturbances thrown up by small temporal events, like looking in a mirror ('How many million times she had seen her face, and always with the same imperceptible

1

contraction!') (Woolf, 1925, p. 55) vie with the natural and social facts of time, such as work rhythms ('There Rezia sat at the table trimming hats. She trimmed hats for Mrs Filmer's friends; she trimmed hats by the hour. She looked pale and mysterious, like a lily, drowned, under water, he thought') (Woolf, 1925, p. 134) or historical eras ('This late age of the world's experience had bred in them all, all men and women, a well of tears.') (Woolf, 1925, p. 13).

It has been almost a century since Woolf wrote *Mrs Dalloway*, during which time the study of organization and its management has become a disciplinary field. Though time is intimate to the emergence of this field (as is witnessed, for example, by Lillian Gilbreth's ground-breaking studies on time and motion in the workplace, and Pitirim Sorokin and Robert Merton's (1937) studies of social time), it is only recently that it has been understood as more than an uncontested, inexhaustible passage of discrete spatial moments marked by a 't' axis. Through the influence of sociologists, social theorists, philosophers of science and social psychologists like Eviatar Zerubavel (1981), Ilya Prigogine and Isabelle Stengers (1988), Barbara Adam (1990), Niklas Luhmann (1995, 2012) and Helga Nowotny (2008), and through journals like *Time and Society*, greater attention is now being paid to the internal, phenomenological experience of time structures, as well as to analyzing how (social) machinery *produces* time. Fact, it seems, is finally catching up with fiction. It is to continuing this study of the intimacy between organization, management and time that the chapters of this book are devoted.

Arguably, time grounds both the practice of managing and the process of organizing (Whipp et al., 2002; Blyton et al., 2017). Management produces nothing; its sole function is to orchestrate and guide productive activity from a set of initial conditions to a desired outcome. As such, it is grounded in what Paul Ricoeur (2014) calls the measured structures of before, now and after, and the experiential structures of past, present and future. In combination, we argue that these two intimately related forms of time constitute the possibility of management. Without them there is neither a sense of progress nor the possibility of being held accountable for such progression. Time also figures as an *a priori* in organization, not in terms of an explicitly stated future toward which managers cybernetically (rationally) steer an organization, but as a raw expression of movement and growth, an inherent mobility in which things are coming into being, and doing so in the company of other beings, all of which beckons organization.

When combined, the intimacy of management, organization and time becomes apparent as an expression of power: the power to grow and move, the power to control and survey, and the power to claim responsibility and authority. For example, in Europe, the idea of a 'working day' emerged with the institution of the Gregorian calendar (Hamann, 2016) (further abetted by developments in factory machinery and architecture and transportation, see Bradbury & Collette, 2009). The seasonally governed growth cycles of agrarian systems gave way to an idea of accumulative growth of capital, which in turn legitimated the overt forms of management needed to oversee and warrant the explicit form that a working day would take. Power shifted from an aristocracy naturally endowed with puissance, and from priests requiring abeyance and sacrifice in exchange for garlanded fate, to managed futures and industrialized factory systems (de Vaujany et al., 2021).

Despite this, and somewhat paradoxically, the field of management and organization studies has tended to separate issues of politics and power on the one hand and issues of time and temporality on the other.[1] Most management and organization scholars interested in politics and power (often, though not exclusively, going by the moniker critical management studies) tend to skew their analytic frame toward space, spacing and spatial practices (Fleming & Spicer, 2004; Kornberger & Clegg, 2004; Dale & Burrell, 2007; Kerr & Robinson, 2016). Historically speaking, perhaps we can blame the long-standing association of human autonomy with an inner sphere, or of sovereignty with a body, or of politics with the maintenance of borders between private and public, self and state, or between regions, or of love and the family with a household. Though he thought it was 'time' (in the guise of historical development) that received too much attention in social science, we might blame the genius of Michel Foucault (1977) for management and organization studies' concern with space, notably in his likening the decentering of attention and the pervasiveness of disciplinary force and surveillance to a panopticon. Power becomes a pervading, atmospheric phenomena, utterly spatial.

This association of power and space sets the scene for much of the critical work being done in management and organization studies. Yet upon examination we find the temporal arising quite naturally from spatial analyses. Zuboff (2019), for example, in her analysis of 'surveillance capitalism' draws extensively on spatialized metaphors such as oversight, instrumentarium, 'the virgin territory of personal experience', 'the architecture of choice' managed through nudge theory, or the closed loop between digital and surveillance capitalism. Yet her critique also hints at the temporal structures, those that we find often absent in many other critical studies, now the Marxist historicism has been largely junked. Zuboff is attentive, for example, to how recommender systems of social media or platform

---

[1] In contrast to other fields, for example, philosophy and anthropology (see Colley et al., 2012; Hassid & Watson, 2014; Akbari-Dibavar & Emiljanowicz, 2019; Portschy, 2020).

organizations contrive a future utterly indebted to a past over which they have control, and to how the history of capitalist development is character-ized by periodic ruptures in common norms that are then concealed through a collective forgetting (transforming farmers into factory workers was as unnatural as harnessing a deer into a plough; that is, she says, until social amnesia set in). Zuboff's work is interesting in this regard because it acknowledges how the spatial is inherently temporal, and, on the other side, how time appears more as a juxtaposition of rhythms and tempos in societal and commercial dynamics.

Lefebvre (2004, see also Beyes & Holt, 2020) is interesting on this issue of multiplicity of rhythms and the intermingling of space and time. He develops a conceptualization of a 'rhythmanalysis' that theorizes the role of rhythms and the conflict between temporalities in daily activities. Rhythms are temporal structures defined by repetition and difference of our activities and social spaces. This temporal analysis is part of a post-Marxist, micro-critique of daily working and social life which fights against the abstractions of social space and time that constrains repetitive activities and gestures in a productive logic of capital translation. Lefebvre distinguishes two kinds of rhythms that both produce repetition: what he names a 'linear rhythm' (i.e repetition that produces similarity) and a 'cyclical rhythm' (i.e. repetition that produces creation). Lefebvre's work is particularly interesting in this regard because it reconsiders the 'linear' as potentially creative. His work calls for considering the rhythm through a political perspective in the struggle between 'linear rhythm' and 'cyclical rhythm'. It would seem that a developed and considered concern with time enriches studies of politics and power.

On the other side, those management and organization studies scholars interested in temporality and time as something more than a background variable (often, though not exclusively, gathered around the moniker process studies) conceptualize organizations and societies as flows, activities, events, force, becoming or lines (see Tsoukas & Chia, 2002; Helin et al., 2014; Hernes, 2014; de Vaujany & Aroles, 2019; Holt & Johnsen, 2019; de Vaujany, 2022a). But politics and power are rarely explicitly part of these discussions. By making them so in this volume we begin to make explicit connections between the humility and connect-ivity implied in process philosophy and what Jacques Rancière (2010, p. 62) has called *the political*, by which he meant the unstructured, open and discursive exchange of the voices of the surplus, the left over, the unlearned, those who have no warrant for their opinion outside of their being a human with a voice. This includes everyone, but only insofar as they embrace the dissensus and refuse the comforts of an informed position with its attendant set of interests.

Relatedly, we tease out the political implications between process philosophy and the time-based categorization of a planet irrevocably touched by human organization, a hybridity most recently made explicit by the unapologetically species-centric concept of 'the Anthropocene'. Against this backdrop, is it right to continue to talk only of flows, flux and force, of affects and sensory immersion, of an ungovernable reality, rather than seek more active organizational structures through which distinct forms can be brought into existence by way of offering resilience, reparation, refuge? We acknowledge process studies has had a critical edge when used in management and organization studies. For example, in the philosophies of Elizabeth Grosz or Rosi Braidotti, who sense how events, in prehending one another, or in continually calling one another or conversing with each other, are caught in relations of mutual captivation, but not capture. This opening up of what is otherwise a fixing, defining and presumably instituted relationship of overt control has allowed them to offer penetrating analyses of the normal, and hence invisible, ways in which female or minority lives are being persistently skewered by prevailing norms and habits. Yet more still might be done from within process studies, notably in attending to how the world, far from being a democracy of things connecting and reconnecting in open networks of mutual agency, is often characterized by stark and abusive hierarchies that emerge from processual forms like networks (see Dean, 2020).

By considering more politically attuned thinkers such as Foucault (*dispositifs*, which settle or sediment subjectivities), process studies can open the way to a more political prehension, so to speak (Eriksson, 2005). Process studies might also consider the political implications of pragmatic philosophy, which has inspired some process studies (see Lorino, 2018), and which has been made organizationally explicit in the writing of Mary Parker Follett (cf. Hernes, 2022), but which seems to have been bypassed by those who espouse a pragmatic framing. The form of inquiry adopted by the likes of John Dewey (1938), for example, stresses the importance of differences, gaps or *écarts*. Without these glitches and ruptures (to recall Rancière's point on dissensus) it is impossible to create a community of inquiry with the flexibility or creativity necessary to solve organizational problems (see also Jullien, 2012). Problematization, transactions and instruments of inquiry are interesting processes to put in conversation with the Foucauldian *dispositifs*. Inquiry fosters a plurality of activities (ahead) instead of a diversity of controlled individuality (in the past and the present).

If some process (and critical) scholars explore the conceptual avenues sketched by Foucault, Deleuze or Dewey, very few define it, and instead link it to a more general conversation between the topics of temporality and the topics of politics (cf. Langley, 2016).

The Structure of the Book

Though we could have fixed on others, we found it interesting to fix on a distinct pairing of the French theorists and writers Gilles Deleuze and Michel Foucault to help orient us to the themes raised in the chapters. They are both thinkers who are alive to the spatial as well as temporal aspects of organization and management, as well as to how neither organization nor management can be understood without a sensitivity to power and politics.

Deleuze (as is expressed, for example, in his work on cinema) finds a world in movement, in the making (see Roets & Braidotti, 2012), and as such, power becomes a raw, natural force of desire and growth which occur spontaneously, and configure *ensembles* (*agencement*). These have a tangibility, but without ever gaining distinct objecthood (see Deleuze, 1988–1989). Given this grounding condition of reality, there is, at root, an indistinguishability of subjects and objects. All occurrence is braided within, and inseparable from, a plane of immanence which itself is being formed in creepages (*lignes de fuite*), ray-like intersections of light express-ing differences in speed and intensity. Politics and power are inseparable from *agencements*, and hence remain in the pre-linguistic or pre-subjective making/folding of a world that is continually underway. Talk of good or bad, fair or unfair, settling justice or not settling justice, yields to talk of connectedness itself, of relations and flow. Freedom is already in the inside of the world. Nothing is frozen, possessed, occupied; the ultimate expression of this being the patient and immobile movement of the nomad: moving but 'not to leave'.

For Foucault, the processuality of the world is also key. But in contrast, and notably during the third and last stage of his intellectual trajectory, Foucault emphasized an ethic of care in the distinct, human subject: an 'attitude' of attending to the emergence of the self from within the agonistic quality of each event (Dews, 1984; Revel, 2015; Stark, 2017; de Vaujany, 2022b). Without the admittedly needy, fragile and explora-tory process of co-appropriating subjectivities being negotiated between multiple beings wrapped in the same situational possibilities, no 'better world' is possible.

This distinction between Foucault and Deleuze epitomizes what we found to be a polarity of influence and emphasis amongst the chapters of the book. Some chapters emphasize care, emancipatory temporalities, creativity or the metaphysical tragedy of existence. Others stress more the importance of alternative *agencements*, intensities in organizing, material vibrations and forces as political *per se* and temporal performativity of managerial assemblages. These divergences should not be exaggerated. Nearly all the chapters stress the importance of non-dualist, post-human, temporal, material and affective views of organizing and managing.

Our book is split into four parts.[2]

Part I – 'The Politics of Time: Ontologies and Metaphysics of Organization as Time' – is devoted to metaphysical discussions around time and power, in particular, through a systematic re-exploration of core processual concepts and how they feed or can feed different ongoing debates in management and organization studies about time and power. In Chapter 1, Tim Barker discusses 'Media Temporalities and the Technical Image'. He comes back to the work of Alfred North Whitehead and explores what is at stake in the temporalities of our digital age. Chapter 2 by Miriam Feuls, Christina Lüthy and Silviya Svejenova is entitled 'Material Temporal Work in Artistic Innovation: How Hilma af Klint Powered Time'. Theirs is an art-based analysis of temporalities in creative practice, one they centre on the making of a 'her'. Chapter 3 – In the Practice *Agencement*: Rhythms, Refrains and Feminist Snaps – focusses on the processual category of practice, finding Silvia Gherardi coming back to core metaphysical debates on post-humanist views of practice. Lastly, Rémy Conche explores the metaphysical tragedy of time, detailing an existential metaphysics in a chapter entitled 'Metaphysics of Tragedy, a Non-Dispositional View of Time'.

Part II – 'Re-orienting Critique in Organization Studies? Exploring Jointly Time and Politics' – is more programmatic, focussing on a more explicit and targeted discussion about politics and time. In Chapter 5, Gabriel J. Costello deconstructs 'supersessionism' in a piece entitled 'Supersessionism and the Politics of Time: Reforming Organisational Studies with Gadamer's Hermeneutic of Trust'. In Chapter 6, François-Xavier de Vaujany, Aurélie Leclercq-Vandelanoitte and Gazi Islam put forward the concept of emancipatory temporalities, inviting scholars to explore the in-betweenness of abandon and dérive in management and organizing in a chapter entitled 'Between Abandon and Inquiry: On the Way to Emancipatory Temporalities in Organizing'. Chapter 7 – 'Future Work: Toward a Practice Perspective' – by Matthias Wenzel Hannes Krämer, Jochen Koch and Andreas Reckwitz focusses on the issue of strategizing and its political as well as organizational

---

[2] Following the 11th Organizations, Artifacts and Practices (OAP) workshop "Politics of Time: From Control to Self-Control in Organizing?" (17th and 18th June 2021). This two-day international event gathered 237 scholars from different fields (Management and Organization Studies, Sociology, Philosophy, STS).

constitution in the experience of envisaging, or imagining, the future. Lastly, Damian O'Doherty analyzes the politics at stake in small, ordinary, organizational events; in this case the appearance of a bob-cut hairstyle in Chapter 8 – 'Towards a Crinicultural Activism in Organization'.

Part III – 'New Ways of Organizing Work, Digitality and the Politics of Time' – covers a key topic of management and organization studies likely to resonate with our inquiry about time and politics: novelty, and in line with that, so-called new ways of working and organizing. Claire Estagnasié, in Chapter 9 entitled – '"Working the Time": Time Self-Management Practices of Remote Workers', explores various forms of temporal practices of remote workers. In Chapter 10, Renata Cherém de Araújo Pereira and André Carlos Busanelli De Aquino analyze 'Temporal Structures Telework in Public Sector Organizations' by emphasizing temporal conflicts. Jonathan Feddersen, Tor Hernes and Silviya Svejenova explore 'Towards a Processual Understanding of Buildings: Temporality, Materiality, and Politics' in Chapter 11. In Chapter 12, Christian Garmann Johnsen considers the temporality of entrepreneurial memory and imagination by examining 'The Temporality of Entrepreneurship: How Entrepreneurs Blend Memories and Projections in the Ongoing Present of New Venture Creations'. Lastly, in Chapter 13, François-Xavier de Vaujany and Elen Riot discuss and offer the concept of 'Management as Dramatic Events: Intense Decentered Organizing (IDO)'.

Part IV – 'History and Duration: Making Things Last, Enduring Politics and Organizing' – covers historical and performative relations. In Chapter 14, Deniz Tunçalp analyzes 'Times *Alla Turca E Franga*: Conceptions of Time and the Materiality of the Late-Ottoman Clock Towers' through a microhistorical perspective. Chapter 15 by Amélie Boutinot, Sylvain Colombero and Hélène Delacour elaborates on 'Temporality and Institutional Maintenance: The Role of Reactivation Work on Material Artefacts'. Chapter 16 by Marco Velicogna offers an historical view on justice through a chapter entitled 'A Time for Justice? Reflecting on the Many Facets of Time and Temporality in Justice Service Provision'. Finally, in Chapter 17, Mike Zundel, Sam Horner and William M. Foster uncover the processes of 'Organizational Memory as Technology'. This volume closes with the concluding chapter by volume editors François-Xavier de Vaujany, Robin Holt and Albane Grandazzi, 'Time and Political Organizing: Five Avenues for Further Research on the Way to Power and Emancipation'.

References

Adam, B. (1990). *Time and Social Theory*. Philadelphia: Temple University Press.
Akbari-Dibavar, A. & Emiljanowicz, P. (2019). Colonial time in tension: Decolonizing temporal imaginaries. *Time & Society*, *28*(3), 1221–38.
Beyes, T. & Holt, R. (2020). The topographical imagination: Space and organization theory. *Organization Theory*. https://doi.org/10.1177/2631787720913880.
Blyton, P., Hassard, J., Hill, S. & Starkey, K. (2017). *Time, Work and Organisation* (Vol. 7). London: Taylor & Francis.
Bradbury, N. M. & Collette, C. P. (2009). Changing times: The mechanical clock in late medieval literature. *The Chaucer Review*, *43*(4), 351–75.
Colley, H., Henriksson, L., Niemeyer, B. & Seddon, T. (2012). Competing time orders in human service work: Towards a politics of time. *Time & Society*, *21* (3), 371–94.
Dale, K. & Burrell, G. (2007). *The Spaces of Organisation and the Organisation of Space: Power, Identity and Materiality at Work*. London: Palgrave Macmillan.
de Vaujany, F-X. (2022a). Imagining the name of the rose with Deleuze: Organizational and self world-making on the screen. *Culture and Organization*. https://doi.org/10.1080/14759551.2022.2105338.
de Vaujany, F-X. (2022b). From Phenomenology to a Metaphysics of History: The Unfinished Odyssey of Merleau-Ponty. In F-X. de Vaujany, J. Aroles & M. Pérezts (eds), *The Oxford Handbook of Phenomenologies and Organization Studies*. Oxford: Oxford University Press.
de Vaujany, F-X. & Aroles, J. (2019). Nothing happened, something happened: Silence in a makerspace. *Management Learning*, *50*(2), 208–25.
de Vaujany, F-X., Leclercq-Vandelannoitte, A., Munro, I., Nama, Y. & Holt, R. (2021). Control and surveillance in work practice: Cultivating paradox in 'new' modes of organizing. *Organization Studies*, *42*(5), 675–95.
Dean, J. (2020). Communism or neo-Feudalism? *New Political Science*, *42* (1), 1–17.
Deleuze, G. (1988–1989). *Abécédaire de Gille Deleuze*, interviews with Deleuze https://youtube.com/playlist?list=PLiR8NqajHNPbaX2rBoA2z6IPGpU0IP lS2 (see entry on 'desire').
Dewey, J. (1938). The pattern of inquiry. *The Essential Dewey*, *2*, 169–79.
Dews, P. (1984). Power and subjectivity in Foucault. *New Left Review*, *144*(1), 72–95.
Eriksson, K. (2005). Foucault, Deleuze, and the ontology of networks. *The European Legacy*, *10*(6), 595–610.
Fleming, P. & Spicer, A. (2004). 'You can checkout anytime, but you can never leave': Spatial boundaries in a high commitment organization. *Human Relations*, *57*(1), 75–94.
Foucault, M. (1977). *Discipline and Punish: The Birth of the Prison*. New York: Random House.
Hamann, B. E. (2016). How to chronologize with a hammer, or, the myth of homogeneous, empty time. *HAU: Journal of Ethnographic Theory*, *6*(1), 261–92.
Hassid, J. & Watson, B. C. (2014). State of mind: Power, time zones and symbolic state centralization. *Time & Society*, *23*(2), 167–94.

Helin, J., Hernes, T., Hjorth, D. & Holt, R. (eds) (2014). *The Oxford Handbook of Process Philosophy and Organization Studies*. Oxford: Oxford University Press.

Hernes, T. (2014). *A Process Theory of Organization*. Oxford: Oxford University Press.

Hernes, T. (2022). *Organization and Time*. Oxford: Oxford University Press.

Holt, R. & Johnsen, R. (2019). Time and organization studies. *Organization Studies*, 40(10), 1557–72.

Jullien, F. (2012). *L'écart et l'entre. Leçon inaugurale de la Chaire sur l'altérité*. Paris: Galilée.

Kerr, R. & Robinson, S. (2016). Architecture, symbolic capital and elite mobilisations: The case of the Royal Bank of Scotland corporate campus. *Organization*, 23(5), 699–721.

Kornberger, M. & Clegg, S. R. (2004). Bringing space back in: Organizing the generative building. *Organization Studies*, 25(7), 1095–14.

Langley, A. (2016). *The SAGE Handbook of Process Organization Studies*. London: Sage.

Lefebvre, H. (2004). *Rhythmanalysis: Space, Time and Everyday Life*. London & New York: Continuum.

Lorino, P. (2018). Pragmatism and *Organization Studies*. London: Oxford University Press.

Luhmann, N. (1995). *Social Systems* (p. 158). California: Stanford University Press.

Luhmann, N. (2012). *Theory of Society* (Vol. 1). California: Stanford University Press.

Nowotny, H. (2008). *Insatiable Curiosity: Innovation in a Fragile Future*. Cambridge, MA: MIT Press.

Portschy, J. (2020). Times of power, knowledge and critique in the work of Foucault. *Time & Society*, 29(2), 392–419.

Prigogine, I. & Stengers, I. (1988) Entre le temps et l'eternité. Paris: Fayard.

Rancière, J. (2010). *Dissensus*. Trans. Steven Corcoran. London: Bloomsbury.

Revel, J. (2015). *Foucault avec Merleau-Ponty: ontologie politique, présentisme et histoire*. Paris: Vrin.

Ricoeur, P. (2014). *Time and Narrative* (Vol. 3). Chicago: University of Chicago Press.

Roets, G. & Braidotti, R. (2012). Nomadology and Subjectivity: Deleuze, Guattari and Critical Disability Studies. In *Disability and Social Theory* (pp. 161–78). London:Palgrave Macmillan.

Sorokin, P. A. & Merton, R. K. (1937). Social time: A methodological and functional analysis. *American Journal of Sociology*, 42, 615–29.

Stark, H. (2017). Deleuze, subjectivity and nonhuman becomings in the Anthropocene. *Dialogues in Human Geography*, 7(2), 151–5.

Tsoukas, H. & Chia, R. (2002). On organizational becoming: Rethinking organizational change. *Organization Science*, 13(5), 567–82.

Whipp, R., Adam, B. & Sabelis, I. (eds.) (2002). *Making Time: Time and Management in Modern Organisations*. Oxford: Oxford University Press.

Woolf, V. (1925). *Mrs Dalloway*. New York: Harcourt Brace.

Zerubavel, E. (1981). *Hidden Rhythms: Schedules and Calendars in Social Life*. Chicago: University of Chicago Press.

Zuboff, S. (2019). *The Age of Surveillance Capitalism*. Boston: Profile Books Ltd.

Part I

The Politics of Time: Ontologies and Metaphysics of Organization as Time

1 Media Temporalities and the Technical Image

Timothy Barker

Introduction

This chapter begins with a rather simple observation: that something has changed in the condition of the image. Over the last two decades or so, one type of image has been coming to an end, in place of another. The photographic image and the cinematic image have been replaced by what scholars such as Steven Shaviro (2010) and Shane Denson (2020) call the 'post-cinematic' imaging regime, which *includes* the cinematic and photographic, but only inasmuch as they are now seen as data to be computed. Once, the photographic and – by extension – the cinematic was dominant in culture. But now that all images are reduced to digital information processed by computers, the images that are the outputs of programs have become the form on which visual culture is produced, whether in films and television, video games, surveillance, art or advertising. This has implications for the way that we discuss the ontology of images, but also for the conditions of representation, particularly the conditions for the representation of time and by extension the conditions for the possibility of being-in-time.

As is no doubt well known to readers of this chapter, discussions of time, the image, and analogue media have a long history: Marshall McLuhan wrote about the temporality of both older inscription technologies and newer electronic media such as television, Roland Barthes wrote about the temporality of the photograph, Gilles Deleuze the temporality of cinema and Mary Ann Doane and Jonathan Crary have linked the temporality of the image to the discourses of modernity, progress and machines. But now, as computers rather than cameras become the be-all-and-end-all of imaging systems, a new type of temporality has replaced the time-image of cinema and the memories expressed in the photographic.

This chapter continues my recent research on the idea of contemporaneity and what it means to live 'in the present' by exploring the conditions for representation produced by such images. Beginning with the media philosopher, Vilém Flusser, I unpack the term 'technical image', which he uses to signify images produced by photographs, films, television and computers. These are images that, according to Flusser, are produced by the automatic function of an apparatus, which breaks images down into smaller elements (pixels, scan lines, frames or grains). Flusser uses this concept to think about the camera as the machine at the start of a new imagining regime, culminating in video and computer-generated images. My use of Flusser's term is slightly different. I would like to use the method for analysing images given to us by Flusser but use the term 'technical image' to unpack and explore the differences between synthetic images – understood as images that present viewers with a unified whole – and images that break a pre-given unity into discrete pixelated elements. I try and go further than Flusser's original formulation of the technical image by tracing its genealogy in much older media used for measurement and the particalisation of events: these are what I refer to in this chapter as *analytical media*. I argue that these types of analytical media, which pre-date the synthesis of the cinema, are now returning in the world produced by technical images. From here, I look at a number of contemporary artworks that further explore what it is to live in the conditions produced by these machines and how this produces a different temporality to that which characterised western modernity.

The conditions for viewing the world through technical images are, according to Flusser, the last in a line of shifts related to techniques of mark making. He writes that first pre-historical man created images to understand the world. A picture of a bull on a cave wall allows you to recognise and hunt one with more precision (Flusser, [1985]2011, pp. 11–12). He goes on to say that historical man then wrote text to explain images, which became non-reversible events in time, where cause followed on from effect. The hunt became a story, a unique event. The world was made comprehensible by projecting onto it the linear structure of the written word. For Flusser, these shifts imply not only a set of key moments in media history, but also a shift in the way time can be represented. In the traditional image, time is circular; the viewer's eyes can wander over its surface, making combinations of objects that are presented all at once. The image is rich with non-linear information flows. The shift to linear writing, for Flusser, then signalled a shift into the time of history, as the eye moves over the text, following a line, with one event following on from another. The shift to the technical image implies a further shift in the way time can be represented and thus understood. No longer gesturing towards the future, no longer a linear progression through information like the printed word, the technical image emphasises the way events can be deconstructed into smaller parts in the present, based on a program.

Although perhaps a little too linear and a little too neat, the shifts that Flusser describes are useful. This is not because we can, in any way, imagine the entire globe caught up in the same shifts between inscription practices (which Flusser might be accused of), but because they introduce to us, as media theorists and philosophers, a new way to address images. It has to be said that it is doubtlessly true that not all images are now technical and not all writing has been overtaken by computation. In fact, as Friedrich Kittler has argued, the electronic binary computer system still processes strings of information and thus remains based on a type of linear reading. But what Flusser gives us is a way of addressing the forms of thinking and relating to technology that are the result of the admission that humans have become functionaries within image-making systems, rather than its authors or audiences. The insight that Flusser gives us is that the way these apparatuses organise information corresponds to the way we come to know the world that they represent. This occurs once the computer outstrips our perception, once we realise that the image can be deconstructed into parts that are only able to be calculated and hence made comprehensible by computers. As Claus Pias (2003) has argued, when images become a sequence of addresses and values, they are no longer the images they once were. At this stage these new types of images become discorrelated from human perception (Denson, 2020).

Ever since the invention of traditional images, humans have used them to understand the world. The image on the cave wall allows for the deciphering of hunted animals. As Flusser argues, we know the animals because we have a picture of them. The image becomes projected onto experience; it is used to make the events of the hunt comprehensible. This was extended and made linear with the widespread adoption of written texts. Flusser often suggested that the world itself was chaotic and that to understand it we needed to process it based on a program, whether this be the program of traditional images, the program of writing or the program of technical images. The difference with the technical image is that its program now outstrips the human, no longer including them as authors of the image. This what leads Flusser to say that, no longer understandable completely, the chaotic events of the world are now only comprehensible if they are first computed, if the program of technical images is projected onto them, which sorts them algorithmically. In this sense, the technical image signals a type of post-humanism, as the image is no longer associated with what the human author or human viewer sees, but rather determined by what the apparatus can pick up, record, process, store and transmit based on its program.

But this is not to say that the technical image offers its viewers immediate access to the world as it is. For Flusser, nothing could be further from the truth. Instead, Flusser is at pains to tell us that the technical image *is an image*; it is a transformation of an event into a scene. This is important to remember because, as he argues, the magic of technical images is that they convince their audiences to project their programs onto the world, so that they begin to see the world through technically produced modes of seeing. We begin to see the world and events through an intense focus on the present, the smallest bits of information, which is supported by our belief in programs. Flusser, ([1983]2014) writes:

... there is something we can say about these images after all. For example, they are not windows but images, ie surfaces that translate everything into states of things; like all images, they have a magical effect; and they entice those receiving them to project this undecoded magic onto the world out there. The magical fascination of technical images can be observed all over the place: the way in which they put a magic spell on life, the way in which we experience, know, evaluate and act as a function of these images. It is therefore important to enquire into what sort of magic we are dealing with here. (p. 16)

Flusser explains that the magic that is involved is related to the technical term 'program', as a form of written instructions, which imposes itself on the world 'out there', in a different way to traditional images and written texts. The program gives its users a way of making images automatically: the camera works according to a program, the television receives and processes signal according to a program, the computer can edit together frames, can create new images that never before existed and can rearrange pixels according to a program. The users of this apparatus produce images on computer screens, they use cameras to record images and computers to manipulate them. They upload these images and are able to store them in an archive, making their memories external. Like Stiegler's work on the technical essence of humans and tertiary memory, Flusser shows how technological apparatuses act as externalisations of memory. In Flusser though, humans act in order that machines can function, becoming themselves parts of the machine, rather than the other way around. These users, rather than the creators of images, are instead seen by Flusser as feedback mechanisms for the apparatus itself and the mechanism for its expansion. As users play with computers, manipulating images, they work within the computer's program and incrementally improve its operability, improving what it can do, improving the program, as they continue to push it further into every aspect of daily life. The important difference between the program of writing or the program of traditional images is that the program of technical images is there for the machine to follow, not the human. Writing and painting follow a set of standard protocols, whether this be grammar or the laws of perspective. The artist creates based on a relationship to these standards. In the case of technical images, the program instructs the apparatus how to produce images, not the human user, who instead has to learn the rules of the interface. As Wendy Chun (2013) puts it, because the programmed rules remain invisible to the user – those intricate pathways, frictions and fissions that control the production and circulation of images, that limit possibilities and veil other possible responses – the user is no longer 'in the picture'. It is in this sense that, for Flusser, society becomes merely a function for the image-making apparatus, extending its capacities and driving the development of its program.

We can now make two claims about Flusser's technical image: (1) the technical image is produced by an apparatus that operates automatically to separate events into segments that can then be reassembled to create an image; this process is based on a program; and (2) human users become functionaries of the technical image by projecting its way of calculating and evaluating events, so that there is no other possibility of understanding the world outside of its program. The result is an intense focus on the present and the measurable, rather than the unformed future. For Flusser, the only way for us to resist becoming functionaries of technical images and subjects of the temporality that they produce is to remain aware of their programs, and to visualise their codes and operations (Ieven, 2003).

Now of course, the existence of the technical image is not always apparently different from traditional images. The pixel, the point, the meaningless image-components, are not usually experienced in any direct way. They are usually hidden behind images, they disappear so that the image itself can appear, circumventing our perception. This is why it is often thought that the processing of images has no effect on us at all. After all, we see images at the end of the transmission chain, after they have been processed. But this is precisely why it is important to think about them. These once invisible things are now the foundation for digital culture and are constantly experienced vicariously through our interaction with technical images. They matter not in the same way that on-screen visual content matters. Instead, they matter precisely because they contribute to what *can be represented* and what we consider as 'real'. As Friedrich Kittler first said, the real is now reduced to that which is switchable and that which is thus able to be read by the technical program of the electronic binary computer (Kittler, [1999]2010, p. 225).

The computer highlights the segmented nature of moving images, whereas in perception, the human senses only pick up and register the moving image, rather than the still frames or separate pixels. But these usually invisible things, although meaningless in the conventional sense, provide the conditions for the possibility of experience, the possibility of communication, the 'imperceptible background' (Hansen, 2015, p. 143), and, as will be argued in what follows, underpin the way time can be represented. In the following, the term *analytical media* is used to describe these machines.

The analytical measures what is thought to be self-evident; it scrutinises what is already there. The synthetic on the other hand produces novelty, it is contingent and moves forward into a field of chaos, creating something new, becoming, producing the unformed, causing things to appear. Analytical media take events as a pre-given occurrence, subtract time and analyse them as discrete instants, no longer moving towards an unformatted future. The computer is not the only analytical medium, but it is the one that provides the most easily identifiable metaphor for the analytical tendencies of digital culture, so much so that theorists have begun arguing that the algorithm actually provides the means with which to understand contemporary life (Beer, 2009; Neyland, 2015; Slavin, 2011; Totaro & Ninno, 2016). This is one aspect of programmable, analytical media, but the other, more worrying aspect, is the temporality that it introduces, where the future is never allowed to exist as a field of potential.

Time

Wolfgang Ernst, one of the key voices in media theoretical considerations of time, has, like Flusser, taken a technico-mathematical approach to reconceiving the time of the digital present. As Ernst (2015) argues:

In digital culture more than ever, the present is immediately quantized, 'sampled and held' (the electronic pre-condition for real-time digital-signal processing). The audiovisual and textual present is being archived as soon as it happens – from Twitter messages and instant photography to sound recording. But even more dramatically undoing the traditional order of times, big data analysis algorithmically predicts the future already as future-in-the-past (futurum exactum). Never has a culture been more dynamically 'archival' than the present epoch of digital media. (p. 22)

The archival, rather than the historical character of the contemporary moment is a product of technical media that is able to process signal based on the von Neumann architecture and store this data along with instructions (algorithms) for processing future signal. The archive not only holds onto the past, but the future perfect as well (what Ernst calls the future exactum), as a future that has not yet but inevitably will (statistically) take place. The present begins to dilate into other spheres of time (past and future). It becomes the condition from which the future and the past are written.

Luciano Floridi, the important philosopher of information, offers a similar formulation in his description of what he terms 'hyperhistory'. According to Floridi, the historical subject lives in a world where information communication technologies (ICTs), since the development of the proto-writing systems around 8,000 BCE, are used to record and transmit data. In so-called 'hyperhistory' ICTs recorded, transmitted and *processed* data autonomously and, because of this, human societies became dependent on them as a vital resource (Floridi, 2015, pp. 51–2). What we find in this element of Floridi's thought, as well as that of both Flusser and Ernst, is the possibility for a media philosophy that offers a way to think about mediated time and temporality as it is related to information storage and processing. To conceptualise and critique the time of the digital, media theory needs to expand discussions beyond historical time and its relation to the 'cinematic time' that marked out modernity. Time, in this era of discourse, was represented by a succession of images, moving towards the ungiven and ungiveable whole. The image, as Deleuze told us, once created a rupture, a line of flight, a torrent towards a deindividuated becoming. But now things have changed; the conditions for the representation of time have shifted. A media philosophy of time now calls for a focus on the non-discursive function of media, which is radically different from an emphasis on the synthesis and push towards an unformatted future of discursive media. This offers a way to describe the new and complex temporalities produced by time-discrete signal processing, which are not so much without time, as Bergson (1950) once argued, as overfull with a type of time that is very different from human, historical time. As Flusser said, we need to remain aware of these programs and become conscious of the possibilities as well as the dangers that they might bring into being. These processes are the materially real. They are also the way that the real is projected onto the possible, in the sense that they are the operations that measure the present and then seek to define the future. They are the opposite of the process of actualisation, as Grosz describes it, as the creation of heterogenous terms (Grosz, 1998, p. 51). The movement of the multiplicity is limited by analytical media, which bases its representation of the objects of the world and its predictions for the future on the measurement of the present. The leap of creativity into the future that Grosz writes about is replaced by the concretisation of a program.

Digital media work on the digital principle of discrete signal processing. However, when we reflect on these processes from a media philosophical perspective, looking past purely human experiences of time to the way it is measured by technical media, it might be considered that the time-discreteness of the digital has the potential to open vastly new, multiple and folded modes of temporality. First, I will look to the reduction of the instant as a discrete moment in time, the negation of an open, unformatted future, and then go into the new possibilities opened up for the representation of time by contemporary media artists and the thinking about media that might follow.

Time-discrete Media

The instant, the supposedly timeless, has been given formal importance in the engineering of media apparatuses themselves. The privileging of the time-discrete occurs most obviously in terms of digital-signal processing, where thanks mainly to the work conducted by the nineteenth-century mathematician Jean-Baptiste Joseph Fourier, samples are taken of a continuous wave function, held and reassembled: a process that is instrumental to the operation of digital-signal processing.

Fourier made the mathematical discovery that any variable could be represented as a series of multiples of the original variable. Periodic functions could be dissected into smaller parts, which may be either time-continuous or time-discrete, and then reconstructed. This was a discovery that was to become fundamental to information theory. This approach, however, of conducting analysis through the segmentation of a whole was an example of a larger cultural technique that was being undertaken in fields such as medicine, criminology, heredity and biometry, largely supported by the new statistical methods introduced by figures such as Francis Galton and Karl Pearson, which emphasised a data science that was focussed on the localised and the discrete, from which inferences could be made. The Fourier transform, as a mathematical operation and a way of computing the world, seems the example *par excellence* of this then new media theory of the world, which would later be represented in the 'particalised' media philosophy of Flusser, and the mathematical theory of information developed in the field of engineering by Claude Shannon.

The Fourier Method is important to scientists and media philosophers alike because it represents a moment when the contingent becomes calculable. It also provides the basis for the realisation of audio and visual recording technologies that, for the first time, began to record previously invisible and inaudible elements of reality, those things that oscillated either too fast or too slowly for human eyes or ears. The purely unrepeatable 'becomes visible as the sum of decimals, and thereby also becomes repeatable' (Krämer, 2006, p. 101). Different to language and the phonetic alphabet, the Fourier transform was based on the calculability of the irregular, the organisation of the chaotic. This, as Mark Hansen (2015) has written, leads to a situation of computational 'feed forward', where micro-sensory functions can be picked up by the computer, bypassing human consciousness, and then processed in a way that influences future decisions.

The Fourier transform refers to an analytical process where a time-continuous wave form is deconstructed into the other time-continuous frequencies of which it is constituted. It is a process where a constant function of time can be separated into sinusoids, its modulating constitutive elements of sine and cosine functions. A numerical variation on the Fourier transform, the discrete Fourier transform, allows time-continuous signal to be processed and transformed to time-discrete samples. By this operation, not only can a waveform be represented as a sum of sinusoids, but it can be further broken into segments and represented as discrete samples. This has proven to be foundational to digital-signal processing and compression, where algorithms can be developed to filter out undetectable frequencies and hence reduce the number of bits needed to transmit a reliable signal. For the material world of vibrating signal, the Fourier Method achieves a numerical dissection. The Fourier Method now gives signal, from sound waves to photography to the analysis of complex change over time functions, a unique temporal character that underpins its capacity for representation. In terms of both the technical qualities of images and the images themselves, it is the instant, the sample, the point, the reliable and the computable that matter.

Measurement and Media

Ernst uses the examples of Éduoard-Léon Scott de Martinville's phonautograph to illustrate the way mass media have roots in measurement and analysis, which owe a great deal to the discoveries made by Fourier (Ernst, 2013, p. 184). Ernst's example is a good one to use to begin to see how the apparatus of measurement, once relatively benign and specialised, becomes tangled up in life and forms part of the elemental surroundings that we now call mass media. Scott's phonautograph (Figure 1.1), patented in 1857 and preceding Edison's and Berliner's inventions, was used to record sounds as a linear inscription on blackened paper. A membrane was set behind a bell mouth, which was used to amplify incoming sounds and direct them in such a way that set the membrane vibrating and caused a wire brush to trace the frequency of the vibrations, hundreds of them per second, onto a cylinder, giving material form to the mathematical theory proved around thirty-five years earlier by Fourier. Scott's device was never intended as a playback medium but was instead

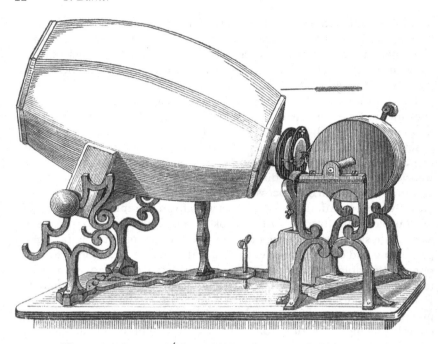

Figure 1.1 Image of Éduoard-Léon Scott Mandeville's phonautograph

developed as a laboratory instrument to study acoustic waveforms that were both audible and inaudible to humans. It was not until later that it was discovered that the recorded inscription contained enough information about the sound to actually be used to play back the recorded sounds. Friedrich Kittler similarly points to the analytical function of the phonograph and gramophone, which retrieve the original function of Scott's invention, where he argues that the analysis of speech – *an analysis of the material rather than the symbolic* – that was afforded by the invention of recorded voice machines was instrumental to the vast changes to discourse seen around the end of the nineteenth century. These machines were able to be used for analytical purposes by slowing down the playback speed to reproduce for human ears sounds previously unable to be notated. The gramophone and phonograph, when used as a talking machine, were able to allow slow-motion studies of single sounds that were previously unavailable. This made the devices ideal in laboratories for measuring hearing. In schools, these devices were instrumental in allowing the analysis of 'the most fleeting, unrepresentable and yet so important, characteristic aspect of language, of line phonetics (speech melody) and of line rhythm' (Surkamp in Kittler, [1985]1990, p. 233). Real phenomena were now able to be stored and played back depending on technical standards, which importantly included the temporality that the medium inscribed on the phenomena. As mentioned earlier, the real began to be defined by what apparatuses could pick up, store and playback, including noise. The real became the property of media, which was no longer solely responsible for the production of the symbolic.

Like the phonograph, the camera was also to be applied as an analytical medium. This is perhaps most obvious in the work of scientists Étienne-Jules Marey and Eadweard Muybridge, who both famously studied movement via the techniques associated with chronophotography. Before the introduction of the photographic to this technique, scientists such as Joseph Plateau and Simon von Stampfer demonstrated the experiment showing how a spinning disk could be used to mobilise still images into apparent continuous motion (Wade, 2016, p. 4). Drawing on earlier work concerning the persistence of vision, Plateau and von Stampfer were able to show how moving reality could be reduced to still images of incremental progression. Scientists such as Albert Londe, working at La Salpêtrière hospital under Jean-Martin Charcot, could then use this discovery to record the movements and disturbances of patients with varying neurological disorders and isolate frames in time that could be studied closely and precisely. As already mentioned, the real became that which could be ordered by the apparatus.

Out of Cinematic Time

Prior to the dominance of analytical media, throughout the twentieth century, it was the synthesis of mass entertainment media that conditioned the mediation of the real. Ever since cinematic images became widespread, and perhaps even before this moment, it has been claimed that civilisation, at least in the West, has begun to occupy 'cinematic time' (Doane, 2002; Stiegler, [2001]2011). By presenting apparent continuity through its framing of time as 'stopped' moments, cinematic apparatus participated in a larger project of modernity where the rhythms of the day were regularised and standardised (Doane, 2002). According to E. P. Thompson's formulation (1967), around the birth of the era commonly referred to as modernity, the workday for much of the population of cities in the West became institutionalised and workers began to base the rhythms of their work on mechanisms. Pre-industrial society waited. They waited for the harvest. They waited for the seasons to change. Industrial society moved things. Like synthetic media, they transformed the environment. One worker in line finished their task. The next commenced theirs. As the product, whether a motor car, a children's toy, furniture or textiles, rolled along the factory line, it was assembled with a repeatable precision. This is a relatively simple example of a technique based on the chronology produced under capitalism, but it could be extrapolated into other contexts such as financial markets that represent time on stock tickers or historical time that represents single events within the narrative chronology of eras, with cause and effect predictably following on from one another in relatively 'shallow' time loops. Industrial time, historical time, is linear, it progresses towards the new. 'It comes from the past and demands the future. Nothing is, everything becomes' (Flusser [1983]2013, p. 119). As Zielinski points out, this is in complete accord with 'the dogged regularity with which the film carrying the photographs was moved on a fraction, sixteen or thirty-two times a second (according to shutter-type), stopped, illuminated, and then transported again' ([1989]1999, p. 79). Movement was towards a future, the medium was synthetic, the focus was on what was about to become, what was about to appear.

A set of cultural techniques was developed for ordering time that was supported by the technical hardware of the cinema, which presupposed a particular 'capturing' of contemporary life by the camera and its transformation and representation as an image always pushing towards the future, towards the next frame. The apparatus acted as a device, that, as Greg Lambert (2016) writes 'literally causes ("makes ready") something to begin to appear – sexuality, power, the state, God, etc.'. In this case it was time that the apparatus caused to begin to appear. Given aesthetic form in the cinema, the time that filtered through modernity was regularised, ordered, packaged and, importantly, able to be represented. The cinema not only participated in the organisation of modern time through its technical function but also, in its self-reflexivity, produced images and stories that reflected the temporalities of life under capitalism, modernity and media machines. This is an argument that is rehearsed in film theory from Deleuze's *Cinema 1* and *Cinema 2* books ([1983]2005 and [1985] 2005) to the important work of Doane. But things have changed. The audio-visual apparatus, the disposition, a time-critical rather than ontological system, has changed and so has the time that it causes to begin to appear. As already mentioned, the present, rather than its becoming, is what is recorded and evaluated by analytical media. 'The present is the totality of the real. In it all virtualities are realised. They "present" themselves' (Flusser [1983]2013, p. 119). Even the past is now stored in the present. Even the future becomes coordinates of the present.

In its concrete actuality, the irreducible flow of time is in fact now made reducible to discrete instants, and hence made less productive. In terms of the way that the dominate apparatus of our time, the digital computer, 'captures', 'downloads' and 'transforms' human subjects, it seems that it is time-discrete data and momentary discontinuities that are now to be privileged, rather than the acoustic, free-flowing environment that McLuhan once described. Perhaps Bergson was right. It is no longer the durational flow that defines contemporary time but rather a return to the function of analytical media that Kittler alerted us to, as time-discrete signal processing. Once the cinema defined its subjects (in images and stories), now the computer defines its users (as data), just as the phonautograph and the chronophotograph defined their subjects. The operations of media such as the cinema, and the techniques that they reflect are, as they always have been, functions that give users a sense of the rhythms of the real. This observation is what led Bernhard Siegert (2015) to argue that it was the material-symbolic infrastructures supplied by techniques of signal processing that have constituted the becoming subject within the world. The mirror of cinema is replaced by the measurement of analytical media.

Siegert, by using Max Bense, argues that the world when defined by computers is determined as a signal processing which replaces beings with frequencies, attributes with functions and qualities with quantities. To arrive at a media theory of the world, objects, processes and attributes need to be redefined in media technical language, as the world is made understandable both by and for the computer (Heidenreich, 2015, p. 137). Lacan once offered film scholars a way of discussing in psycho-analytical terms the subject arrested before cinematic images, as though an infant before a mirror, defined by experiences given through the camera. To know that I am alive, to know what I am worth, I look to the reflections offered by the Other. They tell me what it is like to be alive. Is it now the cultural techniques associated with digital computation that fulfil this role? Does the computer reflect to me what it is to be alive, as data that can be processed?

In the tradition of humanist media studies, however, the computer is, like all other technology, often reduced to a tool. Because of this the humanities have been able to simply describe the tool based on its appearance to a human user, and not on its own characteristics, which condition the way it is used. 'Those who have tried to pour the fuzzy logic of their insights and intentions into computer source code know from bitter experience how drastically the formal language of these codes distort those insights and intentions' (Kittler, 2006, p. 49). Logic is poured into the computer, but it first needs to be transformed in order to be compatible with the formal language of the computer. Feedback loops lead from the machine to the human user, not the other way around.

Rather than the tool being defined from the point of view of the user, we need to start with the other term in the equation. How is the user defined by the computer? What operations are permissible in terms of the rules of the specific coding language?

Let's start to think about this by looking back once more to a key point in the development of computer systems for sorting data: Charles Bachman, one of the first people to realise an effective database management system for computers, stood before a computer at General Electric watching a file run through it. Based on the earlier sequential punch card system, the magnetic tape that he was using contained data in a sequence, with each piece of information attributed a unique number. Bachman requested some data be returned by the computer and it sorted through the sequence in chronological order until the correct number was found. Whether looking at social security numbers, purchase orders or bank account numbers this process was the same. But when Bachman was able to use a new direct access machine and develop a management system to use alongside it, things changed. He no longer stood before the computer as tape passed through it but used the computer to search through a database. The database – the storage system rather than the computer – was at the centre of the information-processing universe (Bachman, 1973, p. 654). Data no longer went through the computer in sequence but went into the database and was stored. An opportunity arose for him to dramatically change the face of information processing. He saw the potential for the machine to access information by probing for a record, rather than sequentially sorting through all the data (Bachman, 1973, pp. 654–5). This was not only a breakthrough in terms of information systems but would also have dramatic consequences for the way all kinds of events could be archived and organised and for the way a subject could come to terms with a world of data. The subject was no longer a stationary figure that watched as things passed before their eyes. The subject was now defined as an operator able to dive into n-dimensional data space.

Dimitris Eleftheriotis (2010) has written that 'a linear, incremental and forward movement of a progressing subjectivity travelling towards ever-increasing knowledge' became the all-pervasive metaphor for life in the eras of modernity (p. 12). In Lutz Niethammer's (1992) words, '[t]he twentieth century is distinguished by the fact that the abstract, linear understanding of time which marked the human sciences in the eighteenth century, as well as the historical conception of nature in the nineteenth, have entered into the everyday life of society' (p. 26). Or as McLuhan (1962) put it, after the Renaissance, a world of multiple durations was replaced by a new lineal world, as people were translated from a world of 'roles' into a world of 'jobs'. At this point, work becomes specialised and the senses fragment. The ear, the eye; touch, taste, smell can be used to develop their own brand of knowledge, with the eye and linear reading being privileged. Both McLuhan and Flusser wrote that the eye moves along a line of print towards ever-increasing knowledge, like the film moves through a projector, towards the future, or like tape moves through the computer at General Electric. But now the contemporary subject knows this experience less and less and is instead presented with a condition that could perhaps only be described as the aftermath of the accumulation and measurement of the stories of modernity. Historical subjects put things in front of themselves. Digital subjects wait and occupy themselves with the stories that have been accumulated in store-houses of data. To put it another way, digital subjects put things in storage. This will be fleshed out with examples in the remainder of this chapter. For now though, we might say that in the face of ubiquitous computing, cinematic time – a time that does not stand still but instead flows – has been replaced by a time that is discrete and instantaneous. This is a time that 'breaks the surface' of cinematic time, that gets 'exposed' and separates itself from the time of succession (Virilio, [1997]2008, p. 27).

Media Art

How does art respond? Given the way analytical media privileges the discrete and separates time from succession, contemporary art has only one option if it hopes to articulate the experience of life in the present. It now turns to the instant. If art today is to be considered contemporary, to embody ways of being, its subject can only be the ontology of the present (Smith, 2009). But taking on this subject, contemporary art seeks to make the present dysfunctional; it seeks to make the present function in a radically different way from what is given to us in digital culture. This has always been the task of what we used to call the avant-garde: Futurism, Dada and formalism all took it upon themselves to make the present dysfunctional by re-ordering the time of the present through the destruction of the past, the undoing of values, the revolutionary value of the dissolution of images (Groys, 2016, pp. 50–2). Contemporary media art continues this tradition by upscaling the processes that define the present as an instant without time – the still, the pixel, the archive – and then reinserts time into these 'post-historical' moments, making them thick with temporalities. In grappling with the present as an instant, a number of media artworks look to the limits of the present, some produce media anachronisms and some expand prior media temporal systems and attempt to view the instant over much more drawn-out moments in time.

Notable artists in this tradition include Douglas Gordon, who radically extends the duration of films to draw attention to both the individual frames and the interstices between frames. The most famous example of this is his work *24 Hour Psycho* (1993). But he also uses this technique, perhaps to more traumatic ends, to re-work the found footage in *10ms-1* (1994), where he slows down footage used to document and study the effects of 'shell shock' on World War I survivors. The work measures trauma, and in a sense reproduces this trauma in that it produces a sense of waiting by further segmenting experience and blocking the progression of time so that it accumulates. We wait for something to happen. But we also know what will happen. We can predict what will happen in the next frame; it is folded into our experience of waiting in the present.

The notion of slowing the forward momentum of duration is also seen in Jeff Wall's photographic work. Images taken over a period of months, sometimes years, are carefully composed by Wall to create photographic montages, which seemingly present samples of time. Durations are not only slowed but stopped and rearranged, as though images in a database, with different times overlapping one another. His most well-known work *A Sudden Gust of Wind* (after Hokusai) (1993), made to resemble Katsushika Hokusai's woodblock print, *Yejiri Station, Province of Suruga* (ca. 1832), was assembled over one year by taking photographs of sets, props and actors, which were then combined into the instant of the photograph. The theatricality of the image, the wind that blows through the photograph, the relationships between the figures from different times, further exemplifies the way movement, in this case the movement of the production over twelve months, is frozen in a multi-temporal present, with the instant represented as a scene that acts like an archive stretching back over the twelve-month production of images and even further, to the original woodblock print.

Wall's more recent work *Listener* (2015) (Figure 1.2), similarly presents a stopped, multi-temporal scene. A shirtless man, whose twisting figure resembles the images of Christ once seen in mannerist paintings, kneels on the ground, victimised, but speaking. A man leans over him, listening. What has just happened? What is about to happen? What words have been said? What will be the response? The theatricality of the image presents us with an agonising extended present. All of the elements in the scene, the rocks, the surroundings, the art historical references, the potential for action, take on significance as the past and future are folded into this temporally thick moment. The photograph, like Gordon's found footage, further alerts us to the way this 'real moment in time' and our experience of the tempos of this reality, is technically produced as

Figure 1.2　Jeff Wall, *Listener,* 2015, inkjet print, 159.4 x 233.0 cm.
© Jeff Wall, courtesy of the artist

a moment that nests within itself multiple temporalities and is at once up to date and already past.

Another figure in this tradition is David Claerbout, one of the most significant artists to give aesthetic form to contemporary philosophies of time. Whereas Wall's works embody the accumulation of time, Claerbout in works such as *Arena* (2007) and *Sections of a Happy Moment* (2007) radically extends the duration of an instant to break the surface of photographic temporality. Where Wall gives us the sense of a stopped moment in time, a break in succession, by folding multiple instants into one image, Claerbout unfolds one instant, one image, allowing it to unravel over time. In these works, the archive of moments such as the instant before a point is scored in a basketball game or significant but seemingly banal moments of happiness, made still in the photographs, are turned into images not of frozen sections of life but mediations that, via a reintroduced duration, extend into the future and become scenes. Claerbout achieves this by photographing the moment from multiple and unexpected perspectives and then introducing duration via montage. Standing before one of these installations the viewer sees the instant from multiple perspectives. It is no longer a frozen section of time but a scene that extends into the future and with each new image of the montage offers us new information, new visions of the scene. In these works, the instant is examined and open to analysis in time. The extension of the instant, the usually fleeting moment, into the future, and the way in which this instant seems to be overfull with information, produce the *affect*, the feeling, of the work.

There is an inescapable sense in these works that, although viewers are offered multiple views of the same still section of movement, there is paradoxically never enough time to grasp the fullness of each instant entirely. There is paradoxically too much time to conceptualise all there is in the work. The temporary has become overfull with significance. These photographic images show, via their continual *re*-presentation of the instant, what it might mean to be with the temporary.

Perhaps the image that shows this best is Claerbout's recently completed video animation *KING (After Alfred Wertheimer's 1956 portrait of a young man named Elvis Presley)* (2015) (Figure 1.3). In 1956 Wertheimer photographed Elvis Presley at the age of twenty-one, just before he reached the heights of popular stardom and transformed into 'the King'. In Claerbout's reworking of Wertheimer's original photo-graph, the body of Presley, the body that will eventually become the King, is, in a computational type of recursive reflection, overlayed with textures of the King's body taken from a digital archive of famous photo-graphs (Claerbout, 2015). The virtual camera in Claerbout's animation circles around the image; it produces the wandering gaze over the surface of the image and comes in for close-ups on the now 3D-animated version of Presley's body, made up from a composite of images only visible in close-up. The King is now able to be closely and methodically inspected at the moment of the original photograph, which is now overlaid by the media autopsy of this body, giving form to the thick multi-temporal event.

Claerbout shows us the ongoing remediation of a temporary instant, not so much in a way that demonstrates Barthes' well-known phrase 'this will be and this has been', but rather demonstrates the way analytical media continue to operate on archives of the past. The work demonstrates 'this once was and is now controlled by a program'. The image, not a record of what once was but now a conceptual abstraction, is based on the careful recomposition of a body based on the archive of photographic data of what that body would eventually become. Flusser once claimed that one's wandering gaze over the photographic surface creates temporal relations between the photographed objects. 'It can return to an image it has already seen and the "before" can become "after"' (Flusser, [1983] 2014, pp. 8–9). In Claerbout's work the computer takes over the role of the gaze and in a controlled way creates disjunctive temporal relations, not just between obviously visible elements of the photograph but

Figure 1.3 David Claerbout, *KING (after Alfred Wertheimer's 1956 picture of a young man named Elvis Presley)*, 2015–2016, single channel video projection, HD animation, black & white, silent, 10 minutes, edition of 7 with 1 AP and 1 AC. © David Claerbout, courtesy of the artist and Sean Kelly, New York

between an archive of data in the form of textures of the King's body parts photographed throughout his career. In this image we do not look at a 'frozen image' but instead see a state of things translated into a *multi-temporal scene*. The technical image acts as a dam into which other images flow and become endlessly reproducible (Flusser, [1983]2014, p. 19).

An artist that looks to the longer scale of the instant, where the experience of being with the temporary and the fragmentary takes form, in a similar manner to Claerbout's found photographs, is Dominique Gonzalez-Foerster. In *TH. 2058* (2008), which was first exhibited as an element in the Unilever Series in the Turbine Hall at the Tate in 2008, Gonzalez-Foerster extends the contemporary moment fifty years into the future, when cultural artifacts, as she puts it, 'take shelter' in the Tate from the catastrophic climate change that has begun to take effect. This work presents the instant rather than the durational in the sense that no change takes place, only the sensation of being locked into an archive of artifacts at what might be considered the end point, or aftermath, of historical time. The Tate in 2058 acts as an archive for the books, films, sculptures and other artifacts of culture and a place that now stands in for the collective memory of a civilisation at the moment of extinction of the extended but still temporary moment. This archiving also speaks to the nesting of time within the work, not only focussed on a type of speculative fiction of what London might look like in 2058, but also nesting within itself the incremental and catastrophic accumulation of present moments, of which we are all as contemporaries implicated, and also nesting within itself, via its archive of cultural artifacts and traces of collective memory, events that stretch back much farther than 2008. The work is analytical because it extends the instant and is intent on carefully analysing what makes up this instant, rather than following vectors or creating the sense of a time that flows through the present to a future. The work engages a media aesthetic because it demonstrates how analytical and archival techniques, using media to preserve the past, creates an environment of storage time. Much like the tradition of archive artworks such as Muntadas' *The File Room*, the series of works conducted by Walid Raad under the banner of The Atlas Group, and indeed Claerbout's *KING*, it presents its archaeology of the present via non-chronological means; it blocks the transmission of events towards a future. What we see is a close analysis of a moment, which has been brought into such a close-up view that it dilates throughout time, and the contemporary, the idea of attempting to grasp and archive a continually fleeting moment, becomes the condition that underpins the work. The temporary instant is extended in this work to the beginning of extinction itself. Where previously the instants of history came to an end, where paradigms would shift and be replaced by something new, now all that is left after the end of the instant, this stretched-out aftermath of history, is extinction itself.

Gordon's and Claerbout's work, which allow small instants to unravel over an extended time period, Wall's photograph, which theatrically assembles instants into a new scene and Gonzalez-Foerster's work, which offers viewers an opportunity to engage with the idea of a very large, non-chronological instant, give form to a condition of a present in the aftermath of time, a condition without a transition to a future, without an actualisation of the virtual, or what Siegfried Zielinski described so perfectly as melancholia, *a being too much with time*. Either in very small or very large instants, where chronology is replaced by the archaeology of the moment, in all the media artworks mentioned above, the present is thick with temporalities that percolate beneath images, where events no longer roll on but instead remain blocked up in scenes. In these artworks, the moment, the instant, is thick with time and it is in this way that these artworks provide a way to reconceptualise the world of analytical media. Where the analytical, as was shown by McLuhan and Flusser, separates time into thin, anaemic points, focussing attention and experience on the present, these artworks, by amplifying the analytical, by making it work harder and that way making it dysfunctional, show how the contemporary moment might be a time in which the past and future get radically reconceptualised as within, rather than beyond, the present.

In this chapter I first offered a description of the technical image and its break from traditional image making. Using Flusser, I asked what happens when events and time are made into particles by the apparatuses that are culturally dominant. I then explored the technical image as an example of analytical media, which works by breaking a continuous signal into smaller parts that can be analysed. I then focussed on the history and epistemological effects of analytical media, including developments such as the Fourier transform and Bachman's discovery of data management systems. The argument here was that, following Flusser, users begin to project technical apparatuses onto the world and begin to know and evaluate the world based on their programs. From here, we were able to generalise that technical images exist as the outcome of an apparatus that works based on a program to separate continuous signal into discontinuous particles of information. I then looked at the way this process introduces a new type of temporality to our contemporary lives, as different to what we in the West think of as modernity and the time of succession and progress. This was argued particularly by exploring the differences between contemporary analytical media and modern synthetic media – media that gestures forward into an unformatted future, into the unformed and the potential. Analytical media now challenge this once dominant form and offer to us new ways to represent time, usually by reducing it to what can be measured. The chapter then ended with the question of time and aesthetics, outlining a number of examples where contemporary artists amplify this programmed function of analytical media, making it visible and by this, the process of making the usually invisible visible, making it dysfunctional. These artworks resist the regularity and precision of analytical media and instead represent the multi-temporal, the non-linear and the thick moments of time that are folded into each moment, offering new ways to represent and conceptualise the time of the contemporary.

References

Bachman, C. W. (1973). The programmer as navigator. *Communications of the ACM, 16*(11), 653–8.

Beer, D. (2009). Power through the algorithm? Participatory web cultures and the technological unconscious. *New Media & Society, 11*(6), 985–1002.

Bergson, H. (1950). *Matter and Memory*. London: George Allen & Unwin.

Chun, W. (2013). *Programmed Visions: Software and Memory*. Cambridge, MA: MIT Press.

Claerbout, D. (2015). Description of *KING (After Alfred Wertheimer's 1956 portrait of a young man named Elvis Presley)*. Available at http://davidclaerbout.com/KING-after-Alfred-Wertheimer-s-1956-picture-of-a-young-man-named. Accessed 21 November 2022.

Deleuze, G. ([1983]2005). *Cinema 1: The Movement Image*. Trans. Hugh Tomlinson & Robert Galeta. London & New York: Continuum.

Deleuze, G. ([1985]2005). *Cinema 2: The Time Image*. Trans. Hugh Tomlinson & Robert Galeta. London & New York: Continuum.

Denson, S. (2020). *Discorrelated Images*. Durham: Duke University Press.

Doane, M. A. (2002). *The Emergence of Cinematic Time: Modernity, Contingency and the Archive*. Cambridge, MA: Harvard University Press.

Eleftheriotis, D. (2010). *Cinematic Journeys: Film and Movement*. Edinburgh: Edinburgh University Press.

Ernst, W. (2013). *Digital Memory and the Archive*. Minneapolis: University of Minnesota Press.

Ernst, W. (2015). Media archaeology-as-such: Occasional thoughts on (més-) alliances with archaeologies proper. *Journal of Contemporary Archaeology*, 2(1), 15–23.

Floridi, L. (2015). Hyperhistory and the Philosophy of Information Policies. In L. Floridi (ed.), *The Onlife Manifesto: Being Human in a Hyperconnected Era* (pp. 51–64). Cham, Heidelberg, New York, Dordrecht & London: Springer.

Flusser, V. ([1983]2013). *Post-History*. Trans. Rodrigo Maltez Novaes. Minneapolis: University of Minnesota Press.

Flusser, V. ([1983]2014). *Towards a Philosophy of Photography*. Trans. Anthony Matthews. London: Reaktion Books.

Flusser, V. ([1985]2011). *Into the Universe of Technical Images*. Trans. Nancy Ann Roth. Minneapolis: University of Minnesota Press.

Grosz, E. (1998). Thinking the new: Of futures yet unthought. *Symplokē*, 6(1/2), 38–55. http://jstor.org/stable/40550421.

Groys, B. (2016). *In the Flow*. London & New York: Verso Books.

Hansen, M. B. N. (2015). *Feed-Forward: On the Future of Twenty-First Century Media*. Chicago: University of Chicago Press.

Heidenreich, S. (2015). The Situation After Media. In E. Ikoniadou & S. Wilson (eds.), *Media After Kittler* (pp.135–54). London & New York: Rowman and Littlefield.

Ieven, B. (2003). How to orientate oneself in the world: A general outline of Flusser's theory of media. *Image and Narrative*, 6. Available at: https://imageandnarrative.be/inarchive/mediumtheory/bramieven.htm Accessed 21 November 2022.

Kittler, F. ([1985]1990). *Discourse Networks 1800/1900*. Trans. Michael Metteer & Chris Cullens. Stanford: Stanford University Press.

Kittler, F. ([1999]2010). *Optical Media*. Trans. Anthony Enns. Cambridge: Polity.

Kittler, F. (2006). Thinking colours and/or machines. *Theory, Culture & Society*, 23(7–8), 39–50.

Krämer, S. (2006). The cultural techniques of time axis manipulation: On Friedrich Kittler's conception of media. *Theory, Culture & Society*, *23*(7–8), 93–109.

Lambert, G. (2016). 'What is a Dispositif?' Available at: https://academia.edu/25 507473/What_is_a_Dispositif?campaign=upload_email Accessed 23 May 2016.

McLuhan, M. (1962). *The Gutenberg Galaxy: The Making of Typographic Man.* Toronto: University of Toronto Press.

Neyland, D. (2015). Organizing algorithms. *Theory, Culture & Society*, *32*(1), 119–32.

Niethammer, L. (1992). *Posthistorie: Has History Come to an End?* Trans. Patrick Camiller. London & New York: Verso.

Pias, C. (2003). Das digitale Bild gibt es nicht. Über das (Nicht-)Wissen der Bilder und informatische Illusion [The digital image does not exist. About the (non-) knowledge of the images and the computer illusion]. *Zeitenblicke*, *2*(1). Available at https://mediarep.org/handle/doc/4845. Accessed 21 November 2022.

Shaviro, S. (2010). *Post-Cinematic Affect.* Winchester: Zero Books.

Siegert, B. (2015). *Cultural Techniques: Grids, Filters, Doors, and Other Articulations of the Real.* Trans. Gregory Winthrop-Young. New York: Fordham University Press.

Slavin, K. (2011). 'How algorithms shape our world'. Available at: http://ted.com/talks/kevin_slavin_how_algorithms_shape_our_world.html Accessed 20 August 2015.

Smith, T. (2009). *What is Contemporary Art?* London & Chicago: University of Chicago Press.

Stiegler, B. ([2001]2011). *Technics and Time, 3: Cinematic Time and the Question of Malaise.* Trans. Stephen Barker. Stanford: Stanford University Press.

Thompson, E. P. (1967). Time, work-discipline, and industrial capitalism. *Past and Present*, *38*, 56–97.

Totaro, P. & Ninno, D. (2016). Algorithms and the practical world. *Theory, Culture and Society*, *33*(1), 139–52.

Virilio, P. ([1997]2008). *Open Sky.* Trans. Julia Ross. London & New York: Verso.

Wade, N. J. (2016). Capturing motion and depth before cinematography. *Journal of the History of the Neurosciences*, *25*(1), 3–22.

Zielinski, S. ([1989]1999). *Audiovisions: Cinema and Television as Entr'actes in History.* Trans. Gloria Custance. Amsterdam: Amsterdam University Press.

2

Material Temporal Work in Artistic Innovation
How Hilma af Klint Powered Time

Miriam Feuls, Christina Lüthy and Silviya Svejenova

> *Don't expect that the signals and symbols that you developed with much effort will be understood by the brothers that you meet, but work hard for the future.*
> Hilma af Klint, Notebooks, February 27–March 2, 1907, in Solomon R. Guggenheim Museum (2018a)

> *Suddenly, more than 50 years after history was written, completely out of the blue, at least for the general public, we discover this woman who painted abstract works before Kandinsky, creating this huge oeuvre, fully independently, and by a kind of miracle it's all stayed together. It's like finding a time capsule in Sweden.*
> Julia Voss, art critic and author of Hilma af Klint's biography, in Halina Dyrschka's (2019) documentary *Beyond the Visible: Hilma af Klint*

Introduction

How is an artwork, conceived ahead of its time, protected from incomprehension and projected into the future to reach receptive audiences? What does to "work hard for the future" (opening quote) entail?

Swedish artist Hilma af Klint (1862–1944) had an intriguing trajectory that makes it possible to explore such questions on organizing radical artistic innovation in time. The praise for her extraordinary work has been abundant in recent years, acknowledging her breakthrough to abstraction ahead of better-known male artists, such as Vasily Kandinsky, Kazimir Malevich, Piet Mondrian, or František Kupka. She signed, sold, and exhibited her conventional paintings, but kept her novel artwork outside the established art world's institutions, "convinced the world was not yet ready to understand her work" (Solomon R. Guggenheim Museum, 2018b). Hoping for her work to reach future receptive audiences, af Klint posited that most of her paintings and notebooks – those marked with the symbol + x – should be stored away for twenty years after her death (Voss, 2020); that is, until 1964. As R. H. Quaytman – the artist who was instrumental in arranging af Klint's first solo exhibition in New York in 1989 – reflected: "Experience cruelly taught her [af Klint] what an 'inappropriate' gift her work offered. But in 1964 the world still was not ready" (in Birnbaum & Noring, 2013, unnumbered page). It would take several more decades for the art world to appreciate af Klint's radical artistic inception.

Hilma af Klint's trajectory is amenable to the 'language' of time and is characterized by a number of 'temporal contrasts' (Zerubavel, 1987). For example, the artist does not fit the customary image of artists of her time, neither the avant-garde (working for the future), nor that of the academy system (Voss, 2018). Her artwork has been defined as "both of its time and ahead of it" (Bashkoff, 2018b, p. 12) and yet "as undefinable today as it was a century ago" (Birnbaum, 2021), an example of one of "these moments of achronicity" (Florman, in Bashkoff, 2018a, p. 43).

Some art historians have framed her story as the rediscovery of a forgotten female artist in a zeitgeist of a broader revival and recognition of women artists' contributions from the early twentieth century (Behr, 2002), one marginalized due to both gender and connections to the occult (Reponen, 2020). Others, such as the artist Quaytman (in Birnbaum & Noring, 2013, unnumbered page), have pointed out that "another explanation for her oblivion is that the work never entered the market. It is quite literally worthless." (The artwork is owned by Stiftelsen Hilma af Klint Verk (The Hilma af Klint Foundation), established in 1972 as a custodian of the artist's legacy.) While these are all plausible framings, they fall short of fully appreciating af Klint's distinctive trajectory and the multiple puzzles it poses, not only for art history and art historians, but also for scholars of organization and time who are interested in how an 'untimely' artistic innovation searches for and reaches the 'right' time over a century after its creation. In this chapter, we examine such self-determinism amidst its temporal embeddedness by posing the question: *How is radical artistic innovation protected from incomprehension and projected towards receptive future audiences?*

Our interest in Hilma af Klint's story was kindled by a recent documentary *Beyond the Visible – Hilma af Klint* (Dyrschka, 2019). It portrayed af Klint's visionary work at the interface of spiritualism, modern science, and the natural world, her unique creative process, as well as the herewith related constraints regarding the reception of her work during and after her lifetime. The documentary also delved into "the process of her mischaracterization and erasure by both a patriarchal narrative of artistic progress and capitalistic determination of artistic value" (Zeitgeist Films, 2019), reclaiming her place in and importance for art history. Following this initial inspiration, we collected books (including a biography) on the artist, exhibition catalogues, and also explored exhibits of her work as far as the pandemic allowed. We also gathered master's theses, media articles, podcasts, and YouTube video presentations on discussions of her work (hosted by museums as well as the Theosophical Society), and sources on an architecture and design competition 'A Temple for Hilma' (Combo Competitions) for a building to house af Klint's work. While we also studied art history books to contextualize af Klint's work, we should emphasize that our exploration is from an organizational perspective, zeroing in on the temporal dimension of organizing processes. Therefore, we focus less on the sources of her inspiration and more on the traveling of her artwork into the future.

In particular, we explore this traveling into the future from the vantage point of temporal agency and material temporal work. We argue that af Klint's temporal agency (her anticipation of and acting upon her own future significance) and, particularly, her and others' (on her behalf) *material temporal work* – that is, influencing, sustaining, or redirecting interpretations of time through materiality (for example, of the art works, the twenty year wait for these, or how they inspire other artists) – enabled the radically novel artwork to reach the future. We elaborate on two main processes of material temporal work – *bifurcating time* and *bridging time* – which we suggest enabled af Klint's novel work to reach receptive future audiences. We conclude by suggesting how powering time (that is, the interplay between bifurcating and bridging time) contributes to the politics of meaning (Slavich et al., 2020), that is the political process of shaping audiences' interpretation and reception of artistic innovation by mobilizing material and discursive elements in the public arena. Powering time contributes to the contested processes of meaning making in the context of innovation involving paintings and notebooks as non-human actants that help to constitute time itself as a political agent.

Our own journey of exploring Hilma af Klint's trajectory and attempting to relate it to and interrogate it through notions of organization and time has been both enriching and challenging. It has been enriching in terms of raising multiple questions and inspiring us to discuss, on multiple occasions, what her trajectory could suggest to us about the technologies, power, and politics in a context of radical artistic innovation, in which artist and audience reach each other, spanning over 100 years. However, while we enjoyed unravelling different stories of her artwork's traveling in time, we also struggled to provide a 'neat' account that weaves the multiplicity of implicated interests and voices. At times, it felt like we were moving along one of af Klint's spirals, constantly arriving at another possible layer of meaning.

Our current settlement on Hilma af Klint's work and trajectory is outlined below. First, we briefly highlight some seminal ideas on temporal agency, temporal work, and materiality that guide the interpretation of af

Klint artwork's traveling in time. We then present two processes of material temporal work that, we argue, helped the artist in powering time, connecting with an unknown future zeitgeist (the mood of the time). We end the chapter by discussing the implications for organization and time in the context of radical artistic innovation.

Temporal Agency and Material Temporal Work

While actors' actions are embedded in time (temporal agency), actors engage in processes to influence, sustain, or redirect their and others' interpretations of time (temporal work). The temporality of agency has been considered as crucial in practices of social engagement (Emirbayer & Mische, 1998). According to Emirbayer and Mische (1998, p. 963), actors' actions are "informed by the past (in its habitual aspect), but also oriented toward the future (as a capacity to imagine alternative possibilities) and toward the present (as a capacity to contextualize past habits and future projects within the contingencies of the moment)." From this perspective, the experiential structures of past, present, and future are necessary for action. In line with Emirbayer and Mische (1998), Pontikes and Rindova (2020) emphasized the temporal embeddedness of actors and their connecting of temporal experiences to craft their "identities and action repertoires, as well as dreams and visions for the future" (Pontikes & Rindova, 2020, p. 154). Temporal agency provides actors with the perspectives to create and transform "the situational contexts within which they act" (Emirbayer & Mische, 1998, p. 1003); it can shape agents' transformative capacities and agendas (Pontikes & Rindova, 2020). Flaherty (2020), in turn, drew on American pragmatism, to emphasize actors' choices, such as when constructing their pasts in anticipation of an imagined future. Flaherty (2020, p. 13) defined temporal agency as "time work" that describes actors' attempts to control, manipulate, and customize their own temporal experience or that of others, to ultimately create a "desired form of temporal experience" and modify the course of (inter)action.

Further research on the temporality of agency has investigated how interpretations of the past, present, and future are connected and how potential conflicts among multiple interpretations are resolved to enable action (Kaplan & Orlikowski, 2013). For instance, actors rethink the past in light of current and anticipated experiences, reconsider and reassess present concerns, and reimagine future alternatives projected from prior experiences. They engage in these forms of "temporal work" to "construct useful lines of action" (Kaplan & Orlikowski, 2013, p. 966). Hence, the way resourceful or skillful actors shape their own and others' temporal experiences has a major impact on their action (Flaherty et al., 2020; Granqvist & Gustafsson 2016), giving them "significant material and/or symbolic advantages" (Emirbayer & Mische, 1998, p. 1000).

Offering a material dimension to the debate on temporal agency, Hernes et al. (2021) advanced the understanding of material temporality. This concept sensitizes us to the materials' movement through time and their performativity in creating time; for example, making futures (cf. Comi & Whyte, 2018), for instance, Duchamp's ready-mades as untimely objects opening new temporalities in conceptual art. According to Hernes et al. (2021, p. 352), material temporality "also illustrates how materiality may be interpreted differently along the dimension of time, from the temporally present to the temporally distant dimensions." This can be illustrated by Christo and Jeanne-Claude's 1995 *Wrapped Reichstag*, which interweaved the building's own winding history with twenty-four years of negotiations by the artists to obtain permission to complete their artwork (Svejenova et al., 2011). The silvery fabric on the Reichstag yielded a quality of impermanence to and an openness to multiple interpretations of the highly symbolic building. Other scholars have discussed the role of material objects in their making of time (Blagoev et al., 2018; Schultz & Hernes, 2013). For instance, Blagoev et al. (2018) discussed how computers as a material technology play an active role in a museum's remembering practices. Thus, materiality becomes constitutive of time rather than being defined by time.

These insights into temporal agency, temporal work, and material temporality are important for our study of Hilma af Klint's relation to time, as they recognize the interplay of temporal determinism (agency as temporally embedded) and self-determinism (temporal work), as well as the importance of materiality. This interplay becomes important when studying interconnections of past, present, and future and their influence on strategic action (Bansal et al., 2022) or their strategic mobilizing to create change or innovation (Feuls et al., 2020). For instance, in the context of artistic innovation, drawing on the case of Spanish painter Joan Miró, Svejenova (2018) highlighted the importance of temporal work, which opens up new temporalities that put the artist's work forward into the future, such as engaging with a new art form, participating at events, or creating a foundation.

Against this backdrop, we outline the material temporal work that powered time and projected Hilma af Klint's unconventional artwork into posterity.

Material Temporal Work in Radical Artistic Innovation

Our exploration of Hilma af Klint's work and trajectory (see Figure 2.1 for a timeline of selected events during and subsequent to her lifetime)

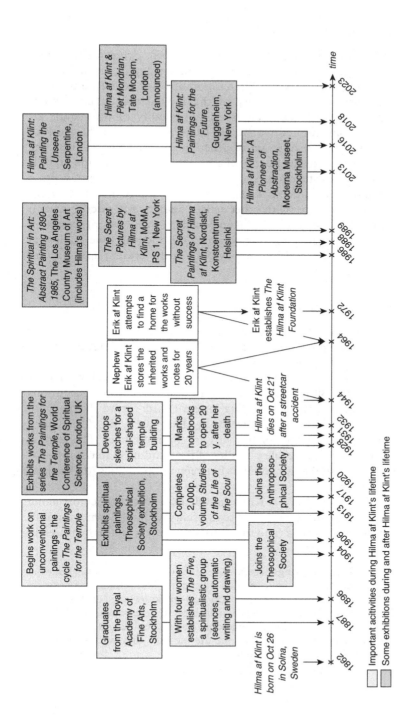

Figure 2.1 Hilma af Klint's timeline

revealed two processes of material temporal work: *bifurcating time* and *bridging time*. *Bifurcating time* is driven by the agency of the artist. It is about embarking on an unknown temporality (yet to be discovered) through the distinctive materiality of the radical artistic innovation, while continuing along the established temporality of the extant art world through conventional works. *Bridging time* is about the work of the artist, as well as a diverse set of other agents that help connect the artwork with the established history of abstract art. Bridging time unfolds through narrative construction (such as by the artist and others), waiting time (for instance, the artist, her family, the Hilma af Klint foundation), and emotional resonance (with other artists, audiences, critics, museum curators, etc.). We suggest that, taken together, these two processes of material temporal work – bifurcating time and bridging time – allow af Klint to power time, exercising agency both in the present and, beyond her lifetime, into the future.

Bifurcating Time

To prepare audiences to accommodate the difference brought about by her unconventional paintings, Hilma af Klint acted with foresight, lending her project a sense of control. She organized and materialized time entrepreneurially, incorporating it in her artistic process, which we denote as bifurcating time. Bifurcating time is a term borrowed from conceptions of entrepreneurial work as "viewing present and future events with entirely different mindsets" (Miller & Sardais, 2015, p. 492), which makes it possible to appreciate and sustain contradictions. The term is also suggestive of the "possible plurality of time and its materialization," and the related possibility for conflicts between temporalities (de Vaujany et al., 2014, p. 5).

In bifurcating time, Hilma af Klint unfolded her artistic trajectory along two very different paths: established temporality and unknown temporality. That bifurcating of time (and the artist's awareness of it) is captured in the following statement:

Af Klint's conventional paintings became the source of financial income, but what she refers to as the "great work", realised during her life, remained a separate activity. Only spiritually interested audiences had any knowledge of this body of works. Her attempts to exhibit these paintings to like-minded individuals remained largely unsuccessful and remarks in her notebooks indicate that she felt that the world was not quite ready for the message they were intended to communicate. (Hilma af Klint Foundation, 2022)

We argue that bifurcating time into an established and an unknown temporality allowed the artist to have control and power over her work, and to exercise temporal agency at a time when female artists' agency was constrained by patriarchal structures and art institutions. Below, we briefly discuss the material temporal work involved in bifurcating time along the two temporalities.

The established temporality involved continuity of conventions, following a progression from learning to mastery, and reproduction of established order that involved educational institutions (such as art academies), galleries, and, not least, art dealers (White & White, 1965), and in that sense was not concerned with artistic innovation. Hilma af Klint was among the first female artists trained at the Royal Academy of Art in Sweden in the art conventions of her time and she worked along extant expectations in terms of conventions and practices. She was considered a successful mainstream artist (Becker, 1976), painting, signing, exhibiting, and selling conventional artworks. She mastered recognized techniques, covered conventional subjects (such as landscapes and portraits), and worked in a naturalistic style, also illustrating scientific books on plants, insects, birds, and even horse surgery. She is thought to have benefitted from engagement with the art institutions of her time, which exhibited and rewarded her conventions-based work at a time when women artists were being subjected to tremendous prejudice (Behr, 2002). Over time, the established temporality of the art world recognized and incorporated in its canon the contributions of male abstract artists, who were af Klint's contemporaries. These artists had been vocal about their innovative art and had created manifestos and other ways of proclaiming their pioneering efforts, and had also counted on the support of promoters from the art world (MoMA's Exhibition History, 2022).

With the start of her work on radically different paintings, which broke the conventions of her time, af Klint opened up an unknown temporality; that is, a trajectory outside the art world, characterized by connections to multiple domains' pasts and presents, such as botany, science, music, mathematics, and spiritual currents (Moderna Museet, 2016), and uncertain possibilities for a present and future(s). Along that unknown temporality, there was both temporal embeddedness and self-determinism; for example, the artist and others seeking to influence the trajectory of her work, as embedded in their own time. Overall, she used time in the process of her artwork being interpreted, absorbed, and made resonant, rather than just as a subject of her work, as her male colleagues (futurists, cubists, surrealists) did. However, there were also the workings of time itself, as indifferent, unmanaged, and ungovernable as well as a sensory and affective concern (Holt & Johnsen, 2019); for example, decaying the artwork in its long wait for a receptive audience or allowing connections to it when in 'the mood' for it (zeitgeist).

Along this new trajectory, the Swedish artist worked 'collectively,' 'on demand,' her hand driven by higher forces, to execute a vast number of paintings in a very short time and in an as yet unknown style that was decades later defined as a form and precursor of abstraction.[1] Various sources have suggested that af Klint's abstract art initially grew out of the séances she held with a circle of women who called themselves *De Fem* (The Five, translation from Swedish). Hilma af Klint engaged in spiritualism and theosophy to establish an "automatic drawing practice, many years before Surrealism validated this as an artistic method and route to self-discovery" (McNab, 2021, p. 35). She paired these heterodox religious beliefs with her scientific interest to create a new pathway in (her) art, experimenting with "circles, spirals, ovals, cones, globes, lines, triangles, shades of color (dark, light, pastel)" and "playing with scalar space and time, collapsing the distinctions between the microscopic and macroscopic" (Friedman, 2020, p. 133). Sources claim that engaging with the spiritual also allowed her to innovate the art process, becoming "almost a technological apparatus – a recording instrument – recording not messages from the other side but her own aesthetic sensibilities" (Fer, 2020, p. 110). Reflecting on the art process, af Klint herself described that "the pictures were painted directly through me, without any preliminary drawings, and with great force. I had no idea what the paintings were supposed to depict; nevertheless I worked swiftly and surely, without changing a single brush stroke" (Moderna Museet, 2013). However, as some sources have suggested, the involvement of spirits could also have been a way of shielding her radically novel work from the harsh criticism directed at her daring to defy conventions. She left her novel artwork unsigned and unknown beyond her closest circle. In terms of time, this

---

[1] For instance, the exhibition "Cubism and Abstract Art" at MoMA, New York in 1936 (during Hilma af Klint's lifetime) brought together 400 art objects by 113 artists and was "key to establishing the pedigree for modern art proposed by Museum of Modern Art Founding Director Alfred H. Barr, Jr. – a narrative that continues to shape the Museum's presentation of modernism to this day" (MoMA's Exhibition History, 2022). In a press release MoMA (1936) announced that "the purpose of the exhibition is to reveal the development of cubism and abstract art by arranging the material in its historical sequence." Barr Jr. (1936) developed a chart of the evolution of modern art, which appeared on the catalogue's dust jacket. The chart organized the different streams in the evolution along the axes of time (from 1890 to 1935) and styles or movements (from Japanese prints, Synthetism and Neo-Impressionism to Geometrical and Non-Geometrical abstract art), also noting the places (cities and regions) in which these developments took place (for example, Paris, but also Berlin, Cologne, Dessau, Leyden, Milan, Moscow, Munich, Pont Aven, Provence, and Weimer). Barr Jr.'s chart was "designed to help a general public unfamiliar with modern art to learn about Cubism and abstraction in order to 'see' that they were not aberrations" (Lowry, 2013, p. 363).

upended the tradition of signature and origin, underpinning her own understanding of her work not as a novelty made manifest in her art, but as an expression of what is already there, an eternal present.

Along the unknown temporality, she operated as a maverick (Becker, 1976) who developed a new universe of signs and symbols: "her imagery proliferated like a language. With each series she layered her recurring motifs with new forms and subjects" (Bashkoff, 2018b, p. 23). As we know from studies of artistic careers, it is not unusual for artists to be initially in the mainstream – learning and using conventions – before they come up with a distinctive new style (Jones et al., 2016) or that they combine both mainstream and maverick trajectories as amphibian artists (Patriotta & Hirsch, 2016). It is also not unusual that this involves some collective experimentation and effort, as in the case of Cubism (Sgourev, 2013). What is unique about af Klint, though, is her temporal agency in relation to these mainstream and maverick trajectories; that is, her engagement with the future through both the established and the unknown temporality, which involved paintings with distinct materiality, such as differences in size, technique, aesthetics, and process of creation. We argue that by bifurcating time, Hilma af Klint took control over her work "through the means of her imagination" (Fer, 2020, p. 110), which allowed her to transform herself as an artist and the perception of her work. In a sense, she was both a technology for and a confident agent of her radical artistic innovation.

Bridging Time

Bridging time is about connecting Hilma af Klint's unknown temporality and her radical artwork to the established temporality of the present art world. Bridging time is enabled by a diversity of agents with their own interests and agendas, from the artist herself and her family, through critics, artists, and museum curators, showing a 'vote of confidence' in her work, to art historians and scholars coming up with theories and challenging extant understandings of abstract art, as well as the media expressing fascination with af Klint's artwork, creative processes, and overall trajectory. Bridging time as material temporal work is supported by three mechanisms, which we unfold below: narrative construction, waiting time, and emotional resonance of artist and artwork with present-day audiences.

Narrative Construction   Hilma af Klint began constructing her narrative through the materiality of her paintings and in her notebooks. In line with Emirbayer and Mische (1998, p. 989), we argue that narrative construction allowed af Klint to visualize the future path (for example, the encounter with future audiences, her plans for a temple, a center of her own, to house her works) and to create "cultural resources" that provided her with a sense of movement forward in time.

Hilma af Klint left behind "an archive of over 1,300 paintings and sketches, supplemented by a self-edited 26,000 pages of notes" (McNab, 2021, p. 35). In creating the archive, she projected her work into the future through the construction of her own narrative, taking certain control of her story. Preparing that archive involved an active work with materiality, such as destroying work that she did not want future generations to encounter, preparing notes, and creating sketches for the temple in which she envisioned her work would be exhibited. It took a decade of reassessment of her own work. With help, she also created a typewritten transcription of her handwritten 1917 analysis of the key period of her art making. "It's over 2,000 pages typed!" exclaimed artist Josiah McElheny (in Bashkoff, 2018a, p. 34).

The narrative construction highlights the artist's efforts in making both artwork and archive, as well as the pioneering nature and purity of her endeavors: "The experiments I have conducted . . . that were to awaken humanity when they were cast upon the world were pioneering endeavors. Though they travel through much dirt they will yet retain their purity" (af Klint's notebooks, quoted in Ferren, 2019). The narrative also involves a "radical concept that all the works . . . were one entity and must always remain together" (Quaytman, in Birnbaum & Noring, 2013, unnumbered page).

However, as aspects of that narrative were picked up by museum curators and critics – for example, referring to af Klint as a "pioneer of abstraction" or as an "artist, researcher, medium" (Moderna Museet, Stockholm and Malmö, respectively) – counter-narratives were used when refusing to give visibility to af Klint's novel paintings or when questioning their value. With the exception of selections from *The Paintings for the Temple* (1906–1915) that were shown at an Anthroposophical conference in London (Editor's note, Bashkoff, 2018a, p. 47), af Klint's novel work was shown for the first time outside Sweden in Los Angeles in 1986 at an exhibition called 'The spiritual art – Abstract paintings from 1890 to 1985'. Although this exhibition put af Klint at the center of the abstract movement, some critics were rather unappreciative of her merits. For example, as a commentary to af Klint's paintings shown in that exhibition, Kramer (1987, p. 1) wrote:

As documents in the history of abstraction, they have a certain interest, to be sure, but it is not an aesthetic interest. . . . To accord them a place of honor alongside the work of Kandinsky, Mondrian, Malevich, and Kupka, in the section of the exhibition devoted to the pioneers of abstraction, is absurd. Af Klint is simply not an artist in their class, and – dare one say it? – would never have been given this inflated treatment if she had not been a woman.

R. H. Quaytman's "pleading" of af Klint's case encountered contempt and ongoing resistance, on the grounds that "this huge body of work was the product of a crazy woman" (in Birnbaum & Noring (2013), unnumbered page). In that sense, af Klint's paintings meet not only time's affirmative role but also time's negativity (Holt & Johnsen, 2019). Reponen (2020, p. 78), who investigated the development of a discursive field around af Klint, noted how, in the late 1980s, the Swedish artist was mostly referred to as a canon-breaker in the United States, whereas Nordic critics started showing curiosity about the artist herself and her artistry, as well as the "feelings of wonder" her paintings triggered in viewers.

It took several attempts by highly reputable institutions to elaborate on her narrative and endorse her value before interest in her work started to grow. By referring to af Klint as an abstract pioneer, the 2013 exhibition at Moderna Museet in Stockholm, for example, sought to serve "a provocation, inviting a discussion about how to understand her work" (curator Iris Müller-Westermann in conversation with Anni Reponen, in Reponen, 2020, p. 85). For the Serpentine Gallery in London, who exhibited af Klint in 2016, she was "the earliest painter to be shown in a one-person exhibition at the gallery" (Kellaway, 2016). Another direction for the elaboration of the narrative was to compare af Klint with consecrated artistic innovators, by exhibiting her artwork "under the same roof as Picasso" at the Picasso Museum in Malaga, Spain (Reponen, 2020, p. 131) or alongside Mondrian, as announced by the Tate Modern, for an exhibition in 2023. This 'vote of confidence' by the art world – namely, highly visible commitments by reputable art institutions to the artist's novelty and importance – has forcefully connected her narrative with current time.

As museums have their own interests and agendas, it is unsurprising that they also sought to give af Klint's narrative their own spin: to both place her in the larger discourses and timelines of art history, and differentiate their perspectives, (re)claiming different aspects of the artist's identity, such as abstract pioneer, medium, or researcher. Their exhibition catalogues and online (re)sources try to both organize and provide interpretations of the artist's trajectory and radical work, not only in the context of other artistic contributions, but also of their own collections and institutions, developing variations of her narrative, which expands its meaning. For example, the catalogue of af Klint's 2018 exhibition at the Guggenheim (Bashkoff,

2018a) established points of intersection between the creation of the museum's distinctive building by F.L. Wright, originally conceptualized by artist Hilla Rebay (an advisor to Solomon R. Guggenheim, who helped shape his art collection and the ways in which it was to be exhibited) as "the temple of non-objectivity and devotion" (Bashkoff, 2018b, p. 26) and af Klint's ideas of a spiral-like "temple of the spirit" (Bashkoff, 2018b, p. 30) for her works, which she described in her notebooks from 1930–1, a year after Rebay's conceptualization.

Artists inspired by af Klint have singled out the community efforts that supported the path-breaking work, allowing her to create, for example, *The Ten Largest* paintings in about sixty days, an impressive outburst of creativity and physical effort that would be challenging for a present-day artist. In relation to that, Josiah McElheny (in Bashkoff, 2018a, p. 38) affirmed: "I think it's really important for us to remember that she spent years and years with four other women, drawing and talking and thinking together," the products of which she coalesced and synthesized in her work. There has also been a curiosity about the influence on that narrative of keeping af Klint's artwork waiting for twenty years and how others further constructed her narrative. For example, in a conversation among artists, curators, and art historians, transcribed from a 2017 meeting, the moderator Helen Molesworth posed the question: "How has af Klint's refusal to show her work until twenty years after she died, along with the prohibition against selling the work, affected our ability to narrativize her historically?" (in Bashkoff, 2018a, p. 33).

Overall, af Klint did not loudly put her narrative forward. Unlike the Futurists, she did not proclaim her radical innovation in manifestos, and "unlike Kandinsky, she . . . did not position her work specifically as a way of reimagining art" (Solomon R. Guggenheim Museum, 2018a, p. 11). However, in her narrative construction of what she called her 'future paintings' (narrative, to which other institutions and actors would contribute), and in her conviction for waiting for the 'right' time to meet the audience, she was no less political, giving temporal agency to future generations to act on behalf of her work. Below, we will briefly explain the nature and role of waiting time as part of the process of bridging time.

Waiting Time   A well-diffused aspect of af Klint's narrative is that her paintings took a century to reach their audience. Waiting is an interstitial time, both a gap and a link between present and future, which is closely related to expectation, and can involve blockage of action as well as meaningful experience (Gasparini, 1995). Gasparini (1995, p. 30) referred to St Augustine's definition of waiting as "the present of the future" and suggested that waiting implies an actor's orientation towards the future.

Confining af Klint's abstract works to waiting was, first and foremost, the artist's own decision, triggered by concern about not "be[ing] understood by the brothers that you meet" (Hilma af Klint, 1907 – opening quotation to this chapter). Waiting happened both during the artist's life time, when the majority of her abstract works were likely seen only by her close circle, and a limited number of them shown in spiritual circles, as well as subsequently, when these works were placed in a twenty-year 'time capsule', "rolled up in a storage, inaccessible to posterity and awaiting to be brought into the light of day" (Müller-Westermann, 2013, p. 33). However, whereas customary time capsules contain something typical of the time when they are sealed, to be rediscovered when opened by later generations, in the case of af Klint, what was made to wait was a radically novel artwork, atypical of its time, which required comprehension and appreciation by later generations. For the artist, that time capsule infused the artwork with expectation and anticipation for the future.

In addition, waiting was sustained by the artist's family who inherited her work with the twenty-year restriction, in particular, her nephew, Erik af Klint, a naval officer who lacked artistic background or proper means to be the works' custodian. Johan af Klint, Erik's son, who inherited the works from his father, explained: "In 1966 my father and I awoke the works from their imposed twenty-year rest and photographed them. It was a remarkable experience to bring out – and for the first time to see – the artist's creations and feel an affinity with her" (af Klint, Artist's Foundation Statement, in Bashkoff, 2018a, p. 9). According to various sources, in the 1960s, the director of the Moderna Museet in Stockholm turned down af Klint family's offer to donate her entire oeuvre on the grounds that she was a medium, not an artist. That led to the establishment of another repository, in which her work could continue waiting in an organized way: the Hilma af Klint Foundation which took upon itself the task of continuing to protect her work and search for interested audiences. The foundation became a technology of waiting, patient and persistent, metaphorically bringing Hilma af Klint's radical works under its roof. In addition to the family, over the years other interested parties have stepped in for the artist and sought to bring her paintings out of their decades-long wait.

The materiality of waiting – being "rolled up in storage, inaccessible to posterity and awaiting to be brought into the light of day" (Müller-Westermann, 2013, p. 33) – implies an opportunity for discovery and expectation for the encounter. For example, Moderna Museet's experts had to restore the paintings during the wait; they "examined each work, cleaned the paintings, painstakingly smoothed out the rolled-up works on paper and pastels, and mounted and framed the works" (Müller-Westermann, 2013, p. 37). They also had to document and digitize large parts of the oeuvre in order to secure its accessibility and enable research (Colstrup & Tøjner, 2014). The digitalization of the oeuvre may, however, not only be affected by the paintings' past, but can also affect their temporality. Through digitalizing, material traces are left that may constrain or at least shape future action (Blagoev et al., 2018).

Emotional Resonance   In addition to narrative construction and waiting time, for the established and unknown temporalities to meet, the material temporal work of bridging time involves emotional resonance with the paintings and the artist's ideas. Here, we draw on aesthetic theorists who have long argued for the importance of emotion and imagination in understanding and appreciating art. For example, Vischer (1873) used the notion of 'Einfühlung' to describe an observer's ability to empathize with and feel through an artwork. Brinck (2018, p. 205), evoking the phenomenologist Merleau-Ponty, noted that, when observing art, we can "meet in things the actions of another and find in these actions a sense" because they are themes of possibility in our own body. According to Brinck (2018), 'Einfühlung' gives rise to our emotional resonance with art; it is scaffolded by technology and material culture, by rituals, habits and norms, as well as by the more intangible affective mood of our time. Hilma af Klint's decision to keep her novel artwork largely private during her lifetime and to subsequently put it to wait for two decades after her death could be a result of the reactions she may have received from the few people with whom she had shared her innovative paintings. Also, the emotional engagement (or lack thereof) she may have experienced could have convinced her that the world was not ready to embrace her non-figurative work.

After bringing these paintings to light, museums were the primary means for encounters and emotional engagement with af Klint's unconventional work (given that it had not been on the art market), as well as for meaning making around it, along with the media that covered these exhibitions, and sparked curiosity in the artist's trajectory and her paintings. The artist McElheny explained that museums "offer us the potential to return and to experience, again and again, how moments become duration and how the contemporary is timeless," and that af Klint's work is "most effective when experienced by a human body, in physical space, for a period of time" (in Bashkoff, 2018a, p. 47). As Mitsuji (2021) noted, "throughout the secular space of the museum, af Klint's works hum with a transcendent intensity."

Hilma af Klint's major recognition came with her 2013 grand presentation at the Moderna Museet in her native Stockholm with the exhibition 'Hilma af Klint: A Pioneer of Abstraction', a century after her artistic breakthrough, in which af Klint's oeuvre could "be seen for the first time ever in all of its protean complexity" (Müller-Westermann, 2013, p. 37). The exhibition's curator, Iris Müller-Westermann (2013, p. 15), recalled how "mysterious wooden crates, old and enigmatic, arrived from the warehouse where they had been biding time." Expert restorers examined, cleaned, and prepared the paintings for framing, making them ready to meet the audience. Müller-Westermann was surprised by how visitors found themselves crying, unable to explain why, "neither happy nor sad, it was as if spending time with Hilma's paintings spurred something inside them that needed an outlet" (Ferren, 2019). As a "bloc of sensation" (Deleuze & Guattari, 1994, p. 167), the paintings became "a portal, an access point, to another world" (O'Sullivan, 2001, p. 128), or rather, our world experienced differently, and invited visitors into a moment of affective becoming.

Hilma af Klint's novel work was a break from convention, not only in artistic terms but also in gender terms, which has made it hard for her to gain attention and acceptance. After all, "[she] was working in a time when women were not allowed to be creative . . . when they weren't supposed to make things that were new and radical" and where a certain machismo dominated the rhetoric of abstract art (Mitsuji, 2021). Decades later, it is this different subjective space and voice carved out by her work that starts connecting with a changing spirit of time and a broad audience, and young artists of many stripes. The artistic director of the Serpentine galleries, Hans Ulrich Obrist (2020, p. 101), argued that "[af Klint's] concerns resonate with so much contemporary practice that we felt it was urgent to represent her vision." Her "fearfully esoteric" art "matches a present mood of restless searching" (Schjeldahl, 2018). It attracts attention and resonates with a collective longing for more meaning and purpose in the hyper-technological, profit-driven, and creative-disruptive landscapes that map the psychic spaces of contemporary societies. Some have suggested that the otherworldly magnetism of af Klint's work is to propose a specific interpretation of modernity, one that offers a return to "a sense of mystery and order in a world that seems dispiriting and beyond control," opening up a different conception of our relationship with the world (Davis, 2018).

Hilma af Klint's work touches audiences differently in the present day, perhaps because the values her work presents – female, spiritual, ecological, collectivist – are values that artists and audiences desperately seek to reclaim. At the same time, af Klint's work speaks to new spiritual, cultural, and technological trends that expand her resonance sphere: her work being aptly absorbed and reverberated by the aesthetic surfaces, occultist, and activist sensibilities promoted by social networks such as Instagram, as well as in popular culture more generally, where her work has featured in films such as *Personal Shopper*, starring Kristen Stewart, and in an ever-expanding series of merchandise. The artist's rise to popularity is reflective of a collective state of mind that longs for something transcendent and that has managed to bring af Klint's work into a 'timely' bloom (Davis, 2019; Ventura, 2018).

While af Klint did not have disciples, she "has a devoted following amongst some of the most exciting artists of the last two decades, and . . . when her work is revisited by a new generation, the process very often starts with artists" (Obrist, 2020, p. 101). Artists' search for forgotten ancestors allow their own work to acquire sense (Ossandón, 2020). For example, Quaytman argued that af Klint "used what artists today also use: temporality, seriality, language, the unconscious, science and sexuality" (in Birnbaum & Noring, 2013, unnumbered page). Hence, she is resonant with contemporary approaches and sensibilities; she is current. Quaytman (in Birnbaum & Noring, 2013, unnumbered page) also affirmed that the dilemma of what she believed seems so inconsequential compared with how the paintings themselves stir her and others; that is the timeliness of their emotional resonance.

In addition to the paintings, the materiality of and ideas in her notebooks is another source of emotional resonance. In a book with a complete facsimile of one of af Klint's notebooks, Birnbaum and Noring (2013) brought together nine artists who share an interest in her artwork. In the book, one of these artists, Eva Löfdahl, reflected on her encounter with af Klint's works of art:

When I first encountered Hilma af Klint's oeuvre in 1989, I found her statements to be liberating. Her lucidity, even if a great deal was completely impenetrable, had an effect. Her statements stimulated speculation, at a time when the question was always more important than the answer. But above all, she helped me realize the importance of delivering something in a form that enables it to have an effect. (Löfdahl, in Birnbaum & Noring, 2013, unnumbered page)

Last but not least, the artist's work and ideas resonate with our digital age. For example, diverse technologies of digital reproduction have made images of af Klint's paintings widely accessible and, in a sense, omnipresent (from notebook covers to art reprints and even shopping bags). YouTube videos, podcasts, and other multimodal resources have brought stories about the artist to life. These technologies can produce engagement and meaning, beyond the powerful voice of reputable art institutions or journalists in prestigious media. They enable each of us to encounter the artist on our own terms and project her further, opening up through her work new futures in art and life. In addition, the digital is not only an enabler of af Klint's trajectory; her ideas also anticipated it. For example, Birnbaum (2021), evoking Walter Benjamin's observation that certain art forms are prophetic, in that their effects require a new technical standard or art form, reflected on how the temple af Klint envisioned for her works (what he referred to as her institutional imagination for the museum as both individual and communal) could be considered an anticipation of virtual space and digital technology.

Discussion and Conclusion: Powering Time to Reach the Future

In this final section, having examined two processes of material temporal work – bifurcating time and bridging time – that enabled Hilma af Klint's novel artwork to find receptive future audiences, we connect the two processes through the notion of powering time (that is, giving agency to time). We suggest that powering time contributes to the politics of meaning (Slavich et al., 2020); that is, to the contested processes of meaning making in the context of radical artistic innovation that make it possible for the novel artwork to be comprehensible to experts and audiences that are distant in time. In that, as we acknowledged earlier, time not only plays an affirmative role, but also reveals its negativity (Holt & Johnsen, 2019) in decaying the works and delaying their connection with the audiences.

Hilma af Klint's temporal agency and the material temporal work in which she (and others on her behalf) engaged, show how time can become a resource (cf. Hernes, 2022), and, through the materiality of different artifacts, can also have political qualities (Winner, 1980) in creating and transforming novel artworks' perception, position, and influence. In envisioning the importance of her novel artwork for future generations and finding ways to ensure that work reaches them, af Klint acted as a temporal architect (cf. Flaherty et al., 2020) of her own and others' temporal agency. However, instead of engaging herself in an overt politics of meaning, putting forward arguments and artifacts related to the radical innovation to the public domain and in reputable institutions (Slavich et al., 2020), af Klint let her paintings and notes, as well as time itself, become political agents and do the politics. That political agency was sustained by an unwavering belief in and temporal foresight for the energy and emotional resonance of her work, captivating and speaking to audiences and artists in a distant future, long after af Klint's lifetime.

While radicality and artistic innovation are often associated with the immediate present and are often encountered through the noise they make and the sense of urgency they convey in their attempt to disrupt the here and now, af Klint's case tells a different story. The trajectory of her work shows that articulating radical novelty can also be a quiet and patient process that bides its time, preparing for and anticipating a receptive future to which it will contribute. Hilma af Klint's double marginality, as innovator and woman, which positioned her at the fringe of the powerful artistic networks of the avant-garde movements of her time, made the material temporal work of waiting time a central element in powering time against the prejudices her work faced. Rather than being a passive act, waiting time became a deliberate and carefully orchestrated strategy that unfolded an unexpected and subversive power, challenging established temporalities.

We can see from af Klint's abstract geoforms, symbols, and color wheels how her paintings invoke and enfold different temporalities (cf. Barad, 2013). They do so by materializing past and present scientific discourse, such as Darwinian evolution, and movements in spirituality, such as theosophy, and projecting a future that combines these elements with a higher spiritual reality. Hilma af Klint's paintings are both materially durable and temporally malleable, similar to Feddersen et al.'s (Chapter 11, this volume) description of the material temporality of buildings. Following the aim of changing society through art, af Klint made use of her paintings to link these different material temporalities and bring her imagined future into being. Her way of future making enables a more sensorial orientation towards the future (cf. Comi & Whyte, 2018).

Furthermore, through af Klint's detaching her conventional from her radical paintings (bifurcating time), as well as anticipating and imagining the latter's encounter with future generations (bridging time), the artist allowed the paintings themselves to "do" time (Barad, 2013; Hernes et al., 2021). Following Barad (2008, p. 139), we could interpret af Klint's paintings as performative, an "intra-active becoming, not a thing, but a doing, a congealing of agency." They give form to imagined futures through the symbols, geoforms, and colors, escaping past and present constraints, such as the male-dominated art world and non-abstract genres. Hence, what we learn from af Klint's work is an imaginative dialogue between human and non-human agency that she uses to shape and power time. On the one hand are the spirits that speak to her which she materializes in her paintings; on the other hand is the imagined interaction between paintings and viewers envisioned to change viewers' perception of the world (bringing together art and life).

According to Emirbayer (1997, p. 294), "agency is always a dialogic process … with others in collectively organized action contexts, temporal as well as spatial." In this case, the paintings create the organized action context that af Klint projects into the future. In this sense, although it is not intended, our study of af Klint is a response to Comi and Whyte's (2018) call for studies of the entwinement of human and non-human agencies in future making. We refer to this process as powering time to emphasize af Klint's work in and through her paintings, and to acknowledge both human and non-human agency that power time. Engaging distant generations with her paintings, she makes a difference to society that is in its continuous becoming: "visual artefacts set transformation in motion, in that they give form to abstract imaginings of the future, and in so doing contribute to make a future that would not otherwise be (or that would perhaps take a different form)" (Comi & Whyte, 2018, p. 1078).

Future making is based on emotional resonance. The sociologist and social theorist Hartmut Rosa (2019) used the notion of 'resonance' to theorize a relationship where humans experience a reciprocal 'touch' and 'being touched' by others, becoming aware of their physical and emotional intertwinement with the world. This notion denotes a more active, dynamic moment of encounter or of being mutually addressed. Rosa noted that art has specific potential to create resonance, but at the same time also acknowledged that resonance as an emotional state needs resonance spheres, hence spatial, temporal, physical, psychological, and social conditions that enable the emergence of such resonance experiences. Clearly, af Klint was betting that new times would make her novel work resonate, sparking a vibration.

This chapter has discussed how temporal agency and material temporal work can protect radically novel artwork from incomprehension and project it towards receptive future audiences, while becoming a vehicle for the making of future. In that, politics of meaning is the subtle, yet powerful act of the paintings' emotional resonance, their ability to bide time and tell new stories about art and life. Politics of meaning is also the organizing power of time itself that makes it possible to connect the meanings that innovators give to their novel work and the public arenas, in which the meanings are renegotiated.

Acknowledgments: The authors wish to thank Gabriela (Gabi) Garza De Linde and José Ossandón for the insightful conversations and for pointing us in the direction of helpful sources, as well as Robin Holt for his inspiring feedback. We gratefully acknowledge funding support for our work on this chapter: Miriam Feuls and Silviya

Svejenova to the Velux Foundation (grant #00021807), and Christina Lüthy to the Swiss National Science Foundation (grant P2SGP1_200037).

References

Bansal, P. Reinecke, J., Suddaby, R. & Langley, A. (2022). Temporal work: The strategic organization of time. *Strategic Organization*, *20*(1), 6–19.

Barad, K. (2008). Posthumanist Performativity: Toward an Understanding of How Matter Comes to Matter. In S. Alaimo & S. Hekman (eds), *Material Feminisms* (pp. 120–54). Bloomington: Indiana University Press.

Barad, K. (2013). Mar(k)ing Time: Material Entanglement and (Re)memberings: Cutting Together and Apart. In P. Carlile, D. Nicolini, A. Langley, & H. Tsoukas. (eds), *How Matter Matters: Objects, Artifacts and Materiality in Organization Studies* (pp. 16–31). Oxford: Oxford University Press.

Barr Jr., A. H. (1936). Cubism and Abstract Art. *The Museum of Modern Art*. New York. Available at: https://moma.org/documents/moma_catalogue_2748_300086869.pdf?_ga=2.242891521.2053702799.1656769981-1314868305.1656622880.

Bashkoff, T. (2018a). *Hilma af Klint: Paintings for the Future*. New York: Guggenheim.

Bashkoff, T. (2018b). Temples for Paintings. In T. Bashkoff (ed.), *Hilma af Klint: Paintings for the Future*. New York: Guggenheim.

Becker, H. S. (1976). Art Worlds and Social Types. *American Behavioral Scientist*, *19*(6), 703–18.

Behr, S. (2002). Differencing Modernism. In C. Widenheim (ed.), *Utopia & Reality. Modernity in Sweden 1900–1960* (pp. 108–21). New York: Yale University Press.

Birnbaum, D. (2021). Lucid dreaming: Daniel Birnbaum on Hilma af Klint's institutional imagination. *Artforum*, *60*(1), https://artforum.com/print/202107/daniel-birnbaum-on-hilma-af-klint-s-institutional-imagination-86326.

Birnbaum, D. & Noring, A-S. (2013). *The Legacy of Hilma af Klint: Nine Contemporary Responses. Moderna Museet*. London: Koening Books.

Blagoev, B., Felten, S. & Kahn, R. (2018). The career of a catalogue: Organizational memory, materiality and the dual nature of the past at the British Museum (1970–Today). *Organization Studies*, *39*, 1757–83.

Brinck, I. (2018). Empathy, engagement, entrainment: The interaction dynamics of aesthetic experience. *Cognitive Processing*, *19*(2), 201–13.

Colstrup, T. & Tøjner, P. E. (2014). Forord. Hilma af Klint – Abstraioneerner. *Louisiana Revy*, *54*(2), 7. Louisiana Museum of Modern Art.

Comi, A. & Whyte, J. (2018). Future making and visual artefacts: An ethnographic study of a design project. *Organization Studies*, *39*(8), 1055–83.

de Vaujany, F-X., Mitev, N., Laniray, P., & Vaast, E. (2014). Introduction: Time and Materiality: What is at Stake in the Materialization of Time and Time as a Materialization? In F-X. de Vaujany, N. Mitev, P. Laniray, & E. Vaast. (eds), *Materiality and Time. Technology, Work and Globalization* (pp. 1–13). London: Palgrave Macmillan.

Davis, B. (2018, October 23). Why Hilma af Klint's occult spirituality makes her the perfect artist for our technologically disrupted time. *Artnet News*. Available at: https://news.artnet.com/art-world/hilma-af-klints-occult-spirituality-makes-perfect-artist-technologically-disrupted-time-1376587.

Davis, B. (2019). Here's how the Hilma af Klint show played perfectly into the current zeitgeist to become the Guggenheim's most-visited exhibition ever. *Artnet News*. Available at: https://news.artnet.com/art-world/hilma-af-klint-breaks-records-guggenheim-1522192.

Deleuze, G. & Guattari, F. (1994). *What is Philosophy?* Trans. H. Tomlinson & G. Burchell III. New York: Columbia University Press.

Dyrschka, H. (2019). *Beyond the Visible – Hilma af Klint*. Zeitgeistfilm. Available at: https://zeitgeistfilms.com/film/beyondthevisiblehilmaafklint.

Emirbayer, M. (1997). Manifesto for a relational sociology. *American Journal of Sociology*, *103*(2), 281–317.

Emirbayer, M. & Mische, A. (1998). What is agency? *American Journal of Sociology*, *103*(4), 962–1023.

Feddersen, J., Hernes, T., & Svejenova, S. (2023). Towards a Processual Understanding of Buildings: Temporality, Materiality, and Politics. In F-X. de Vaujany, R. Holt, & A. Grandazzi (eds), *Organization as Time: Technology, Power and Politics* (Chapter 11, this volume). Cambridge: Cambridge University Press.

Fer, B. (2020). Hilma af Klint: The Outsider Inside Herself. In K. Almqvist & L. Belfrage (eds), *Hilma af Klint: Seeing is Believing* (pp. 105–13). Stockholm: Bokförlaget Stolpe.

Ferren, A. (2019, October 21). In search of Hilma af Klint, who upended art history, but left few traces. *The New York Times*. Available at: https://nytimes.com/2019/10/21/travel/stockholm-hilma-af-klint.html.

Feuls, M., Stjerne, I., Reinecke, J., Garud, R., Ravasi, D., Schultz, M., & Slawinski, N. (2020). Temporality of innovations: How do different concepts of time further our understanding of managing and organizing innovations? Showcase Symposium, Academy of Management Annual Meeting Proceedings.

Flaherty, M. G. (2020). The Lathe of Time: Some Principles of Temporal Agency. In M. G. Flaherty, A. L. Dalsgård, & L. Meinert (eds), *Time Work: Studies of Temporal Agency* (pp. 13–30). New York & Oxford: Berghahn Books.

Flaherty, M. G., Dalsgård, A. L., & Meinert, L. (2020). Introduction. In M. G. Flaherty, A. L. Dalsgård, & L. Meinert (eds), *Time Work: Studies of Temporal Agency* (pp. 3–12). New York & Oxford: Berghahn Books.

Friedman, S. S. (2020). Scaling planetarity: Spacetime in the new modernist studies – Virginia Woolf, HD, Hilma af Klint, Alicja Kwade, Kathy Jetñil-Kijiner. *Feminist Modernist Studies*, *3*(2), 118–47.

Gasparini, G. (1995). On waiting. *Time & Society*, *4*(1), 29–45.

Granqvist, N. & Gustafsson, R. (2016). Temporal institutional work. *Academy of Management Journal*, *59*(3), 1009–35.

Hernes, T. (2022). *Organization and Time*. Oxford: Oxford University Press.

Hernes, T., Feddersen, J., & Schultz, M. (2021). Material temporality: How materiality 'does' time in food organizing. *Organization Studies*, *42*(2), 351–71.

Hilma af Klint Foundation (2022). About. Available at: https://hilmaafklint.se/a bout-hilma-af-klint/.

Holt, R. & Johnsen, R. (2019). Time and organization studies. *Organization Studies, 40*(10), 1557–72.

Jones, C., Svejenova, S., Pedersen, J.S., & Townley, B. (2016). Misfits, mavericks and mainstreams: Drivers of innovation in the creative industries. *Organization Studies, 37*(6), 751–68.

Kaplan, S. & Orlikowski, W. J. (2013). Temporal work in strategy making. *Organization Science, 24*(4), 965–95.

Kellaway, K. (2016, February 21). Hilma af Klint: A painter possessed. *The Guardian.* Available at: https://theguardian.com/artanddesign/2016/feb/21/hil ma-af-klint-occult-spiritualism-abstract-serpentine-gallery.

Kramer, H. (1987). On "The Spiritual in Art" in Los Angeles, 5(8), 1. Available at: https://newcriterion.com/issues/1987/4/on-the-aoespiritual-in-arta-in-los-angeles.

Lowry, G. D. (2013). Abstraction in 1936: Barr's Diagrams. In L. Dickermann, (ed.), *Inventing Abstraction, 1910–1925: How a Radical Idea Changed Modern Art* (pp. 359–63). New York: Museum of Modern Art.

McNab, J. (2021). Hilma af Klint and the need for historical revision. *Religious Studies Review, 47*(1), 35–40.

Miller, D. & Sardais, C. (2015). Bifurcating time: How entrepreneurs reconcile the paradoxical demands of the job. *Entrepreneurship Theory and Practice, 39*(3), 489–512.

Mitsuji, T. (2021, June 15). Hilma af Klint's 'miraculous' art: "In dialogue with spirits, she found her own voice." *The Guardian.* Available at: https://theguar dian.com/artanddesign/2021/jun/15/hilma-af-klints-miraculous-art-in-dialogue-with-spirits-she-found-her-own-voice.

Moderna Museet (2013). Hilma af Klint: A pioneer of abstraction. Topics and central works. Available at: https://modernamuseet.se/stockholm/en/exhib itions/hilma-af-klint-2013/topics/.

Moderna Museet (2016). *Nu visar vi verk av Hilma af Klint.* Available at: https:// modernamuseet.se/stockholm/sv/2016/02/05/verk-av-hilma-af-klint-visas/.

MoMA (1936). Museum of Modern Art's press release on the Exhibition of Cubism and Abstract Art. Available at: https://moma.org/documents/moma_ press-release_325049.pdf.

MoMA's Exhibition History (2022). Cubism and Abstract Art, Mar 2–Apr 19, 1936. Available at: https://moma.org/calendar/exhibitions/2748.

Müller-Westermann, I. (2013). Paintings for the Future: Hilma af Klint – A Pioneer of Abstraction in Seclusion. In I. Müller-Westermann & J. Widoff (eds), *Hilma af Klint – A Pioneer of Abstraction* (pp. 33–51). Stockholm: Moderna Museet and Hatje Cantz Verlag.

Obrist, H. U. (2020). An Extraordinary Opportunity. In K. Almqvist & L. Belfrage (eds), *Hilma af Klint: Seeing is Believing* (pp. 101–2). Stockholm: Bokförlaget Stolpe.

Ossandón, J. (2020). Reading as Theorizing: A Conjecture Based on the Savage Detectives' Mode of Inquiry. In C. De Cock, D. O'Doherty, C. Huber, & S. N. Just (eds), *Organization 2666: Literary Troubling, Undoing and Refusal* (pp. 45–61). Wiesbaden: Springer VS.

O'Sullivan, S. (2001). The aesthetics of affect: Thinking art beyond representation. *Angelaki*, 6(3), 125–35.

Patriotta, G. & Hirsch, P. M. (2016). Mainstreaming innovation in art worlds: Cooperative links, conventions and amphibious artists. *Organization Studies, 37* (6), 867–87.

Pontikes, E. G. & Rindova, V. P. (2020). Shaping markets through temporal, constructive, and interactive agency. *Strategy Science*, 5(3), 149–59.

Reponen, A. (2020). Breaking Myths! Unveiling the storytelling processes in the reception of Hilma af Klint from the 1980s and 2010s. Stockholms Universitet, Institutionen för kultur och estetik. Available at: http://su.diva-portal.org/sma sh/get/diva2:1469894/FULLTEXT01.pdf.

Rosa, H. (2019). *Resonance: A Sociology of Our Relationship to the World*. Trans. J. Wagner. Medford, MA: Polity.

Schjeldahl, P. (2018, October 15). Hilma af Klint's visionary paintings. *New Yorker*. Available at: https://newyorker.com/magazine/2018/10/22/hilma-af-klints-visionary-paintings.

Schultz, M. & Hernes, T. (2013). A temporal perspective on organizational identity. *Organization Science*, 24(1), 1–21.

Sgourev, S. V. (2013). How Paris gave rise to Cubism and Picasso: Ambiguity and fragmentation in radical innovation. *Organization Science*, 24(6), 1601–17.

Slavich, B., Svejenova, S, Opazo, M. P., & Patriotta, G. (2020). Politics of meaning in categorizing innovation: How chefs advanced molecular gastronomy by resisting the label. *Organization Studies*, 41(2), 267–90.

Solomon R. Guggenheim Museum (2018a). Hilma af Klint: Paintings for the future. Teacher Resource Unit. Available at: https://guggenheim.org/wp-content/uploads/2018/10/guggenheim-education-hilma-af-klint-teacher-resource-unit-10-5.pdf.

Solomon R. Guggenheim Museum (2018a). Hilma af Klint: Paintings for the future. Available at: https://guggenheim.org/exhibition/hilma-af-klint.

Svejenova, S. (2018). "It Must Give Birth to a World": Temporality and Creative Leadership for Artistic Innovation. In C. Mainemelis, O. Epitropaki, & R. Kark (eds), *Creative Leadership: Contexts and Prospects* (pp. 171–88). New York: Routledge Studies in Leadership Research.

Svejenova, S., Strandgaard Pedersen, J., & Vives, L. (2011). Projects of Passion: Lessons for Strategy from Temporary Art. In G. Cattani, S. Ferriani, L. Frederiksen, & F. Täube (eds), *Project-Based Organizing and Strategic Management (Advances in Strategic Management)* (Vol. 28, pp. 501–27). Bingley, UK: Emerald Group Publishing Limited.

Ventura, A. (2018, October 11). Secret séances and high masters: The making of mystic painter Hilma af Klint. *Frieze*. Available at: https://frieze .com/article/secret-seances-and-high-masters-making-mystic-painter-hilma-af-klint.

Vischer, R. (1873). *Über das optische Formgefühl: ein Beitrag zur Aesthetik*. Leipzig: Credner.

Voss, J. (2018). The Traveling Hilma af Klint. In T. Bashkoff (ed.), *Hilma af Klint: Paintings for the Future* (pp. 49–63). New York: Guggenheim.

Voss, J. (2020). *Hilma af Klint. Biographie.* Frankfurt: S. Fischer.
White, H. C. & White, C. A. (1965). *Canvases and Careers: Institutional Change in the French Painting World.* New York: John Wiley & Sons.
Winner, L. (1980). Do artifacts have politics? *Daedalus, 109*(1), 121–36.
Zeitgeist Films (2019). Film synopsis. Available at: https://zeitgeistfilms.com/film/beyondthevisiblehilmaafklint.
Zerubavel, E. (1987). The language of time: Toward a semiotics of temporality. *The Sociological Quarterly, 28*(3), 343–56.

3

In the Practice *Agencement*
Rhythms, Refrains and Feminist Snaps

Silvia Gherardi

Introduction

To introduce the reader to the conceptualization of practice as an *agencement*[1] of humans, materials, objects, discourses, times, spaces and affect all becoming together and morphing into each other, I tell a short, personal story of how I became aware of the practical importance of time, materiality and power long before becoming a feminist new materialist scholar.

My first fieldwork took place in the fitting shop of a firm that made batteries, and I still vividly remember that one of the first things the workers told me was how important it was at the beginning of the morning shift to meet a workmate who shared the same pace. The meaning of 'the same pace' was very clear and very specific:

You must report for work at 6.00 in the morning and work non-stop until 9.15. When you enter to take my place,[2] the first thing you must do is check on the large board at the end of shop to find out what type of battery is being assembled today and what the quota is. Then you go and meet your workmate. You'll be taking turns with him to weld the terminals onto the batteries and beat the plates. When you are the beater, lay the separators on the bench, put the negative plates on the left, the positive plates in the centre, and the separators on the right. Then lay the separators on top of the negative plates and then the positive plates on top of them. Repeat the action several times to build up the units. Then put the units on the bench for your mate to pick up and weld the terminals. You have to put your back into it, so that you can keep the last hour free: in the first few hours you keep up a good work-rate, taking turns at beating and welding with your workmate every four batches. It's the older one of the pairs who fixes the work-rate when both

---

[1] The reason for preferring to keep Deleuze and Guattari's (1987) French word *agencement*, poorly translated into English as assemblage, is that the French term retains its root in agency and has a processual connotation – the idea of establishing or forming an assemblage – and is not a fixed state of assembled things. My aim is to shift the attention away from what is interconnected towards the way the elements that are entangled achieve agency by being interconnected (Gherardi, 2016).

[2] Here I am using the "interview with the double," a projective technique based on the following instruction for the interviewee: "I want to imagine myself as your double, completely the same as you, and that tomorrow morning I shall be going to work in your place. How should I behave, what should I do so that no one discovers the switch?"

agree. When you have done three hours' hard work and the daily quota is in the bag, you can slow down, take a ten-minute break every hour and go out for a cigarette, a coffee or a chat. After the lunch break you don't work like you did in the morning: you finish your quota, you catch up a bit if you've fallen behind, and you try to finish earlier so you can clean your work station and take a well-earned rest. It's important to work fast in the morning so that you don't have to worry about your daily quota and you can relax in the afternoon (Gherardi, 1995b, p. 12).

It is easy to imagine that not all the workers understood, in the same way, the meaning of 'same pace' (and the normativity implied in it). Moreover, the daily differences in the materiality of the plates put at risk obtaining the quota and therefore interfered with the regularity of the daily work rhythm. A complex social ritual was in place for negotiating the 'right' quota of production. However, still in my ears is the sound and the cadence of the 'beating of the plates' and how that sound was recognizable amid all the noises, human and mechanical, of an assembly line. It was not music, but it had a specific tempo.

Sharing this personal memory has the aim of sharing my understanding of a working practice as an *agencement* of entangled elements that achieve agency in their being interconnected. Although *agencement* is very close to assemblage or arrangement, the English concepts nonetheless imply a divide between agencies and arrangements, while Deleuze and Guattari (1987) wanted to stress that agencies and arrangements are not separate. Thus, the notion of *agencement* allows for tracing agency in the configuration of the practice instead of tracing it in sole actors. Moreover, the French term *agencement* points to the 'becoming' of practices, to practic*ing*.

The collective achievement of the daily quota is the effect of how different humans embody different temporalities, how the speed of the assembly line has a linear temporality, how the variability of the materials contrasts the human desire to regulate the rhythm. Moreover, workers and management use time as a strategic resource, and this multiplicity and plurality of times[3] (often conflictual and dyschronic) is inscribed in the history of that factory in which the workers' past struggles legitimized the tacit reduction of daily working hours. Times, spaces, materialities, discourses, rules and powers are not only entangled but flow as entangled elements that achieve different configurations according to the capacity of those elements to affect and to be affected, while becoming together.

---

[3] When referring to the plurality of times (Gherardi and Strati, 1988), I consider multiple time including time as dyschronic: "made of multiple conflicts of temporalities in a present that is not shared anymore" (de Vaujany et al., 2021, p. 687). An example of dyschronic time is the multiple time of digital world, for example, time without the experience of the duration as in the digital world (López, 2019).

In introducing an image of practice as an *agencement*, I suggest also a posthumanist definition of practice in which humans are de-centered (they are not the main nor the only source of agency), and more-than-humans (the world that we are of including humans, animals and earth others) play an agentive role in their ongoing materialization. In particular I wish to explore, through a feminist new materialist lens, how the entanglement of time, the complex materialities of bodies and power are practiced into being (Hopwood, 2014), that is to say, how they are performed in working and in research practices as well as through the researchers' conceptualizations. It is important to notice that the researchers' practices are part of the same *agencement* since their epistemic practices draw the boundaries around the 'objects' they study thus operating inclusions and exclusions, or, what matters and what is excluded from mattering.

The chapter proposes this intention by means of two concepts – refrain and feminist snap – that I understand as being linked to a qualitative tone of time and rhythm. In this choice I follow the post-qualitative approach to the use of 'concepts as method' (Lenz Taguchi & St. Pierre, 2017), that is, how concepts create orientations for thinking. Following Deleuze and Guattari (1994), concepts are devices that draw on the complexities of the empirical world in order to open "our theoretical imagination to things as they might be, rather than to represent or capture these complexities in knowledge. Concepts deal with possibilities" (Gane, 2009, p. 87).

In the following sections I consider first the relationship between time, practice and agentive materiality, then introduce the concept of refrain and feminist snap. In the conclusion, I discuss the contribution of these two concepts to theorizing the flow of agency within a practice *agencement* as performative and affective.

Time and Practice

We may consider that a main characteristic of practice is its constitutive recursiveness. Giddens (1984) considers the essential recursiveness of social life, as constituted in social practices. There is an idea of time when we say that something is recursive, implying doing or saying the same thing several times in order to produce a particular result or effect. The same idea of iterative time and practice distinguishes between theories of action and theories of practice (Cohen, 1996). While the theories of action privilege the intentionality of actors, from which meaningful action derives (in the tradition of Weber and Parsons), the theories of practice locate the source of significant patterns in how conduct is enacted, performed or produced (in the tradition of Schutz, Dewey, Mead, Garfinkel and Giddens). While theories of action start from individuals and from their intentionality in pursuing courses of action, theories of practice view actions as 'taking place' or 'happening,'; as being performed through a network of connections-in-action, as life-world and dwelling (as the phenomenological legacy calls them; see Chia & Holt, 2006; Dall'Alba et al., 2018; Holt & Sandberg, 2011). The adoption of an ecological model that gives ontological priority to neither humans nor nonhumans nor discursive practices, constitutes the fundamental difference between theories of action and those of practice, as Cohen (1996) argues, and as a posthumanist practice theory, develops further, considering a practice as an *agencement* of human, nonhuman, more-than-human and discursive elements (Gherardi, 2019).

In other words, practices are not actions, nor are they just activities; they are also the configuration of the world in which such activities are significant. Practices not only develop and persist in time: they constitute time. Practices are order-producing devices thanks to the expectation that they will take place over and over again as long as they continue to be practiced and thus reproduced in a changing continuity in time, so that they are once again performed "for another first time" (Garfinkel, 1967, p. 9).

Temporality inscribed in practices and practicing is a theme that has received much consideration in practice-based studies of consumption. Shove (2009, p. 17) writes: "temporal arrangements arise from the effective reproduction of everyday life, or, to put it more strongly, practices *make* [emphasis in original] time." Therefore, three orientations towards time can be followed: one to the production of time, one to the consumption of time and the third to forms of substitution in the use of time. Shove, for example, mentions the changing habit of daily showering as opposed to weekly bathing as a social way of squeezing time and as an example of inquiring about how some practices emerge and others disappear (2009, p. 17).

However, the relation between time and practice is quite complex also because time and space are analytically inseparable; rather, we should think in terms of the timespace of social practices (Schatzki, 2006, 2010). For example, Hernes' (2022) definition of time includes four dimensions: experience, events, resource and practices, which evolve through mutual interplay. In elaborating on time-as-practice, Hernes supplements the 'stretched-outness' of practices with their 'reach-outness': "Whereas stretched-outness signifies a direct projection from the present to what is to come, a reach-outness assumes that practices address a future and a past that lie beyond the temporal structures of actors" (Hernes, 2022, p. 69). We may conclude this point about time-as-practice by saying that the temporal micro-dynamics of the stretched-outness and reach-outness is an iterative movement of continually bridging past and future in the present of an ongoing practice.

In this chapter I am interested in the relation between time and practice that concerns the multiplicity of times and the enactment of cyclical time as rhythm, tempo and repetition in situated practices and fleeting moments of time. While pluralism assumes that there is a single objective time of which a plurality of perspectives can exist, multiplicity assumes that there are multiple ways of practicing it. Each way of practicing performs a different version of 'the' time. Hence, time is not 'one,' but more than one: a time multiple.

Rhythms and their institutionalization have been studied mainly by Blue (2019) as the emergence, establishment and entrenchment of connections between returning practices. With this approach, based on Lefebvre's rhythmanalysis, entrainment of institutionally inscribed rhythms is the outcome of the movements of rhythms within a polyrhythmia as they crash into one another, disrupt, adjust to, absorb and affect each other. When a given set of rhythms is reproduced and strengthens its connections in returning, this movement enables and supports further repetition. In particular, my intention is to explore the rhythmic and affective flow of practice, looking for the entanglement of power and temporality.

In order to delineate my argument, I need to make explicit that my conceptual approach to practice theory is grounded in a feminist post-humanist epistemology (Gherardi, 2019) that defines practice as an *agencement* of humans, nonhumans, discourses, times and spaces. A posthumanist practice theory participates in the conversation about post-epistemologies which blurs the boundaries between ontology and epistemology (Barad, 2007) and which includes feminist posthumanism, feminist new materialisms and feminist affect theories (Ringrose et al., 2019). This conversation decentres the human as the sole source of agency, challenges the anthropocentric ideals of the human as sovereign over the world and dismantles binary thinking that separates nature from culture, among other dualist pairings. When a practice is approached as an *agencement* of entangled components, at the forefront is sociomateriality; a conception of agency as a temporal flow emergent in situated material–discursive practices; and affect as the capacity to affect and be affected. The power of affect within an *agencement* is formed as the elements' capacity to affect and be affected, thus affective flow within a practice can be seen as the agentic capacity of linking or dissolving entangled relationships.

In the following sections I follow Lenz Taguchi and St. Pierre's (2017) methodological suggestion of using 'concepts as method,' meaning that a concept is 'an act of thought' (Deleuze & Guattari, 1994, p. 21) that creates orientations for thinking. I have been inspired by two concepts – refrain and feminist snap – and my aim is to explore how these two concepts can offer an orientation for thinking through the entanglement of time, materiality, power and affect within research practices in a way that frames, differently, the rhythmic happening of social practices.

Refrain

A refrain is a regularly recurring phrase or verse at the end of a poem or in music between stanzas, or just any phrase that is often repeated. Thus, refrain relates to recurrence, repetition and repetition with a cadence, a melody, a rhythm. As a philosophical concept it has been elaborated by Deleuze and Guattari (1987) in their plateau 11 "1837: Of the refrain." Their chapter opens with an example of refrain: a child in the dark, gripped with fear, comforts himself by singing. Other examples are the birds that sing to mark a territory, a housewife that sings to herself, or listens to the radio, as she marshals the antichaos forces of her work. Deleuze, in the video *Abécédaire*, in which he is in conversation with Claire Parnet, uses onomatopoeia in order to explain this concept:

Let's say, the ritornello is a little tune, "tra-la-la-la, tra-la-la-la." When do I say "tra-la-la?"

I am doing philosophy here, I'm doing philosophy in asking when do I sing "tra-la-la," when do I sing to myself? I sing to myself on three occasions: I sing to myself when I am moving about in my territory, wiping off my furniture, radio playing in the background, that is, when I am in my home (*chez moi*). Then, I sing to myself when I am not at home and I am trying to reach home (*regagner le chez moi*), at nightfall, at the hour of agony, I'm seeking my way, and I give myself courage by singing, "tra-la-la," I'm going toward my home. And then, I sing to myself when I say "farewell, I am leaving, and I will carry you with me in my heart," it's a popular song [Deleuze softly sings these words] (Deleuze & Parnet, 1988, p. 77).

Refrains emerge as the differential patterning through the relations between milieu, rhythm and territory. Milieus are made of activities and spaces, and ongoing movement among milieus creates territories and rhythm; this movement is the creative act of making connections with and within (and between and among) milieus. Rhythm connects milieus and is about becoming, and a milieu exists by virtue of a periodic repetition, but "it is the difference that is rhythmic, not the repetition, which nevertheless produces it" (Deleuze & Guattari, 1987, p. 314). Rhythm is in the in-between space – the intermilieu where difference is generated and a refrain involves an element of recurrence, but it is not a repetition or a copy of the same, rather it is "a repetition with a difference," whose "significance is in what it *does*, in its expressive qualities." (Springgay & Zaliwska, 2017, p. 279). The concept of refrain has inspired several scholars who have illustrated the plasticity of the concept (Bertelsen & Murphie, 2010; Charteris & Jones, 2020; Jackson, 2016; McCormack, 2013; Springgay & Zaliwska, 2017; Stengers, 2008), working mainly within post-qualitative inquiry and informed by a feminist reading of Deleuze and Guattari.

I wish to explore the potential of the concept of refrain to discuss how it ties together critical, rhythmic moments, those threshold moments in which repetition and difference are nested. I consider the dilemma 'equality versus diversity' as an organizational refrain whose effect is to consolidate a normative embodiment around the image of the employee as a 'Man': white, abled-bodied, heterosexual and head of the family. The critique of normative embodiment may be grounded in the critical posthumanist project (Braidotti, 2019) that is triggered by the convergence of feminist anti-humanism (focused on the critique of the humanist ideal of the 'Man of Reason' as the allegedly universal measure of all things), and anti-anthropocentrism (which critiques species' hierarchy and human exceptionalism). Moreover, feminist new materialism offers a particular contribution in bringing to the fore the vital materiality of embodiment, thus complementing the Foucauldian perspective on norms and discipline and the phenomenologist understanding of normative embodiment as a sense that is generated within and through experience and manifests itself as a habitual style of experiencing (Wehrle, 2016). Thus, the materiality of embodiment participates in the flow of agency, in relation to other materialities of the workplace, and the discursivity of how bodies fit or do not fit in the organization.

Bodily differences are not neutral facts since people have to live up to standards of embodiment (in terms of size, appearance, fitness, gender, sexual orientation, dressing and so on) sustained by cultural narratives that shape the material world and by systems of representation that inform human and nonhuman interactions. Those who do not conform to the standardized body norms are exposed to various forms of marginalization through oppressive practices. However, non-intentional oppressive practices – such as various diversity policies – also produce marginalization by their materialization of social categories inscribed in differentiating practices. Organizational programs conceived as a contrast to discrimination, in application of anti-discriminatory laws and for inclusion of 'diversity', materialize social categories that mark people as requiring protection or promotion, thus segmenting their workers and employees according to different targets. Their effect is to produce, by means of documentation, a territorialization of differential subjectification. We may consider, as one example among many, programs targeted at people who are in the process of changing sex and identity attribution or to the 'inclusion' of LGBTQ+ people. The fragility and contradictory character of the notion of inclusion is illustrated by Priola et al. (2018) who show how the power of heteronormativity produces specific meanings of inclusion within which some lesbian, gay, bisexual, transgender and queer workers are included and normalised, while others remain excluded because they do not conform to normative conventions and flaunt their 'diversity.' Thus, 'inclusive' organizations might continue to exclude lesbian, gay, bisexual, transgender and queer individuals. The vulnerability of these employees may change in relation to the type of occupation, industry and organizational culture they are in; however, the risk of being exposed to hate crimes, not only in social settings but also at the workplace, is a real danger. The use of abusive language, disdain or violence is inscribed within a heterosexualizing practice that aims to cement the bond between members of a group and its values. A hate crime is usually "not directed at an individual, or person; rather, it is directed at a group, or category of people, where a specific group is seen to embody each one of its members' (dis)identification on the grounds of religion, ethnicity, physical appearance, gender, and sexual orientation" (Rinaldi, 2020, p. 100). It is worth noting how differentiating practices and the mobilization of stigma are oriented more towards groups of people assigned to a specific category rather than to the individual who often is treated according to the 'exception' clause (Gherardi, 1995a).

Normative embodiment and its unexpected effects materialize in and through organizational artifacts, an example of which can be seen in the texts, training program and bureaucratic tools used for human resource management of the 'Strengths' program, based on the premise that every employee should work within the areas of their 'natural' strengths which will make them productive, effective and happy. A strengths-based company would actively put employees in situations that suit their strengths and that would benefit both the company and the individual. The program begins with an assessment to determine an individual's strengths and instructs individuals to focus their work around their 'natural' talents. The analysis of popular management texts and the auto-ethnography conducted by a trainer (Blithe, 2019) unveils how embedded ideologies about gender and work reproduce discursively and materially the normative embodiment of gender and evoke significant historical power structures of inequality.

The participation of things, discourses and the material world in enacting power structures of inequality has been widely explored. I do not invoke this literature here; rather, I wish to stress that what a feminist new materialist approach contributes to this literature is the stress on the bodies' materiality. For example, bodies come in different sizes (apart from all the other differences) and bodies change status (a pregnant or breastfeeding body assumes this particular positioning only for a certain period of time). Fat bodies are often stigmatized as unhealthy and by extension lazy, unproductive and unprofessional and van Amsterdam et al. (2022) offer a feminist new materialist analysis of the production of difference in organizations related to size as an entanglement of bodies, discourses, organizational materials and affect. The participants in that study became for the most part shameful and their 'bad fit' with their jobs was the effect of the intra-action of their large bodies with obesity discourses and organizational materials, such as chairs and workwear. Indeed, social norms for appropriate behaviour and appearance are enforced especially on women as part of a more general effort to control women's bodies and those bodies, organizationally materialized as a 'bad fit,' employ specific strategies of embodied identity work at their workplace (van Amsterdam and van Eck, 2019a).

I offer a last example of a recurrent refrain in organizations that territorializes a normative embodiment while also catalyzing anxieties and deep fears. The female body is never neutral in an organization since it is always an unpredictable body, potentially suspicious of child birthing, shameful, sexualized or abject (Gatrell, 2011, 2013; Huopalainen & Satama, 2020; Kristeva, 1984). Organizations express archetypical elaboration of the fear of the maternal and of the omnipotent and devouring mother (Höpfl & Kostera, 2003; Poggio, 2003). Maternal bodies are objects of differentiating practices that may evoke feelings of disgust or abjection (Gatrell, 2019). Pregnancy and breastfeeding recall the flesh of the body (a 'leaky' body), materialize the ghost of sexuality, show the equivocality of embodied fleshy experience in relation to the natural time of reproduction intertwined with production. These bodies are positioned at the threshold of nature and culture. Motherhood is the effect of the intra-actions of bodies, discourses, materiality and affects (Katila, 2019).

The concept of abjection-as-practice (Gatrell, 2019) has been offered for enhancing understandings of how marginalization operates in organizations in relation to the 'othering' of minority groups of workers, not only breastfeeding bodies but also gay workers, the chronically ill, and migrant and/or ethnic minority employees. The fear of difference creates a pressure on certain groups of workers to minimize their 'differences' for fear of co-workers' reactions. Abjection derives from bodies considered improper because they do not respect borders, positions or rules, because they are ambiguous and do not fit in with social norms in specific working contexts. Within institutionalized practices of differentiating bodily materiality, social categories and relative forms of subjectification are produced.

However, a refrain territorializes and deterritorializes. Deleuze and Guattari have developed a vocabulary that emphasizes how things connect rather than how they are, and thus focusses on how things move in creative mutations, considering things in terms of unfolding forces with their powers to affect and be affected. A path of mutation in the refrain is a 'line of flight' that releases new powers in the capacities of those bodies to act and respond. The translation of the French word *fuite* in Massumi's (1987) notes as translator of *A Thousand Plateaus* comes with a commentary:

FLIGHT/ESCAPE. Both words translate *fuite*, which has a different range of meanings than either of the English terms. *Fuite* covers not only the act of fleeing or eluding but also flowing, leaking, and disappearing into the distance (the vanishing point in a painting is a *point de fuite*). It has no relation to flying. (p. xvi).

The lines of flight that I can see in relation to the normative embodiment enacted by organizational differentiating practices are in relation to art and the changed rhythm thus introduced in the refrain. I give some examples, in which bodies and dance, bodies and photography and bodies and poetics, illustrate the feminist new materialist methodology for deterritorializing the refrain of equality or diversity.

Within disability studies, dance is a methodology for working with matter that can transform living in, with and through a body, and that can explore how a body affects and is affected (Blockmans et al., 2020). In the work of dance, heterogeneous bodies, some of which identify as being impaired or having an intellectual disability, the times and spaces in which the work is created and the different subjects and experiences of the dance are connected (Hickey-Moody, 2015). We can look at dance as a practice *agencement*. Dance is a means for knowing the social differently and for reinventing it, since the histories and identities of individuals with intellectual disability are specific aspects of these individuals' embodiment. The embodiment of temporality is materialized in "points of a body that tell a particular story – prostheses, shunts, scars, tattoos, piercings, stretch marks and corporeal brandings of various forms, create different intensities, lines of latitude and longitude along which to read and feel life stories" (Hickey-Moody, 2015, p. 187).

Moreover, dance as a profession catalyzes the embodied agency of passion and vulnerability. Professional dancers feel like 'feathers on fire' (Satama, 2016); they experience a burning enthusiasm towards their career on the one hand, and move like brittle feathers in the air on the other, thus working continuously between the tensions of passion and vulnerability. Another example is the study of the real-time practicing of a dance production where intergenerational diversity is central. In this context Janssens and Steyaert (2020, p. 1143) describe the accomplishment of "multiplicity through practices and their associations in time and space, highlighting the necessity to understand 'practice' as the entanglement of bodily, discursive and material components, and approaching context as comprised of mutually constituting relations instead of micro/macro levels."

The line of flight that deterritorializes bodies in and through dance induces a few considerations. Organization studies may learn from dance and dancers the practice of collaborative creativity, as the entanglement of a mental and a highly intimate bodily practice (Satama et al., 2022). Embodied agency is a concept that may advance the study of working and organizing. Lastly, socially engaged art practices are a political resource through which people co-create and communicate complex ideas (Hickey-Moody, 2020).

Another line of flight takes a different medium and, in this case, picturing and photography constitute a methodology dealing with images and their specific materialities. In a book collection of methodologies for teaching with new materialisms (Hinton & Treusch, 2015) we find an overview of very different approaches that recently have appeared in educational practices and education research. For example, 'thinking through picturing' uses an agential-realist methodology, in which ontology and epistemology are intertwined through a series of photographs associated with interviews in order to produce a material–discursive arrangement that describes how interprofessional practices are understood and enacted by Social Education students. The aim is to present them with the idea of going "'from learning about practices' to producing situated knowledges in and through practices" (Sauzet, 2015, p. 42). In working across the nature–culture divide, photographs may be useful in exploring the aesthetic and embodied dimension of processes of organizing (Strati, 2019; Warren, 2002). Dance, pictures, drama, queering clownness, poetry and potentially all forms of art-based practices have the advantage of overcoming the limitations of language as a medium of articulating aesthetic experience. As Warren (2002) argues for contrasting the overreliance on text and language, embodiment and the representation of bodies necessitate the employment of a more 'sensually complete' methodology. Photography is one step towards this end, keeping in mind that photographic images are partial, selected and subjective interpretations of one reality wholly dependent on the photographer's 'visual culture' (Pink, 2001).

To illustrate another line of flight, I refer to poetry to argue that it has the power of disturbing – through words – the linearity of what is written, and displaces it in between words and images and the evocation of what eludes the speaking subject. In introducing a special issue on poetry for organizing, Bachani (2021) states that poetry reading, like organizing, is not passive, but active. Writing poems is, for van Eck and van Amsterdam (2021), a process of engaging with the research data in an affective way, one that sparks joy and creativity. With the poems that explore the actions of airport security, they argue that poetry in organization studies can better capture the material agencies that constitute organizing and can better address the readers, sparking an affective engagement from them. A good way to understand the difference that poetry makes when writing research articles is to read van Amsterdam and van Eck (2019b) and 2019a, used to illustrate the sedimentation of a process of subjectivization as the "fat female employee." In van Amsterdam and van Eck (2019b) the authors offer six poems, five of which are written by them, while the sixth poem is written by one of the participants, voicing her first-person experiences and perspective. In this article the reader may 'feel' – rather than understand – how it feels to be stigmatized based on body size. The affective responses and stigma management strategies that the participants in the research project talk about – from feeling anxious, supersmart, impeccable and funny, to rebellious and confident – could get under the reader's skin. In writing this poetry, the authors' aim is to do justice to the emotions that circulate in job interviews and to make a political statement on the stigmatizing practices related to size and health that are conducted in organizations.

In using the concept of refrain as method, I wish to show how thought, knowledges and representations of the world are embedded in different bodies and materialities and are the effect of organizational differentiating practices through which power is unevenly distributed and politically enabled. The project of feminist new materialism is to propose a method, a conceptual frame and a political positioning that challenges the linguistic paradigm and is instead, one which favours the concrete yet complex materiality of bodies immersed in social relations of power (Coleman, Page & Palmer, 2019). To explore this project, I use a second 'concept as method': feminist snap.

Feminist Snap and Digital Activism

To snap means to break suddenly and completely, typically with a sharp cracking sound; as a noun it refers to the act of breaking something stiff or the cracking sound made when it breaks. As an adjective it means done suddenly without allowing time for careful thought or preparation. As a verb, a noun and an adjective, snap refers to time and to the moment when a change takes place suddenly.

Sara Ahmed's concept of 'feminist snap' (Ahmed, 2017a, 2017b) refers to a critical breaking point useful for understanding participant involvement in affective ways that consider sudden jolts of awareness that are significant and 'glow' for participants in particular ways (MacLure, 2013). A snap is ephemeral; sometimes it is only in the aftermath of a snap that we realize it has happened (Ahmed, 2017a). A snap might be both a breaking point and also a creative and affirmative action.

Ahmed, in her writing, has mainly black feminism images in mind and a feminism of colour when she defines feminist snaps as

those moments when you can't take it anymore, when you just can't take it anymore, we are thinking about worlds; how worlds are organised to enable some to breathe, how they leave less room for others. You have to leave because there is nothing left; when there is nothing left (Ahmed, 2017a).

A snap is not a starting point, but a snap can be the start of something. It was, indeed, the start of something when a seminar prompted by this concept – Feminism, Activism, Writing! – took place at the Copenhagen Business School in November 2017 and a special section in the journal *Ephemera* grouped articles dealing with the neologisms 'snaptivism' (Basner et al., 2018) and 'snap.tivism' as a workshop format (Antonakaki et al., 2018).

I wish to take up the concept of feminist snap for exploring digital activism in relation to temporality, materiality and power. My entry point is through the observation that 'feminist snap' is a transversal concept that crosses the binary individual/collective. The intensity and the experience of snap as a breaking point is personal but seeing or hearing somebody else snapping activates a process of affective resonance with the Other and a felt participation in a common history. An example is offered by Mendes and Ringrose (2019, p. 40): "As one woman shared after joining the #MeToo hashtag: It felt like it was the tipping point for me. I could no longer just stand by and do nothing." Thus, adding a voice to #MeToo is not simply about individual empowerment, but is done for the recognition of collectively doing 'something.' The feeling of a breaking moment, of a tipping point, the affective urge to take action, gives to temporality a qualitative connotation. The use of digital technologies change and have changed the social perception of time. Taking part in digital activism, as an individual feminist snap and as a collective snapping experience, implies a modality of engagement that is affective and political at the same time. Feminist digital activism is a practice in which digital networking technologies, active participants, textual written expressions, affective publics and social imageries are entangled in the same practice *agencement*, which also comprises the researchers and the research methodologies of those who study digital activism.

Digital activism may be defined as a social practice that enacts affective publics, that is to say, "public formations that are textually rendered into being through emotive expressions that spread virally through networked crowds" (Papacharissi, 2016, p. 320). Whereas women previously took to the streets to protest against patriarchy and misogyny, they are now taking their activism online. The materiality has changed and we cannot understand contemporary social movements without considering the power of inclusion and exclusion enacted by digital technologies. Life and liveliness are re-mediated by new media which enable the possibility of generating unprecedented connections and unexpected events (Kember & Zylinska, 2012) that make consciousness raising and social transformation possible. However, there is the risk of rendering technology invisible by focusing on textual media analyses alone. While a considerable amount of research on digital activism is underway (Mendes et al., 2019; Ringrose & Renold, 2014) we should remember that it is still predominantly directed at contemporary western digital feminism, and traditionally marginalized groups such as gender non-confirming communities, LGBTQ+ and BAME women are often silenced, unrecognized or ignored, despite the visibility of #MeToo. For this reason, I prefer to give an example more grounded theoretically in new feminist materialism and one which is empirically based in research-activism that involves schools and teenagers using Twitter to oppose rape culture. Rape culture can broadly be defined as a socio-cultural context in which an aggressive male sexuality is eroticized and seen as a 'normal' part of sexual relations. Ringrose and Mendes (2018) have analyzed how teens use Twitter to contrast rape culture and create affective solidarity. An example they give concerns a London school where

the girls created a joint Twitter handle, stating Twitter was central in documenting and sharing experiences granting them some greater force and urgency due to the immediacy of the platform. For example, Kelly (16, London) told the interviewer in response to a discussion of how male teachers had 'lined them up like cows' to scrutinize their outfits during a non-uniform day at school: Kelly: "So it's like, say if something sexist happened within school we can tweet about it and make people aware of it straightaway ...." (Ringrose & Mendes, 2018, p. 90)

These girls found ways to combat and cope with the rape culture: they learnt to 'tweet like professionals,' to look for consensus within the group to tweet effectively and to avoid engaging with 'hurtful' comments. Also, discursive and material categories, such as 'slut' and 'acting slaggy,' have been appropriated both as stigmatized subjectivities and activist forms of protest like SlutWalk,[4] showing how they have powerful affective, and violent force in a wider socio-historical assemblage of classed and raced sexual meanings of femininity (Ringrose et al., 2013). Digital activism illustrates at the same time how girls are sexually regulated (by boys and by girls) through the use of words like 'slut' or 'acting slaggy' and how these regulations could be disrupted and possibly transformed from their injurious norm. A feminist snap can take form, meaning and time in the moment when, for example, 'slut' and 'whore' became usernames on the girls' social networking site profiles in response to 'slut shaming' at school. Complex negotiations and re-significations of 'slut' can be read as an ongoing affective intensity within a technologically mediated practice that is both disruptive and generative.

When we consider contemporary young people's sexualization we have to consider how technological social mediation is entangled in everyday life and intertwined with a digital corporeal culture. In particular, mobile digital technologies cannot be treated like some add-on to young people's lives: we are now dealing with what has been called a posthuman, digitally mediated cyborg body. Studies of socially mediated digital images show how selfies go beyond the representational paradigm and are construed as networked material–discursive entanglements wherein bodies, photos, cameras and expressed selves are always and already touching (Warfield & Demone, 2018).

The inventiveness of diverse digital feminist activism has generated different ways of enacting feminism through affective relations that connect and challenge silence (Keller et al., 2018). Through contemporary social movements we have been able to see the power of vibrant forms of matter in inspiring and building affective solidarity (Baxter, 2021), albeit precarious and ephemeral.

Discussion: In the Flow of Agency

In this chapter I aim to disturb the smooth linearity of Chronos and suggest an image of crumpled time. In the beginning, while introducing the concept of practice *agencement* through the example of the fitting shop, the temporality of that working practice is pace, when time has a cadence and is dyschronic. In thinking through the concept of refrain,

---

[4] In January 2011, a Toronto police officer told students at York University that if women wanted to avoid rape they should not dress like sluts. This incident sparked international outrage, with protests spreading quickly throughout the world under the name SlutWalk.

time has a cadence and a cyclical dynamic: first the refrain creates stability in a field of chaos; second it marks a stable habitat (it territorializes) around that point of stability; and third the refrain opens out into cosmic uncertainty (it deterritorializes). Finally, in thinking through the concept of feminist snap we see time as discontinuity, the breakdown that is open to difference and differing. I am not arguing for a typology of temporality, rather for how the multiplicity of temporality, spatiality and materiality is enacted in relation to the flow of agency. Here, I am referring implicitly to Barad's (2007) conceptualization of spacetimemattering,[5] a neologism that visually suggests the entanglement of time, space and matter as intra-active elements.

When a practice is conceptualized as an *agencement* of intra-acting material–discursive elements, it means that we have left a *being* ontology for a relational one of *becoming* in which a practice and its possibilities for becoming are remade in each iterative practicing. Therefore, we are not only interested in the flow of agency but also in the specific material configurations of the practice's becoming. The concepts of refrain and of feminist snap are expressions of the entanglement of stability and change, of conditions of possibilities that lie in the in-between of virtuality and actualization. I have explored them in relation to the materiality of bodies and the normative embodiments in material–discursive practices. The materialization of subject positionings – like 'fat woman' or 'slut' illustrates the flow of agency that configures how material bodies are interlaced with discourses on health, appearance and sexuality, with the material artifacts they encounter in the world and how that configuration materializes a power of control over bodies. However, we can follow Braidotti's (2013) Foucauldian perspective, according to which power it is not only negative or confining (*potestas*), but also affirmative (*potentia*) and productive of alternative subject positions and social relations. With such a perspective we can look at the flow of agency that stabilizes a configuration of practice elements in terms of domination or control over (*potestas*) and also look at configurations that enable affirmative positionings. I have discussed how different art-based practices have been explored as configurations in which normative embodiment is subverted. Moreover, in relation to the control of teenagers' images,

---

[5] Barad (2007, p. 179) writes: "Intra-actions are nonarbitrary, nondeterministic causal enactments through which matter-in-the-process-of-becoming is iteratively enfolded into its ongoing differential materialization. Such a dynamic is not marked by an exterior parameter called time, nor does it take place in a container called space. Rather, iterative intra-actions are the dynamics through which temporality and spatiality are produced and iteratively reconfigured in the materialization of phenomena and the (re)making of material–discursive boundaries and their constitutive exclusions."

appearance and sexuality I have discussed how digital technologies have an agentic power (*potestas* and *potentia*) in different configurations of digital practices. With both the concept of lines of flight or with feminist snap we can account for a qualitative leap in the actual configuration of the flow of agency. However, for a better understanding of how agency flows we need to qualify the idea of flow with the adjectives performative and affective.

Through the concept of performativity, we may understand how a subject does not precede the process of subjection; rather it becomes through the iterative enactment of a subject position. Barad (2007), who considers the entanglement of nonhuman and human elements in the construction of both subject and object positions, starts from Butler's (2011) conception of performativity as a regularized and constrained repetition of norms. This repetition is not performed by a subject, rather it becomes through the iterative enactment of subject positions. Thus, the performative flow of practice is what enables a subject and constitutes the temporal condition for the subject to emerge. In methodological terms it means that instead of focusing on what (human) actors say, do or think we have to look at what gives them ways of acting that are already assumed to be appropriate and legitimate by the circulating flow of agency through material–discursive practices (Hultin, 2019). In the circulating flow of agency, repetitions, connections and disconnections take place as an affective capacity to affect and be affected.

Through the concept of affect, in the Deleuzian–Spinozist tradition, we may describe a moment of intensity, a reaction in/of the body at the level of matter. Affect is immanent to matter: it is the matter in us responding and resonating with the matter around us. It is, in this sense, "*transcorporeal*," substantially and perpetually interconnected with the flow of substances and the agencies of the environments (Alaimo, 2008). Methodologically, an affective lens implies that the researcher is less involved in making sense of the world and more involved in exploring the possibilities of being and becoming in/with the world. The focus then is on the in-betweenness of virtuality and realization. In the circulating performative flow of agency, affect elucidates the elusive dimensions of connections-in-action and the becoming and transformations of practice configurations.

In conclusion, what this chapter contributes to the conversation about organizing as time is a feminist new materialist lens that operates three moves. First, it de-centers the human in order to recognize the agency of the other-than-human and more-than-human bodies, objects, things and matter with which we (humans) share the world (Cozza & Gherardi, forthcoming). Second, it re-centers the focus on practices, doings and vital materialities as material–discursive enactments of the real in all its messiness. Third, it allows us to see the work of power (*potestas* and *potentia*) and the material aspects of power as the effect of the temporal, affective flow of agency.

Acknowledgement: I wish to thank my colleagues Marie Manidis and Antonio Strati for reading and discussing with me a first draft of this chapter. They have been very generous with me. It is understood that the responsibility for the final chapter is mine alone.

References

Ahmed, S. (2017a). Snap! In *Feministkilljoys*. Available at: https://feministkilljoys .com/2017/05/21/snap/.

Ahmed, S. (2017b). *Living a Feminist Life*. Durham: Duke University Press.

Alaimo, S. (2008). Trans-corporeal feminisms and the ethical space of nature. In S. Alaimo and S. Hekman (eds), *Material Feminisms* (pp. 237–64). Bloomington: Indiana University Press.

Antonakaki, M., French, J. E. & Guner, C. (2018). Realising Sara Ahmed's 'feminist snap': Voices, embodiment, affectivity. *Ephemera*, *18*(4), 923–54.

Bachani, J. (2021). Poetry for organizing. *Organizational Aesthetics*, *10*(1), 1–8.

Barad, K. (2007). *Meeting the Universe Halfway: Quantum Physics and the Entanglement of Matter and Meaning*. London: Duke University Press.

Basner, K., Christensen, J. F., French, J. E. & Schreven, S. (2018). Snaptivism: A collective biography of feminist snap as affective activism. *Ephemera*, *18* (4), 901–22.

Baxter, L. F. (2021). The importance of vibrant materialities in transforming affective dissonance into affective solidarity: How the Countess Ablaze Organized the Tits Out Collective. *Gender, Work & Organization*, *28*(3), 898–916.

Bertelsen, L. & Murphie, A. (2010). An Ethics of Everyday Infinities and Powers: Félix Guattari on Affect and Refrain. In M. Gregg & G. J. Seigworth (eds), *The Affect Theory Reader* (pp. 138–61). Durham: Duke University Press.

Blithe, S. J. (2019). "I always knew I was a little girly": The gendering of skills in management training. *Management Learning*, *50*(5), 517–33.

Blockmans, I. G., De Schauwer, E., Van Hove, G. & Enzlin, P. (2020). Retouching and revisiting the strangers within: An exploration journey on the waves of meaning and matter in dance. *Qualitative Inquiry*, *26*(7), 733–42.

Blue, S. (2019). Institutional rhythms: Combining practice theory and rhythmanalysis to conceptualise processes of institutionalisation. *Time & Society*, *28*(3), 922–50.

Braidotti, R. (2013). *The Posthuman*. Cambridge: Polity Press.

Braidotti, R. (2019). A theoretical framework for the critical posthumanities. *Theory, Culture & Society*, *36*(6), 31–61.

Butler, J. (2011). *Bodies that Matter: On the Discursive Limits of Sex*. London: Routledge.

Charteris, J. & Jones, M. (2020). Replete Sensations of the Refrain: Sound, Action and Materiality in Agentic Posthuman Assemblages. In M. Thomas & R. Bellingham (eds), *Post-Qualitative Research and Innovative Methodologies* (pp. 187–202). London: Bloomsbury Publishing.

Chia, R. & Holt, R. (2006). Strategy as practical coping: A Heideggerian perspective. *Organization Studies*, 27(5), 635–55.

Cohen, I. J. (1996). Theories of action and praxis. In B. S. Turner (ed), *The Blackwell Companion to Social Theory* (pp. 111–42). Cambridge: Blackwell Publishers.

Coleman, R., Page, T. & Palmer, H. (2019). Feminist new materialist practice: The mattering of methods. *MAI Feminism and Visual Culture*, Spring(3).

Cozza, M. & Gherardi, S. (forthcoming). Posthuman Feminism and Feminist New Materialism: Towards an Ethico-onto-epistemology in Research Practices. In S. Katila, E. Bell & S. Meriläinen (eds), *Handbook of Feminist Methodologies in Management and Organization Studies*. Cheltenham: Edward Elgar.

Dall'Alba, G., Sandberg, J. & Sidhu, R. K. (2018). Embodying skilful performance: Co-constituting body and world in biotechnology. *Educational Philosophy and Theory*, 50(3), 270–86.

De Vaujany, F-X., Leclercq-Vandelannoitte, A., Munro, I., Nama, Y. & Holt, R. (2021). Control and surveillance in work practice: Cultivating paradox in "new" modes of organizing. *Organization Studies*, 42(5), 675–95.

Deleuze, G. & Guattari, F. (1987). *A Thousand Plateaus: Capitalism and Schizophrenia*. Trans. B. Massumi. Minneapolis: University of Minnesota Press.

Deleuze, G. & Guattari, F. ([1991]1994). *What Is Philosophy?* Trans. H. Tomlinson & G. Burchell. New York: Columbia University Press.

Deleuze, G. & Parnet, C. (1988). L'Abécédaire de Gilles Deleuze [The ABCs of Gilles Deleuze]. Produced and directed by P-A. Boutang. France: Semiotext(e).

Gane, N. (2009). Concepts and the 'new' empiricism. *European Journal of Social Theory*, 12(1), 83–97.

Garfinkel, H. (1967). *Studies in Ethnomethodology*. Englewood Cliffs, NJ: Prentice Hall.

Gatrell, C. (2011). Managing the maternal body: A comprehensive review and transdisciplinary analysis. *International Journal of Management Reviews*, 13(1), 97–112.

Gatrell, C. (2013). Maternal body work: How women managers and professionals negotiate pregnancy and new motherhood at work. *Human Relations*, 66(5), 621–44.

Gatrell, C. (2019). Boundary creatures? Employed, breastfeeding mothers and "abjection as practice". *Organization Studies*, 40(3), 421–42.

Gherardi, S. (1995a). *Gender, Symbolism and Organizational Cultures*. London: Sage.

Gherardi, S. (1995b). When will he say: "Today the plates are soft"? Management of ambiguity and situated decision-making. *Studies in Cultures, Organizations and Societies*, 1(1), 9–27.

Gherardi, S. (2016). To start practice-theorizing anew: The contribution of the concepts of *agencement* and formativeness. *Organization*, *23*(5), 680–98.

Gherardi, S. (2019). *How to Conduct a Practice-based Study: Problems and Methods*, (2nd ed.). Cheltenham: Edward Elgar.

Gherardi, S. & Strati, A. (1988). The temporal dimension in organizational studies. *Organization Studies*, *9*(2), 149–64.

Giddens, A. (1984). *The Constitution of Society: Outline of the Theory of Structuration*. Cambridge: Polity Press.

Hernes, T. (2022). *Organization and Time*. Oxford: Oxford University Press.

Hickey-Moody, A. (2015). Manifesto: The Rhizomatics of Practice as Research. In A. Hickey-Moody & T. Page (eds), *Arts, Pedagogy and Cultural Resistance: New Materialism* (pp. 169–92). London: Rowman & Littlefield.

Hickey-Moody, A. C. (2020). New materialism, ethnography, and socially engaged practice: Space-time folds and the agency of matter. *Qualitative Inquiry*, *26*(7), 724–32.

Hinton, P. & Treusch, P. (eds) (2015). *Teaching with Feminist Materialisms*. Utrecht: ATgender, The European Association for Gender Research, Education and Documentation.

Holt, R. & Sandberg, J. (2011). Phenomenology and organization theory. In M. Lounsbury (ed), *Philosophy and Organization Theory*. Bingley, UK: Emerald Group Publishing Limited.

Höpfl, H. & Kostera, M. (eds.) (2003). *Interpreting the Maternal Organization*. London: Routledge.

Hopwood, N. (2014). The Fabric of Practices: Times, Spaces, Bodies, Things. In L. McLean, L. Stafford & M. Weeks, *Exploring Bodies in Time and Space* (pp. 137–46). Oxford: Inter-Disciplinary Press.

Hultin, L. (2019). On becoming a sociomaterial researcher: Exploring epistemological practices grounded in a relational, performative ontology. *Information and Organization*, *29*(2), 91–104.

Huopalainen, A. & Satama, S. (2020). Writing birthing bodies: Exploring the entanglements between flesh and materiality in childbirth. *Culture and Organization*, *26*(4), 333–54.

Jackson, A. Y. (2016). An ontology of a backflip. *Cultural Studies Critical Methodologies*, *16*(2), 183–92.

Janssens, M. & Steyaert, C. (2020). The site of diversalizing: The accomplishment of inclusion in intergenerational dance. *Journal of Management Studies*, *57*(6), 1143–73.

Katila, S. (2019). The mothers in me. *Management Learning*, *50*(1), 129–40.

Keller, J., Mendes, K. & Ringrose, J. (2018). Speaking "unspeakable things": Documenting digital feminist responses to rape culture. *Journal of Gender Studies*, *27*(1), 22–36.

Kember, S. & Zylinska, J. (2012). *Life after New Media: Mediation as a Vital Process*. Cambridge, MA: MIT Press.

Kristeva, J. (1984). *Powers of Horror: An Essay on Abjection*. New York: Columbia University Press.

Lenz Taguchi H. & St. Pierre, E. (2017). Using concepts as method in educational and social science inquiry. *Qualitative Inquiry*, *23*(9), 643–8.

López, D. T. (2019). The Society of the Digital Swarm: Microblogging and Construction of Subjectivity in Homo Digitalis. In V. González-Prida Diaz & J. P. Zamora Bonilla *Handbook of Research on Industrial Advancement in Scientific Knowledge* (pp. 95–110). Hershey, PA: IGI Global.

MacLure, M. (2013). Classification or wonder? Coding as an analytic practice in qualitative research. In B. Coleman & J. Ringrose (eds), *Deleuze and Research Methodologies* (pp. 164–83). Edinburgh: Edinburgh University Press.

Massumi, B. (1987). Translator's Foreword: Pleasures of Philosophy. In G. Deleuze & F. Guattari (eds), *A Thousand Plateaus: Capitalism and Schizophrenia*. Minneapolis: University of Minnesota Press.

McCormack, D. (2013). *Refrains for Moving Bodies*. Durham: Duke University Press.

Mendes, K. & Ringrose, J. (2019). Digital feminist activism: # MeToo and the everyday experiences of challenging rape culture. In B. Fileborn & R. Loney-Howes (eds), *# MeToo and the Politics of Social Change* (pp.37–51). London: Palgrave Macmillan.

Mendes, K., Ringrose, J. & Keller, J. (2019). *Digital Feminist Activism: Girls and Women Fight Back Against Rape Culture*. Oxford: Oxford University Press.

Papacharissi, Z. (2016). Affective publics and structures of storytelling: Sentiment, events and mediality. *Information, Communication & Society, 19* (3), 307–24.

Pink, S. (2001). *Doing Visual Ethnography*. London: Sage.

Poggio, B. (2003). Who's Afraid of Mothers? In H. Höpfl & M. Kostera (eds), *Interpreting the Maternal Organizations* (pp. 13–26). London: Routledge.

Priola, V., Lasio, D., Serri, F. & De Simone, S. (2018). The organisation of sexuality and the sexuality of organisation: A genealogical analysis of sexual 'inclusive exclusion' at work. *Organization, 25*(6), 732–54.

Rinaldi, C. (2020). Homophobic Conduct as Normative Masculinity Test: Victimization, Male Hierarchies, and Heterosexualizing Violence in Hate Crimes. In A. Balloni & R. Sette (eds), *Handbook of Research on Trends and Issues in Crime Prevention, Rehabilitation, and Victim Support* (pp. 100–23). Hershey, PA: IGI Global.

Ringrose, J., Harvey, L., Gill, R. & Livingstone, S. (2013). Teen girls, sexual double standards and "sexting": Gendered value in digital image exchange. *Feminist Theory, 14*(3), 305–23.

Ringrose, J. & Mendes, K. (2018). Mediated Affect and Feminist Solidarity: Teens Using Twitter to Challenge "Rape Culture" In and Around School. In T. Sampson, S. Maddison & D. Darren (eds), *Affect and Social Media: Emotion, Mediation, Anxiety and Contagion*. London: Rowman & Littlefield International.

Ringrose, J. & Renold, E. (2014). "F**k rape!" Exploring affective intensities in a feminist research assemblage. *Qualitative Inquiry, 20*(6), 772–80.

Ringrose, J., Warfield, K. & Zarabadi, S. (eds) (2019). *Feminist Posthumanisms, New Materialisms and Education*. London: Routledge.

Satama, S. (2016). "Feathers on Fire": A study of the interplay between passion and vulnerability in dance. *Organizational Aesthetics, 5*(1), 64–93.

Satama, S., Blomberg, A. & Warren, S. (2022). Exploring the embodied subtleties of collaborative creativity: What organisations can learn from dance. *Management Learning*, *53*(2), 167–89.

Sauzet, S. (2015). Thinking through Picturing. In P. Hinton and P. Treusch (eds), *Teaching with Feminist Materialisms* (pp. 37–51). Utrecht: AtGender, The European Association for Gender Research, Education and Documentation.

Schatzki, T. R. (2006). The Time of Activity. *Continental Philosophy Review*, *39* (2), 155–82.

Schatzki, T. R. (2010). *The Timespace of Human Activity: On Performance, Society, and History as Indeterminate Teleological Events*. Plymouth, UK: Lexington Books.

Shove, E. (2009). Everyday Practice and the Production and Consumption of Time. In E. Shove, F. Trentmann & R. Wilk (eds), *Time, Consumption and Everyday Life: Practice, Materiality and Culture*. London: Routledge.

Springgay, S. & Zaliwska, Z. (2017). Learning to be affected: Matters of pedagogy in the artists' soup kitchen. *Educational Philosophy and Theory*, *49*(3), 273–83.

Stengers, I. (2008). Experimenting with refrains: Subjectivity and the challenge of escaping modern dualism. *Subjectivity*, *22*(1), 38–59.

Strati, A. (2019). *Organizational Theory and Aesthetic Philosophies*. New York: Routledge.

van Amsterdam, N. & van Eck, D. (2019a). "I have to go the extra mile." How fat female employees manage their stigmatized identity at work. *Scandinavian Journal of Management*, *35*(1), 46–55.

van Amsterdam N. & van Eck, D. (2019b). In the flesh: A poetic inquiry into how fat female employees manage weight-related stigma. *Culture and Organization*, *25*(4), 300–16.

van Amsterdam, N., van Eck, D. & Meldgaard Kjær, K. (2022). On (not) fitting in. Fat embodiment, affect and organizational materials as differentiating agents. *Organization Studies*. https://doi.org/10.1177/01708406221074162

van Eck, D. V. & van Amsterdam, N. V. (2021). Affective engagement with airport security work: Wor(l)ding material agencies through poetry. *Organizational Aesthetics*, *10*(1), 36–41.

Warfield, K. & Demone, C. (2018). Writing the Body of the Paper: Three New Materialist Methods for Examining the Socially Mediated Body. In Z. Papacharissi, (ed), *A Networked Self and Human Augmentics, Artificial Intelligence, Sentience* (pp. 133–52). New York: Routledge.

Warren, S. (2002). "Show me how it feels to work here": Using photography to research organizational aesthetics. *Ephemera* *2*(3), 224–45.

Wehrle, M. (2016). Normative embodiment. The role of the body in Foucault's genealogy. A phenomenological re-reading. *Journal of the British Society for Phenomenology*, *47*(1), 56–71.

4   Metaphysics of Tragedy, a Non-Dispositional View of Time

Rémy Conche

> We, as late modern human beings, aim to make the world controllable at every level – individual, cultural, institutional, and structural – we invariably encounter the world as … series of objects that we have to know, attain, conquer, master, or exploit.
>
> Hartmut Rosa, 2020 (pp. 3–4)

"Vanity of Vanities"

In his last book, Hartmut Rosa (2020) develops the idea that late modernity is characterised by a new sort of relationship to the world. This relationship is based on the availability of the world, availability of nature, of the other, and even if Rosa touches on it only briefly, availability of time. Indeed, as Rosa wrote in his last essays, modernity could "potentially [produce] 'mute' or 'alienated' relationships (among individuals as well as to the world of things and to nature, to time and space, to one's own experiences, needs, and actions, and finally to one's own body)". Therefore, the problem of the world's availability includes the availability of time. Management is a good example of this phenomena: from the beginning Management and Organisational Science have wanted to make time an available resource, or as Holt and Johnsen say a *time-for-us* (2019). However, this fiction carefully elaborated within the literature for decades does not correspond to reality. Everyday, people suffer from time, have pathologies which could be described as temporal (first and foremost *burnout*). In other words: they endure time. This fundamental experience of the independence of time and its dominion over us can be find in our most ancient literature:

> Vanity of vanities, says the Preacher,
> vanity of vanities! All is vanity.
> What does man gain by all the toil
> at which he toils under the sun?
> A generation goes, and a generation comes,
> but the earth remains forever.
>
> (Ecclesiastes 1)

Here *vanity* is the translation of the word *hevel* which can also be translated to *fog* or *steam*. The author, named Qoheleth by the tradition, makes here a value judgement through which he gives to every human work a negative connotation. This word *hevel*, in texts already available at the time of writing (known as the books of *Genesis, Jeremiah* and *Job*), points to the vanity of idols, to their nothingness, but also designates what is illusive (because it is ephemeral). In our context, *hevel* qualifies all that exists. This all has a common characteristic: to be destined to insignificance. As the author says "All go to one place. All are from the dust, and to dust all return" (Ecclesiastes 3:20). According to Jacques Ellul ([1987] 2016), a French protestant philosopher, theologian, historian, and sociologist, who wrote a monograph about this text, it is more interesting to translate *hevel* to vanity, and not to *fog* or *steam*, because a person who displays vanity is a person who has illusions, or more precisely, is a person who is covering up reality with illusions; this is, in the words of Ellul, a "parry". *Vanity* is also something that has no destiny, that is useless, that has no future. In the term *vanity* there's also a tragic connotation which exists in the word *hevel*. *Hevel* is tragic destiny: not the tragic destiny that depends on gods (known as fate) but the tragic destiny which is the very condition of humankind. In this sense, "destiny can only be known, not mastered" (Ellul, [1987]2016). Finally, when Qoheleth asks "what does man gain?" he does not speak about money but about meaning. Nothing that man can do or produce will answer his existential questions.[1]

To sum up, Qoheleth tackles the issue of time and its negativity in this text. This time conceptualisation and its existential dimension are foreign to Management and Organisational Science. In this chapter I want to restore in management (and its discourse about temporal issues) the idea of a time that undoes, that makes all beings tend towards nothingness, and for which everything is in vain. A time which is similar to destiny and inherent to the human condition: a tragic time, so to speak, from which humankind, through illusion, tries to escape.

Time and Management Literature: The Conceptual Pluralisation of Time

The history of management and its science could be seen as a long-running attempt to master time. From Taylor (1911) to Reinecke and Ansari (2015) management science has aimed to dominate time. Whether it is objective, subjective, social, or processual, time is conceptualised by management as a resource or as a place of creativity.

---

[1] We have summarised here some of the interpretations of Ellul's ([1987]2016) work.

Management and Organisational Science have focused on individuals' temporal agency over the agency of time itself. However, managers' daily experience, the literature in social sciences (Rosa, 2015), and some authors in management science (Holt & Johnsen, 2019; Johnsen et al., 2019) have shown that individuals are not masters of time, and may even suffer from attempting to master it. In this chapter I want to take seriously the agency of time itself, which implies taking up again the question of the ontology of time. This should make it possible to build a new managerial position where managers no longer dominate time but learn to "deal with it".

Time has long been an under-studied subject in management science (Reinecke & Ansari, 2015), although many researchers implicitly considered time as the backdrop of management (from Taylor during the twentieth century to Eisenhardt in 1990). Time has been an underlying obsession of management for decades (Tsoukas & Chia, 2002) but only as the x-axis of our existences' chart. Since the 1990s, a great deal of research in sociology has studied time as a subject per se (Adam, 1990; Gurvitch, 1964; Melbin et al., 1986; Nowotny, 1992). Even if there are early works about time in management (Roy, 1959; Sorokin & Merton, 1937; Taylor, 1911), this literature about time in sociology has facilitated the recent emergence of a "more systematic representation of time and temporality in organization studies" (Pulk, 2022), represented for example by the works of Allen C. Bluedorn (Bluedorn, 2002), and more recently by scholars interested in "the other time" (Shipp & Jansen, 2021). Two streams of research are more significantly related with the study of time: practice studies (Orlikowski & Yates, 2002; Rowell et al., 2016) and process studies (Hernes, 2014; Reinecke & Ansari, 2015). Practice studies have applied Giddens' "structuration theory" (1986) to the study of time. It led to the theory of "temporal structuring" in which "people in organizations experience time through the shared temporal structures they enact recurrently in their every-day practices" (Orlikowski & Yates, 2002). According to the authors, "temporal structures here are understood as both shaping and being shaped by ongoing human action, and thus as neither independent of human action (because shaped in action), nor fully determined by human action (because shaping that action)" (Orlikowski & Yates, 2002). A large part of the processual studies on time is based on those contributions which they prolong through the concept of "temporal work" (Kaplan & Orlikowski, 2013) defined as "any individual, collective or organizational effort to influence, sustain or redirect the temporal structures" (Special Issue of Strategic Organization, 2019).

In the vein of different scholars (Holt & Johnsen, 2019; Johnsen et al., 2019), we argue that this perspective, which focuses on individuals' temporal agency has done a lot "toward affirming time" but has tended to ignore the agency of time itself. This whole literature has created a "time-for-us" (Holt & Johnsen, 2019). However, individuals cannot simply "master time", they have to "deal with it". Some will say that managers can enact representations of time in order to control it. But these representations of time are not time. They are answers to the inherent negativity of time, a way to cope with it. There is an infinite number of techniques and devices to manage time, but practice shows that there is always an unmanageable time. This unmanageable time does not exist in management literature, or if it does, it is only very briefly mentioned because individuals can, with a little effort, take control over it. This simple observation shows that management sciences need a negative conceptualisation of time. That is to say, a conceptualisation that considers time as a force which exercises an imperious domination over individuals.

The Subjectivising Shift of Management Literature

Research has only slightly highlighted time as a negative force. Researchers are more interested in the multiplicity of times, their different properties, and therefore the conflicts that could result (Reinecke & Ansari, 2015). The most recent research in Management and Organisational Science effectively suggests that organisations and individuals live within a multitude of temporal structures, each of which has different attributes or properties. The presence of these different structures inevitably causes conflicts (Biesenthal et al., 2015; Yakura, 2002). There can be conflicts, for example, between different hierarchical levels within a company, top managers, and middle managers (McGivern et al., 2018); between different functions such as marketing, research and development, or strategy (Ancona and Chong, 1996; Dougherty et al., 2013); and between actors internal and external to the company such as managers and investors (Gersick, 1994). Reinecke and Ansari (2015) also pointed out that time conflicts can appear when the organisation seeks to manage different processes.

In those publications, the purpose of "temporal structuring" or "temporal work" is therefore to reconcile temporal structures. This stream of research considers temporal conflicts only in the context of their resolution. It presents time as a place of creativity for individuals and organisations. They ignore the agency of time itself. However, as recent research has shown (Holt & Johnsen, 2019), time is not at our disposal, and cannot be fully controlled. Holt and Johnsen write:

Time is conceptualized as affirmative, either as a tool-for-use in human lives, or as an open space for play and hence creative possibility. This "lyrical and therapeutic anthropomorphism of the Absolute", as Eugene Thacker (2014, p. 114) calls it, unthinkingly finds in the human an unchallenged ascendency, with the objective (or at least presubjective) force of time being reduced to "clock time" coupled to the "possibility of enacting different temporal structures" (Orlikowski & Yates, 2002, p. 686) by way of organized riposte ... After all, exposing the grounds of time's destructive presence in the midst of organized life is the first step towards a comprehension of the world in which we live as both human and non-human – or simply as more than us. (2019)

The theories of "temporal structuring" or "temporal work" do not take seriously the possibility that time may have its own agency. This agency cannot be considered because management sciences present a metaphysical bias. As Theunissen and Sagnol (2013) show in their text "Can we be happy through time?", there exists a specific stream of thinking about time which has emancipated itself from the metaphysical (2013, p. 41); that is to say, for which the "whole of reality" is no longer its problem (Conche, 2012, p. 7). It leads to four phenomena regarding the conceptualisation of time (we will speak only about the three that are relevant for this chapter). First, the idea that we are in time. According to Kant, time is considered one of the "pure forms of intuition" (Kant, 1781); this *subjectivisation* of time led to its dissolution in the subject and, as a consequence, to its *pluralisation,* so there are as many times as there are individuals. Finally, there is *total affirmation,* where time became "the condition of possibility of everything for which we can say yes" (Theunissen & Sagnol, 2013, p. 42). It no longer bothers us; it is no longer marked by vanity but becomes the place of self-realisation.

These deviations created a conceptualisation of time which is emancipated from metaphysics, and which can be found in a large part of the literature about management sciences. This literature generally considers that time is only the product of individuals' and groups' norms, beliefs, and customs.

However, these three phenomena are incompatible with the agency of time. By agency of time, we mean the domination, already studied via its sociological consequences (Rosa, 2015), that time has over us. The domination of time is the reign that it exercises over us, its "non-liberating" and "alienating" domination (Theunissen & Sagnol, 2013, p. 44). Time reigns over us and makes us tend towards non-being.

Here the theoretical issue is major. By taking a closer look at the management literature on time we can see that it has always considered time as a resource, as an object available for human use (Johnsen et al., 2019). This resource was first a quantitative one (Eisenhardt, 1990; Perlow et al., 2002) but over a course of decades it became a more qualitative one. According to this secondary literature, time is a structure shaped through practices (Orlikowski & Yates, 2002). In doing so, management research has completely eluded this obvious fact: time exercises an imperious domination over humanity. Marx in *The Philosophy of Misery* (1847) already remarked: "Time is everything, man is nothing; he is, at most, time's carcass." Hartmut Rosa's work (2015) has also shown that social acceleration has caused individuals to lose their temporal agency. The increase in the number of diseases that some authors have called chronopaties (Johnsen et al., 2019) – namely burnout, anxiety, and depression – is a symptom of this loss of temporal agency. Similarly, some authors in Management and Organisational Science, without necessarily being interested in the agency of time, have shown that individuals can experience time without meaning and, as a consequence, are confronted with boredom and spleen (Johnsen, 2016). Consequently, time is not necessarily at our disposal; it affects our lives and sometimes (maybe all the time) we cannot do anything about it.

The Agency of Time as an Existential Dimension

Hans-Georg Gadamer in "Concerning empty and ful-filled time" (1970) considers the famous Saint Augustin interrogation about time[2] as the prototype of the philosophical question:

The great fundamental questions of philosophy all have this structure: they do not allow themselves to be held at bay in a way which makes possible an unequivocal answer to them. They seem to evade the grasp of our concepts and nevertheless continue to attract in their evasiveness. To be attracted by something which retracts itself constitutes the basic movement of philosophical interest. This attraction-retraction calls into question the conceptuality in terms of which one inquires. We can indeed say: the philosophical problem is a question which one does not know how to "raise."

According to Gadamer then, time is a philosophical question that individuals constantly face during their lifetime. Every experience of time is an answer to this question. Therefore, by their very existence, individuals cannot help but consider it. The answers they give are answers within which they live.

Taking seriously time as a research question, and therefore recognising its agency, ultimately leads the individual to ask existential questions. It also leads to the study of its negative impact and the solutions that individuals deploy to cope with it. However, we must distinguish between time itself and what is in time. As the French philosopher Marcel Conche

---

[2] "What is time? If no one asks me, I know; but if someone asks me and I want to explain it, I don't know anymore." Saint Augustin, *Confessions*, XI.

(2012) explains, we can speak of multiple times "if we consider not time, but what is in time – the content, or rather the contents of time. Because these contents are multiple: they are all beings and their modes of being ... If therefore we multiply the times, we end up with the fact that their number is infinite" (p. 101).[3] There is on the one hand the multiple perceptions of time by beings, and on the other hand time itself. For Conche, the latter is linked to the passage of things from being to non-being. As Luhmann (1995) stated: "the question of time, in essence, has repeatedly proved unanswerable and is probably the wrong question". A good way to tackle the time definition issue is to define it by its action. And, as Conche (2011) wrote: "our fundamental experience of time holds in one movement: annihilation ... as the nothingness of what was or of what it was" (p. 153). Here time is identified with the finitude of things and beings. Time – and this is a common point between Theunissen and Conche – reigns over us. In consequence, its *pluralisation* is not to be understood as a diversity of time, but as a diversity of time perceptions. There is only one time, but from the point of view of what is in time, there is an infinity of times.

The question of time is therefore eminently existential. Giving an answer to the question "what is time?" is not easy because we tend to confuse time and its different perceptions. But saying what it does, what its action is, is simpler:

What is the action of time? What is to come does not remain to come, it becomes past. Tomorrow I'm going to the seaside. The day after tomorrow, tomorrow will have become yesterday. Time is a power: if after one hour there is another, nothing can be done against that. It is a universal power: there is nothing of human experience that is not under the yoke of time. By the effect of time, I say, what is to come becomes past. Hence the definition: time is the universal power that transforms what is to come.[4] (Conche, 2012, p. 329)

Time is a "universal destinal power"[5] (Conche, 2022, p. 328). It is a power which drags us along and cancels us. We are victims of it, and this experience is part of all other experiences. In other words, all human experiences are marked by the independence of time.

The Human Being in the Face of Time

This affirmation of time and its domination over us also confirms that we suffer from it. The alienating domination that we pointed out above creates suffering. This alienating domination being the experience of time, it is the experience of time that creates suffering. Suffering is

---

[3] Our translation.   [4] Our translation.   [5] Our translation.

not an accidental feature of time; it is one of its necessary characteristics. To explain the origin of this suffering, Theunissen and Sagnol remind us that when we talk about time, we tend to use the adjectives "filled" and "empty" (Theunissen & Sagnol, 2013):

> So-called "ful-filled" time, which we usually distinguish from empty time, borrows its plenitude, as we have seen, from life; its full character is verily the meaningful character of life. This is why we don't think about time. But when the meaning of our life becomes empty, time becomes noticeable. We can also reverse the sentence: the more time is noticed, the more our life is meaningless. The life of a scientist who spends his time measuring time seems to me the most desolate of all possible lives. The suffering that time becoming objective produces is called boredom. But boredom is the state of mind most appropriate to time immediately experienced, fixed on oneself . . . In boredom, time appears for us as naked.[6] (pp. 47–48)

According to Theunissen and Sagnol, time is "ful-filled" for an individual when his life has meaning; that is to say, when time is not noticeable. Montaigne (2004) in his *Essays* wrote: "For why do we derive the title of being from this instant, which is but a flash in the infinite course of an eternal night, and so short an interruption of our perpetual and natural condition, death possessing all the before and after this moment, and also a good part of the moment itself?" Individuals, in order to give meaning to their existence, must live in a time shorter than the infinite time of nature. As Marcel Conche says:

> The individual cannot live in the immense Time of Nature, because he must believe he is, and he cannot live in what makes him almost nothing, a "flash" in the infinite time. He must limit time, giving himself time on a human scale. He must think that living a hundred years is having a long life. . . . Man gives himself the time he needs to be able to believe that it is worth living. . . . In Time of innumerable days, I'm delimiting a portion and I'm living in a reduced, shrunken time, where I am myself and where I deal with beings.[7] (2022, p. 339)

Theunissen and Sagnol (2013) talk about the "dimensioning of time in future, past and present". What must be understood here is that time is not a social structure, it is rather a force that makes all beings tend towards nothingness. It is the destiny of the whole of humankind. However, the human being, unlike all other living beings, is aware of being in time. And in order to give meaning to their very ephemeral existence, humans define a "temporal span", build a significant temporality, or using the vocabulary of Management and Organisational Science they "structure time" (Orlikowski & Yates, 2002). "Temporal structuring", in our view, is

---

[6] Our translation.   [7] Our translation.

a human response to the negativity of time. Individuals give meaning to their existence by assigning properties to time (properties it does not in reality have): these are the different properties of temporal structures. Research has attempted repeatedly to define these properties. Halbesleben, et al. (2003) have, for example, retained the temporal horizon, the tempo, the temporality, the synchronisation, the sequence, the pauses, the simultaneity with the *zeitgebers*, the temporal personality, and the absence of time (timelessness). Ancona et al. (2001) considered the timing, the recurrence of cycles, the rhythms, the flow, the temporal orientation, and the cultural significance of time.

To summarise, time is not a social structure (Orlikowski & Yates, 2002) but something in which individuals try to live through a process of temporal structuring. Individuals try to inhabit time through the elaboration of different temporal structures. This reasoning forces us to rethink the managerial posture built by the literature in Management and Organisation Studies with respect to time.

The Foundations of a Tragic Management

Management and Organisational Science literature about time, and particularly about subjective time, has confused time and what is in time (or time and temporality). While temporal structuring is an answer to time negativity, Management and Organisational Science has taken temporal structuring for time, thus ignoring time as a force that makes all beings tend towards nothingness. This is why, in our opinion, this literature has so much difficulty in considering agency specific to time, and in recognising that in organisations there can be a time that creates suffering. Finally, what Management and Organisational Science lack is a tragic vision of time. From the moment we understand that time makes non-being being, that it condemns things to disappear, we become aware of time as finitude. To use the words of Marcel Conche (2012), it is the finitude of being that teaches us what time is. Admitting this, we develop a tragic ontology of time that Clément Rosset (1991) illustrates in an early essay:

I'm walking down the street, at the foot of a building under construction, a mason stumbles on a scaffolding, falls 20 meters at my feet and kills himself. Nausea rises in my throat, but as the body is carried away on a stretcher and I gaze at the pool of blood on which sand is being spread, I realize that I am immersed in intellectual horror and not under the blow of a psychological upheaval. Indeed, I am not only in the presence of a tragic spectacle, I am not the witness of a 'situation', as would be the passer . . .. In fact, I am the only one to have grasped the tragedy of death, not because the mason crashed at my feet, but because I saw him, in the space of a second, alive, dying, then dead …. The tragedy … is that this heap of bloody flesh is the same as the one that fell a moment ago … this subsequent representation from one state to another is the tragic mechanism.[8] (pp. 8–9)

We can see it clearly: the vision of one and the same being, alive and then dead, teaches us what time is. The illusion of free time, the free succession of events, is substituted with a determined, rigid, necessary time.

Faced with tragedy, one would be tempted to act to thwart it. However, in a tragic ontology, any possibility of acting on the world is rejected. The individual, when he acts, brings "a certain modification" to what exists, but this modification is hazardous and "does not modify the nature of what it acts on" (Rosset, 2013). According to Rosset, "the approval of the real" is the "only act capable of affecting human lives with a minimal coefficient of modification …. It only concerns the mode according to which a person represents their thoughts and their actions". Johnsen et al. (2019) describe the time sufferance of prisoners: we realise that those prisoners have no choice but to admit that they are dominated by time which they do not fight but synchronise with prison's time. They do not want to dominate time but are in a reality from which they cannot run. It is when this synchronisation with prison time fails (for example when the meal does not arrive at the scheduled time) and gives way to waiting, that time is suffered and appears as "empty". We come back to the teaching of Qoheleth: destiny, defined as time and its negativity, cannot be mastered, it can only be known. In consequence, it is necessary to redefine the temporal structuring to re-embed it in this tragic ontology of time. We should consider temporal structuring not as a way to dominate time, but as an answer to tragic time, a way to approve it. That is to say, a way to inhabit it.

So, how can we explain the situations where individuals endure time? An individual or a group of individuals may be forced to adopt external practices which could come into conflict with their own practices (those practices being the actualisation of underlying temporal structures). If those practices come into conflict, so do the temporal structures and it is therefore the temporal structuring that is defeated. The individual then finds himself/herself exposed to the negativity of time; tragic time reminds him/her. In consequence, endured time is a destructured time because this endured time is a time that escapes the temporal structuring of individuals. Those individuals are caught up in routines and practices that participate in the reproduction of a temporal structure that does not suit them, or they are prevented from updating their own temporal structures and are thus exposed to tragic time.

[8] Our translation.

We understand why Management and Organisational Science is unable to think about the agency of time and endured time. If time is only a social structure, there is no reason why individuals cannot modify it as they want (as in Reinecke & Ansari, 2015). But if time is a force full of negativity and in consequence individuals are compelled to define a "temporal span" (i.e. to structure time) they also take the risk that this structuring may fail, thus revealing the agency of time. This is how we see the possibility of thinking of endured time.

When we confuse time and temporal structuring, we take our desires for reality, and think that we can create images of time as controllable. But we cannot dominate time and emancipate ourselves from it because this wrenching of the individual from tragic time is "always unstable and is only possible to a certain extent. The time we have, and which is 'our' time, the one we do not want to be robbed, is in fact surrounded and limited by the time which we cannot have because it has us" (Theunissen & Sagnol, 2013, pp. 73–4). The image of time as controllable is only the result of temporal structuring which creates a duplicate reality, which is an illusion. As Rosset (1991) says, it is "taking upon us not to see a reality whose existence we have recognized". It is covering the reality with illusions: ultimately, it is the vanity of Qoheleth.

Conclusion

What is problematic is the ability of Management and Organisational Science to tackle the concept of time in its negativity. Because management literature expresses a certain form of solutionism that has led to the subjectivising of time, it has completely eluded the tragic dimension of time and therefore its own agency. We must return to a definition of time as a negative force in order to restore the balance between the temporal agency of individuals and the agency of time and get away from the theories that make the individual an omniscient and omnipotent being with no constraints and no limits. We must create a managerial posture that does not amount to dominating, but to 'dealing with it'. It is this daily 'dealing with' that unfolds within organisations that we must study and theorise. We must consider that the action of the individual does not unfold over time but through it, thanks to time. This is the idea of the philosopher Michael Theunissen who wrote in his *Negative Theology of Time* (Theunissen & Sagnol, 2013) that "human life is successful not because of time but in spite of it" (p. 72). According to this idea, we think that Management and Organisational Science should not consider how to master time, but how to succeed despite time. The question remains: how to change this posture ('dominating time') so rooted in management literature? The fact that Theunissen was able to theorise negative time within the framework of a theology, and not of a philosophy, points to an approach that could be interesting to follow in future research: a "theology of organization" (Dyck, 2021). Theology is useful for the management researcher in three ways (Sørensen et al., 2012): it makes it possible to find the origins of modern concepts (because they are secularised theological concepts); some of its ideas can be "imported unchanged in[to] management sciences"; and finally, the researcher can also "redeem forgotten or repressed theological concepts". We believe that eschatology, as a theological discourse on the "last ends", can allow us to theorise a negative time. As the French historian François Hartog (2020) has pointed out, the modern world is affected by presentism, a "regime of historicity" (Hartog, 2015) in which the present has absorbed the past and the future and is valuing only the "now". Within this regime we buy time with money to endlessly stretch the present, saying to ourselves "as long as it lasts". As a consequence, we abolish duration and death. We totally deny the negative force that is time; in short, "time no longer passes". Managerial literature does not escape this trend. As we have seen, it considers time as a place of creativity and subjective creation. Reconnecting with eschatology, particularly a Christian one, would make it possible to take time and its negativity seriously and perhaps develop a managerial posture that doesn't deny the agency of time, but thinks it an "assent to life as a whole" (Ratzinger, 2005, p. 101) including death and suffering, both inherent in the human experience of time.

References

Adam, B. (1990). *Time and Social Theory*. Philadelphia: Temple University Press.

Ancona, D. & Chong, C-L. (1996). Entrainment: Pace, cycle, and rhythm in organizational behavior. *Research in Organizational Behavior, 18*, 251–84.

Ancona, D. G., Goodman, P. S., Lawrence, B. S., & Tushman, M. L. (2001). Time: A new research lens. *Academy of Management Review, 26*(4), 645–63. https://doi.org/10.5465/amr.2001.5393903.

Biesenthal C., Sankaran S., Pitsis T., & Clegg S. (2015). Temporality in organization studies: Implications for strategic project management. *Open Economics and Management Journal, 2*(1), 45–52.

Bluedorn, A. C. (2002). *The Human Organization of Time: Temporal Realities and Experience*. Stanford: Stanford University Press.

Conche, M. (2011). *Orientation Philosophique: Essai de Déconstruction*. Paris: Les Belles Lettres.

Conche, M. (2012). *Métaphysique*. Paris: Presses Universitaires de France.

Conche, M. (2022). *L'infini de la Nature: Oeuvres Philosophiques*. Paris: Éditions Bouquins.

Dougherty, D., Bertels, H., Chung, K., Dunne, D. D., & Kraemer, J. (2013). Whose time is it? Understanding clock-time pacing and event-time pacing in complex innovations. *Management and Organization Review*, *9*, 233–63.

Dyck, B. (2021). Organization and Management. In *Routledge Handbook of Economic Theology*. London: Taylor & Francis.

Eisenhardt, K. M. (1990). Speed and strategic choice: How managers accelerate decision making. *California Management Review*, *32*(3), 39–54. https://doi.org /10.2307/41166616.

Ellul, J. ([1987]2016). *La raison d'être: Méditation sur l'Ecclésiaste* (pp. 61–73). Paris: Éditions du Seuil.

Gadamer, H-G. (1970). Concerning empty and ful-filled time. *The Southern Journal of Philosophy*, *8*(2), 341.

Gersick, C. J. G. (1994). Pacing strategic change: The case of a new venture. *Academy of Management Journal*, *37*(1), 9–45. https://doi.org/10.2307/256768.

Giddens, A. (1986). *The Constitution of Society: Outline of the Theory of Structuration*. Cambridge: Polity.

Gurvitch, G. (1964). *The Spectrum of Social Time*. Dordrecht: D. Reidel Publishing Company.

Halbesleben, J. R. B., Novicevic, M. M., Harvey, M. G., & Buckley, M. R. (2003). Awareness of temporal complexity in leadership of creativity and innovation: A competency-based model. *The Leadership Quarterly*, *14*(4–5), 433–54. https://doi.org/10.1016/S1048-9843(03)00046-8.

Hartog, F. (2015). *Régimes d'historicité: Présentisme et Expériences du Temps*. Paris: Éditions du Seuil.

Hartog, F. (2020). *Chronos: L'Occident aux Prises avec le Temps*. Paris: Gallimard.

Hernes, T. (2014). *A Process Theory of Organization*. Oxford: Oxford University Press.

Holt, R. & Johnsen, R. (2019). Time and organization studies. *Organization Studies*, *40*(10), 1557–72. https://doi.org/10.1177/0170840619844292.

Johnsen, R. (2016). Boredom and organization studies. *Organization Studies* *37* (10), 1403–15.

Johnsen, R., Berg Johansen, C., & Toyoki, S. (2019). Serving time: Organization and the affective dimension of time. *Organization*, *26*(1), 3–19. https://doi.org /10.1177/1350508418763997.

Kant, E. (2021). *Critique de la raison pure*. Paris: Flammarion.

Kaplan, S. & Orlikowski, W. J. (2013). Temporal work in strategy making. *Organization Science*, *24*(4), 965–95. https://doi.org/10.1287/orsc.1120.0792.

Luhmann, N. (1995). *Social Systems*. Stanford: Stanford University Press.

McGivern, G., Dopson, S., Ferlie, E., Fischer, M., Fitzgerald, L., Ledger, J., & Bennett, C. (2018). The silent politics of temporal work: A case study of a management consultancy to redesign public health care. *Organization Studies*, *39*(8), 1007–30. https://doi.org/10.1177/0170840617708004.

Melbin, M., McGrath, J. E., & Kelley, J. R. (1986). Time and human interaction: Toward a social psychology of time. *Contemporary Sociology*, *16* (6), 860–1. https://doi.org/10.2307/2071593.

Montaigne, M. de. (2004). *Les Essais* (p. 526). Paris: PUF.

Nowotny, H. (1992). Time and social theory. *Time & Society*, *1*(3), 421–54. https://doi.org/10.1177/0961463x92001003006.

Orlikowski, W. J. & Yates, J. A. (2002). It's about time: Temporal structuring organizations. *Organization Science, 13*(6), 684–700. https://doi.org/10.1287/o rsc.13.6.684.501.

Perlow, L. A., Okhuysen, G. A., & Repenning, N. (2002). The speed trap: Exploring the relationship between decision making and temporal context. *The Academy of Management Journal, 45*(5), 931–55. https://doi.org/10.2307 /3069323.

Pulk, K. (2022). *Time and Temporality in Organisations: Theory and Development.* Basingstoke: Palgrave Macmillan.

Ratzinger, J. (2005). *La mort et l'au-delà.* Paris: Fayard.

Reinecke, J. & Ansari, S. (2015). When times collide: Temporal brokerage at the intersection of markets and developments. *Academy of Management Journal, 58* (2), 618–48. https://doi.org/10.5465/amj.2012.1004.

Rosa, H. (2015). *Social Acceleration: A New Theory of Modernity.* New York: Columbia University Press.

Rosa, H. (2020). *The Uncontrollability of the World.* Medford, MA: Polity Press.

Rosset, C. (1991). *La Philosophie Tragique.* Paris: Presses Universitaires de France.

Rosset, C. (2013). *Logique du pire. Éléments pour une philosophie tragique* (pp. 42–4). Paris: Presses Universitaires de France.

Rowell, C., Gustafsson, R., & Clemente, M. (2016). How institutions matter "in time": The temporal structures of practices and their effects on practice reproduction. *Research in the Sociology of Organizations, 48A.* https://doi.org/10 .1108/S0733-558X201600048A010.

Roy, D. F. (1959). "Banana time" job satisfaction and informal interaction. *Human Organization, 18*(4), 158–68. http://jstor.org/stable/44124108.

Shipp, A. J. & Jansen, K. J. (2021). The "other" time: A review of the subjective experience of time in organizations. *Academy of Management Annals, 15*(1), 299–334. https://doi.org/10.5465/annals.2018.0142.

Sørensen, B. M., Spoelstra, S., Höpfl, H., & Critchley, S. (2012). Theology and organization. *Organization, 19*(3), 267–79. https://doi.org/10.1177/1350508 412437464.

Sorokin, P. A. & Merton, R. K. (1937). Social time: A methodological and functional analysis. *American Journal of Sociology, 42*(5), 615–29. https://doi .org/10.1086/217540.

Special Issue of Strategic Organization. (2019). Temporal work: The strategic organization of time. *Strategic Organization, 17*(1), 145–9. https://doi.org/10 .1177/1476127018824166.

Taylor, F. W. (1911). *The Principles of Scientific Management.* New York & London: Harper & Brothers.

Thacker, E. (2014). *Starry Speculative Corpse.* Hants, UK: Zero Books.

Theunissen, M. & Sagnol, M. (2013). *Théologie Négative du Temps* (pp. 39–87). Paris: Les Éditions du Cerf.

Tsoukas, H. & Chia, R. (2002). On organizational becoming: Rethinking organizational change. *Organization Science 13*(5), 567–82.

Yakura, E. K. (2002). Charting time: Timelines as temporal boundary objects. *Academy of Management Journal, 45*(5), 956–70. https://doi.org/10.5465/3069324.

Part II

Re-orienting Critique in Organization
Studies? Exploring Jointly Time and Politics

5   Supersessionism and the Politics of Time
Reforming Organisational Studies with Gadamer's Hermeneutics of Trust

Gabriel J. Costello

Introduction

Brad Gregory (2012) in *The Unintended Reformation* defines historical supersessionism as follows: "the distant past is assumed to have been left behind, explanatorily important to what immediately succeeded it but not to the present". This chapter will argue that Positivism, a child of the Enlightenment, and a dominant paradigm in management and organisational research, has resulted in a supersessionist assessment of Aristotelian thought. Consequently, it proposes Hans-Georg Gadamer's *hermeneutics of trust* as a means to rehabilitate prejudice and engage in productive dialogue. The argument will draw on Alasdair MacIntyre's (2007) *After Virtue*, which has instigated a revival of Aristotelian philosophy that continues to gather momentum (Murphy, 2003). Chapter five of *After Virtue* has a provocative title: *Why the Enlightenment Project of Justifying Morality had to Fail*. At the beginning of the next chapter MacIntyre is very direct: "The problems of modern moral theory emerge clearly as the product of the failure of the Enlightenment project" (2007, p. 62). Beadle and Moore (2011, p. 85) have recently concluded that MacIntyre "has always taken organizations seriously as objects of philosophical attention" and consequently, organisational studies can benefit from his work. The study contends, following MacIntyre, that the uncritical acceptance of Enlightenment thinking with its dogmatic rejection of Aristotelian philosophy, has impoverished organisational research. Furthermore, it argues that this case of historical supersessionism provides a contemporary example of the *politics of time*. In the *Nicomachean Ethics*, Aristotle describes three approaches to knowledge: *episteme*, *techne* and *phronesis*. Flyvbjerg (2001, p. 56) explains that "whereas *episteme* concerns theoretical know-why and *techne* denotes technical know-how, *phronesis* emphasizes practical knowledge and practical ethics". Consequently, a reformation in organisational studies will be proposed based on a contemporary revival of Aristotle's concept of *phronesis* presented in the framework of Gadamer's *hermeneutics of trust*. This chapter will proceed as follows. First, the historical development of the concept of supersessionism will be discussed. Then, a brief introduction to the Enlightenment and its next of kin, Positivism, will be presented with a focus on its supersessionist approach to Aristotelian philosophy. Next, MacIntyre's critique of the Enlightenment and his arguments for the restoration of Aristotle will be outlined. Following this, the relatively recent discovery of Aristotle's concept of *phronesis* in the social sciences will be charted. Finally, the chapter will discuss how Gadamer's hermeneutics of trust can provide the opportunity for dialogue between Aristotle (mediated by MacIntyre), and the Enlightenment (mediated by Comte's Positivism). Furthermore, this engagement can result in a fruitful reformation in the study of organisations, artefacts, and practices.

Supersessionism and the Politics of Time

The aim of this section is to explain what is meant by supersessionism in the context of this study and how it impacts "the politics of time". First, I will examine the origin of supersessionism as a theological concept and more recently as a historical concept. Then, I will look briefly at the philosophy of time and how it has developed from the Greeks to the phenomenologists. Supersessionism originated as a religious notion that the Old Covenant was superseded by the New Covenant. Currently there are many definitions of the concept and D'Costa (2017) suggests that the taxonomy of R. Kendal Soulen (1996) is helpful. Soulen proposes three forms of supersessionism: 'economic', 'punitive', and 'structural'. The concept of historical supersessionism is presented by Gregory (2012, p. 7) as a mode of thinking where knowledge of the distant past "is widely assumed to be largely dispensable for those who want to understand the present". This he contends is a great mistake and has resulted in periodisation becoming an "intellectual prison" for students of history. Supersessionism is embedded in time, so I will undertake a brief exploration of the challenging quest to understand "time".

The study of time is as old as philosophy itself with Parmenides and Zeno holding what is regarded as a "static" view, since they considered the appearance of temporal change to be an illusion. However, Heraclitus and Aristotle argued for a "dynamic" view of time where reality was being constantly added to as time passed (Lowe, 2005). In particular, Aristotle's concept of time was closely linked with his account of motion, with his conclusion that we perceive time and motion together (Kenny, 2010). Aristotle provides an analysis of time in IV Book Delta of his *Physics* (Aristotle, 1961). According to Aristotle, nothing comes into being independently of some activity or process (1961, p. 86). Consequently, time is not independent of the process of change and Aristotle provides a definition. "For this is what time is: the number of precessions and successions in process" (1961, p. 80). Furthermore "the present is time's continuity since it holds past and future together" (1961, p. 85). However, according to Jancar (1966, p. 78), Aristotle holds that "the process of change does not depend upon our experiencing of it. Growth, decay, and motion would take place without us". Nevertheless, our sense of time is not equal with our sense of motion for "if it were, it would be common to all animals" (Kahn, 1979, p. 8 n. 23). Randall (1961, p. vii) concludes that Aristotle's concept of time is "not an absolute but rather a dimension" and hence relative. Furthermore, his conceptualisation "is suggestive in the attempt to escape the difficulties of Newton's Platonistic views" (1961, p. vii). Jancar (1966, p. 76) proposes that Aristotle's concept of time is noteworthy in that it considers it as something relative, a view which was not generally accepted until Einstein proposed his theory of relativity over 2,000 years later. An influential discussion of the problem of time is contained in Book XI of Saint Augustine's Confessions (1961) where he opens by stating that there is "no quick and easy answer" to the question of what time is (1961, p. 263). He goes on to say that there are three *times*: "a present of past things, a present of present things, and a present of future things". He explains: "The present of past things is memory; the present of present things is direct perception; and the present of future things is expectation" (1961, p. 269).

Moran and Cohen (2012, p. 320) propose that the question of temporality was a "foundational element of Edmund Husserl's entire phenomenological project" and subject to "profound and constant revisions, precisions and clarifications". A conundrum that he struggled with was how to relate "objective time" with the "subjective" consciousness of time and he regarded time as the "most difficult of all phenomenological problems" (2012, p. 321). From the beginning of the twentieth century Husserl began to have a great interest in the "temporal character of acts and their objects, and in the temporal 'streaming' of the ego itself" (Moran, 2005, p. 139). He began to study the way in which consciousness is framed by temporal experience. Similarly, Brough (1977) points out that an examination of relatively recent editions of the *Husserliana* indicates the development of Husserl's idea of time-consciousness: "In the new position which then appeared, around 1909, the absolute flow of time-constituting consciousness, and its distinction from temporal objects both immanent and transcendent was unequivocally affirmed (1977, p. 83).

Bergson defines "the immediate data of consciousness as being temporal, in other words, as the duration (*la durée*). In the duration, there is no juxtaposition of events; therefore there is no mechanistic causality"(Lawlor & Moulard-Leonard, 2021), a statement that has implications for our discussion of Positivism below. Another influential phenomenologist, Merleau-Ponty, "rejected classic approaches to time that treat it either as an objective property of things, as a psychological content, or as the product of transcendental consciousness". He proposed the concept of the *field of presence* as our foundational experience of time (Toadvine, 2019). This chapter will proceed to review both the Enlightenment and Positivism to support my argument that they are agents of historical supersessionism.

The Enlightenment: A Short Introduction

Kenny (2010) describes the intelligentsia of the seventeenth and eighteenth centuries as self-styled heralds, bringing the light of reason to a Europe darkened by ignorance and superstition. They contended that this dullness had resulted, to a large extent, from the religious beliefs of those whom Hume was wont to describe as "the vulgar". Pointedly, Hume viewed himself as "doing for psychology what Newton had done for physics, by applying the experimental method to moral subjects" (Kenny, 2010, p. 563). Having begun in England, and been given impetus in Scotland, the Enlightenment had, by the end of the eighteenth century, become an international movement "with important social and political ramifications" (Brittan, 1999, p. 266). According to MacIntyre (2007, p. 160), a direct consequence of the Enlightenment was the expulsion of Aristotle from European culture. In *After Virtue*, MacIntyre studies the historical and theoretical origins of the idea of virtue. He also proposes reasons for the post-Enlightenment absence of the concept of virtue from both personal and public life. Finally, he proceeds to sketch out a strategy for its recovery. In *A Short History of Ethics*, MacIntyre argues that Luther's opinion that "the community and its life are no longer the area in which the moral life is lived out" (2002, p. 117) could not be further away from Aristotle's worldview. MacIntyre quotes Luther's portrayal of Aristotle as "that buffoon who has misled the Church" (2002, p. 118) in the context of the general opinion of reformers that virtuous Christian behaviour did not contribute to one's eternal salvation. Gregory makes a strong historical argument that the Reformation had a direct bearing on the Enlightenment and remains "substantively necessary to an explanation of why the Western World today is as it is" (Gregory, 2012, p. 7). Furthermore, he posits that the influence of Max Weber's ahistorical conclusion, that "science and religion are incompatible" (2012, p. 26), has excluded any discussion of God from polite academic discourse. This ahistoricism was evident in the writings of French Enlightenment philosophers such as d'Alembert and Diderot who "shared a faith in the inevitability of scientific progress, a belief that the Christian religion was a great obstacle to human betterment, and a fundamentally materialist view of human nature" (Kenny, 2010, p. 570). According to Brittan (1999), a central Enlightenment belief was that any actions prompted by traditional authority, whether religious or political, could not be termed "free". Inwood (2005a, p. 252) contends that the Enlightenment is in one sense "unhistorical" and distils a number of Enlightenment doctrines (sic) such as: "Beliefs are to be accepted only on the basis of reason, not on the authority of priests, sacred texts or tradition." As a result, Enlightenment thinkers are disposed to being atheists. Furthermore, he offers an example of the Enlightenment's ahistoricism by contending that "the Enlightenment devalues local prejudices and customs, which owe their development to historical peculiarities rather than to the exercise of reason" (2005a, p. 253). This chapter now goes on to argue that the Positivist movement is an offspring of the Enlightenment, and that it promotes a supersessionist worldview.

Positivism: Child of the Enlightenment

The Positivist movement originated with the French philosopher and sociologist, Auguste Comte, who in the mid-nineteenth century formed a grand theory of the three supersessionist stages of human thought: religious, metaphysical, and scientific; with the final stage being the most productive and valuable (Lacy, 2005). This is sometimes referred to as Comte's "law of three stages". He was greatly influenced by the *philosophes* who were an eclectic group of intellectuals that instigated what is now termed the Enlightenment (Ruse, 2005). Comte believed that social reality can be explained only through science, and that society's behaviour can be *determined and governed* (my italics) by natural laws. According to Waliaula (2022), "Comte regarded all factual knowledge and phenomena a result of a predictable set of relations or a combination of relations". Positivism has had a significant influence on social science research, and understanding its tenets is important for the arguments in this chapter. However, despite his zeal for the primacy of the scientific method based on observation and a rejection of metaphysics, Comte found it necessary to found a "religion of humanity" towards the end of his life, complete with its saints such as Frederick the Great and Adam Smith (Wernick, 2001). Comte's categories and hierarchies, of which he was rather fond, rejected Aristotle's philosophical universe where physics and metaphysics could orbit harmoniously in their different spheres (Daintith & Gjertsen, 1999). Donald Schön (1983, p. 32) argues that Comte's formulation of his philosophy of *Positivism* contains three principal doctrines: empirical science is not just a form of knowledge but the only source of positive knowledge of the world; men's minds need to be cleansed of mysticism, superstition, and other forms of pseudo-knowledge; and scientific knowledge and technical control should be extended to human society in order to make technology "no longer exclusively geometrical, mechanical or chemical, but also primarily political and moral". Schön (1983) laments that the seeds of Positivism were firmly planted in the curricula of American universities and professional schools; a factor which he argues has contributed significantly to the contemporary fissure between research and practice. Furthermore, he concludes that the present difficulty in accommodating contemporary phenomena such as "complexity, uncertainty, instability, uniqueness, and value conflict" stems from the Positivist origins of technical rationality. It is worth noting that, according to Fotion (2005), logical Positivism is now regarded as having run its course and has little support among professional philosophers. This is a very salient point for the social science researchers who are still positivistic in outlook. However, it must be stated that this chapter is not a rejection of the empirical achievements of Enlightenment thinkers, but rather considers that its ahistorical agenda has impoverished scholarship. The specific case of ahistoricism being examined is the Enlightenment's refutation of Aristotelian thought. This chapter now examines the influence of Positivism on organisational and management research using the example of management information systems (MIS).

Positivism in Management Research

The role and importance of philosophy continues to be a matter of lively debate within the MIS discipline (Butler, 1998; Davison & Martinsons, 2011; Dobson & Love, 2004). Opinions in leading journals have called for researchers to have a firm philosophical basis to justify their research strategies. Presently, the MIS philosophical landscape consists of two streams: quantitative and qualitative. In this taxonomy, qualitative research admits three philosophical perspectives: Positivist, interpretive, and critical while the quantitative method firmly ties its adherents to Positivism (Myers, 2022). It should be borne in mind that there are also emerging perspectives in MIS philosophy such as Realism and Phenomenology (Costello, 2017; Mingers, 2004; Mingers et al., 2013). However, the dominant genre is Positivism which will be the focus here.

The Positivist perspective is accompanied by a broad commitment to the idea that the social sciences should emulate the natural sciences (Lee, 1989). The researcher is seen to play a passive, neutral role, and does not intervene in the phenomenon of interest. Klein and Myers (1999 p. 69) point out that generally speaking, MIS research can be "classified as positivist if there is evidence of formal propositions, quantifiable measures of variables, hypothesis testing, and the drawing of inferences about a phenomenon from a representative sample to a stated population". The goal of Positivism is to replicate the success of natural science in explanation, prediction, and control. A study by Dube and Pare (2003) found that the majority of studies in MIS were conducted from a Positivist philosophical perspective. Despite signs of waning, some highly respected MIS researchers have recently attested to the prevalence of the positivistic system in the discipline by concluding that "in numerous institutions around the world, IS investigators are expected to test theories in a positivist fashion" (Kock et al., 2017). Now, having set out my critique of the philosophical underpinning of the Enlightenment and Positivism, I will argue for a reformation that includes reinstating Aristotle's thought into the sphere of organisations, artefacts, and practices. Therefore, I will proceed with a brief introduction to Aristotle, his treatment by the Enlightenment thinkers, and the current interest in his concept of *phronesis* by some social scientists.

Aristotle

Dante considered Aristotle as epitomizing the pinnacle of human reason and his references to Aristotle came second only to that of the Bible (Dante, 1984 translation). Without doubt, Aristotle is one of the most influential thinkers in the history of western civilisation. His works have covered a vast range of subjects such as logic ethics, metaphysics, politics, natural science, and physics (ODE, 2006). Aristotle's science was not superseded until the scientific revolution of the sixteenth and seventeenth centuries (ODS, 1999). Critchley (2001) points out that among other things, ancient philosophy endeavoured to amalgamate knowledge and wisdom: "namely, that knowledge of how things were the way they were, would lead to wisdom in the conduct of one's life. The assumption that ties knowledge and wisdom together is the idea that the cosmos as such expresses a human purpose. This is called the 'teleological view of the universe'" (2001, p. 7) and the idea of attainment of goals or contributing to optimal states (Bogen, 2005) implies a concept of time. The basic structure of the moral scheme that had dominated the Middle Ages in Europe was that which Aristotle had proposed in the *Nicomachean Ethics*.

Alasdair MacIntyre laments the spread of emotivism or feelings in a variety of philosophical guises that has resulted in its gaining a dominant position in our contemporary culture. According to MacIntyre, one consequence is that the "idioms of therapy have invaded all too successfully such spheres as those of education and of religion" displacing truth as a value, a central tenet of Aristotle's virtue ethics in the notion of teleology, that is, that humans have a purpose and a goal. Ethics, in this schema, is the teleological science that enables a man or woman to transition from the state of "man-as-he-happens-to-be" to the state of "man-as-he-could-be-if -he-realised-his-essential-nature" (MacIntyre, 2007, p. 52). Chapter eight of *After Virtue*, MacIntyre's critique of the present-day view of managerial expertise, with its resulting consequences for organisational studies, is relevant to the debate on the politics of time. He argues that the conventional understanding of organisation science, derived from the Enlightenment through luminaries such as Comte and Mill, is to provide managers with law-like solutions to their problems in the same way that the laws of physics are applied to natural phenomena. In contrast, Aristotle's concept of the virtues supports a person's achievement of *eudaimonia*, variously described as happiness and wellbeing. Virtues provide a disposition to both act and feel in particular ways to support the attainment of *eudaimonia*. Decisions in organisations are summarised succinctly by MacIntyre when he says that "choices demand judgement and the exercise of virtues requires therefore a capacity to judge and to do the right thing in the right place at the right time in the right way" (MacIntyre, 2007, p. 150). Consequently, judgement has an indispensable role in the life of a virtuous man which it does not or could not have in, for example, the life of merely law-abiding or rule-abiding man. Thus, it is the person with practical intelligence, intelligence informed by virtues, that we meet in history. MacIntyre proposes that a central virtue is that of *phronesis* and that "it comes to mean more generally someone who knows how to exercise judgement in particular cases" (2007, 154). Consequently, the next section of this chapter will examine the concept of *phronesis* and its application to organisational studies.

Phronesis and Its Implications for Organisational Studies

I will now discuss the implications for organisational studies of Aristotle's concept of *phronesis*, presented in the managerial and social science literature by Flyvbjerg (2001), Kinsella and Pitman (2012), Thomas (2011), and Van de Ven (2007). Aristotle's ethical writings synthesise the ideas of knowledge and wisdom, and their application in practice. This he achieved through the concept of *phronesis* (*phronēsis*) which can be described simply as practical wisdom. Aristotle used the term to represent the complete excellence of the practical intellect. It was the equivalent in the practical sphere of *sophia* in the theoretical sphere. Taylor (2005) explains *phronesis* as having, in ancient Greece, connotations of intelligence and soundness of judgement and he defines *phronesis* as comprising a true conception of the good life and the deliberative excellence necessary to realise that conception in practice through choice. Flyvbjerg describes *phronetic social science* as an approach to the study of social phenomena based on a *contemporary* interpretation of the *classical* Greek concept *phronesis*, variously translated as practical judgement, practical wisdom, common sense, or prudence. Phronetic planning research is phronetic social science employed in the specific study of policy and planning (Flyvbjerg, 2018). In *The Sage Dictionary of Qualitative Management Research*, Flyvbjerg points out that Phronetic Organisational Research effectively provides answers to the following four value-rational questions, for specific problems in management and studies:

1 Where are we going with this specific management problem?
2 Who gains and who loses, and by which mechanisms of power?
3 Is this development desirable?
4 What, if anything, should we do about it?

Thus, in his view, *Phronetic Organizational Research* concerns deliberation, judgement, and praxis in relation to these four questions. Praxis is the process by which *phronesis*, as a concept, becomes lived reality. Kinsella and Pitman (2012) state that their book on *phronesis* originated from a continuing conversation in which

we voiced concern (bordering on distress) regarding the instrumentalist values that permeate (often without question) our professional schools, professional practices, and policy decisions. Like others, we were grappling with a sense that something of fundamental importance – of moral significance – was missing in the vision of what it means to be a professional, and in the ensuing educational aims in professional schools and continuing professional education. (2012, p. 1)

Furthermore, they explain that *phronesis*, "is an intellectual virtue that implies ethics. It involves deliberation that is based on values, concerned with practical judgment and informed by reflection. It is pragmatic, variable, context-dependent, and oriented toward action" (2012, p. 2). In thinking about how practitioners might enact *phronesis*, Kinsella (2012) argues in a related chapter that attention to reflection and judgement is key. In management scholarship, the influential Andrew Van de Ven (2007) also uses Aristotle's theory of knowledge when he distinguishes between *techne* (applied technical knowledge of instrumental or means-ends rationality); *episteme* (basic knowledge in the pursuit of theoretical or analytical questions); and *phronesis* (practical knowledge of how to act prudently and correctly in a given immediate and ambiguous social or political situation). According to Van de Ven, saying that the knowledge of science and practice are different is not to imply that they stand in opposition, or that they are a substitute for each other; rather, they complement one another (2007, p. 3). I now go on to discuss *phronesis* in the context of the 'case study' which is an important instrument in organisational research.

Thomas (2011) argues that the case study is concerned with *phronesis* rather than with theory and that this has far reaching implications for social science research. As a result, he contends that there is a pressing need to move from generalisable knowledge and development of theory associated with the dominant inductive approach, which is unattainable in the complex world of practice. Instead of talking about theory when examining case studies, we should be talking about *phronesis*. Drawing on MacIntyre and others, Thomas argues that the prevailing deduction-induction nexus leads to a dead end. He provocatively proposes – after Fish (1990) – that much of what passes for theory in the social sciences is not theory at all but is just some kind of *theory talk*. In its place, he proposes a move towards the "exemplary" knowledge of abduction and *phronesis* which provides meanings which are malleable and interpretable in the context of diversities of experience. It is interesting that Flyvbjerg (2011) makes a similar point in his chapter on the "Case Study" in *The Sage Handbook of Qualitative Research*. Previously he argued for Aristotle's insight that case knowledge is crucial to the practice of *phronesis*, and on this basis he clarifies the status and uses of case studies in social science (Flyvbjerg, 2001, p. 4). This chapter will now discuss a proposal to initiate a dialogue between Enlightenment Positivism, and neo-Aristotelian philosophy, through the mediation of Hans-Georg Gadamer.

Discussion: Gadamer's Hermeneutics of Trust

This section will argue that the historical supersessionism inherent in Enlightenment and Positivist thinking has excluded Aristotelian philosophy and will propose the work of Hans-Georg Gadamer as a path for dialogue. Furthermore, organisational studies can look to Gadamer for ways to come to terms with the bias that is intrinsic to historical supersessionism. Malpas (2018) has described Gadamer as the decisive figure in the development of twentieth-century hermeneutics and indeed his long life spanned the whole of this period from his birth in 1900 to his death in 2002. An important theme of Gadamer's was that speech, language, interpretation, and understanding is embedded in our historical context and is subject to our prejudices (or pre-judgements). Gadamer alters the normal pejorative view of *prejudice* into a positive conception that both Moran and Malpas term as the rehabilitation of prejudice. Consequently, the uncovering of our normally concealed prejudices through dialogue opens us up to new viewpoints, understandings, and, indeed, questions. Moran (2000, p. 278) describes Gadamer as encouraging us to engage in dialogue in order to uncover our presuppositions and pre-judgements: "We cannot eliminate prejudice, but we can make it visible and thus make it work for us." According to Gadamer, "prejudices are biases of our openness to the world. They are simply conditions whereby we experience something" (2000, p. 278). It is worth noting here that Burke's anti-Enlightenment critique included his "belief that society depends on what he called 'prejudice', that is, on instinctive feelings of love and loyalty" (Dowie, 2005, p. 115) and that the "accumulated wisdom of past generations is more likely to be correct than the ideas of an individual philosopher" (Inwood, 2005a, p. 253). An important facet of Gadamer's work was his immersion in the Greek tradition and the programme proposed by Socrates, Plato, and Aristotle, of pursuing philosophy through dialogue and engagement with the *practical*. In fact, both Plato and Aristotle saw philosophy as engaging with practice (Moran, 2000, p. 268). Tredennick (1969) points out that Socrates insisted that he was not a teacher but a sort of intellectual midwife who helped "others to bring their thoughts to birth". The Aristotelian concept of *phronesis* (practical wisdom), described earlier, is central to the development of hermeneutical understanding in Gadamer's major philosophical work *Truth and Method* (Dostal, 2002, p. 8). Heidegger's early analysis of Aristotle's *phronesis* helped Gadamer see that Aristotle's practical philosophy exemplifies integral hermeneutics. According to Lawrence (2002), when Gadamer makes *phronesis* the heart of his philosophical hermeneutics, he removes all the ambiguity from Heidegger's insight into the relevance of *phronesis* for a philosophy of human historicity. On the contrary, Gadamer maintains, reading Plato in light of Aristotle's critique, "we see how close the knowledge of the good sought by Socrates is to Aristotle's phronesis" (Zuckert, 2002, p. 212). Whether we are dealing with morality, ethics, or politics, Gadamer advocates the necessity of cultivating hermeneutics sensitivity and *phronesis* in all dimensions of human life. According to Bernstein (2002), Gadamer prescribes the practical philosophy of Aristotle and his concepts of *phronesis* as an antidote to the growing pervasiveness of somnambulism, that is, blind technological thinking. Understanding *understanding* was a major theme running through Gadamer's work and he contrasted the "phenomenon of understanding (Verstehen)" with "the explanation (Erklären) characteristic of the natural sciences"(Inwood, 2005b). Paul Ricoeur described Gadamer's vision of the philosophical dialogue as a hermeneutics of trust rather than suspicion; thus rejecting the Nietzschean standpoint that "all understanding is really an attempt at mastery and will-to-power" (Moran, 2000, p. 253).

A method that could facilitate this hermeneutics of trust is the practice of Husserl's idea of *epoché* (suspension of judgement) which employs a set of procedures that Husserl called "reduction" (from the Latin *reducere* "to lead back"). As Moran (2000, p. 146) explains, it allowed Husserl to detach from such influences as conventional opinion and scientific consensus: "We must put aside our beliefs about our beliefs, as it were." Furthermore, Husserl considered that philosophy should be carried out as a rigorous science using the structured methodology of reason, and his vision was that the phenomenological approach (of bracketing the natural world and a reduction to pure consciousness) could overcome and synthesise the radical disagreements of contemporary philosophy. This chapter ends by summarising my argument that supersessionism is a contemporary example of the politics of time, and that Gadamer's hermeneutics of trust can assist the task of reconciling the Enlightenment worldview with Aristotelian philosophy.

Conclusions

This chapter is not a broad rejection of the Enlightenment programme; rather, it acknowledges the outstanding achievements of the scientific method. However, it does argue that the supersessionist predisposition of Enlightenment thinking, and, in particular, the influence of Comte, has resulted in a rejection of any philosophical engagement with the transcendent, a perennial fault-line among philosophers (Priest, 2005). Ruse (2005, p. 153) cautions that one should not underestimate the influence of Comte or neglect the fact that there is an identifiable chain from Comte down to the twentieth-century positivists of various hues. My proposed antidote is an engagement with Aristotle, as presented by neo-Aristotelians such as Alasdair MacIntyre, using Gadamer's hermeneutics of trust as a vehicle for such a reformation. The discussion on *phronesis* above provides evidence of the contemporary relevance of Aristotle's explication of "knowledge" and its growing impact on management and organisational research. This is also relevant to debates on education, as the Enlightenment views its main purpose as imparting knowledge in contrast with the Aristotelian view of development of character. Another significant influence of Aristotle can be seen in Heidegger's (1962, p. 21) *Being and Time*, which begins with the statement that the question of Being "has today been forgotten" but that the "question we are touching upon is not just any question". This central question had "provided a stimulus for the researches of Plato and Aristotle, only to subside from then on as a theme for actual investigation" (1962). Furthermore, "a dogma has been developed which not only declares the question about the meaning of Being to be superfluous, but sanctions its complete neglect" (1962). I argue that these statements by Heidegger support the thesis that Aristotelian ontology has been the object of a supersessionist mindset. Technological artefacts and practices are a vital part of the modern organisation, and its philosophical examination is an important undertaking. Heidegger (1977) contends that "technology is a human activity" and pointedly observes that its "threat to man does not come in the first instance from the potentially lethal machines and apparatus of technology. The actual threat has already affected man in his essence". Heidegger proposed that our knowledge and basic ways of encountering the world are obtained through the use of technology rather than by means of its scientific description. A hammer is not just a tool to look at or theorise about but an implement to experience, often unconsciously, in the act of creating something. Gadamer was a student of Heidegger, as well as being a learned interpreter of Plato, Aristotle, and the poetic texts (Sokolowski, 2000, p. 224). However, it is worth noting that when Husserl got around to reading *Being and Time* he was alarmed at its propositions and wrote on his copy of the book Aristotle's famous words: *amicus Plato, magis amica veritas* [Plato is a friend, but truth is a greater friend] (Moran, 2000, p. 207).

Finally, I suggest that future work in organisational studies must have the confidence and ambition to examine an urgent example of the politics of time: the rise of fundamentalism. This includes atheistic fundamentalism, which has resulted in a confessional secularist agenda that has mirrored the rise of religious (or rather *ideological* religious) fundamentalism. However, Aristotle can provide common ground for dialogue given his significant influence on Ibn Sina (Avicenna) in Islam; Maimonides (Moses ben Maimon) in Judaism; St. Thomas Aquinas in Christianity; and atheistic Aristotelian scholars such as Edith Hall (2018). As Jancar (1966, p. 26) points out,

under Aristotle, Plato's idea of a common life shared by friends in search of wisdom became the basis for the first university in Europe. It is ironic that Marx, who prophesised that the coming of a socialist society would render both philosophy and religion obsolete (McLellan, 2005), also considered that "we are not able to shed our history the way a snake sheds its skin" (Moran, 2000, p. 278).

Gadamer's hermeneutics of trust can make a helpful contribution to the study of organisations, artefacts, and practices as it advocates the necessity of cultivating hermeneutics sensitivity and dialogue in all dimensions of human life. Furthermore, Husserl's idea of *epoché* can be used to examine historical supersessionism and assist the work of resolving contemporary prejudices and misunderstandings. By embracing a hermeneutics of trust, organisational research can address MacIntyre's concern (2006, p. 4) about the current irrelevance of philosophy for social science disciplines.

Imprisoning philosophy within the professionalisations and specialisations of an institutionalised curriculum after the manner of our own contemporary European and North American culture is arguably a good deal more effective in neutralising its effects than either religious censorship or political terror.

References

Aristotle (1961). *Aristotle's Physics with an Analytical Index of Technical Terms.* Trans. Richard Hope. Nebraska: University of Nebraska Press.

Beadle, R. & Moore, G. (2011). MacIntyre, neo-Aristotelianism and Organization Theory. In H. Tsoukas & R. Chia (eds.), *Philosophy and Organization Theory Research in the Sociology of Organizations* (Vol. 32, pp. 85–121). Bingley, UK: Emerald Publishing Limited.

Bernstein, R. J. (2002). The Constellation of Hermeneutics, Critical Theory and Deconstruction. In R. J. Dostal (ed.), *Cambridge Companion to Gadamer.* West Nyack, NY: Cambridge University Press.

Bogen, J. (2005). Teleological Explanation. In T. Honderich (ed.), *The Oxford Companion to Philosophy* (2nd ed., p. 911). Oxford: Oxford University Press.

Brittan, G. G. J. (1999). Enlightenment. In R. Audi (ed.), *The Cambridge Dictionary of Philosophy* (p. 266). New York: Cambridge University Press.

Brough, J. B. (1977). The Emergence of an Absolute Consciousness in Husserl's Early Writings on Time-Consciousness. In F. A. Elliston & P. McCormick (eds.), *Husserl: Expositions and Appraisals.* Indiana: University of Notre Dame Press.

Butler, T. (1998). Towards a hermeneutic method for interpretive research in information systems. *Journal of Information Technology*, *13*(4), 285–300.

Costello, G. J. (2017). Phenomenological realism: A pragmatic lens for information systems research. *Systems, Signs & Actions SYSIAC (An International Journal on Information Technology, Action, Communication and Workpractices)*, *10*(1), 34–53. Available at: https://sysiac.org/?pageId=45

Critchley, S. (2001). *Continental Philosophy: A Very Short Introduction.* Oxford: Oxford University Press.

D'Costa, G. (2017). Supersessionism: Harsh, Mild or Gone for Good? *European Judaism: A Journal for the New Europe*, *50*(1), 99–107.

Daintith, J. & Gjertsen, D. (eds.) (1999). *Oxford Dictionary of Scientists* (2nd ed.). Oxford: Oxford University Press.

Dante (1984 translation). *The Divine Comedy, Volume 1: Inferno by Dante Aligheri.* Trans. Mark Musa. New York: Penguin Classics

Davison, R. M. & Martinsons, M. G. (2011). Methodological practice and policy for organisationally and socially relevant IS research: An inclusive–exclusive perspective. *Journal of Information Technology, 26,* 288–93.

Dobson, P. & Love, P. (2004). Realist and postmodernist perspectives on information systems research: Points of connection. *Australasian Journal of Information Systems, 12*(1). Available at: https://doi.org/10.3127/ajis .v3112i3121.3107

Dostal, R. J. (2002). Introduction. In R. J. Dostal (ed.), *Cambridge Companion to Gadamer.* West Nyack, NY: Cambridge University Press.

Dowie, R. S. (2005). Burke, Edmund. In T. Honderich (ed.), *The Oxford Companion to Philosophy* (2nd ed.). Oxford: Oxford University Press.

Dube, L. & Pare, G. (2003). Rigor in information systems positivist case research: Current practices, trends, and recommendations. *MIS Quarterly, 27*(4), 597–635.

Fish, S. (1990). *Doing What Comes Naturally: Change, Rhetoric, and the Practice of Theory in Literary & Legal Studies.* Durham, NC: Duke University Press.

Flyvbjerg, B. (2001). *Making Social Science Matter: Why Social Inquiry Fails and How It Can Succeed Again.* Trans. Stephen Sampson. Cambridge: Cambridge University Press.

Flyvbjerg, B. (2011). Case Study. In N. K. Denzin & Y. S. Lincoln (eds.), *The Sage Handbook of Qualitative Research* (4th ed., pp. 301–16). Thousand Oaks, CA: Sage.

Flyvbjerg, B. (2018). What is Phronesis and Phronetic Social Science? Available at: https://linkedin.com/pulse/what-phronesis-phronetic-social-science-bent-flyvb jerg-%E5%82%85%E4%BB%A5%E6%96%8C-/. Accessed February 2022.

Fotion, N. (2005). Logical Positivism. In T. Honderich (ed.), *The Oxford Companion to Philosophy* (2nd ed.). Oxford: Oxford University Press.

Gregory, B. S. (2012). *The Unintended Reformation: How a Religious Revolution Secularized Society.* Cambridge, MA: Harvard University Press.

Hall, E. (2018). *Aristotle's Way: How Ancient Wisdom Can Change Your Life.* London: Bodley Head.

Heidegger, M. (1962). *Being and Time.* Trans. John Macquarrie & Edward Robinson. New York: Harper.

Heidegger, M. (1977). The Question Concerning Technology. In *The Question Concerning Technology: And Other Essays* (pp. 3–35). New York & London: Garland Publishing Inc.

Inwood, M. J. (2005a). Enlightenment. In T. Honderich (ed.), *The Oxford Companion to Philosophy* (2nd ed., pp. 252–3). Oxford: Oxford University Press.

Inwood, M. J. (2005b). Gadamer, Hans Georg. In T. Honderich (ed.), *The Oxford Companion to Philosophy* (2nd ed.). Oxford: Oxford University Press.

Jancar, B. (1966). *The Philosophy of Aristotle.* New York: Monarch Press.

Kahn, C. H. (1979). Sensation and Consciousness in Aristotle's Psychology. In J. Barnes, M. Schofield, & R. Sorabji (eds.), *Articles on Aristotle.* London: Duckworth.

Kenny, A. (2010). *A New History of Western Philosophy.* Oxford: Oxford University Press.

Kinsella, E. A. (2012). Practitioner Reflection and Judgement as Phronesis. In E. A. Kinsella & A. Pitman (eds.), *Phronesis as Professional Knowledge: Practical Wisdom in the Professions*. Rotterdam: Sense Publishers.

Kinsella, E. A. & Pitman, A. (eds.) (2012). *Phronesis as Professional Knowledge: Practical Wisdom in the Professions*. Rotterdam: Sense Publishers.

Klein, H. K. & Myers, M. D. (1999). A set of principles for conducting and evaluating interpretive field studies in information systems. *MIS Quarterly, 23* (1), 67–94.

Kock, N., Avison, D. & Malaurent, J. (2017). Positivist information systems action research: Methodological issues. *Journal of Management Information Systems, 34*(3), 754–67. DOI: 710.1080/07421222.07422017.01373007.

Lacy, A. (2005). Positivism. In T. Honderich (ed.), *The Oxford Companion to Philosophy* (2nd ed.). Oxford: Oxford University Press.

Lawlor, L. & Moulard-Leonard, V. (2021). Henri Bergson. In E. N. Zalta (ed.), *The Stanford Encyclopedia of Philosophy* (Fall 2021 ed.). Available at: <https://plato.stanford.edu/archives/fall2021/entries/bergson/>. Accessed January 2022.

Lawrence, F. (2002). Gadamer, the Hermeneutic Revolution, and Theology. In R. J. Dostal (ed.), *Cambridge Companion to Gadamer*. West Nyack, NY: Cambridge University Press.

Lee, A. (1989). A scientific methodology for MIS case studies. *MIS Quarterly*, March, 33–50.

Lowe, E. J. (2005). Time. In T. Honderich (ed.), *The Oxford Companion to Philosophy* (2nd ed., pp. 919–20). Oxford: Oxford University Press.

MacIntyre, A. C. (2002). *A Short History of Ethics: A History of Moral Philosophy from the Homeric Age to the 20th Century*. London: Taylor & Francis.

MacIntyre, A. C. (2006). *Edith Stein: A Philosophical Prologue, 1913–1922*. Lanham, MD: Rowman & Littlefield.

MacIntyre, A. C. (2007). *After Virtue* (3rd ed.). Indiana: University of Notre Dame Press.

Malpas, J. (2018). Hans-Georg Gadamer. In E. N. Zalta (ed.), *The Stanford Encyclopedia of Philosophy* (Fall 2018 ed.). Available at: https://plato.stanford.edu/archives/fall2018/entries/gadamer/. Accessed February 2022.

Mingers, J. (2004). Real-izing information systems: Critical realism as an underpinning philosophy for information systems. *Information and Organization, 14*, 87–103.

Mingers, J., Mutch, A., & Willcocks, L. (2013). Critical realism in information systems research. *MIS Quarterly, 37*(3), 795–802.

Moran, D. (2000). *Introduction to Phenomenology*. London & New York: Routledge.

Moran, D. (2005). *Edmund Husserl: Founder of Phenomenology*. Oxford: Polity.

Moran, D. & Cohen, J. (2012). *The Husserl Dictionary*. London & New York: Continuum.

Murphy, M. C. (ed.) (2003). *Alasdair MacIntyre*. Cambridge: Cambridge University Press.

Myers, M. D. (2022). Qualitative Research in Information Systems. Available at: https://qual.auckland.ac.nz/. Accessed February 2022.

ODE. (2006). Aristotle. In *Oxford Dictionary of English* (Rev. 2nd ed.). Oxford: Oxford University Press.

ODS. (1999). Aristotle. In J. Daintith & D. Gjertsen (eds), *Oxford Dictionary of Scientists* (2nd ed.). Oxford: Oxford University Press.

Priest, S. (2005). Transcendence. In T. Honderich (ed.), *The Oxford Companion to Philosophy* (2nd ed.). Oxford: Oxford University Press.

Randall, J. H. (1961). Foreword. In *Aristotle's Physics with an Analytical Index of Technical Terms*. Trans. Richard Hope. Nebraska: University of Nebraska Press.

Ruse, M. (2005). Comte, Isidore Auguste Marie Francois Xavier. In T. Honderich (ed.), *The Oxford Companion to Philosophy* (2nd ed.). Oxford: Oxford University Press.

Saint Augustine. (1961). *Confessions*. Trans. R. S. Pine-Coffin. London: Penguin Classics.

Schön, D. A. (1983). *The Reflective Practitioner: How Professionals Think in Action*. New York: Basic Books.

Sokolowski, R. (2000). *Introduction to Phenomenology*. Cambridge, UK & New York: Cambridge University Press.

Soulen, R. K. (1996). *The God of Israel and Christian Theology*. Minneapolis: Fortress Press.

Taylor, C. C. W. (2005). Phronēsis. In T. Honderich (ed.), *The Oxford Companion to Philosophy* (2nd ed.). Oxford: Oxford University Press.

Thomas, G. (2011). *How To Do Your Case Study: A Guide for Students and Researchers*. Thousand Oaks, CA: Sage.

Toadvine, T. (2019). Maurice Merleau-Ponty. In E. N. Zalta (ed.), *The Stanford Encyclopedia of Philosophy* (Spring 2019 ed.). Available at: https://plato.stanford.edu/archives/spr2019/entries/merleau-ponty/. Accessed January 2022.

Tredennick, H. (1969). Introduction. In *Plato: The Last Days of Socrates*. Harmondsworth, UK: Penguin Classics.

Van de Ven, A. H. (ed.) (2007). *Engaged Scholarship: A Guide for Organizational and Social Research*. Oxford & New York: Oxford University Press.

Waliaula, A. J. P. (2022). Positivism. *Salem Press Encyclopedia Research Starters*. EBSCOhost. Accessed March 27, 2018.

Wernick, A. (2001). *Auguste Comte and the Religion of Humanity: The Post-Theistic Program of French Social Theory*. Cambridge: Cambridge University Press.

Zuckert, C. H. (2002). Hermeneutics in Practice: Gadamer on Ancient Philosophy. In R. J. Dostal (ed.), *Cambridge Companion to Gadamer*. West Nyack, NY: Cambridge University Press.

6   Between Abandon and Inquiry
On the Way to Emancipatory Temporalities in Organizing

François-Xavier de Vaujany, Aurélie Leclercq-Vandelannoitte and Gazi Islam

Introduction

In most post-Marxist and critical perspectives on organizing, domination and emancipation have often been described in terms of spaces and spacing (Dale, 2005; Dale & Burrell, 2008). With such treatment, the space of our cities, the space of capitalism, and the spacing of our activities and practices, are dominated, controlled, manipulated, and instrumentalized (see e.g. Lefebvre, 1991). With the "spatial turn", space (and organizational space in particular) has been presented as political rather than merely aesthetic (Dale & Burrell, 2008), and described as a materialization of power relations (Fleming & Spicer, 2004; Taylor & Spicer, 2007). The politics of organizing have thus often been conceptualized in management and organization studies as spatial issues, often obscuring the temporal dimensions of power, such that power is often linked to a spatial target (the "space" of our activities) and a spatial medium (the "organizational space").

Time, by contrast, has been mostly understood through space as movement or episodes of spacing, contributing to a "spatialization of time" (Portschy, 2020). More rarely, management and organization studies have investigated time and temporality as important dimensions of organizational politics, power dynamics, and emancipation (e.g. Bailey & Madden, 2017; Dawson & Sykes, 2018). If space is often acknowledged as politically agentive, this is less the case for time, which is rarely acknowledged as a source of agency in organizational scholarship. This omission is problematic given that organizing itself is increasingly recognized as a process of temporalization, a duration, a living process, a temporal work, fields of events, or depth of experience (see Chia, 2002; Tsoukas & Chia, 2002; Deroy & Clegg, 2011; Helin et al., 2014; Hernes, 2014; Reinecke et al., 2021; de Vaujany, 2022b). Temporality is then a force by itself (Holt & Johnsen, 2019), the locus of an 'agency'

(Hernes, 2014), in and/or beyond practices, and even the true source of power in organizations and organizing.

As suggested by Foucault (1977), time is indeed highly political, fundamentally related to the exercise of power and embedded in social relations (Portschy, 2020): power directly intervenes in the social organization of time, as shown by Foucault's (1977) emphasis on the fundamental connection of power with practices of temporalization and timing (though as diverse time-dispositives and time-norms that shape bodies, affect identities, and fundamentally alter the conduct of conducts) (Zerubavel, 1985). However, beyond Foucault's (1977) famous consideration of time as a technology of power (or technology domination), time can also be interpreted and used as an instrument of self-government and resistance; a technology of the self (Foucault, 1988), a way to transform oneself, and even a practice of freedom and emancipation from domination (Lilja, 2018). In the late "ethical" Foucault of the late 1970s and 1980s (Foucault, 1985), time is considered an important element in his investigation of ancient literature on techniques of the self, involving specific meditations and practices directed towards establishing a certain ethics towards time and temporality (Portschy, 2020). Foucault (1982) thus paves the way to possibilities of resistance against dominant articulations of time, power, and knowledge, and envisions strategies to live time differently, implying a refusal to be governed by and through time, in ways that help people turn their life and times into a work of art (Portschy, 2020). This perspective suggests considering specific temporal self-relations, diverse experiences of being present, and forms of retrospections and prospection, enabling control of individual life-times.

Thus, in light of these developments on the interconnectedness of time and power, temporality and emancipation (Lilja, 2018) and the recognition that time is inherently plural, heterogeneous, and relational (Portschy, 2020), exploring the intersection between temporality and power seems crucial; it even becomes a key way to explore power, perhaps even the most relevant and important one. How do temporality and events foster, contribute to, actualize, and matter, (new) agentive subjectivities, emancipations, and resistance within organizing processes? This is the issue we will analyse in this chapter.

Addressing the relative neglect of politics of time in management and organization studies (Holt & Johnsen, 2019), the current chapter elaborates on two main conceptualizations of temporality that we contend help us make sense of political views of time, in particular, of emancipatory conceptualizations of temporalities. On the one hand, "abandon" (de Vaujany, 2022a), "dérive" (Debord, 1956, 1967; Fabbri et al., 2016), flânerie (Nash, 2018a, 2018b; Pelurson, 2019; Aroles & Küpers, 2022), and "reverie" (Helin, 2020; Helin et al., 2020) can be considered paths towards an authentic voice, a *verticality*[1] inside the permanent change in our cities, organizations, and in capitalism and other structuring mechanisms. In these approaches, actors must create their own anchoring, and search for their own ground. Emancipation in this conceptualization involves a temporal suspension as actors abandon themselves to the moment. The writing process serves as one way to cultivate such verticality (Helin, 2020). More embodied activities such as the practice of walking can also open this proximity to a self that is agonistically built from the "within of our present" (Fabbri et al., 2016; de Vaujany & Vitaud, 2017; de Vaujany, 2022a) and help elaborate new pedagogies of affects (Beyes & Steyaert, 2021).

On the other hand, inquiry, deconstruction, and active reflexivity constitute much more active temporal stances. In contrast to the previous approaches, what matters here is the movement from indeterminacy to determinacy, from concerns to problematization and solution (see Dewey, 1938; Zask, 2015; Lorino, 2018). Chaos can be a part of the process, but only insofar as it grounds attempts to correctly interpret a real problem by a collectivity and works towards a progressive determination and solution. Here, the social and material aspects of an ongoing social construction are engaged in a social process of collective problem-solving. Inquiry is at the heart of temporalization in such cases. Its movement is far from cybernetic, that is, made of feedbacks and circular loops that maintain a pre-existing social system (see Otley, 1983 or Flood & Jackson, 1988).[2] Rather, this pragmatist orientation is auto-poetic and self-creative. Emancipation is sought in the process of defining problems and solutions that are important to everyday life, with a democratic suspicion of expert prescription or other forms of top-down domination.

"Abandon" and "inquiry" visions of emancipatory temporalities may seem, *prima facie*, to be incompatible. This apparent incompatibility derives from the divergence in their respective positions, temporal

---

[1] The bulk of process studies deals with flat duration or events, that is, the flat and continuous horizontalities of organizing. Following Bachelardian or Foucaldian stances, some other studies explore what can stand in the present (see Helin, 2020; Helin et al., 2020) or the differential depth of organizing (de Vaujany, 2022a). According to this alternative approach, everything flows, but sometimes, is cut such that the flow of organizing can be suspended. Events are crowned by something. Immobility, flânerie, and drift, move around the expanded site, this spacing inside the events of the world, to make visible what is at stake in our cities in the present.

[2] Although cybernetics has been paradoxically influenced by pragmatism (see de Vaujany, 2022a).

orientation, and objectives, auguring a tense, if not impossible, dialogue. Abandon emphasizes spontaneity and self-delivery to the fluid moment; inquiry, to structured (if flexible) pragmatism. The two approaches seem to diverge in that the first (abandon, dérive, or flânerie) involves drifting collectively and spontaneously in urban spaces, through an undefined and opened temporality. This drifting re-instils a quality of passivity, fragility, ambiguity, and freedom to the experience of the world. In contrast, inquiry involves active problematizing and experimenting with co-constituted solutions to converge towards an outcome for the collectivity, in the frame of a well-defined, organized, chronological, and horizontal temporality.

In this chapter, we contend that despite their divergences, abandon and inquiry might coincide or de-coincide in ways that are fruitful for theory generation. This matters as emancipation itself is often conceptualized in what appears to be polarized views. In the search for verticality, emancipation (e.g. through the process of writing) appears as an abandon and surrender to (individual) reverie. Beyond the spectacle imposed by our societies, each one could and should come closer to his/her true self by wandering through the process of true personal reverie and creative activities. In the quest for pragmatic truth, emancipation lies, in contrast, in the melting-pot of the community itself (that is, in the transaction of inquiring). Collective activity, as a common objectification of and for activity, is what matters. Individuals then emancipate themselves from the confines of community. On the one hand, emancipation appears as a kind of oneiric transcendence done with abandon. On the other hand, it follows a strict logic of immanence with inquiry.

Aiming at reconciling the two in this chapter, we argue that an integrative view supports social research in management that seeks to better grasp "politics of time" and identify emancipatory temporalities. Drawing on the respective philosophies of Guy Debord (1958) and John Dewey (1938) to anchor our interpretations of these two views, we suggest that each one is the necessary process of the other, the hiatus of it. The activity of inquiry requires the joint work of reverie, drift, and abandon. The passivity of our oneiric exploration of the world requires the activity of a bodily engagement and an open inquiry of what is going on.

We argue, in fact, that the emancipatory potential for organizing temporalities may be found in the generative tensions between abandon and inquiry, and suggest a productive, agonistic relationship between each emancipatory temporality. Specifically, we describe this as the tension between "vertical" and "horizontal" temporalities. We illustrate our approach with a short auto-ethnographic vignette, involving the first author's experience with an open learning expedition in an urban environment. Using the results of this experimentation, we further conceptualize what we call an "ethic of odyssey", which points to a possible combination of the vertical temporality of dérive and the horizontal temporality of inquiry in the emergence of emancipatory temporalities. We conclude by inviting researchers to cultivate the generative tensions or productive differences between dérive and inquiry (as vertical and horizontal temporalities), to further conceptualize and experiment with the politics of time.

Polarities of Emancipatory Temporality: Walking with Debord and Dewey

Guy Debord (1967) is known for his work on the spectacular nature of capitalism, and its related processes of domination. In a more specific work, Debord (1956) conceptualizes the process of drift (dérive) in the public space, defining it in the following way: "One or several persons involved in a dérive renounce, for a short or long period of time, their habitual reasons for moving and acting. They give up their own relations, work, leisure to let go and abandon themselves to the field, encountering while on the field" (p. 3). A dérive is a suspension, an *epoche*. The agentivities of urban situations,[3] often unfelt or even avoided, are explicitly and exclusively discussed by a small group (more likely to reach a consensus through a discussion about the consequences of the urban situations encountered) just in the doing of the walk. In many ways, Debord's approach is consequential (what matters is what happens emotionally, affectively, and materially in the flow of the walk) and is the obvious heir of Beaudelaire's flânerie.

Debord invokes a geo-psychology of spaces, to explore their specificities, their emotional invocations, what they are likely to hide or to make visible, and their broader social and psychological processes (Debord, 1958). In this approach, emancipation is based on urban "flânerie", an exploration with no specific goal and no destination. Emancipation is alive in the time-space of this process, in the conversation with fellow walkers, but there is also a "verticality" involving the sedimented, seated, immobile time that follows. Through the process of walking in urban space, people accumulate a memory (and reverie) of the place encountered. The places and atmospheres people come across are accumulated

---

[3] Debord (1956) adds: "there is a psychogeographic relief of the cities, with constant currents, fixed points, and whirlpools which make access to or exit from certain areas very difficult".

vertically in the present of their exploration and are given a density and depth.

Moreover, Debord invites those experiencing the dérive to a cartography of atmosphere, to subsequently visualize the space of the city differently, to make the visible invisible or the too visible, invisible. Writing, mapping, describing the urban space is another aspect of verticality. It happens in the immobile times between and most of all, after the walk. It keeps the landmark of a vertical body walking in the city to constitute or rather, re-constitute public space. It sheds light on what appears as the shocks and frictions endured by bodies in movement. In many senses, dérive is a suspended temporality: that of a sociality which usually does not give a voice to the walker stuck in routine trajectories in socially compatible spaces. In the time-space of dérive, all this is at the vertical aspect of the walk; it is suspended in traditional beliefs and habits.

Debord's view of dérive is not directional or progressive in one way or another. Nothing is solved or problematized: reverie appears as the embodied exercise of walking itself, and as an interesting way to unveil the geo-psychology in and through the process of walking. Clearly, something is suspended, and the passivities of our urban habits are made visible. In contrast, Dewey (1938) defends a much more active, radical, problem-oriented, and processual view of temporality. From a pragmatist's perspective, traditional temporalities are not suspended to be made visible. New necessary temporalities are co-constituted by all entities wrapped into the process of inquiry.

The group contributing to a public[4] debate and inquiry should not be pre-constituted (even randomly). The concerns and problematizations themselves should be the locus of the inquiry. Problems, concerns, and communities of inquiry are co-constituted by the process of inquiry itself. No specific entities are awaiting their exploration in an external public space. The public and publicity of our world is fully emergent, fully conversational. Inquiry is clearly in the immanent world in a process of construction, and not a reverie explored by mysterious poetical flux. Thus, concreteness does not mean that art, affects, emotions, and imagination are not part of the process of inquiry. But imagination appears in the pragmatist landscape mainly as the ongoing process of inquiry itself, this flow of activities co-constitutive of concerns, problems, and sometimes, provisional solutions built through collective experimentation.

---

[4] Interestingly, public space and publicity are much more processual in the perspective offered by Dewey (1938). They are the open process of spacing co-constituted by inquiry. Each problem corresponds to a specific public and publicity.

Put this way, both abandon and inquiry seem to correspond to very different emancipatory temporalities. On the one hand, dérive is an undefined, passive temporality, a fully open one that is unbound to any specific activity. It is the dialogical exploration of an outside and an inside, a subjectivation that is authentic in relation to the mimicry of the society of spectacle. People have a pre-assigned 'me' in the public space which is not (yet) a sensed, true, personal 'I' (Mead & Schubert, 1934). Letting exploration and self-exploration evolve spontaneously, like a poetic dérive, helps build agentive citizens and small-scale political actors to become reflexive of their own power and closer to their own needs in a vertical relationship with the world. Verticality is here the sedimentation and cultivation of a personal memory made of possessed, sensed souvenirs and reveries beyond the society of spectacle and the pre-packaged memory and images it offers.

In contrast, pragmatic inquiry involves more active, experimental, goal-oriented activities within the frame of a defined, organized, and agent-oriented temporality. Inquiry follows the problems of a neighborhood, of a collective which becomes agentic in the pragmatic exploration of its problems and its solutions. Pragmatic temporality involves a flat real world under construction, a world immediately material, transformative of itself and of the relationships at stake in its present. What matters is what continuously and horizontally surfaces in the visibilization of concerns and the problems at hand.

Given these differences, it is tempting to contrast the passive, vertical temporalities of reverie and dérive on the one hand, and the active, horizontal temporalities of inquiry on the other hand. One is the infinite, undefined poetic space of oneiric wandering. The other is the concrete, experimental, exploratory process of provisional solutions to collective problems (see Table 6.1).

Despite their differences, the two temporalities are more compatible and mutually generative than this preliminary summary might suggest. Both temporalities transform subjectivity and subjectivation as the consequence of a process. Subjects are the events of our world. Temporality is primordial to subjectivation, as already shown by philosophers such as Foucault (1982), who offers an insightful analysis of the temporality of resistance, in a theorizing text displaying how time, power, and resistance are always intertwined (Lilja, 2018, p. 420; Portschy, 2020). Temporality can indeed be conceived of as a way to resist regimes of historicity or dominant visions of time that attempt to impose time intensification for example (through, for instance, time deceleration, Rosa, 2013). Technologies of the self (Foucault, 1988) can indeed be interpreted as strategies to create one's own temporalities to experience time differently;

Table 6.1 *A comparison of the emancipatory temporalities of dérive and inquiry*

Type of emancipatory temporality	Dérive	Inquiry
Temporal orientation	Sequential, follows successive atmospheres until a sense of finitude is reached and the walk is stopped. No goal and keeps the absence of goal as an important part of the process.	Transactional, rhizomic, driven by the move from concerns to problems and solutions and the co-constitution of a community of inquiry. Each inquiry process follows its own temporalities.
	Vertical process: process of mapping and writing the geo-psychology of the places encountered.	Horizontal process: everything flows on the plane of immanence of inquiries and the entities put into trans-action.
Connectivity of events	Not necessarily. The different spaces and atmospheres of the city can be fully different worlds, with their own time-spaces, rhythms, tempos, and temporal structures.	Yes. Inquiry eventalizes and links events. Inquiry is by itself constitutive of fields of events.
Nature of the exploratory process	An embodied reverie, i.e. oneiric and imaginary process, during the walk and in times of immobility during or after it.	A pragmatic convergence from an indeterminate situation to a determinate situation.
Sources	Debord (1958), Bachelard (1936, 1948, 1969, 1988)	Dewey (1938), Zask (2015), Lorino (2018)

they are crucial in the subjectivation process through which the subject acts to "promote new forms of subjectivity" (Foucault 1982, p. 785). This subjectivation process, as a historical movement, draws on technologies of the self that mix the past, present, and future in order to make a difference: "technologies of the self, as a political practice, involve remembering the past and narrating the present, as well as embracing ethical considerations that involve the future" (Lilja, 2018, p. 428). Memory, present time, and anticipation of the future are thus essential to free oneself from attempts of domination and regimes of truth, as well as to know who one wants to be in the agonistic subjectivation process described by Foucault. Power here is the resistance experienced in and through the present on the way to an agentive self. It is the dynamic memory of inquiry and forgetting of abandon, developed in the making and mattering of this self from the within of our present, in the process of its opening.

In the next section, we explore the intertwining of the temporalities of dérive and inquiry, presenting a new walking-based ethnographic research protocol. We aim at building hereafter an "ethics of travel" or "odyssey" that can render as generative the tensions between dérive and inquiry, particularly between their vertical and horizontal temporalities. We suggest that emancipatory temporalities are made of paradoxes that nurture the flow towards resistance, self-fulfilment, and authentic inhabiting of the world. Both abandon (or dérive) and inquiry matter in the process of subjectivation necessary for true freedom to exist in the world. The new wisdom of the dispositive is needed which is part of our exploration of the world.

An Ongoing Experimentation: Exploring the Indeterminate Duration of the City

In 2016, one of the authors of this chapter participated in elaborating a research protocol based on the practice of walking in the public and semi-public spaces of a city. The practice of walking has long been cited as a method for social researchers, especially ethnographers (Ingold & Vergunst, 2008; Yi'En, 2014; Pierce & Lawhon, 2015; Macpherson, 2016) but also organizational scientists interested in the exploration of public space, its rhythms, and processes of domination (Nash, 2018a, 2018b), or the more pragmatic issues of learning and affects (Beyes & Steyaert, 2021; Juhlin & Holt, 2021). The very process of walking is indeed central to our exploration of emancipatory temporalities. It is explicitly part of the thought of Debord (1958), Lefebvre (1991), or Bachelard (1948). Beyond conversations and instrumental activities, it is also more and more part of the process of inquiry conceptualized by pragmatists themselves (see Hall, 1996; Stratford et al., 2020).

Walking is a way of exploring a place, a space, and an aesthetic, to develop an embodied experience of it, to foster a smooth, fluid, in-context conversation. In contrast to a "seated" or "immobile" ethnography, a walking ethnography makes it possible to share the very movements and becoming of a society. The experimentation described in this chapter relied on learning expeditions based on walking ethnographies that aimed to explore entrepreneurial and innovative places in the city. We aimed to discover new places for innovation and entrepreneurship in the city, in the context of the new world of work (Aroles et al., 2019), and to come closer to local problems encountered by workers and managers. Driven by a deliberate non-choice between dérive and inquiry, the objective was to walk with a group of people (including both local and non-local people, as well as academics, students, practitioners, and workers) according to the principles of exploring and drifting in the city, with the goal of identifying and problematizing key issues of the area.

These open learning expeditions included two parts: one relatively planned venture, integrating specific places and people likely to be encountered. The second, fully improvised, during which the local people participating in the walk could co-design with the others the elements to be seen and discussed by the group. This approach thus included aspects of both logics of inquiry and the logic of dérive. On the one hand, it followed the logic of inquiry in its attempt to identify local problems encountered by innovators and entrepreneurs. Concerns, problems, and small experimentations embedded into activities (e.g. workshop or future projects) were at the heart of these walked conversations. In this way, the protocol relied on a strong sense of focus and time, organized in a chronological manner through *horizontal temporalities*, in a heavy program driven by the move from problems to solutions.

On the other hand, the open learning expeditions were punctuated by numerous spontaneous visits and seated moments. Among them, some time slots were devoted to collaboratively reflecting on and reporting what was going on in collaborative articles, videos recorded with camcorders or more simply, the sharing of posts, likes, and re-tweets on social media. These collective activities were *vertical temporalities*. They punctuated the broader narrative of the open learning expeditions. They built links between these expeditions with a narration. They also contributed to a sedimentation, an embodied memory, a present likely to be opened by ongoing events of the learning expedition (see Revel, 2015; de Vaujany, 2022b).[5] The built and extended present was continuously opened and re-opened by our events (i.e. the tweets, unexpected encounters, workshops, short stops to use public transportations, etc.).

Thus, verticality and horizontality were largely interwoven in most of our learning expeditions and in the broader process and narrative connecting them. Verticality, reverie, and dérive augmented the strata at stake in the present, and horizontal temporality, of our collective activities. At the same time, this verticality was meaningless outside of the broader duration and horizontality of our walks. Vertical temporality was made operative through its relation to this ongoing horizontality.

---

[5] These views are epitomized in the works of the late, political Merleau-Ponty and the third, ethical, Foucault (see Revel, 2015). The present we live in is both horizontal and vertical. It is the experience continuously re-opened by events, the continuity in and of discontinuity.

To abandon oneself, to cultivate emancipatory temporalities grounded vertically in an immobile moment, could not make sense outside the flow of the other people, posts on social media, or the discourse of the community managers. *Inhabiting the fragility of the moment was impossible without the ceaseless flux of the world.* Bachelard needs Bergson and Bergson[6] needs Bachelard. As stated in his logbook by the leading author:

> To enjoy and feel my immobility, to taste the pleasure of just sitting here or walking on a straight line in a walk or reverie, I had to feel all these forces pushing constantly ahead. Indeed, to cultivate deeply myself, I needed to resist these forces that suddenly became not a part of my self and just go away. (Extract 1 from logbook)

Indeed, as most open learning expeditions organized for this experimentation (32 between 2016 and 2020) took place far from the home of the author, the whole event was itself a punctuation of an ongoing life that was suddenly suspended.

> I had to go thousands of kilometers away from home to be truly lost. But what a strange adventure. Often, in Tokyo, Lisbon, Singapore, or New York, I was just wondering what I was doing here. I was just abandoning this powerful rhythm of life which was the temporality of my job itself. And sometimes, walking to nowhere in the middle of nowhere, I enjoyed deep moments of reverie. My body was walking for so long that it disappeared in the process of walking. I was the pure process of exploring these unknown cities and their problems. (Extract 2 from logbook)

Getting lost, or getting willingly lost with or without local people leading the walk, was always an amazing experience. In this context, it was not possible to control anything. But it was possible to inquire and abandon oneself.

Both the possible convergent process of inquiry and the process of dérive cohabited in the present of the walk. Paradoxically, bodies both abandoned themselves and could not avoid finding reasons to go where they were going while walking. Conversations (in particular with local people) often highlighted the problems experienced by those who live there, with words, expressions, and logics. For example, during an open learning expedition in Barcelona, an inhabitant of a gentrified area told us the story of his despair, mentioning that the prices and atmosphere had completely changed over the past years. Most of his friends had already left the neighborhood. Some of his cousins and his parents still lived in a building he showed to us; the kind of building we would not have been aware of without his direction. It was a clear vestige of the pre-gentrified era. Coworkers and managers of coworking spaces were walking with us.

---

[6] For reasons of space, we will not discuss here the presence of verticality in Bergson's writings, which we see as obvious in his work about memory and materiality (see Bergson, 1896).

What could they do? How could they build new conversations with their neighbors? How, as a community of collaborative spaces in the same city, could they avoid strengthening these trends? How could they become a voice for these people? A conversation started. It was possible that it could result in specific actions far later, one month, ten months, and two years later, as happened for several conversations focussed on problems raised during the process of walking. As the co-author explained in their logbook:

It is strange, as this description happened during the walk; it was not a complaint or even a criticism. For those sharing with us their suffering, it was the opportunity to make us feel their suffering and to experience the situation itself. Subtly, we moved into the time-space of all those invisible people suffering in one of the most glamorous cities in the world. This conversation suspended the usual touristic temporality to make us enter into a very interesting political odyssey. (Extract 3 from logbook)

Towards an "Ethic of Odyssey"

Based on the experiences described above and our theorization of drift and inquiry, we may conceptualize further what could be an "ethic of odyssey" likely to feed an emancipatory temporality. An odyssey is defined as "a long trip or period involving a lot of different and exciting activities, especially while searching for something",[7] in reference to the title given to the "ancient name of the Homeric poem telling tales of the ten-year wanderings of Odysseus, king of Ithaca, seeking home after the fall of Troy".[8] An odyssey is not a touristic experience. It is based on an intensity and an authenticity. In contrast to simple travel, an odyssey is not predefined, and remains open to discovery and unexpected turns. It involves an acknowledged and searched for joint verticality and horizontality, regular encounters with numerous differences akin to 'our' difference; and multiple events on the way to a quest for a true, agentive, sensed, sensible self.

It is a radically open temporality far from the usual cybernetic, control-oriented world of management we live in. Once involved in an odyssey, it is impossible to know when, where, and how it will stop. It is not even possible to dictate when, where, and how it will start. One just "lets go" (see Chia, 2010) and travels as much as dictated by the odyssey. He/she moves with all the people, objects, and situations encountered as much as

---

[7] Cambridge Academic Content Dictionary.
[8] Online Etymology Dictionary: https://etymonline.com/word/odyssey#etymonline_v_2504

he/she is moved by them. Odyssey is just like life itself; always exploring, renewing, encountering.

As adventures, odysseys are by nature open and require situated decisions in the face of unfamiliar events. They involve solving numerous ongoing issues and overcoming multiple concerns. These are pragmatic and poetic processes, and these two aspects involve temporalities of dérive and inquiry, verticality and horizontality, which are mutually constitutive. They are generated at the poles of experience itself, as expressions of its tensions.

Management and organization studies (MOS) are too often on one side of the generative tension described here.[9] On the way to emancipation and resistance, temporalities are too often theorized as active rhythms and deliberate events moving towards a stronger felt presence, or a poetic, imaginary wandering towards a true self. Organizational ethnography is thus rarely seen as a pragmatic inquiry by itself, and creative, art-based approaches to management are rarely inquiry-oriented. Likewise, pragmatist approaches of qualitative methods or pragmatic conceptualizations of organizing rarely combine the Dewey interested in art with the Dewey interested in solving societal issues, although the philosopher himself never separated the two ventures. We argue here that understanding and experimenting in depth the emancipatory temporalities at stake in organizations and organizing requires a joint involvement in inquiry and reverie.

The temporality of experimentation has both vertical and horizontal dimensions: vertical, in that multiple temporalities are layered; and horizontal, in that a set of deep moments are connected by a duration. As illustrated by our empirical experimentation, walking is not only a movement toward horizontality. It is also a process of digging into the layers accumulated by the becoming of a city, its historical strata, its poetical and imaginary layers below common experience. In this way, the "ethic of odyssey" we describe reveals the importance of depth (emphasizing both horizontality and verticality) in our understanding of the politics of time, processes of resistance, and emancipation.

Indeed, most of all – and making possible a major rupture for organizing processes – there is no coloniality in an ethic of odyssey. An odyssey implies that one does not travel to settle. Exploration does not seek possession. The relationship with the planet does not flow as a resource-based logic. It is symbiotic and non-proprietary. Inhabiting means inhabiting the fragility of the world (de Vaujany, 2022a). Extended, pushed, regenerated by the tensions between abandon and dérive, managers, citizens, researchers,

---

[9] MOS often become caricatures. Indeed, there is a poetry and imaginary dimension in Dewey's (1938) pragmatism and there is pragmatism in Bachelard's (1936) or Debord's (1956, 1958) philosophies. But the way all these philosophies are appropriated is too often polarized.

activities, students, and artists give more and more depth to their experience. Their nomadism becomes central to the process of resistance and emancipation within the world (Deleuze & Guattari, 1980).

The non-durational nature of poetic experience and subjectivation described by Bachelard (1936, 1948, 1969) does not need to be opposed here to the processual and durational stance of Bergson (1896). There is no verticality without flow and no flow without verticality. There is no present without actuality and actualization and no actuality or actualization without a shared present built during the walk and from one walk to another. With this in mind, it is then possible to conceptualize and experiment with a politics of time.

Our description of the intertwining of dérive and inquiry within the method of experimental walking opens up a space for discussing the complexity of experienced time by researchers as well as social actors. Such a discussion contributes to understanding time and temporality in management and organization studies (Lee & Liebenau, 1999; Chia, 2002; Costas & Grey, 2014; Holt & Johnsen, 2019). This literature often remains attached to horizontal considerations of temporality (Helin, 2020). Vertical temporality as cuts, suspensions, reverie, and encounters with our present has recently appeared as a new concern, but without explicit cross explorations of organizing and political phenomena (Helin, 2020; Singh, 2020; de Vaujany, 2022b). In line with this growing trend, our chapter suggests that verticality, in conjunction with horizontal temporality, is fundamental to our political experience of the world. Both moments of dérive and processes of inquiry are crucial in the subjectivation process that is necessary for emancipation as a process from the within of our present of management and organizing.

If power is time, subjectivation as the agonistic making of subjectivity from within, is its necessary counter power. Emancipatory temporalities are the folds, holes, and dark bubbles inside the lights of time and becoming. They are in-between events of inquiry and abandon, joint moves in-between determination and indetermination. Emancipatory temporalities are relational times built willingly and courageously, from and against our time. They emerge from the intersections as differences in speed and intensities of movements. This intersectionality and "differentiality" in becoming can be cultivated. The self can work on itself to happen effectively, to build its own ways and suspensions from the within of time.

Given the urgency of the current moment in terms of the temporality of climate change and environmental crisis, it is tempting to link our discussion to the ongoing debates about the Anthropocene. When applying the ideas of the current chapter to this key question of temporality, two different approaches seem to be at stake with regards to humankind's relation to the surrounding world.

The first approach, linked to abandonment, passivity, strolling, and wandering in the world involves drifting in the movement of aimless walking or daydreaming. Time is infinite, endless, continuously flowing. We give ourselves time. All of nature and its flows pass by. Emancipation is characterized by this suspended temporality which is also a connection to the universe. Humans do not dominate the world but participate as one flux among the ceaseless flux of the universe.

The other approach is linked more to an ethics of activity. If the whole universe is indeed in flux, it is also made of irreversible and damaging fluxes and assemblages ("agencements"). The recent GIEC report[10] underlines that there are only three years left before climate change becomes irreparable. This other political temporality is more urgent. It presupposes an investigation whose time is running out. Emancipation is here in the temporality and the very process of the investigation and in all that it transacts.

In this chapter, we emphasized, from a practice that combined both abandonment and inquiry, that these modalities should not be opposed, but reconciled. Their differences can be very generative for organizations and their more or less symbiotic relationships with the planet and nature. Our emancipation also depends on the temporality of our planet. Its continuity is our continuity, but more importantly, its emancipation from an endless consumption is also our own emancipation.

Conclusion

This chapter, illustrated by our experimentation, shows the extent to which both dérive, (poetry, abandon) and inquiry – and their respective temporalities (verticality and horizontality) – empirically coincide in ways that are fruitful for conducting research in management and organization. A possible cross-fertilization between them is possible through what we call an "ethic of odyssey", paving the way to a more open approach to social science, where openness relies on, and means, the emergence of a shared temporality, more than a shared space. We thus call for considering simultaneously dérive and inquiry, vertical and horizontal temporalities, in management and organization studies, in order to co-produce an embodied knowledge (Jarzabkowski et al., 2010; Reed et al., 2020). In many ways, this invitation is close to a Nietzschean philosophy: a philosophy of life. As explained by Stiegler (2021, p. 17), in his research on the conditions of life, Nietzsche

---

[10] See www.forbes.fr/environnement/rapport-du-giec-trois-ans-pour-eviter-les-effets-les-plus-devastateurs-du-changement-climatique/.

discovered very early on that the living need both to expose themselves to the ever new flow of what happens to them, since it is what nourishes them and pushes them to evolve and to transform, but also to resist this flow, to defer it or to delay it, by manufacturing a whole arsenal of stasis and closures allowing it to be slowed down, filtered, digested, in short, incorporated, which also means fitting it out and transforming it to make it visible.

Cultivating inquiry and drift, horizontality and verticality, could thus be a way to keep a research process 'alive'.

Despite its contributions, this chapter presents some conceptual and empirical limitations. First, it is not an easy task to synthesize and counterpose the thoughts developed by Debord and Dewey, whose concepts are complex and difficult to operationalize. Furthermore, our empirical experimentation, which has been only briefly explained in the frame of this chapter, focussed on urban environments: other observations could have been made in other spatial and geographical settings. In particular, future research could explore the relationship between digital and offsite wandering, online and offline explorations.

Nevertheless, we hope to offer new perspectives on the emancipatory temporalities of dérive and inquiry, to serve future research in management and organization studies, where political issues of temporality have long been neglected, or, at least often stuck in a horizontal temporality of a flat, ceaseless flux; a world of continuous mobilities and unbounded materializations (Helin, 2020). Indeed, although time and temporality have long been an important, perennial subject for organizations and a central issue in social sciences (see Butler, 1995; Orlikowski & Yates, 2002; Hernes et al., 2013), "the more time [has] been attended to in organization studies, the more it [has been] concealed" (Holt & Johnsen, 2019, p. 1557), such that "there has been a progressive forgetfulness of time in organization studies" (Holt & Johnsen, 2019, p. 1557). We thus hope to offer in this chapter an interesting and original perspective that future research could develop, in order to better explore the politics of time, notably the emancipatory potential of temporalities. In particular, by combining the verticality of dérive with the horizontality of inquiry, assembled in our suggested "ethic of odyssey", we invite management and organization researchers to further experiment with this important aspect of a politics of time.

References

Aroles, J. & Küpers, W. (2022). Flânerie as a methodological practice for explorative re-search in digital worlds. *Culture and Organization*, DOI: 10.1080/14759551 .2022.2042538.

Aroles, J., Mitev, N. & de Vaujany, F-X. (2019). Mapping themes in the study of new work practices. *New Technology, Work and Employment, 34*(3), 285–99.

Bachelard, G. (1936, 2022). *La dialectique de la durée: Édition établie par Élie During*. Paris: Presses Universitaires de France.

Bachelard, G. (1948). *La terre et les rêveries du repos* (p. 86). Paris: J. Corti.

Bachelard, G. (1969). *The Poetics of Reverie: Childhood, Language, and the Cosmos*. Boston: Beacon Press.

Bachelard, G. (1988). *Air and Dreams: An Essay on the Imagination of Movement*. Dallas: The Dallas Institute Publications.

Bailey, C. & Madden, A. (2017). Time reclaimed: temporality and the experience of meaningful work. *Work, Employment and Society, 31*(1), 3–18.

Bergson, H. (1896). *Matière et mémoire. Essai sur la relation du corps à l'esprit*. Paris: Félix Alcan.

Beyes, T. & Steyaert, C. (2021). Unsettling bodies of knowledge: Walking as a pedagogy of affect. *Management Learning, 52*(2), 224–42.

Butler, J. (1995). Subjection, Resistance, Resignification. In J. Rajchman (ed.), *The Identity in Question* (pp. 229–50). New York: Routledge.

Chia, R. (2002). Essai: Time, duration and simultaneity: Rethinking process and change in organizational analysis. *Organization Studies, 23*(6), 863–8.

Chia, R. (2010). Shifting Paradigms through "Letting Go". In C. Wankel & B. DeFillippi (eds), *Being and Becoming a Management Education Scholar* (pp. 11–42). Charlotte, NC: Information Age Publishing Inc.

Costas, J. & Grey, C. (2014). The temporality of power and the power of temporality: Imaginary future selves in professional service firms. *Organization Studies, 35*(6), 909–37.

Dale, K. (2005). Building a social materiality: Spatial and embodied politics in organizational control. *Organization, 12*(5), 649–78.

Dale, K. & Burrell, G. (2008). *The Spaces of Organisation and the Organisation of Space: Power, Identity and Materiality at Work*. New York: Palgrave Macmillan.

Dawson, P. & Sykes, C. (2018). Concepts of Time and Temporality in the Storytelling and Sensemaking Literatures: A Review and Critique. *International Journal of Management, 21*(1), 97–114.

de Vaujany, F-X. (2022a). *Apocalypse managériale*. Paris: Éditions Les Belles Lettres.

de Vaujany, F-X. (2022b). The Process of Depth: Temporality as Organization in Cinematographic Experience. In F-X de Vaujany, J. Aroles & M. Pérezts (eds), *The Oxford Handbook of Phenomenologies and Organization Studies*. Oxford: Oxford University Press.

de Vaujany, F-X. & Vitaud, L. (2017, July). Re-inventing management research with learning expeditions. *LSE Business Review*. Available at: https://blogs .lse.ac.uk/businessreview/2017/07/04/re-inventing-management-research-with-learning-expeditions/.

Debord, G. (1956, 1958). Theory of the Dérive. *Internationale situationniste*, 2 (20.05), 2015. Available at: https://larevuedesressources.org/theorie-de-la-dérive,038.html).

Debord, G. (1967). *La société du spectacle*. Paris: Les Éditions Gallimard.

Deleuze, G. & Guattari, F. (1980, 2004). *A Thousand Plateaus*. London: A&C Black.

Deroy, X. & Clegg, S. (2011). When events interact with business ethics. *Organization, 18*(5), 637–53.

Dewey, J. (1938, 2018). *Logic - The Theory of Inquiry*. New York: Read Books Ltd.

Fabbri, J., Mukherjee, A. & de Vaujany, F-X. (2016). Management and the Practice of Walking: An Exploration of Organizations and Organizing with Legs. In *Academy of Management Proceedings, 2016*(1), 17741. Briarcliff Manor, NY: Academy of Management.

Fleming, P. & Spicer, A. (2004). "You can check out any time you want, but you can never leave": spatial boundaries in a high commitment organization. *Human Relations, 57*(1), 75–94.

Flood, R.L. & Jackson, M.C. (1988). Cybernetics and organization theory: a critical review. *Cybernetics and Systems: An International Journal, 19*(1), 13–33.

Foucault, M. (1977). *Discipline and Punish: The Birth of Prison*. New York: Vintage.

Foucault, M. (1982). The Subject and Power. In H.L. Dreyfus & P. Rabinow (eds), *Beyond Structuralism and Hermeneutics*, (pp. 208–26). Chicago: University of Chicago.

Foucault, M (1985). *The Use of Pleasure*. New York: Pantheon.

Foucault, M. (1988). Technologies of the Self. In L.H. Martin, H. Gutman & P. H. Hutton (eds), *Technologies of the Self: a Seminar with Michel Foucault* (pp. 16–49). Amherst, MA: The University of Massachusetts Press.

Hall, R. (1996). Representation as shared activity: Situated cognition and Dewey's cartography of experience. *The Journal of the Learning Sciences, 5*(3), 209–38.

Helin, J. (2020). Temporality lost: A feminist invitation to vertical writing that shakes the ground. *Organization*, 1350508420956322.

Helin, J., Dahl, M. & Guillet De Monthoux, P. (2020). Caravan poetry: An inquiry on four wheels. *Qualitative Inquiry, 26*(6), 633–8.

Helin, J., Hernes, T., Hjorth, D. & Holt, R. (eds.) (2014). *The Oxford Handbook of Process Philosophy and Organization Studies*. Oxford: Oxford University Press.

Hernes, T. (2014). *A Process Theory of Organization*. Oxford: Oxford University Press.

Hernes, T., Simpson, B. & Söderlund, J. (2013). Managing and temporality. *Scandinavian Journal of Management, 29*(1), 1–6.

Holt, R. & Johnsen, R. (2019). Time and Organization Studies. *Organization Studies, 40*(10), 1557–72.

Ingold, T. & Vergunst, J.L. (eds) (2008). *Ways of Walking: Ethnography and Practice on Foot*. London: Ashgate Publishing Ltd.

Jarzabkowski, P., Mohrman, S.A. & Scherer, A.G. (2010). Organization studies as applied science: The generation and use of academic knowledge about organizations. *Organization Studies, 31*(09/10), 1189–207.

Juhlin, C. & Holt, R. (2022). The sensory imperative. *Management Learning, 53* (4), 640–51.

Lee, H. & Liebenau, J. (1999). Time in organizational studies: Towards a new research direction. *Organization Studies, 20*(6), 1035–58.

Lefebvre, H. (1991). *The Production of Space*. Trans. D. Nicholson-Smith. Oxford: Blackwell.

Lilja, M. (2018). The politics of time and temporality in Foucault's theorisation of resistance: ruptures, time-lags and decelerations. *Journal of Political Power*, *11* (3), 419–32.

Lorino, P. (2018). *Pragmatism and Organization Studies*. Oxford: Oxford University Press.

Macpherson, H. (2016). Walking methods in landscape research: moving bodies, spaces of disclosure and rapport. *Landscape Research*, *41*(4), 425–32.

Mead, G.H. & Schubert, C. (1934). *Mind, Self and Society*. Chicago: University of Chicago Press.

Nash, L. (2018a). Gendered places: Place, performativity and flânerie in the City of London. *Gender, Work & Organization*, *25*(6), 601–20.

Nash, L. (2018b). City Rhythms: Walking and Sensing Place through Rhythmanalysis. In K. Dale, S.F. Kingma & V. Wasserman (eds), *Organizational Space and Beyond* (pp. 161–88). London: Routledge.

Orlikowski, W.J. & Yates, J. (2002). It's about time: Temporal structuring in organizations. *Organization Science*, *13*(6), 684–700.

Otley, D.T. (1983). Concepts of Control: The Contribution of Cybernetics and Systems Theory to Management Control. In T. Lowe & J.L.J. Machin (eds), *New Perspectives in Management Control* (pp. 59–87). London: Palgrave Macmillan.

Pelurson, G. (2019). Flânerie in the dark woods: Shattering innocence and queering time in The Path. *Convergence*, *25*(5–6), 918–36.

Pierce, J. & Lawhon, M. (2015). Walking as method: Toward methodological forthrightness and comparability in urban geographical research. *The Professional Geographer*, *67*(4), 655–62.

Portschy, J. (2020). Times of power, knowledge and critique in the work of Foucault. *Time & Society*, *29*(2), 392–419.

Reed, G., Dagli, W. & Hambly Odame, H. (2020). Co-production of knowledge for sustainability: an application of reflective practice in doctoral studies. *Reflective Practice*, *21*(2), 222–36.

Reinecke, J., Suddaby, R., Tsoukas, H. & Langley, A. (eds) (2021). *Time, Temporality, and History in Process Organization Studies*. Oxford: Oxford University Press.

Revel, J. (2015). *Foucault avec Merleau-Ponty: ontologie politique, présentisme et histoire*. Paris: Vrin.

Rosa, H. (2013). *Accélération. Une critique sociale du temps*. Trans. Didier Renault. Paris: La Découverte.

Singh, P.K. (2020). The Quest for Verticality: An Inquiry into the Infinite Nature of Self-Perfection. *Philosophy of Management*, *19*, 387–408.

Stiegler, B. (2021). *Nietzsche et la vie*. Paris: Gallimard.

Stratford, E., Waitt, G. & Harada, T. (2020). Walking city streets: Spatial qualities, spatial justice, and democratising impulses. *Transactions of the Institute of British Geographers*, *45*(1), 123–38.

Taylor, S. & Spicer, A. (2007). Time for space: A narrative review of research on organizational spaces. *International Journal of Management Reviews* 9(4), 325–46.

Tsoukas, H. & Chia, R. (2002). On organizational becoming: Rethinking organizational change. *Organization Science, 13*(5), 567–82.

Yi'En, C. (2014). Telling stories of the city: Walking ethnography, affective materialities, and mobile encounters. *Space and Culture, 17*(3), 211–23.

Zask, J. (2015). *Introduction à John Dewey.* Paris: La Découverte.

Zerubavel, E. (1985). *Hidden Rhythms: Schedules and Calendars in Social Life.* Berkeley and London: University of California Press.

7 Future Work
Toward a Practice Perspective

Matthias Wenzel, Hannes Krämer, Jochen Koch and Andreas Reckwitz

It is quite true what philosophy says: that life must be understood backwards. But then one forgets the other principle: that it must be lived forwards.
(Translated by Hannay, 1996, p. 161; Kierkegaard, 1843)

Introduction

Perhaps one of the most astonishing characteristics of the future is that it is an elusive temporal category – one that lies ahead. As Luhmann (1976, p. 130) suggested, "the future cannot begin" because it is constantly pushed forward by an ongoing present and, thus, remains inaccessible. Therefore, as the comic illustrates, one might attempt to background the future in everyday life, focusing on the "here and now" rather than the "yet-to-come." However, Søren Kierkegaard reminded us that even if, in the present, we pay less attention to the future, we are constantly opening up and closing off possible futures through the performance of our day-to-day activities. Therefore, *any* organizational activity that actors perform in the present carries a past, but also casts a shadow on the future (e.g., Bakken et al., 2013; Hernes, 2014; Hjorth et al., 2015; Holt & Johnsen, 2019).

In addition to the inherent imbrication of the future in organizational activities, actors in all types of organizations – from Indigenous tribes to multinational corporations – engage in activities that are dedicated more or less explicitly to reflecting on and acting upon the future. The ways in which organizational actors do so can take many shapes: a CEO's Christmas address on the company's goals and desires for the following year, entrepreneurs' pitches about new ventures that do not yet exist, activists' fights for a better world, shamanic visions and ceremonies, meteorologists' weather forecasts, populist politicians' dystopic images of societal trends, the construction of vanguard office buildings, the development of technology roadmaps by actors across entire industries, a director's

136

realization of a science-fiction movie, and press articles by celebrated 'experts' on economic outlooks, among others. One of the most prevalent contemporary manifestations of the yet-to-come is the "future of work" (e.g., Adler, 1992; Donkin, 2010; Malhotra, 2021), a constellation of typically fluid and seemingly flexible, transparent, and inclusive ways of working. By making a difference to extant ways of working that are typically characterized as hierarchical, stiff, opaque, and non-inclusive, performances of the "future of work" in the present can stage what work could be like in the future. As these illustrations indicate, conceptions of the future often serve as a key orientation for action (Beckert, 2016, 2021), which is why modern organizations spend "a multibillion-dollar [fortune each year to] employ . . . hundreds of thousands of people" (Sherden, 1998, p. 2) who dedicate most of their work to engaging with the future (Wenzel, 2022). For example, founders of early-stage start-ups invest much of their time scripting and rehearsing pitches that aim to convince others of the future viability of a new venture (Wenzel & Koch, 2018), which may help them attract funding from investors in expectation of viable business opportunities (Garud et al., 2014). Artists and engineers may scan the visions of science-fiction movies as a source of inspiration for futurist creations (Reckwitz, 2017). Even winemakers' seemingly small-scale daily look at the weather forecast may motivate them to protect their grapevines by means of costly and perhaps even hazardous pesticides in response to the prognosis of a rainy day.

These are just a few examples of the consequential activities through which organizational actors engage with the future almost every day. These activities are so ubiquitous that they are almost taken for granted – perhaps, as is the temporal mode of the future itself. However, what do we really know about the discursive formations that organizational actors mobilize to construct and persuade others of their conceptions of the future? Which types of material artifacts do organizational members use to 'present' events that are to come? How do they, more or less consciously, in interactions with others, orchestrate discursive, material, and bodily resources to underline aspects of their understanding of the future in order to visualize and mobilize support for it? This chapter invites organization scholars to gain a deeper understanding of the activities through which organizational actors imagine and process the future.

In fact, in spite – or perhaps because – of the ubiquity of future-related activities, a deeper engagement with the temporal mode of the future remains at the fringes of organization research. Despite promising beginnings (e.g., Comi & Whyte, 2018; Thompson & Byrne, 2022; Tsoukas & Shepherd, 2004), the nascent or resurgent future-related debates on topics such as forecasting (Bacon-Gerasymenko et al., 2016), foresight

(Gavetti & Menon, 2016), and risk (Bromiley et al., 2017) translate futures into 'manageable' categories by relying on concepts that "enable managers to understand and act upon future environmental uncertainty [to achieve a] competitive advantage" (Rohrbeck et al., 2015, p. 1), for example, through "visionary" cognitive skills (Schilling, 2017) or "strategic intelligence" (Levine et al., 2017). In doing so, they turn engagement with the future into a planning problem (e.g., Brinckmann & Sung, 2015); one that can be tamed through scenario techniques, design thinking, and other planning tools and techniques (Holt, 2004). Thus, in keeping with March's (1995, p. 427) warning that "predictions of the future . . . are variations on a theme of fantasy: reliably incorrect," these conceptualizations of "envisioning futures [cast organizational actors into] epic [roles]" (Hjorth et al., 2018, p. 164) to achieve the unachievable: the "anticipation of uncertain futures" (Augier & Teece, 2008, p. 1192). This does not mean, however, that organizational actors have responded to ongoing critiques of planning activities (e.g., Barry & Elmes, 1997; March, 1995; Mintzberg, 1994) by stopping the performance of these activities; in fact, as Wolf and Floyd (2017, p. 1754) reiterated, "planning is [still] one of the most widely used management tools in contemporary organizations." However, in response to the experience of an ever-increasing acceleration of social life, which "has massively heightened the cost of planning [due to] the surrender of collective [and, thus, predictable] rhythms and time structures" (Rosa, 2013, p. 126) in contemporary societies, actors have pluralized the ways in which they engage with the future (Koselleck, 1989; Wagner, 1994). This turns planning into one among many ways in which organizational actors engage with the yet-to-come, all of which deserve to be explored in greater detail (Wenzel et al., 2020).

How can organizational actors' engagement with something as elusive as the future be explored, if at all? Frankly, the theoretical and methodological affordances for empirical examinations of such a phenomenon have not been fully elaborated. We argue that this has changed along with the ongoing advancement of practice theory (e.g., Feldman & Orlikowski, 2011; Nicolini, 2013; Reckwitz, 2002; Schatzki et al., 2001; Vaara & Whittington, 2012). Practice theory draws attention to the enactment of specific activities and their temporal unfolding through which organizing is accomplished in the present. In doing so, practice theory provides a window into the manifold, performative, relationally bundled, and situationally enacted practices through which organizational actors constantly imagine and process the future. Therefore, we argue that practice theory provides a valuable conceptual apparatus for examinations of temporality and the future in organization research.

This chapter invites organization scholars to build on practice theory to draw a more complex picture of organizational actors' engagement with the future; one that extends beyond a unidimensional focus on planning. To facilitate practice-based examinations of the future in and for organizing, we first introduce the foundational terms and concepts of practice theory. Second, we outline the methodological principles of a practice-based examination of organizational actors' engagement with the future. The final section outlines implications of a practice-based research agenda on engaging with the future for organization research. As we suggest, such an agenda not only helps us gain a better understanding of an important but under-researched organizational phenomenon; it also challenges the underlying future-related assumptions of many organizational concepts and theories as well as the predominant understanding of what organizing *is*.

Foundations of a Practice-based Understanding of Engaging with the Future

In contemporary organizations, the future serves as a point of orientation for actions in the present – be it hopeful expectation, strategic positioning, entrepreneurial disruption, or apocalyptic fear. Much of the literature on planning (at least implicitly) treats the future as "a separate entity" (Tsoukas & Shepherd, 2004, p. 10) that organizational actors can forecast through "accurate" planning techniques. However, as Sherden (1998, p. 2) suggested, "it is sometimes hard to distinguish science from paranormal, and professional from amateur, because the track records [of predicting or foreseeing the future] are often so similar."

The impossibility of building courses of action on unequivocal anticipations of the yet-to-come turns organizational actors' engagement with the future into a phenomenon of the present, in that conceptions of the future and their enactment must be constantly imagined, revised, reworked, and renegotiated. Therefore, we argue that the future is not simply a 'thing' that is 'out there' waiting to be predicted. Specifically, we propose that, to overcome the elusiveness of this temporal mode, we must observe how the future is 'produced,' or how the future is constantly imagined and processed in and through the discursive, bodily, and material enactment of social practices in the present. As we argue, practice theory lends itself to opening up these dynamics. This is because practice theory affords engagement with ways of producing and enacting the future not only in the sense of an "anthropomorphic *time-for-us*" that actors categorize, organize, and manage through purposive activity, but also in the spirit of "*time-beyond-us*, or just time," which "organize[s] us" by guiding day-to-day activities (Holt & Johnsen, 2019, p. 1558, emphases in original).

Practice Theory: Core Elements of a Bundled Perspective

Practice theory refers to a "family of theories" (Reckwitz, 2002, p. 244) that includes a number of related theoretical approaches (see also Feldman & Orlikowski, 2011; Nicolini, 2013; Rasche & Chia, 2009). That is, although practice theory is nurtured by different perspectives, such as Bourdieu's praxeology, ethnomethodology, social-constructionist approaches in various research streams, and philosophical thoughts by Theodore Schatzki and Bruno Latour, there are similarities in their theoretical approach to social life. Practice theory does not lure with extensive theoretical vocabulary but stands out for having a slim conceptual apparatus that spawns empirical research in various fields.

Practice theory draws attention to social practices – for example, structured activity, which is action and structure at the same time – as the smallest unit of social life. Thus, practice theory is not grounded solely either in intentional action or in the determinism of social structures and rules. Rather, practice theory emphasizes the routinized sequences of activities that point to a trajectory of their emergence through routine behavior and *performatively* (re)produce these structures and rules in and through action. Thus, practice theory builds on a practice ontoepistemology, which considers that social life is produced and recreated in and through the enactment of social practices.

Relatedly, the enactment of social practices is *situationally embedded* and, thus, changeable. More specifically, although practice theory considers social life to be structured through social 'practices,' it is the very enactment in response to the specific situation at hand – for example, social "praxis" (Reckwitz, 2002) – through which variations in the performance of social practices can occur. Social practices include two forms of materiality, namely, human bodies and artifacts, both relevant for the performance of social praxis. This implies that individuals, or "practitioners" (Whittington, 2006) are not the (only) core of social praxis. In the end, social practices consist of the multimodal interplay of the bodies of interconnected practitioners, discourses, and material artifacts (Streeck et al., 2011).

Another premise of practice theory is that the social world consists of a complex web of *heterogeneous*, interconnected social practices. For example, practices as types of activities can relate to practices of cooperation, that is, the ways of jointly working on a task. A subform of such cooperation practices could be meetings, agreements, and feedback rounds. Some of these practices are so-called dispersed practices (Schatzki, 1996, p. 91), which reappear in different areas. For example, meeting practices are enacted in different social fields, such as in universities or commercial firms. In contrast, "integrated practices" (Schatzki,

1996, p. 98) are tied more closely to specific social fields and, similar to dispersed practices, are historically grounded. For instance, the practice of mastering scientific evidence may be found mainly in academia, albeit with different qualities today compared with past centuries.

Referring once again to Schatzki, social practices constitute a "nexus of doings and sayings" (Schatzki, 1996, p. 89). This means, on the one hand, that social practices are performed and recreated through material carriers, such as bodies and artifacts. On the other hand, this nexus points to a dimension of knowledge because practices are always skilled and recognizable forms of doing. Such knowledge – usually implicit knowledge – organizes the respective social practice and is, in turn, reproduced as "knowing" in and through action (e.g., Gherardi, 2000). Thus, such organizing of activities manifests in practical orders that are *relationally entwined* in and through performing social practices.

Consequently, practices are always *cultural* practices in that they contain specific cultural orders of knowledge. They are always *material* practices in that they are anchored in two types of materiality – bodies and artifacts – and they are always *social* practices in that they are produced and recreated in a similar way by diverse individuals across different places and different times. In this way, the practice perspective does not depart from acting individuals; rather, it runs its own version of a decentralization of individuals: in a way, social practices avail themselves of the bodies and minds of individuals who are 'subjectified' in a Foucauldian sense.

Toward a Practice-based Understanding of Time and the Future: Beyond Objectivism and Subjectivism

A practice theory of the future operates beyond the conventional interpretations of temporality. In organization research (see Reinecke & Ansari, 2017) and the social sciences more broadly (Reckwitz, 2016), time is usually understood either as an objective or a subjective category. From an *objective* point of view, time is a neutral background against which events occur. In this vein, time is a standardized, measurable, and comparable unit and is, in principle, the same for all processes. Such a perspective on time puts quantity at center stage and hinges upon Taylorism, according to which work steps are partitioned into measurable time units and compared with other work steps based on performance. This leads to measuring and evaluating the time needed for tasks such as opening drawers or cleaning the floor, and so on. In planning concepts, this understanding of time becomes manifest in the emergence, sequencing, and outcomes of different plans (e.g., Arend et al., 2017; Hopp & Greene, 2018) which conceive of time in the same way.

In contrast, a *subjective* position considers the individual, social, and cultural character of time. This perspective puts the quality of time at center stage; that is, the specific forms of experiencing and understanding time. Thus, a subjective conception of time is a matter of perception, like duration. For example, actors may perceive that opening a drawer takes longer at a later point in the day. Such subjective perceptions of time are not limited to individuals. Similarly, social groups may have their own perceptions of time. For example, the "time culture" in consulting firms (Costas & Grey, 2014) and start-up accelerators (Wenzel & Koch, 2018) is characterized by a higher short-term orientation, spontaneity, and frequency of change than in car manufacturers (Maielli, 2015) and news-publishing companies (Koch, 2011) with their orientation toward temporal stability.

The practice perspective is positioned beyond an 'objective' temporal structure and a 'subjective' perception of time. From this perspective, time is neither an objective precondition for social action nor just a subjective perception; rather, it is the product of enacting social practices. That is, social practices have their own temporal structures and 'temporal effects' in that their temporal structures are produced and recreated in and through their enactment. Such a perspective by no means implies that it is positioned within subjectivism. In contrast to the idea of (collective) mental structures that structure perceptions of time, the practice-based understanding of time emphasizes the structuration of time in and through corresponding social practices. In this sense, even a seemingly 'objective' time is produced by performing social practices and is therefore culturally loaded like any other. Thus, in practice theory, time is not a precursor of social praxis that is deposited in mental dispositions, but rather the product of performing activities. In this vein, a practice perspective implies considering time as a routinized, or repetitive, way of dealing with time that is shared by several people.

The Temporality of Social Praxis, the Temporality of Social Practices, and Temporal Practices

What does the temporality of practice theory imply for the examination of how organizational actors engage with the future? From a practice perspective, references to the future in social life can be found in three different but interrelated ways: the temporality of social praxis in general, the temporality of each social practice, and 'temporal practices' in the narrow sense (see also Reckwitz, 2016).

The first form relates to the overall temporality of social praxis. This refers to the foundational and inherent role of time in social praxis, which is always temporally structured. Social praxis is a sequence of activities that has a future and a past in that each activity refers to previous activities and is succeeded by further activities. Thus, as a "temporally unfolding and spatially dispersed nexus of doings and sayings" (Schatzki, 1996, p. 89), social praxis is conceived as a stream of activities that have a 'before' and an 'after.' Social praxis (re)produces a reference to the past through repeated, rehearsed bodily performances of activities. However, in its situational enactment, social praxis is repeatedly subject to both smaller and larger changes that create scope for something new – even for changes of social praxis. Garfinkel (1967, p. 9) called this "for another first time" and later, "for another next first time" (Garfinkel, 2002, p. 182). Such reenactments of social praxis give rise to a host of potential futures that cannot be conceived as linear projections of the past. Rather, through the momentary performance of social praxis, actors (re)interpret the past and give sense to possible future events to make sense of and enact the present situation (e.g., Kaplan & Orlikowski, 2013; Schultz & Hernes, 2013).

In contrast to this foundational temporality of social praxis, we can distinguish a second way in which time is relevant in social practice: the temporality of specific social practices. Just as every social praxis has a foundational temporal dimension, social practices can be distinguished in terms of their specific temporality. This then relates to the specific temporal structures that are produced and recreated in and through the enactment of each social practice (Orlikowski & Yates, 2002) – not its foundational ontological structure of activities. Here, we can distinguish between two forms. First, the enactment of specific social practices always precedes other activities and events. For example, in a board meeting, managers can lay the foundations for organizational change, or the board meeting itself may constitute a response to organizational challenges. In this sense, such meetings always constitute an (enacted) anticipation of the yet-to-come and refer back to the past in that they are the outcome of previously performed social practices. However, both temporal references – toward the future and the past – do not deplete in the immediate temporal proximity but make more distant temporal references. For example, it may take several years for a board meeting to be acknowledged as a decisive event, and at the same time, the cultural meeting praxis is historically grounded in a long-standing practice of cooperative debate (Sennett, 2012). Second, social practices can themselves structure time. For example, during the enactment of board meetings, actors typically distinguish between times allotted for speaking and those for silence, which are allocated to different participants. In addition, actors usually formulate a specific beginning and an approximate ending. Additionally, the dramaturgical sequence of activities is often organized such that the content-related climax is separated from other, less important aspects (see also Jarzabkowski & Seidl, 2008). Thus, through the enactment of such meeting practices, board meetings obtain a ritualized (Johnson et al., 2010) temporal rhythm that structures the flow of activities therein (see also Gilbreth & Gilbreth, 1917).

These two ways of manifesting future in practice theory represent "time-beyond-us" (Holt & Johnsen, 2019) in that the present, past, and future are immanently and inevitably reproduced in and through social praxis and practice. From these two forms, we can distinguish a third way of interpreting the interplay between time and social practice, which represents "time-for-us" (Holt & Johnsen, 2019). This way refers to those practices that are related to time in the narrow sense – the so-called temporal practices. One prominent example is the social practice of remembering (e.g., Gioia et al., 2002; Hatch & Schultz, 2017). This practice refers to the specific routinized activities through which actors in the present bring to life and connect with previous events. Remembering includes the enactment of rituals such as the (staged) performance of commemoration events at a company's anniversary and the materialization of an organization's history in movies and books, which commemorate past events such as the establishment of the company. In turn, "future-making practices" can be understood as "a set of practices through which actors produce and enact the future" (Wenzel et al., 2020, p. 1441). Future-making practices thus include the streams of activities of imagining, including, and processing future events and occasions that are performed in the present. Together, they constitute a bundle that we call 'future work,' that is, constellations of future-making practices that participate in the production of the yet-to-come.

Future Work: Performativity, Situationality, Heterogeneity, Relationality

This overview of the foundations of a theory of social practice points to four dimensions relevant to practice-based examinations of how organizational actors engage with the future through 'future work.' In the following, we describe these dimensions and explicate their role in the analysis of future-making practices.

First, practice theory highlights the *performativity* of the future. By taking into account the specific social practices through which actors imagine and process the yet-to-come, it draws attention to the *(un) doing* of the future. This implies that a practice-based examination of engaging with the future describes and explains not only how organizational actors imagine and process the yet-to-come but also which conceptions of the future emerge in and through this process. For instance, whereas actors produce and recreate future projections of the past through the enactment of prognostic-probabilistic procedures, visionary narratives of the future explicitly refer to a structural break with contemporary and past experiences. Thus, these procedures are consequential for the emergence of different conceptions of the future; in turn, these conceptions initiate further activities, such as passively bearing, actively pursuing, or defending against these images of the yet-to-come. Taken together, the performativity of the future implies that conceptions of the future are closely entwined with the future-making practices through which they come into being, and set in motion a stream of subsequent activities through which they may or may not become 'realized.'

The second dimension relates to the *situationality* of future work. Practice theory considers engaging with the future as a contemporary phenomenon. Specifically, it draws attention to future-making practices as ways in which actors imagine and process the yet-to-come in the present. As such, this is not a novelty in debates on time and temporality in organization research (e.g., Hernes, 2014) and the social sciences more broadly. Even the philosophical stream of pragmatism (Mead, 1932) and the theory of social differentiation refer to such "contemporary futures" (Luhmann, 1976), which organizational actors enact "as if" they were already a matter of the present (Koch et al., 2018; Pitsis et al., 2003). At the same time, however, practice theory draws attention to 'future presents,' which are always bound to the present as imaginations, expectations, or forecasts. Such an emphasis on situationality often evokes the critique that practice theory would delimit itself to a situationalism that does not take into account 'macro' or societal structures (see Seidl & Whittington, 2014). Here, we note that practice theory does not decouple the situational enactment of specific streams of activities from broader social structures. It just locates the latter differently; not as a precursor of, but as being relationally entwined with, social praxis (e.g., Giddens, 1984). Thus, if broader social structures, such as organizational cultures, hierarchies, or broader principles of social order, play a role in and for the situational enactment of future-making practices and other social practices, they become manifest as such in social praxis.

Third, the *heterogeneity* of social praxis is relevant for the examination of future work. Given that practice theory draws attention to the specific practices through which the future is 'made,' it does not stop at the identification of prescriptive conceptions of the future (e.g., Lê, 2013), but takes into account the empirical diversity of future praxis through which such conceptions come into being. Thus, a practice perspective focusses not only on those procedures that are explicitly dedicated to imagining and processing the future – such as planning procedures – but also those mundane activities that are not explicitly oriented toward the yet-to-come but are, nonetheless, consequential for the ways in which actors imagine and process the future. This coarse-grained grid for the identification of future-making practices precludes antecedent theoretical decisions: it is through the empirical analysis of social praxis that the specific ways in which organizational actors engage with the future are identified. In this way, practice theory takes seriously the possibility of 'surprise' and makes it generative in that a practice perspective sustains openness for exploring the manifold ways in which future-making practices become manifest in social praxis. Through such an approach, multiple future-making practices may be identified – and, with them, different futures.

Fourth, practice theory points to the *relationality* of future work. Understanding social praxis as "nexus" (Schatzki, 1996) and, therefore, as the interplay of several streams of activities reminds us that future-making practices are never just stand-alone entities but are processually embedded in a web of practices.

The relationality of future-making practices highlights several analytical categories that are of special interest. First, practice theory puts special emphasis on the materiality of social life in a double sense: it is interested in human bodies and artifacts in and through which social practices are enacted. As routinized performances, social practices rely on competent bodies through which they come to life. In the process of acquiring a practice, humans learn to move their bodies in a skillful way. However, from a practice perspective, humans do not instrumentally use their bodies, given that practice theory does not privilege the mind over the body. Rather, humans learn to 'be' a body in a certain way (Reckwitz, 2002). Likewise, artifacts play an important role because their enactment structures social practices to a significant extent. Therefore, both human bodies and material objects are carriers of social practices that have to be there, and be used to perform and reproduce social practices, and human bodies and material objects are inseparably interconnected (see also Stiegler, 1998). For future-making practices, this means that actors produce and recreate the future in and through bodily performances and the inclusion of artifacts. For example, actors (may) move their bodies differently to imagine and process the future in weekly management meetings than they do in shamanic ceremonies. Furthermore, they include different material objects through which actors produce and recreate the future: whereas the former case typically involves ubiquitous office supplies, flipcharts, and electronic tablets, the latter case presumably includes 'natural' material objects outside of a work context.

In addition to this material dimension, the enactment of social practices is guided by a "practical sense" (Bourdieu, 1980) that can only be observed in and through their performance. Thus, the sense and meaning of a social practice can only be found in and emerge through its enactment. This processual understanding of sense, again, points to the examination of specific situations of imagining and processing the future *in actu*. At the same time, it relates to collective knowledge orders that are fundamentally entwined with this practical sense. Through a shared knowledge horizon, social practices refer to practically meaningful rules that display their ordering power in social praxis. For instance, the structuring of an organization's future based on planning principles may not be reflected in the organizational chart but in the 'know how' of performed practices, that is, in the development and pursuit of a plan.

An interesting case of future-making practices can be found in temporal discourses. From a practice perspective, discourses are a special case of social practices. They can be understood as ways of representing social reality in and through which actors produce and recreate sign systems, arguments, narratives, and visualizations. In the case of future-making practices, this relates to specific discourses of broaching and representing the future (e.g., Crilly, 2017; Stjerne et al., 2022). Such discursive representations of the future can be found in vision and mission statements, strategic plans, speeches at company anniversaries, prognostics of the research and development department, and futurologies of popular science. For practice-based examinations, such future-related discourses are part of discourse/practice complexes in which they are entwined with other discursive and nondiscursive practices. In this way, written or articulated predictions become a material foundation for discussions about organizational futures – as apocalyptic messages for some and hopeful messages for others. It is important to note here that such discourses are not just neutral comments but are also part of the social praxis in organizations.

Being thought of as relationally entwined, future-making practices are to be considered as a complex of all these parts and components. Future praxis always has a material dimension, which consists of various human bodies and artifacts that come to life through their enactment (e.g., Comi & Whyte, 2018). Therefore, it includes and is entwined with future-related discourses, structured by a practical sense, and, therefore, relates to collectively shared knowledge orders. However, empirical observations of future-making practices not only focus on these complexes in an isolated way but also take into account how they are relationally interconnected with other social practices. More specifically, the enactment of future-making practices evokes the performance of other practices. For example, in public administrations, planning procedures are now highly institutionalized and regulated by laws. However, the ritualized performance of related practices can also be observed in less regulated contexts. For example, company anniversaries include and evoke a host of practices that are enacted in a routinized way – such as giving a speech, invoking a vision, and performing a ceremonial act – which actors discuss in the in-house magazine or in the cafeteria for example. Thus, the idea of relationality creates an opportunity to observe a network of numerous practices that enable and constrain the production and recreation of future-making practices. Notably, such relations can also be observed and traced by examining their history. For example, one may identify specific 'quotes' in prior performances of future-making practices that actors consciously or unconsciously rely on later.

Prospection: Organizing (for) the Future and Future Work

In this chapter, we began by highlighting the ubiquitous role of the future as a key orientation in organizations in general and in the 'future of work' in particular. Organizational actors have always engaged with the yet-to-come and will always do so – be it in the form of creative action, research and development, strategic positioning, or the entrepreneurial pursuit of (future) opportunities. However, as we also suggested, the future is an elusive temporal category that denies any direct access, which turns organizational actors' engagement with the future into a phenomenon of the present in that the future must be constantly imagined, revised, reworked, and renegotiated. Practice theory, then, opens a window into the situationally enacted, performative, heterogeneous, and relationally entwined ways through which organizational actors engage with the future. This turns the 'future of work' into 'future work,' that is, a bundle of practices through which futures are continually made, unmade, and remade. Therefore, this chapter invites organization scholars to gain a practice-based understanding of how organizational actors engage with the yet-to-come.

A practice-based understanding of engaging with the future generates a number of questions, such as: Which kinds of explicitly dedicated or mundane, everyday 'future-making practices' do organizational actors enact? How does the enactment of future-making practices performatively evoke organizational futures, and which kinds of futures do the different future-making practices 'make'? How do organizational actors coordinate the enactment of several, potentially even numerous future-making practices? In which ways are the discursive, bodily, and material aspects of future-making practices consequential for engaging with the yet-to-come and the conceptions of the future that are produced and recreated? What specific narratives do organizational actors mobilize in this process? Finding answers to these and other questions allows organization scholars to gain insights into engaging with the future as a key challenge of contemporary organizing.

However, both the ubiquitous nature of the future in organizations and the practice perspective on this phenomenon imply more than drawing attention to an under-researched aspect of organizing: they question the way in which the future is, at least implicitly, conceptualized in many prevalent theories of organizing and organization. Specifically, much of the organizational literature still conceives of the future as a plannable and, thus, 'manageable' temporal mode. For example, in the resource-based view, the effective use of organizational assets is based on "a very clear vision of the future [that] reflect[s] firms' systematic, company-wide strategic planning process" (Barney, 1991, p. 111). Similarly, the theoretical statements by organization scholars interested in dynamic capabilities (Teece et al., 1997) largely build on "up-front planning" (Arend, 2015, p. 79). In turn, parts of the institutional literature (Meyer & Rowan, 1977) consider planning-based responses to institutional forces as key to achieving legitimacy (Honig & Karlsson, 2004). And despite the openness of strategy-as-practice (SAP) scholars for a practice-based understanding of engaging with temporal categories (e.g., Kaplan & Orlikowski, 2013), "[s]trategic planning has taken a central place in SAP research" (Vaara & Whittington, 2012, p. 292). This planning-based approach to the future reflects recent observations of the continued enactment of conventional planning activities in organizations (e.g., Wolf & Floyd, 2017). However, it underplays the plurality of the ways in which organizational actors engage with the future (e.g., Wagner, 1994), which turns classical planning procedures into one among various future-making practices – perhaps only with the purpose of creating spectacular illusions of rational anticipations of the yet-to-come, while actually engaging with the future in different ways (Flyverbom & Reinecke, 2017). This implies that conventional explanations for organizational survival and demise based on the (non)ascription of competences to 'correctly' anticipate and act upon the future (e.g., Levine et al., 2017; Schilling, 2017) are not just incomplete; they might also be problematic in that they confound the symbolic management of the future on the front stage with the 'real' activities through which organizational actors engage with the yet-to-come on the back stage. A practice perspective on engaging with the future in organizations helps organization scholars uncover such activities and, in doing so, provide richer explanations for the dynamics of stability and change through which organizational actors respond to but perhaps even performatively cocreate and shape futures.

More broadly, reconceiving the notion of the future in organizing has implications for our understanding of what organizing *is*. The growing interest in the temporal mode of the past (e.g., Godfrey et al., 2016; Hatch & Schultz, 2017; Suddaby & Foster, 2017) indicates that organizing is still conceived mainly as *historically grown* processes through which work is coordinated and order is (re)created. However, in light of the ubiquity and consequentiality of the future in organizations, organizing may also be conceived as a "future-oriented *dwelling*" (Chia & Holt, 2009, p. 128, emphasis in original), one that is directed toward the (re)production of (dis)order in light of, or despite, the ongoing inaccessibility of the future, which eludes itself from being 'managed' through planning techniques alone. When considering the present as a space between the future and the past, such dwelling can occur in and through the constant inhabitation of 'spaces for play/invention,' that is, in-between "space[s] of actualization, actuated by movements toward future creation" (Hjorth, 2004, p. 421; Hjorth, 2005), which results in continual "speculative movement[s] towards the future" (Hjorth et al., 2018, p. 157). From this perspective, organizational structures and processes are not (only) the outcomes of past activities and events but (also) constitute organizational actors' responses to their imaginations of the yet-to-come and are constantly 'in-the-making.' Evidently, such a perspective sympathizes with process views of organizing (e.g., Bakken et al., 2013; Hernes, 2014; Hjorth et al., 2015; Holt & Johnsen, 2019; Langley et al., 2013; Tsoukas & Chia, 2002) and puts the driving force of engaging with the future at center stage. Therefore, examining the future more systematically in organization research implies conceiving of organizational phenomena as processes and exploring the prevalence of the future therein. We hope that the practice-based approach to engaging with the future will help future research do so.

References

Adler, P. S. (ed.) (1992). *Technology and the Future of Work*. Oxford: Oxford University Press.

Arend, R. J. (2015). Mobius' edge: infinite regress in the resource-based and dynamic capabilities views. *Strategic Organization*, *13*(1), 75–85. DOI: 10.1177/1476127014563051.

Arend, R. J., Zhao, Y. L., Song, M., & Im, S. (2017). Strategic planning as a complex and enabling managerial tool. *Strategic Management Journal, 38*(8), 1741–53.

Augier, M. & Teece, D. J. (2008). Strategy as evolution with design: The foundations of dynamic capabilities and the role of managers in the economic system. *Organization Studies, 29*(8&9), 1187–208. DOI: 10.1177 /0170840608094776.

Bacon-Gerasymenko, V., Coff, R. W., & Durand, R. (2016). Taking a second look in a warped crystal ball: Explaining the accuracy of revised forecasts. *Journal of Management Studies, 53*(8), 1292–319.

Bakken, T., Holt, R., & Zundel, M. (2013). Time and play in management practice: An investigation through the philosophies of McTaggart and Heidegger. *Scandinavian Journal of Management, 29*(1), 13–22.

Barney, J. B. (1991). Firm resources and sustained competitive advantage. *Journal of Management, 17*(1), 99–120.

Barry, D. & Elmes, M. (1997). Strategy retold: Toward a narrative view of strategic discourse. *Academy of Management Review, 22*(2), 429–52.

Beckert, J. (2016). *Imagined Futures: Expectations and Capitalist Dynamics.* Cambridge, MA: Harvard University Press.

Beckert, J. (2021). The firm as an engine of imagination: Organizational prospection and the making of economic futures. *Organization Theory, 2*(2). DOI: 10.1177/26317877211005773.

Bourdieu, P. (1980). *Le Sens Pratique.* Paris: Les Éditions de Minuit.

Brinckmann, J., & Sung, M. K. (2015). Why we plan: The impact of nascent entrepreneurs' cognitive characteristics and human capital on business planning. *Strategic Entrepreneurship Journal, 9*(2), 153–66.

Bromiley, P., Rau, D., & Yu, Z. (2017). Is R&D risky? *Strategic Management Journal, 38*(4), 876–91.

Chia, R. & Holt, R. (2009). *Strategy without Design: The Silent Efficacy of Indirect Action.* Cambridge: Cambridge University Press.

Comi, A. & Whyte, J. (2018). Future making and visual artefacts: An ethnographic study of a design project. *Organization Studies, 39*(8), 1055–83.

Costas, J. & Grey, C. (2014). The temporality of power and the power of temporality: Imaginary future selves in professional service firms. *Organization Studies, 35*(6), 909–37.

Crilly, D. (2017). Time and space in strategy discourse: Implications for temporal choice. *Strategic Management Journal, 38*(12), 2370–89.

Donkin, R. (2010). *The Future of Work.* London: Palgrave Macmillan.

Feldman, M. S. & Orlikowski, W. J. (2011). Theorizing practice and practicing theory. *Organization Science, 22*(5), 1240–53. DOI: 10.1287/orsc.1100.0612.

Flyverbom, M. & Reinecke, J. (2017). The spectacle and organization studies. *Organization Studies, 38*(11), 1625–43.

Garfinkel, H. (1967). *Studies in Ethnomethodology.* Englewood Cliffs, NJ: Prentice-Hall.

Garfinkel, H. (2002). *Ethnomethodology's Program: Working Out Durkheim's Aphorism.* Lanham, MD: Rowman and Littlefield.

Garud, R., Schildt, H., & Lant, T. K. (2014). Entrepreneurial storytelling, future expectations, and the paradox of legitimacy. *Organization Science, 25*(5), 1287–571.

Gavetti, G. & Menon, A. (2016). Evolution cum agency: Toward a model of strategic foresight. *Strategy Science*, 1(3), 207–33.

Gherardi, S. (2000). Practise-based theorizing on learning and knowing in organizations. *Organization*, 7(2), 211–23.

Giddens, A. (1984). *The Constitution of Society: Outline of a Theory of Structuration.* Berkeley, CA: University of California Press.

Gilbreth, F. B. & Gilbreth, L. M. (1917). *Applied Motion Study: A Collection of Papers on the Efficient Method to Industrial Preparedness.* New York: Sturgis & Walton.

Gioia, D. A., Corley, K. G., & Fabbri, T. (2002). Revising the past (while thinking in the future perfect tense). *Journal of Organizational Change Management*, 15(6), 622–34.

Godfrey, P. C., Hassard, J., O'Connor, E. S., Rowlinson, M., & Ruef, M. (2016). What is organizational history? Toward a creative synthesis of history and organization studies. *Academy of Management Review*, 41(4), 590–608.

Hannay, A. (1996). *Søren Kierkegaard – Papers and Journals: A Selection.* London: Penguin.

Hatch, M. J. & Schultz, M. (2017). Toward a theory of using history authentically: Historicizing in the Carlsberg Group. *Administrative Science Quarterly*, 62(4), 657–97.

Hernes, T. (2014). *A Process Theory of Organization.* Oxford: Oxford University Press.

Hjorth, D. (2004). Creating space for play/invention: Concepts of space and organizational entrepreneurship. *Entrepreneurship & Regional Development*, 16(5), 413–32.

Hjorth, D. (2005). Organizational entrepreneurship: With de Certeau on creating heterotopias (or spaces for play). *Journal of Management Inquiry*, 14(4), 386–98.

Hjorth, D., Holt, R., & Steyaert, C. (2015). Entrepreneurship and process studies. *International Small Business Journal*, 33(6), 599–611.

Hjorth, D., Strati, A., Drakopoulou Dodd, S., & Weik, E. (2018). Organizational creativity, play and entrepreneurship: Introduction and framing. *Organization Studies*, 39(2–3), 155–68.

Holt, R. (2004). Risk management: The talking cure. *Organization*, 11(2), 251–70.

Holt, R. & Johnsen, R. (2019). Time and organization studies. *Organization Studies*, 40(10), 1557–72. DOI: 10.1177/0170840619844292.

Honig, B. & Karlsson, T. (2004). Institutional forces and the written business plan. *Journal of Management*, 30(1), 29–48.

Hopp, C. & Greene, F. J. (2018). In pursuit of time: Business plan sequencing, duration and intraentrainment effects on new venture viability. *Journal of Management Studies*, 55(2), 320–51.

Jarzabkowski, P. & Seidl, D. (2008). The role of meetings in the social practice of strategy. *Organization Studies*, 29(11), 1391–426.

Johnson, G., Prashantham, S., Floyd, S. W., & Bourque, N. (2010). The ritualization of strategy workshops. *Organization Studies*, 31(12), 1589–618.

Kaplan, S. & Orlikowski, W. J. (2013). Temporal work in strategy making. *Organization Science*, 24(4), 965–95.

Kierkegaard, S. (1843). *Søren Kierkegaards Skrifter* (Vol. 18). Copenhagen: Søren Kierkegaard Research Center.

Koch, J. (2011). Inscribed strategies: Exploring the organizational nature of strategic lock-in. *Organization Studies, 32*(3), 337–63.

Koch, J., Wenzel, M., Senf, N. N., & Maibier, C. (2018). Organizational creativity as an attributional process: The case of haute cuisine. *Organization Studies, 39*(2–3), 251–70. DOI: 10.1177/0170840617727779.

Koselleck, R. (1989). Vergangene Zukunft der frühen Neuzeit. In R. Koselleck (ed.), *Vergangene Zukunft: Zur Semantik geschichtlicher Zeiten* (pp. 17–37). Frankfurt: Suhrkamp.

Langley, A., Smallman, C., Tsoukas, H., & Van de Ven, A. H. (2013). Process studies of change in organization and management: Unveiling temporality, activity, and flow. *Academy of Management Journal, 56*(1), 1–13. DOI: 10.5465/amj.2013.4001.

Lê, J. K. (2013). How constructions of the future shape organizational responses: Climate change and the Canadian oil sands. *Organization, 20*(5), 722–42.

Levine, S. S., Bernard, M., & Nagel, R. (2017). Strategic intelligence: The cognitive capability to anticipate competitor behavior. *Strategic Management Journal, 38*(12), 2390–423.

Luhmann, N. (1976). The future cannot begin: Temporal structures in modern society. *Social Research, 43*(1), 130–53.

Maielli, G. (2015). Explaining organizational paths through the concept of hegemony: Evidence from the Italian car industry. *Organization Studies, 36*(4), 491–511.

Malhotra, A. (2021). The postpandemic future of work. *Journal of Management, 47*(1), 1091–102.

March, J. G. (1995). The future, disposable organizations and the rigidities of imagination. *Organization, 2*(3–4), 427–40.

Mead, G. H. (1932). *The Philosophy of the Present*. London: Open Court Company.

Meyer, J. W. & Rowan, B. (1977). Institutionalized organizations: Formal structure as myth and ceremony. *American Journal of Sociology, 83*(2), 340–63.

Mintzberg, H. (1994). *The Rise and Fall of Strategic Planning: Reconceiving Roles of Planning, Plans, Planners*. New York: Free Press.

Nicolini, D. (2013). *Practice Theory, Work and Organization: An Introduction*. Oxford: Oxford University Press.

Orlikowski, W. J. & Yates, J. (2002). It's about time: Temporal structuring in organizations. *Organization Science, 13*(6), 684–700.

Pitsis, T. S., Clegg, S. R., Marosszeky, M., & Rura-Polley, T. (2003). Constructing the Olympic dream: A future perfect strategy of project management. *Organization Science, 14*(5), 574–90.

Rasche, A. & Chia, R. (2009). Researching strategy practices: A genealogical social theory perspective. *Organization Studies, 30*(7), 713–34.

Reckwitz, A. (2002). Toward a theory of social practices: A development in culturalist theorizing. *European Journal of Social Theory, 5*(2), 243–63. DOI: 10.1177/13684310222225432.

Reckwitz, A. (2016). *Zukunftspraktiken. Die Zeitlichkeit des Sozialen und die Krise der modernen Rationalisierung der Zukunft.* In A. Reckwitz (ed.), *Kreativität und soziale Praxis. Studien zur Sozial- und Gesellschaftstheorie* (pp. 115–35). Bielefeld, Germany: transcript.

Reckwitz, A. (2017). *The Invention of Creativity: Modern Society and the Culture of the New.* Hoboken, NJ: Wiley.

Reinecke, J. & Ansari, S. (2017). Time, temporality, and process studies. In A. Langley & H. Tsoukas (eds.), *Sage Handbook of Process Organization Studies* (pp. 402–16). London: Sage.

Rohrbeck, R., Battistella, C., & Huizingh, E. (2015). Corporate foresight: An emerging field with a rich tradition. *Technological Forecasting and Social Change, 101,* 1–9.

Rosa, H. (2013). *Social Acceleration: A New Theory of Modernity.* New York: Columbia University Press.

Schatzki, T. R. (1996). *Social Practices: A Wittgensteinian Approach to Human Activity and the Social.* Cambridge: Cambridge University Press.

Schatzki, T. R., Knorr Cetina, K., & von Savigny, E. (2001). *The Practice Turn in Contemporary Theory.* London: Routledge.

Schilling, M. A. (2017). The cognitive foundations of visionary strategy. *Strategy Science, 3*(1), 335–42.

Schultz, M. & Hernes, T. (2013). A temporal perspective on organizational identity. *Organization Science, 24*(1), 1–21. DOI: 10.1287/orsc.1110.0731.

Seidl, D. & Whittington, R. (2014). Enlarging the strategy-as-practice research agenda: Towards taller and flatter ontologies. *Organization Studies, 35*(10), 1407–21.

Sennett, R. (2012). *Zusammenarbeit: Wie unsere Gesellschaft zusammenhält.* Berlin: Hanser.

Sherden, W. A. (1998). *The Fortune Sellers: The Big Business of Buying and Selling Predictions.* New York: Wiley.

Stiegler, B. (1998). *Technics and Time, 1: The Fault of Epimetheus.* Stanford, CA: Stanford University Press.

Stjerne, I. S., Wenzel, M., & Svejenova, S. (2022). Commitment to grand challenges in fluid forms of organizing: The role of narratives' temporality. *Research in the Sociology of Organizations, 79,* 129–60. https://doi.org/10.1108/S0733-558X20220000079012.

Streeck, J., Goodwin, C., & LeBaron, C. (2011). *Embodied Interaction: Language and Body in the Material World.* Cambridge: Cambridge University Press.

Suddaby, R. & Foster, W. M. (2017). History and organizational change. *Journal of Management, 43*(1), 19–38.

Teece, D. J., Pisano, G., & Shuen, A. (1997). Dynamic capabilities and strategic management. *Strategic Management Journal, 18*(7), 509–33. DOI: 10.1002/10 97-0266.

Thompson, N. A. & Byrne, O. (2022). Imagining futures: Theorizing the practical knowledge of future-making. *Organization Studies, 43*(2), 247–68.

Tsoukas, H. & Chia, R. (2002). On organizational becoming: Rethinking organizational change. *Organization Science, 13*(5), 567–82. DOI: 10.1287/orsc.13.5.567.7810.

Tsoukas, H. & Shepherd, J. (2004). *Managing the Future: Foresight in the Knowledge Economy.* Malden, MA: Blackwell.

Vaara, E. & Whittington, R. (2012). Strategy-as-practice: Taking social practices seriously. *Academy of Management Annals, 6*(1), 285–336. DOI: 10.1080/194 16520.2012.672039.

Wagner, P. (1994). *A Sociology of Modernity: Liberty and Discipline.* London: Routledge.

Wenzel, M. (2022). Taking the future more seriously: From corporate foresight to "future-making". *Academy of Management Perspectives, 36*(2), 845–50. https://doi.org/10.5465/amp.2020.0126.

Wenzel, M. & Koch, J. (2018). Acceleration as process: A strategy process perspective on startup acceleration. In I. Drori & M. Wright (eds.), *Accelerators* (pp. 21–36). Cheltenham, UK: Edward Elgar.

Wenzel, M., Krämer, H., Koch, J., & Reckwitz, A. (2020). Future and organization studies: On the rediscovery of a problematic temporal category in organizations. *Organization Studies, 41*(10), 1441–55. DOI: 10.1177 /0170840620912977.

Whittington, R. (2006). Completing the practice turn in strategy research. *Organization Studies, 27*(5), 613–34.

Wolf, C. & Floyd, S. W. (2017). Strategic planning research: Toward a theory-driven agenda. *Journal of Management, 43*(6), 1754–88.

8 Towards a Crinicultural Activism in Organization

Damian O'Doherty

Introduction

Outside its own specialist industry hair is a neglected aspect of most management and organization, barely acknowledged as a presence let alone deemed a significant feature of management. However, in its multiple forms, hair is a complex material–temporal phenomenon in organization. We cannot do without it. As we shall see, it acts in a variety of ways: it grows, thickens and thins; it ages, falls out, accumulates and explodes. It is also an incredible achievement of organization.

In this chapter I want to introduce the reader to ways of thinking and speaking that help foreground hair in organization. I do this because hair allows us to extend and renew politics in organization, and to *politicize* organization in ways that might help stimulate and animate forces that can be harnessed to challenge the taken-for-granted. To leave dormant the taken-for-granted means that organization can only ever be superficial, resting on an unspoken set of practices and assumptions which are always liable to burst through the thin veneer of order and process (Garfinkel, 1967). Learning to see and act with hair can help revitalize and strengthen organization – not through the usual economies of scale and the mechanisms of bureaucracy or networks that modern organization theory teaches us (Clegg, 1990; du Gay & Vikkelsø, 2016), but in ways that extend relations and agencies to a wider spatial and temporal conception of organization, beyond the limited confines of management as it is currently practiced in 'formal' organization. Building on recent developments in process theory in organization (Tsoukas & Chia, 2002; Hernes, 2014; Sandberg et al., 2015; Langley & Tsoukas, 2016), we propose that hair gives access to process. More specifically, we understand hair to be an artefact and medium of organization, but also an agent and occasion through which something like the temporality of 'event' can begin to work in and on organization.

These preliminary statements allow us to ask: What are the politics of the merkin, or the bob-cut? 'That's a *wig*!' you might say, seized by an opening statement that aims to speak out about what we might call a ruptural 'event' and so follow the work of contemporary philosophers from Deleuze through Badiou (Raffoul, 2020). However, in line with current editorial guidance, this is an opportunity you have been denied. No doubt it is the corrosive influence of the commercial academic journal and the deification of the published article that is responsible for the deskilling of the reader who now must be told what they are reading. The work of active interpretation is no longer entrusted to the reader and the opening paragraphs now *prepare you* for the question: What are the politics of the merkin? Hence, the question loses its shock value. Ah, yes, I get it! (you might now say). By following this procedure, the kind of temporality in organization I want to acknowledge and introduce has been lost, namely the temporarily of event (see also O'Doherty, 2020). This acknowledgement entails and demands a performative happening of the event – a happening, moreover, in which we are seized by time, but also emptied, exhausted by its forces. The event demands we reinvent or renew organization outside its familiar discourse practices (the journal article, the book chapter, the research monograph). To be seized by the event is not an unconcealing in any revelatory sense, as popular in certain Heideggerian readings in contemporary organization theory, but the elaboration of the effects and affects arising from a rupture of Being that is coterminous with the event. This unravelling of being forms part of an event in these terms and finds itself located in the subject in whose being one world is forever transforming into others under the twisting, skewing force of event. The event is a tear (of the crying sort as well (Caputo, 1997)) and a process, and its politics is the process of such a tearing, the study and elaboration of events (ruptures).

The hair that is the merkin should shock. It asks us to look at organization anew, which requires some skewering out of the familiar discourse practices that help make and reproduce organization (Chia, 1996). This skewering produces a kind of *wervinding* familiar to the Heideggerians (see also Costea & Amiridis, 2014), a twisting out of or unwinding from the form of the academic book chapter, but it is a twisting out that leaves traces of the familiar and does not transcend in any great revelation or emancipation beloved of the Heideggerians and critical management studies alike. Like the merkin, this chapter has to pretend to be something it is not, an ex-stasis of representational control and dictation, or a formal narrative that instructs the reader what to think about the topic at hand. Intimately related to the world of the film and sex industry, the merkin of course betrays the modesty or hides the shame of its wearer, and this either/or remains undecidable, or at least this undecidable rings once its reader is able to insert a definition into the word 'merkin'. Such events then demand change to the way one normally proceeds with introductions to an academic paper. It is rare enough in management and organization studies to ask, 'What is Politics?', let alone *what are the politics of the merkin?*

It is a question, we might say, that is untimely. It is one that is certainly avoided by the mainstream. However, 'What is Politics?' is so obvious and basic a question that one might argue that it is at the very least *implicit* in everything studied about organization (O'Doherty & De Cock, 2019). The merkin forms part of a long and elaborate set of objects, practices and artefacts that can help us develop this question of politics and which I address thematically in this chapter by reference to the broader concept of 'the crinicultural' – a concept without the precision of the merkin, but which includes, if not contains, the merkin as a discrete feature of organization. The claim then, is made that in learning how to attend to the crinicultural we might stimulate a return and revitalisation of politics, and specifically activist politics in organization analysis. Such a revitalisation of politics is needed because it remains inhibited and increasingly programmatic, if not dogmatic, in its use by organization analysis. Hence, the doubtless double shock caused when mention is made of a *politics of* the merkin.

It is in many respects difficult to think of organization that does not make use of hirsutal objects and matters, either for business enterprise or managerial control. The power and authority of the high court judge, for example, would be much diminished without the peruke; the film industry relies on a retinue of couturiers and wig designers; popular music and fashion design are intricately entangled with accompanying hair design; there is a global industry in the harvest and distribution of hair and hair products (Tarlo, 2016), whilst barbers, stylists and hair salons make up a significant part of modern economies in terms of both jobs and taxation revenue. There are only a few, however, who have turned to hairstylists and their salons for the advancement of organization studies (Chugh & Hancock, 2009; Shortt 2012, 2015; Shortt & Warren, 2012), but without exception the salon and especially the matter of hair (its materiality) has been notable for its absence in the analysis employed by these studies. The salon, and hair, have simply served as the backdrop in this research against which new forms of emotional and aesthetic labour are discovered but within the customary dynamics of management control and resistance.

This chapter seeks to grant hair a much greater autonomy and significance. We find that it is less a product *of* organization than it is a hidden agent of organization and especially a politics of organization – which we call here a follicle politics of organization. What can be done with hair, we ask? What political difference does hair make and what political difference

can be made by thinking with hair? This is an unusual move in management and organization studies where we are still constrained by
the presumed sovereignty of a bald idealism that grants human thinking
an autonomy and potency it does not deserve. How can hair possibly
make us think differently? Taking materialism seriously and drawing on
ethnographic work undertaken in Manchester Airport (O'Doherty,
2017), I pose the question: What political *difference* does the crinicultural make, taking a point of departure from a chance encounter
with a bob-cut in the Escape Lounge inside the airport? How is the bob-
cut alive in contemporary organization and what are its politics? We
find that one is unable to identify this difference if we subordinate
analysis (difference) to the *identity* provided by the established lexicon
of 'politicalese' in management and organization studies. To be critical
politically, one typically tackles bad things like 'neo-liberalism'. One
seeks emancipation from oppressive and subjugating power relations
and presses for the acknowledgement of value differences, seeking
debate and resolution that might make room for the oppressed and
marginalized. It makes us feel worthy and good to be on the side of
those subordinate to dominant elites and hierarchies of power and
inequality. The bob-cut will seem frivolous and irrelevant in these
terms. It won't even be seen.

Working against this critical panoptic which silences the bob-cut, this
chapter develops the ethnographic material collected during two-and-a-half
years of fieldwork to explore some of the activist possibilities of the bob-cut
and its allied crinicultural phenomena. We explore the unruly qualities of
hair, both an unstable object of representation and group identification
(Hebdige, 1979), but also an active object and a vital materiality, partially
independent of human cognitive and stylistic interventions. Learning to
harness and embody this vitality can mark the difference between a politics
that works within established categories of identity and struggle and
a politics that draws on conditions of possibility that give rise to new
energies of creative struggle and innovation alongside new forms of subjectivity and agency. I seek to write on the seam of this evental temporality,
resisting the urge to write from a perspective of completion. The chapter
remains untimely in this respect, both *towards* a crinicultural politics, but
also suspended in a temporal hiatus where linearity and chronology give
way to a writing with time that is 'out of joint' (Derrida, 1994).

In so doing we are enjoined to follow the curls that entangle the creative
energy of hair-people with a particular approach to descriptive practice in
ethnographic writing (Atkinson, 2020). As such, the writing necessarily
curls and bends in its own way, in part to respect a crinicultural 'mode of
existence' (cf. Latour, 2013) but also to tease out the lineaments of an

'event' in which activist possibilities become charged and animated. To think with the curls and tangles effaced as an absent-presence by the bob-cut demands a sensitivity to the materiality of human hair, to comb into its roots and to follow the actors and agencies involved in a crinicultural politics that remains just beyond the fringe of our everyday work organizations.

The Concern with Politics in Organization Studies

It is safe to say that organization studies has struggled to *inspire* politics, despite a return to forms of a 'praxis' of sorts through a self-labelled critical performative 'turn' (Spicer et al., 2009; Cabantous et al., 2016; Learmonth et al., 2016; King & Land, 2018), a turn that is certainly not cited in mainstream academic political studies. It has attracted even less attention outside academia amongst the most innovative of recent radical political movements – one thinks of Los Indignados, Syriza, or the Extinction Rebellion movement, for example. More promising perhaps has been the recent interest in 'event' in organization studies (Böhm, 2006; Deroy & Clegg, 2011; Islam, 2015; Mauksch, 2020; O'Doherty, 2020) which promises to help identify moments of radical contingency and suspense in organization where established political thinking and practice proves inadequate to the challenges posed by the struggles and practices of members of organization. Whether we follow the work of Blanchot, Derrida, Deleuze or Foucault in their different ways of thinking of event (Buchanan, 2000; Bryant, 2011; Davies, 2013; Raffoul, 2020), we can generalize a little and say that an event is a ruptural moment in one's discursive practice from which we have to start inventing politics anew absent of all established rules and foundations. As a relatively ill-disciplined or post-disciplinary intellectual space that has migrated from the social sciences into the business school (Parker, 2000; Augier et al., 2005; Adler, 2009) we might make the additional claim that the body of work in organization studies provides the fertile conditions of possibility to nurture and cultivate sensitivity to events of this kind. Organization studies might very well be itself an 'event' in the social sciences (O'Doherty, 2007). However, some caution would be prudent.

First, despite the promise of 'evental' thinking inspired by the work of Deleuze or Derrida, the lessons drawn since Böhm's (2006) preliminary theoretical account have been disappointing. Event is often understood in only the most mundane and empirical of ways and this fails to do justice to the challenges posed to our thinking as organization theorists and social scientists by the 'thinking of event' in contemporary continental philosophy (see Raffoul, 2020). On the other hand, there are those pursuing an explication of event who might consider their work evental in its thinking, but their treatment has remained derivative and mainly explicative of the philosophy of others – whether Whitehead, Spinoza, Peirce or Merleau Ponty (Küpers, 2015; Hernes, 2016; Holt & Hjorth, 2016; Lorino, 2018) and has been less successful when developed or deployed empirically (Hussenot & Missonier, 2016). Apart from work on Nietzsche (Holt & Hjorth, 2016), the event tends to get subsumed into various understandings of a processual whole, not an open whole as Deleuze or Derrida might understand it, where event is not a transition or turning point giving onto a greater or more encompassing (processual) whole, but rather a more radical ontological rupture that obstructs the achievement of meaning, purpose or sense-making.

Second, we need to be cautious in building on those attempts to advance politics in management and organization studies because these have normally been sought in a dogmatic critical register which has found expression in a strange mix of overreaching theoretical ambition and naval-gazing as noted by many over the years, most recently by Silverman (2021). Indeed, Silverman makes the broader case that organization studies writ large suffers from a disjuncture between the theoretical and empirical arising out of a lack of methodological rigour. It is allied to an instructional literature that seeks to outline 'what is to be done', in which critical scholars typically end up pulling out their hair in despair, reciting the perennial question: 'what's wrong with critical management studies?' (Grey, 2005; Parker, 2013). The advance of politics in organization studies is also hampered by a parting that divides those who wish to ignore politics as an irrational feature of organization or an extraneous value-judgement introduced by the analyst, and those who, generally coming from critical management studies, pursue a politics of 'emancipation' (Alvesson & Willmott, 1992). This politics of emancipation seeks to improve the lot of whomever is deemed to be suffering the most from the current political–economic system which comes close to an ideological or an *a priori* commitment that seems to duplicate the lack of engagement in the practical messiness of doing politics. Practical politics must allow for the construction of emancipation in which what emancipation might entail is not known but is up for question, and possible compromise and a working order amongst contending interpretation. Ironically, in both the critical and non-critical (itself a too severe parting of the ways) politics is excised in two different ways. In the first, by what is deemed its irrelevance, and in the second, by virtue of the application of *a priori* commitments to certain collective interests, groups and identities, which becomes a programmatic version of identity politics that avoids the very necessary work of finding room for 'the event' which subtends and destabilizes any collective formation or lines of division based on class or other alliances and divisions.

In part, this failure of politics and political thinking/action might be explained by a failure to explore or fully *realize* the question: *what* is the *organization of politics*, or what is the possibility for political *experience* when thinking organizationally? In other words, we need to think about the entanglement of organization and event, to understand politics as ongoing concern with event which is always'immanent with the emergence of hitherto unimaginable forms of organization – and perhaps why those who have reached this understanding have turned to literature rather than the academic discipline of politics, and specifically to forms of literature always preoccupied with the paradoxes of time – Borges for De Cock, for example (De Cock, 2000), Stanislav Lem for Case (1999), Burroughs for Land (2005), or Calvino for De Cock and Land (2006). When thinking, at its most literal, the 'what' suggests we look for things observable, or what can be seen and heard – materials, objects, talk and practices. This reminds us that politics is 'material' (Barry, 2013; Marres, 2016) in the sense that issues triggering political mobilization are things which *object* – and the infrastructure of pipelines, energy, transport, military and so on are in this sense the classic materials around politics and in which political thinking is mobilized and shaped. We also think and practice in the very same material conditions of possibility. We do not float free in an ethereal ideal realm immune from material conditions of possibility. What it is possible to think with electricity and a computer is very different to what can be thought with the horse and plough. In this chapter, the materials we are thinking with are hirsutal in nature and we find their materials inflect networks with particular qualities of resonance. I later draw on Michael Taussig's (1992) study of the tense and febrile conditions of the social 'nervous system' to show how apparently minor and insignificant materials and events (a defaced stone statue of the Queen in his example (see also Taussig, 1999)) can radiate throughout the social body to snowball with affects and unpredictable consequences, much of which can charge the political landscape with new 'matters of concern' (Latour, 2004). In a different register, Joseph Roach (2007) shows a similar '*It* affect' which operates through media image and style with the capacity to mobilize an entire social body. The 'stacked, lacquered hair' of UK Prime Minister Margaret Thatcher, for example, helped establish 'the principles of control, constraint and economy of force' associated with Thatcher's economics and politics. Interventions and changes in apparently frivolous domains of fashion and appearance help bring this 'It' affect to life and to make it 'flash through the aether' of communication media helping to mobilize cults and cults of personality.

Ethnography provides perhaps the most generous method for the study of this quiddity, this 'whatness' of politics in organization. If there is 'politics in a sausage' as Saraiva (2016) shows, then there is politics everywhere, albeit much of it latent or virtual. There is also a lot that is marginalized and disdained (O'Doherty et al., 2013), simply not seen or registered, and much of this blindness can perhaps be explained as a 'willed ignorance' inspired by a new set of forces that promote intellectual conservatism, or worse, an anti-intellectualism. The commodification of knowledge production has been long predicted (Lyotard, 1984), but as this becomes supervised by an increasingly disciplined and coherent managerial logic, there emerges an underlying homogeneity in theory and method, despite the superficial diversity and proliferation of subject matter.

How can management studies be shaken out of its torpor and indeed from its very own academic implication in an organization of politics? Something like this event of thought, at least in Derrida's (1996) sense might be promising, in which the event is experienced as a shock to thought and an experience (right at the limit of what is *experience-able*) for which we have no preparation, the results of which can leave us wondering who we were before we endured the shock or trauma of this experience (O'Doherty, 2020). That shock, which turns hair grey, might be one candidate for such an event. In perhaps the most famous account of such an event, Henriette Campan's memoirs as lady-in-waiting to Marie Antoinette, recalls seeing Antoinette for the first time after the failed Varennes escape attempt in June 1791. On taking off her cap, Marie Antoinette's hair "had become, in one single night, as white as that of a woman of seventy" (Campan, 2018, p. 16).

In turning to the ethnographic material in the next section we are in quest of methods and practices that trace that immanence or potentiality at work in matters pertaining specifically to the crinicultural. Drawing on the resources of recent 'fashion theory' (Entwistle, 2000; Craik, 2003; Barnard, 2020) and its hybridization with studies of politics (Behnke, 2016), a range of methods and theories are available that include the pioneering studies of 'the fashion industry' by Roland Barthes (1990) and the semiotic system of consumer culture in Baudrillard (1970). Progressively inhabiting the material–semiotic properties of airport hair, the research traces the surprising twists and turns of the hirsute and crinicultural, catching sparks of the 'it affect' as it flashes 'through the aether' (Roach, 2007) of communication media connecting up that which is normally separated into the macro and micro – hair practices, an airport lounge, local government and economy. Can politics be made by combining or seeing the connections between phenomena normally considered irrelevant and separated by scale? Only in something like an event as we have articulated here could connections or an equivalence be found in phenomena hitherto conceived as separate and incommunicado. And in this regard, the potential of hair should not be underestimated. Like the automobile as a political resource for subversion (Davis, 2017), lacquered hair is only ever seconds away from bursting into flames (as Hollywood star Nicole Richie recently discovered). As we shall see, for many airport staff, hair is best treated as a fire hazard. Such frangibility and combustibility gives charge and leverage to the affective political possibilities of hair – as a site for acts of protest or potential terrorist activity.

The Bob-Cut

The airport lounge is humming to a collective synthesis of early morning background sounds, coming to life. Soft, curated wallpaper muzak drifts over the periodic hiss of the coffee maker which mingles with TV chatter and the noises coming from small clusters of people as they variously inhabit the lounge, sitting in scoop-sculpted Tom Dixon armchairs, tapping away on laptops, all coming and going in a slow early morning drone. It is a scene that is familiar to many amongst the kinetic elite and the emerging class of 'loungers' and other travellers and holiday flyers circulating in airport space (Augé, 1995; Gottdiener, 2001; O'Doherty, 2017). But then – Flash! Or rather, a blackout. A black geometric shape blooms out of this indifferent background, causing a blackout. At least it does in close-up. I been engulfed by something like Malevich's black square. Are there others who have been similarly ensnared? Everything else disappears. It cuts a space and slices through the lounge. With more conventional perspective, the black is a glossy bob-style haircut. It moves in a strong and deliberate trajectory from left to right, cutting a straight line like the snip of a pair of hairdresser's scissors. It can also be seen to frame the face of an 'angel' as the philosopher Michel Serres (1995) calls the workers who help mediate and orchestrate the movements of people and things in airports.

She radiates. Looking like actress Louise Brooks or the fictional film character Mia Wallace in the 1994 Quentin Tarantino film, *Pulp Fiction*, this airport angel cuts a dramatic figure in which the bob-cut represents the culminating point of a logic that has been identified elsewhere as 'loungification' (O'Doherty, 2017). Her name is Edie, and she is my first entrance into the world of the crinicultural, teaching me how to navigate its hirsutal ways. As we speak, soft lounge music plays on the PA system, 'Sailing' by the soft-funk band, Land, Air and Blaze – 'Sailing on a trip to your heart, sailing every secret little part, Sailing to the sky that is free, fireworks exploding across the sea, the clocks on the wall set free'. The passengers are being transported in more ways than one, the acoustic space and experiential atmosphere programmed with the help of playlist algorithms. Edie smiles, but almost imperceptibly, and her eyes look right through me. Perhaps we are being invited to dance. This is the Escape Lounge, after all, and we have been encouraged to think that anything is possible and to dwell in 'duty-free' (Gottdiener, 2001; Pascoe, 2001). Most business and management studies will find it unusual, if not a little transgressive, vesting so much attention and descriptive practice to body and appearance. The ethnographer, however, must worry about their possible entanglement in hairs that bind.

The cultivation of the female body and the commodification of private emotions in customer service work has also attracted considerable critical attention from feminists and exponents of critical studies of work (Williams, 2003; McRobbie, 2004; Skeggs, 2005; Wolkowitz, 2006; Barry, 2007; Hancock & Tyler, 2007). Specialists in the study of 'aesthetic labour' (Warhurst et al., 2000; Witz et al., 2003; Hancock & Tyler, 2007; Nickson & Korczynski, 2009) and 'emotional labour' and who follow in the wake of Hochschild's seminal work (Hochschild, 1983; Bolton, 2000; Bolton & Boyd, 2003; Korczynski, 2003; Williams, 2003; Brook, 2009) would have little trouble explaining the politics at work in the possible play of sexual allure, innuendo and promise performed in the lounge. Marked by a strong moral foundation, this work makes short shrift of what is at stake politically in the way sense is made of the lounge and, on its basis, the experiences that can be articulated. McRobbie's (2004) study of the popular television makeover program *What Not To Wear*, for example, explains how women are subjected to class forms of prejudice, and indeed violence, in how they are made to understand and present their bodies.

In an effort to avoid the application of these ready-to-hand concepts and to suspend the reassurance that comes with the deployment of such grand-sounding concepts as 'neo-liberalism', 'capitalism', or 'society' – deemed to act behind the backs of the actors – I decided to avoid this work – to forget it if I could – and focus my attention on the immediacy of the bob-cut. Instead of providing an empirical instantiation of an already known 'political economy', I wondered whether a myopic focus on the bob-cut might shift our analytical perception and open up gaps or holes in this thing we call political economy. Might this myopia help make new connections and relations available for inspection and description, changing what is foreground and background, or relevant or irrelevant, part and whole, even opening up 'text' that wasn't housed or determined by a more encompassing 'con- text' (see also Cooper & Fox, 1990)? Either that macro context where the machinations of society and political economy make their determinations, or the micro context of agency where some fixed interior subjective will acts out its freedom and autonomy. These structure/agent and macro/micro-oppositions carve up the world into the familiar 'empirical' domain of discrete entities and bounded objects (Chia, 1996), but they reduce our appreciation of contingency and change. By elevating the bob-cut to the centre of my analysis, might we bring into focus a more elaborate configuration of connections and relations than would be possible with too much *a priori* theoretical knowing? Might we be able to detect agential becomings unique to the difference made by the hirsutal? Such a strategy might then help extend or multiply the points where vulnerability and contingency might be found in organization and thereby help *politicize* a far greater range of phenomena, at least insofar as we can seize upon the ways in which collectives can be formed around objects and practices.

Bringing the Bob-Cut to Life

'It's important, though, isn't it . . . how you dress for work . . . ?' Edie asks me. She goes on to explain how management had designed a 'grooming training' programme which had involved the appointment of fashion consultants and hair designers. It was unclear whether she was telling me this because she was offended by the presumption that she needed 'grooming training' or whether the efforts to train style were somehow doomed to failure. Experts in grooming were employed to help the newly appointed lounge staff think about the way visual impressions are important in creating the right experience for the loungers. Lounge staff were variously styled and trained in how to dress their hair, and how to deploy these stylistic resources to help create the right 'customer experience' in the lounge. The customer is perhaps made to feel clever, for example, if they can see the reference to Louise Brooks or Mia Wallace in Tarantino's *Pulp Fiction*.

From where comes the fashion for bob-cuts? We do not know. We do know that Vidal Sassoon was an early pioneer, inspired by the elevation and 'impossible' suspensions of Bauhaus architecture. Some argue it was the Parisian couturier Antoine who first shaped the bob-cut, whilst others point to the depictions in ancient art of Cleopatra and Joan of Arc (Cox & Widdows, 2005; McMurtrie, 2010). If we don't know its origins, where is it going? And what might be its effects? Again, we cannot be certain. 'Fashion is evolution without destination', according to Agnes Brooks Young, writing in 1937. Without obvious destination or origin, we can only follow the weaves of the bob-cut where we find we have to consider a multitude of actors, agencies and materials distributed across long chains of relations and associations: magazines, photographs, new cutting techniques, grooming instruments, digital media, professional style counsellors, couturiers and global supply chains of hair harvesting, purchasers and experts. Here we find a whole range of new expertise and new forms of seemingly obscure and arcane language that gives life to quite remarkable forms of conceptual innovation, all of which feed off and intensify an obsession with hair. We are soon entangled in complex imbroglios of hair matter. The language here speaks of 'shake-age' and 'snags', 'frontals', 'closures', baby hair, flow and lustre where the subtle distinctions that are to be found in the 'tapered swoop bang' versus the 'butchered' bang will be lost on many in management and organization studies.

Consider the work of grooming experts and the practices that have proliferated through contemporary social media with the rise of influencers and YouTube celebrities helping to popularize and 'democratize' the formerly exclusive world of high fashion (Ouellette, 2017; Pinchera & Rinallo, 2021). The sheer quantity of online 'channels' and social media review 'shows' specializing in hairstyling is staggering, marked by an extremely rapid turnover in novelty and originality. In studying these worlds, one is confronted by a potency and runaway dynamic that appears out of control and which Tarlo (2016) has captured in her ethnography of the social practices and global business market for hair products. Each practitioner has to develop difference and distinction at the same time as they are compelled to participate in collectively shared understandings and conversations. This distinction is achieved by way of developing intricately fine nuances and differences; but what they all share is a highly cultivated and attuned discursive and aesthetic discrimination characterized by infinite invention, borrowings, appropriations and reappropriations.

'Malibu Dollface' is a celebrity in these worlds. Actually, Malibu Dollface is part character, part YouTube channel. The person (should we still want to hold onto these familiar categories in this digitally mediated world) behind Malibu Dollface appears to be someone called Bejean Horowitz, who plies their trade as couturier and hair-maker. Their review of an 'Isee Hair' (a hair merchant brand) bob is particularly instructive, if we can find ways of engaging with it (Dollface, 2017)! Here, Dollface introduces us to the problems of 'static' and 'tangling' which subdivides in a number of ways including into something that is called 'low-key tangle'; they explain issues around 'shedding', 'blending', the intricacies of 'the bump', bleaching knots, the dangers of 'broom-like properties' and the 'orangey effect'. Elsewhere in their catalogue, Dollface introduces a review with the explanation that today they are 'rocking four bundles', a 'two by twenty-six', a 'twenty-four', and 'an eighteen' (this refers to the length of the woven bunches).

To achieve the bob-cut effect Malibu Dollface is sporting requires an incredibly dense scholarship; part citizen science and part art. Problems of what sounds like the 'pouff up' (only spoken) needs to be considered when shaping a bob-cut, for example; brown rinse is also needed; and careful colouring or bleaching of the front to hide the knot of the weave (which can be manufactured from either lace, silk or a combination, each with their own opportunities and pitfalls). Blending a 'one B with a two and a four' can be noticeable under certain lighting and so one must inspect carefully the various conditions under which you are going to display your hair. One should also consider the necessity of having different hair for different occasions, Dollface explains, sometimes during the same 'event'. One can have a 'red carpet wig', but also a 'performance wig', the transition from public display to private, or transitioning through various degrees of public presence may need its own hair. Malibu Dollface describes the effect they have achieved with their own bob-cut hair as a 'corporate 10 o'clock news': it has 'body', 'it moves' and it is apparently 'sexy'.

The sheer complexity of these practices and preoccupations is bewildering – to the outsider, at least – but part of the appeal and dynamism of these worlds of the bob- cut is precisely their very mutability and eccentricity. The politics is equally fraught and powerful, made complex by virtue of the fact that these practices are enrolled in questions of race, ethnicity, identity and sexuality. For black women, in particular, a monthly hair budget for weaves costs anything from US\$1,500 upwards. The investment of time and money, which often involves partners funding the hair, might strike some as remarkable, especially as in urban black working-class communities it is typically the male partner who is expected (by both men and women) to fulfil their gender role by funding their girlfriend's hair budget. More remarkable still is the fact that men are expressly prohibited from touching their girlfriend's hair, as explored in the 2009 documentary film *Good Hair* by Chris Rock.

Black hair of course becomes an object of incredible political charge as some are accused of seeking to mimic white girl's hair and thereby erasing or silencing the distinctive curl and texture of the Afro, retrieved and celebrated in the black power movement during the 1960s. Similarly in Jewish culture, the sheitel is a complex object that in this case is both seen and not seen, shown and not shown. For many, the ideal is to achieve a sheitel display that precisely reproduces what we might call the natural hair or style of its wearer (Tarlo, 2016). When the wig is removed, one is confronted with a double take, a reveal that is in effect no reveal. Complex and controversial politics in the Jewish community have also been escalated in recent years as some Rabbis have banned the sheitel as idolatrous – brought to light by studies that show the origins of hair in temples where it has been shorn or tonsured as a sacrificial offering.

Back in the Escape Lounge, Edie's bob-cut's shine and lustre does not appear quite so effortless now. Part of this is the complex semiotics inscribed into the bob-cut, all of which carries political charge. It appears both formally sculpted, self-consciously mannered and at the same time an uncomplicated and no-fuss wake up and ready-to-go style that has rapidly become an icon or even a precursor to minimalism. Look again at Edie's hair. Our ethnographic enquiries might of course be rendering us ever more sensitive to its qualities and the work that hairstyle is achieving. You might see that the bob-cut achieves lift but somehow without structure or foundation. This is of course highly appropriate at an airport. It seems to exist in its own wonderful and splendid autonomy, a deus ex machina that might stimulate volumes of hermeneutical exegesis and dialectical analysis. For many, the bob-cut also emancipates, it manages to neuter gender ascription – and in the heyday of the 'flappers' in the 1920s, the bob-cut helped promote a world of queer experimentation and androgyny. Without foundation it is a clever trick, full of feint and disguise, such that one can never be certain how to read its message. Indeed, it plays with meaning, attracting and repelling the (male) gaze. It is far from the violence or subjugation attributed to female fashion by certain critical academics. Indeed, the male gaze will look without return, that is, the bob-cut helps make the gaze aware of itself, staring into mystery, threat and perhaps also nothingness. These are key features of Roach's (2007) analysis of the 'It effect'. However, whilst it might seem that Edie manages her clients with her bob-cut, there are other dangers. One invites a gaze and then has to manage the misunderstandings and mistakes that might follow. In this context it would be a stretch to call the bob emancipatory (even if to gently mock the pretensions of certain 'political' voices in critical management studies), but it would be a mistake to ignore the medium and resource it offers to struggles for power within gender and class relations.

The Becoming Unruly of Hair

These wider forces at work in the bob-cut allow for a certain de-centering of the sovereign political agent we assumed of the terminal projects team and thereby give access to more eccentric movements across organization. As we brush deeper into the material properties of hair, we discover much more disconcerting qualities and more complex politics. Hair requires constant attention and management as it can rapidly get out of control under the influence of its own agential-like attributes. So big a problem in fact that Escape Lounge customers are constantly reminded of the facilities offered by the Be-Relax Spa including manicure, pedicure and massage. The new Cloud Spa in Terminal 2 also provides 'nail, brows, lash and massage treatments'. Consider the urgent and perhaps anxious tone of 'Keela' from England who posts a request for help on the website TripAdvisor prior to her visit to Manchester Airport: 'Is there a hairdresser at Manchester Terminal 1 Airport. I see on the shops it does say adult child men's hairdresser but no link to it. My flight is 1pm but staying overnight in airport hotel so if there was I could do an early Appt [sic] prior to check in for flight Advice and information would be appreciated.' The tone of ever so slight desperation is telling here, but hair is getting out of hand in other ways. Soon after the lounge is opened, management are forced to introduce a code of conduct for lounge users which requires customers to sign a contract that stipulates the right of management 'to refuse admission to any guest/person dressed in a way that might be deemed inappropriate' and that '[b]aseball caps, shorts above the knee and football shirts are not permitted, or any other item of clothing likely to cause offence to other Guests'.

One day the lounge manager subtly invites me to look at a gentleman wearing a Manchester City football top with the name Tevez written on the back. Tevez is sporting a shaved and sculpted low Mohawk that resembles a tyre tread. The lounge manager's eyebrows rise and her lips purse slightly as I return her look to acknowledge I have seen it. Lounge managers are vigilant and minutely attentive to the slightest transgression of dress and behaviour code and maintain a constant behind-the-scenes conversation with each other about various 'guests'. Indeed, the airport can be mapped as an extraordinarily intensive organization of hair which helps explain the aisles of hair products from various gels, mousses, sprays and lacquers through to the specialist magazines catering to the hair market: *Hypehair*, *YourHair*, *Perfect Hair* and *BlondHair*, not to mention all the high-end fashion magazines from *Vogue* to *Cosmopolitan*.

We all know that hair grows of its own accord – and in all directions; it falls out, it thickens, and it thins; it changes colour; it attracts bugs and insects; soaks up sweat and other ambient smells; and in certain environments it dries out or greases up. Throughout the day one's hair is changing. I sit watching someone playing on a Nintendo Wii computer game in the airport lounge. Every thirty seconds or so she adjusts her hair, first stroking her hair up and back towards her left ear lobe, and then thirty seconds later she repeats the manoeuvre, this time moving her hair upwards and towards the right and rear, to loop behind her other ear lobe. She sits down and uses her phone mirror to check her alignments. A brush appears from her baggage as she pulls the hair back into some semblance of order. Again, she adjusts her hair, first stroking her hair up and back towards her left ear lobe, and then thirty seconds later she repeats the manoeuvre, this time moving her hair upwards and towards the right and rear to loop behind her other ear lobe.

With a nod to Heraclitus one might say 'you can never wear the same hair twice'. 'Sometimes when I've had it cut though it just sort of does its own thing' one respondent claimed in a recent study of hairdressing salons (Holmes, 2014, p. 98). 'It seems to have a life all of its own [Sounds of agreement from others]', she concludes (Holmes, 2014, p. 98). It is a recurring motif in the discourse of hairdressing expertise that hair is vested with a will and authority of its own. Pick up any issue of *Vogue* magazine and you will read countless articles addressing issues that invest agency in hair. In another genre we read 'My hair wants to be free, to grow, to play in the ocean just like the rest of me. I consider it a natural community leader: the one on top of the head', as Ginny Jordan writes in her startling account of what is quite clearly a politics involved in the 'journey into her body' following extended chemotherapy treatment (Jordan, 2011, p. 42).

Most beguiling of all perhaps is the fact that hair can also be made to speak, at least if we can lend an ear and cultivate sensitivity to its non-linguistic mode of communication. For some aficionados hair speaks about moods that might otherwise be inchoate or unknown – the ubiquitous bad hair day of course, but also tired-looking, frizzy and frazzled. Hair can also affect work performance. *Newsweek* famously reported in 2010 that in a poll of 212 corporate hiring managers 57 per cent admitted that unattractive people find it more difficult to find work and a further 68 per cent felt that job performance is affected by 'looks'. Hair make-overs are now being recommended for treatment of all kinds of performance inhibition, from lack of confidence to a failure to achieve promotion. Consultant Dan Rust (2014) cites a recent Harvard Business review research study showing that 'bad leaders who were given a new hairstyle (or plugs) saw a 22% to 38% increase in perceived leadership effectiveness over the next 6 months'.

Crinicultural Ontology and the Politics of Regeneration

I begin to see hair is everywhere in the lounge. There are even strands that tangle the Escape Lounge into city hall politics in Manchester. Let me show how hair gets into the cracks at city hall where it is once again seen and not seen, forming part of an ongoing discourse-practice associated with local economic 'regeneration'. Trying to explain this regeneration, a senior officer in Manchester City Council hands me a copy of *Manchester: Shaping the City* (RIBA, 2004), which recounts and celebrates the renaissance of the urban fabric that includes the now iconic architecture of the Northern Quarter, No. 1 Springfields, Urbis, No. 1 Deansgate and Beetham Tower. The airport is part of this city-wide makeover and much of its funding and strategic design is being led by members of the city council. As I flick through the pages of the RIBA publication, I am suddenly struck by the swish of a bob-cut. It leaps out of the opening pages. Two black-suited women, both carrying large leather folio document briefcases, one of whom is modelling a version of Malibu Dollface's 'corporate 10 o'clock news' bob-cut, are caught from behind in a blur of strident animation. Walking purposively towards the glass-towered atrium of the Harvey Nichols store in Manchester, the bob-cut is mirrored and reflected in a cascade of mirrored and abyssal images. It is not the questionable assumptions in the models of economic multiplier effects that attract my attention now but the stylistic resonances of the bob-cut in the sweeping vistas of construction and redevelopment in Manchester (the International Convention Centre, Bridgewater Hall, Hulme Arch Bridge, the City of Manchester Stadium). The photomontage gives the impression of dynamism and energy, of towers soaring, strict verticals and angular horizontals reaching out, cantilevered bridges swooping, suspended over vertiginous heights. And then there are the Deansgate arches. Is it possible they too are bob-cuts (see Figure 8.1)?

All aligned in standing order, it seems the whole city is being made over in the image of the bob-cut, a becoming crinicultural of the city, perhaps, but one suggestive of something bigger, of forces at work here outside the control of the erstwhile politicos trying to spearhead economic regeneration. The much-vaunted creativity of Manchester is being enrolled and leveraged here but in ways that give sustenance to that ancient Greek notion of 'tuchē' (chance, unpredictability) which another bob-cut, this time Cooper (1993), drawing from Heidegger, shows the haunting of modern technology and its assumptions or aspirations of detachment, abstraction and control.

Lurking in these archways, in the folds and weaves of the bob-cut might be found unsavoury adventures and possibilities. Frivolous as it may at first appear, the bob-cut can mobilize and enrol in ways that cannot be contained or controlled and which threaten established values and hierarchies. At the time of its first rise to prominence in the 1920s women sporting bob-cuts were labelled 'flappers', a term which was deployed with opprobrium to describe a new urban cosmopolitan group of women.

Figure 8.1 City centre bob-cuts (photos by author)

Giving voice to the anxieties and prejudices of the time, journalists and novelists preoccupied with contemporary social mores were quick to note that these new urban sophisticates enjoyed a predilection for short skirts and 'listening to jazz', amongst other such foibles that marked them out as indulging in a hedonistic and decadent lifestyle (Malcolmson, 2013). According to some accounts, flappers 'wore excessive make-up, drank hard liquor, smoked cigarettes, drove cars, generally flouted conventional social and sexual norms *and wore Bobs*' (McMurtrie, 2010, p. 414; emphasis added).

Manchester tarries with the danger of this excess and decadence when it enrols and promotes the bob-cut. In the same boosterist publications handed out by members of the economic regeneration unit at Manchester City Council, one can, for example, read noir crime writer Cath Staincliffe (2002, p. 13) who tells us that the much-celebrated makeover of the Northern Quarter takes us to a new boundary: 'Beyond here stretches the northern territories, poor, flat lands running up to the hills of Oldham and Rochdale. The wrong side of the tracks. Northern Quarter – time as this was a sorry place; neglected, low rents, vacant lets. The warren of streets and crumbling buildings offered a whiff of opportunity to entrepreneurs, specialists, idealists, fanatics, desperadoes, collectors, rebels, pioneers. Risky business. Fashionable now. The edge of town, spitting distance. Des Res. Though there's still an edge'.

Staincliffe offers a gentle warning that prompts us to ask what reactions and activisms might be stimulated by this ersatz appropriation of popular culture by Manchester City Council. Twenty years before Brexit and populist political rhetoric, there is menace in these words, their telegraphic style scrying inchoate energies in the fringes of Manchester where fomenting matters of concern find nurture and expression. And what role might the bob-cut play in all this? Poised on the edge of the avant-garde and corporate appropriation, couturier, haute coiffure and impresario, Charlie Le Mindu, offers a possible answer with his sensitivity to the agencies and potencies available when *thinking with hair*. Most famous for his styling of Lady Gaga and Lana Del Rey, Le Mindu sculpts incredible bodies of hair, putting things together in ways that are as shocking today as the juxtaposition of a sewing machine and umbrella was in the heyday of surrealist art. His practices involve a constant 'haptic' immersion in hair, working with his hands in communication with the materiality of hair in ways that are suggestive of a certain 'possession'. Not unusual in theories of creativity (Kaufman & Sternberg, 2021), and since Plato, artistic creativity has been associated with something akin to a 'divine possession' – Le Mindu certainly seems possessed. Often his work borders on the aesthetics of popular science fiction and we might see reference to afro-futurism and other avant-gardes in his designs (Womack, 2013). If 'possessed' – and Le Mindu is widely regarded as obsessive in his work habits – then it would certainly appear to be a possession by otherworldly forces, or maybe we could venture the possibility that he is possessed by hair, that his thinking is a communication with hair?

'What does this hair want to do?', he seems to ask. It is a question that registers something of the event, coming to articulation as the border between the human and hair is transgressed and reconfigured. Following Deleuze (1989, pp. 150–4) on the *fabulation* narratives of ethnographic filmmaker Jean Rouch, we might see the power of the crinicultural as harnessed by Le Mindu as sculpting images of a people yet to come, a rallying call for those today who are otherwise maligned and marginalized as the decadent and effete. In this sense we might say there is a certain *emancipation* of hair in Le Mindu's creations, the designs of which come to 'possess' the wearer, inspiring acts of equal creativity and challenge. He invites us to imagine new forms of human-hair couplings and becomings that extend the power of hair, a 'speculative fabulation' in Haraway's (2011) terms that expands the range of companion species, 'helpers' and other critters that might come to form new kin formations with the human. Le Mindu teases us with the possible dangers of out-of-control hair and conveys the sheer sense of possibility embodied in its potency and unpredictability. Tinged with highlights that also portray a sense of the ridiculous, it is a practice that dares to invest or retrieve latent agency in hair and to harness its animacy and fabulative possibilities. In this regard we might recall the tale told in the *Origo Gentis Langobardorum* (as recorded by Paul the Deacon in the eighth century (see Foulke, 1907) of how the women of Winnili, before a crucial battle with the Vandals, arranged their hair in ways that made it appear as if they had beards. By disguising their gender, this helped create the impression that their army had a greater number of men in battle which helped intimidate the Vandal army and secure their defeat in battle. This became the founding date of the formation of the Lombard people (from the Latin *longabardi*, or long beards). If this tale is to be believed, one wonders what other reserves of strength and power might be roused by the deployment of hair. At the same time that the Winnili tale is one of ingenuity, it is also the tale of a ridiculous and barely credible ruse; but it is often in minor things – the overlooked and eccentric – that brings down the might of armies, and something for which the best management in the world cannot be prepared, but against which it is also renewed and reinvigorated.

Split Ends: Towards a Final Cut

These extensions, angular cuts, weavings and enrolings are possibly the product of an eccentric thinking given licence to roam laterally in association and connection by the hiatus of time that puts a halt to more conventional forms of organization analysis and the era of *progressive* politics that were the conditions of possibility for its emergence. However, the shock to thought caused by the temporal paradoxes associated with the Anthropocene (Chakrabarty, 2009; Latour, 2017) are surely sufficient to persuade many that the assumption of onwards and upwards, of linearity and progress, are well and truly over; or rather, over in the ever-eternal return of the same that brings to the front of stage the *Aion* of time – as Deleuze (1994) understood it. Aion replaces Chronos and installs a chaos of times and temporalities, of simultaneous pasts, presents and futures, opening up a future that has already happened, and a past that we are yet to realize. This is also the Garden of Forking Paths as told by Borges.

In such conditions, conventional forms of democratic politics are beginning to show their limits and the limited forms in which they 'represent' the public are increasingly called into question. Unless we understand the way in which politics is organized and the way in which we are organized politically, there can be little hope of a way out of the current impasse. Organization studies might be considered uniquely placed to re-think politics, unencumbered as it is with the curricula and syllabus that define the study of political science and political theory. At the crossroads of social science and the reinvention of the university through the business school, the discipline escapes the territorial supervision of the master social sciences (O'Doherty & De Cock, 2019). Much quicker to read and seize the radical and subversive lessons taught by eccentric and anarchic thinkers like Foucault, Derrida and Deleuze, with all the attendant dangers that this entails, we are perhaps able to see that the practice of politics and the possibility of its reinvention lies with things like the crinicultural. Coming to terms with the results of the ethnographic research at Manchester Airport, I was forced to entertain a kind of thinking that made hair and its design and performance politically significant, to see it as a means through which alliances and dividing lines were made and power accumulated. These apparent trivialities have their populist appeal, but they also open up other worlds of potentiality and design. A more unstable and unsettling world, no doubt, but one that seizes the openness of a more processual view of organization.

We think and act differently when we think with hair and allow ourselves to admit and acknowledge its agential non-human properties. This is one way in which we achieve greater fidelity to the processual in organization as we face the possible embarrassment of coining a phrase or inventing a concept. In making these moves, establishing the crinicultural in this case, we are also made aware that we are not sovereign over all we survey and are in fact subject to the demands the crinicultural makes of us. At this point we have perhaps arrived at a moment where we are beginning to think or practice a form of *crinicultural organization*, but as a mode of analysis. Returning to 'the bob-cut' we might see its light and lustre now infused with agencies and forces that extend to practices, products and materials that form part of its ongoing production and maintenance. When thought of as a carefully orchestrated performance, placing the bob-cut at the centre of our attention allows organizational analysis to build transversal relations that cut across what might otherwise be deemed to be the all too solid and established realms of politics, economy and society. In so doing we extend our repertoire of objects as we begin to appreciate an extended terrain in which politics is conducted, but also to reimagine the weaving of relations that takes place between those all too easily reified neat back-and-side realms of politics, economy and society. Hair is a generator and differentiator in organization that alerts us to new patterns of difference and repetition that might otherwise remain occluded. From where comes the fashion for bob-cuts? We do not know. Where is it going? And what might be its effects? Again, we cannot be certain.

In this chapter we have followed the weaves of the crinicultural that gave access to a multitude of actors, agencies and materials. We have seen that hair contributes or inflects agency in an extended network of non-human agency and complexly distributed causality and effect. It is an agency missing from management and organization studies and yet it flashes through networks of social media and association in unpredictable and volatile ways, giving rise to new energies and creativity. When the crinicultural strikes it strikes like an event and gives chance to the future. Shaven and left bare by the ravages of such an event we might wonder how we could have been so moved by hair? So acted upon, and enjoined into acting, by the cut of our hair?

As we have followed its cuts and rupture, we have harnessed the forces of becoming in organization that make the future unknowable whilst giving opportunity to – or learning to pay our dues to – raw chance. Without such events the future has already happened; it is utterly predictable, preserved in a space insulated from time as open future. The event can never be finished, only ever renewed. Here, a new alignment of the bob-cut with the arch and its plinth, the cantilevered executive summary that takes leave from its evidential basis and support with the media circulation of a new 'It affect', are brought together to form part of a new mytho-poetic resource for organization, a resource upon which all organization hitherto has depended. Perhaps it is time for new myths and fables, drawing on the relations and practices forming around these emerging energies so that we might sketch out the lineaments of a renewed activism around 'im/possible' organizations of the future: impossible because they keep us thinking and working towards something we suspect might never be fulfilled. Either/or, it must remain for now undecidable.

References

Adler, P. S. (2009). (ed.), *The Oxford Handbook of Sociology and Organization Studies: Classical Foundations*. Oxford: Oxford University Press.

Alvesson, M. & Willmott, H. (1992). *Critical Management Studies*. London: Sage.

Atkinson, P. (2020). *Writing and Reading Ethnography*. London: Sage.

Augé, M. (1995). *Non-places: Introduction to an Anthropology of Supermodernity*. London: Verso.

Augier, M., March, J. G. & Sullivan, B. N. (2005). Notes on the evolution of a research community: Organization studies in Anglophone North America, 1945–2000. *Organization Science, 16*(1), 85–95.

Barnard, M. (2020). *Fashion Theory: A Reader*. Abingdon, UK: Routledge.

Barry, A. (2013). *Material Politics: Disputes Along the Pipeline*. Oxford: Wiley-Blackwell.

178   D. O'Doherty

Barry, K. (2007). *Femininity in Flight: A History of Flight Attendants*. Durham, NC: Duke University Press.

Barthes, R. (1990). *The Fashion System*. Berkeley, CA: University of California Press.

Baudrillard, J. (1970). *The Consumer Society. Myths and Structures*. London: Sage.

Behnke, A. (ed.) (2016). *The International Politics of Fashion: Being Fab in a Dangerous World*. Abingdon, UK: Routledge.

Böhm, S. (2006). *Repositioning Organization Theory: Impossibilities and Strategies*. Basingstoke: Palgrave Macmillan.

Bolton, S. C. (2000). Emotion here, emotion there, emotional organisations everywhere. *Critical Perspectives on Accounting*, *11*(2), 155–71.

Bolton, S. C. & Boyd, C. (2003). Trolley dolly or skilled emotion manager? Moving on from Hochschild's managed heart. *Work, Employment & Society*, *17*(2), 289–308.

Brook, P. (2009). In critical defence of 'emotional labour' refuting Bolton's critique of Hochschild's concept. *Work, Employment & Society*, *23*(3), 531–48.

Bryant, L. R. (2011). The Ethics of the Event: Deleuze and Ethics Without Αρχή. In D. W. Smith and N. Jun (eds), *Deleuze and Ethics* (pp. 21–43). Edinburgh: Edinburgh University Press.

Buchanan, I. (2000). *Deleuzism: Transcendental Empiricist Ethics*. Edinburgh: Edinburgh University Press.

Cabantous, L., Gond, J. P., Harding, N. & Learmonth, M. (2016). Critical essay: Reconsidering critical performativity. *Human Relations*, *69*(2), 197–213.

Campan, M. (2018). *The Memoirs of Marie Antoinette, Queen of France* (Vol. 6). Frankfurt: Outlook Verlag.

Caputo, J. D. (1997). *The Prayers and Tears of Jacques Derrida: Religion without Religion*. Bloomington, IN: Indiana University Press.

Case, P. (1999). Organizational studies in space: Stanislaw Lem and the writing of social science fiction. *Organization*, *6*(4), 649–71.

Chakrabarty, D. (2009). The climate of history: Four theses. *Critical Inquiry*, *35*(2), 197–222.

Chia, R. C. H. (1996). *Organizational Analysis as Deconstructive Practice*. Berlin: Walter de Gruyter.

Chugh, S. & Hancock, P. (2009). Networks of aestheticization: The architecture, artefacts and embodiment of hairdressing salons. *Work, Employment & Society*, *23*(3), 460–76.

Clegg, S. (1990). *Modern Organizations: Organization Studies in the Postmodern World*. London: Sage.

Cooper, R. (1993). Technologies of Representation. In P. Ahonen (ed.), *Tracing the Semiotic Boundaries of Politics* (pp. 279–312). Berlin & New York: Mouton de Gruyter.

Cooper, R. & Fox, S. (1990). The 'texture' of organizing. *Journal of Management Studies*, *27*(6), 575–82.

Costea, B. & Amiridis, K. (2014) Martin Heidegger (1889–1976). In J. Helin, T. Hernes, D. Hjorth & R. Holt (eds), *The Oxford Handbook of Process Philosophy and Organization Studies*. Oxford: Oxford University Press.

Cox, C. & Widdows, L. (2005). *Hair & Fashion*. London: Victoria & Albert Museum.

Craik, J. (2003). *The Face of Fashion: Cultural Studies in Fashion*. Abingdon, UK: Routledge.

Davies, C. J. (2013). *Ethics and the Event in Deleuze, Derrida, and Badiou*. Nashville, TN: Vanderbilt University.

Davis, M. (2017). *Buda's Wagon: A Brief History of the Car Bomb*. London: Verso Books.

De Cock, C. (2000). Essai: Reflections on fiction, representation, and organization studies: An essay with special reference to the work of Jorge Luis Borges. *Organization Studies, 21*(3), 589–609.

De Cock, C. & Land, C. (2006). Organization/literature: Exploring the seam. *Organization Studies, 27*(4), 517–35.

Deleuze, G. (1989). *Cinema 2: The Time-Image*. Trans. H. Tomlinson & R. Galeta. London: Athlone.

Deleuze, G. (1994). *Difference and Repetition*. Trans. P. Patton. London: Athlone.

Deroy, X. & Clegg, S. (2011). When events interact with business ethics. *Organization, 18*(5), 637–53.

Derrida, J. (1994). *Given Time Volume 1: Counterfeit Money*. Trans. P. Kamuf. Chicago: University of Chicago Press.

Derrida, J. (1996). Remarks on Deconstruction and Pragmatism. In S. Critchley & C. Mouffe (eds), *Deconstruction and Pragmatism* (pp. 79–88). London & New York: Routledge.

Dollface, M. (2017). 'ISee Hair (Aliexpress): Brazilian Straight Review'. Available at https://youtube.com/watch?v=-hTrmdzkW10 (last accessed 3rd February 2022).

Du Gay, P. & Vikkelsø, S. (2016). *For Formal Organization: The Past in the Present and Future of Organization Theory*. Oxford: Oxford University Press.

Entwistle, J. (2000). Fashion and the fleshy body: Dress as embodied practice. *Fashion Theory, 4*(3), 323–47.

Foulke, W. D. (1907). *History of the Langobards by Paul the Deacon*. Trans. W. D. Foulke, LL.D. With Explanatory and Critical Notes, a Biography of the Author, and an Account of the Sources of the History. Philadelphia: University of Pennsylvania Press.

Garfinkel, H. (1967). *Studies in Ethnomethodology*. Englewood Cliffs, NJ: Prentice-Hall.

Gottdiener, M. (2001). *Life in the Air: The New Culture of Air Travel*. Lanham, MD: Rowman & Littlefield.

Grey, C. (2005). Critical Management Studies: Towards a More Mature Politics. In D. Howcroft & E. M. Trauth (eds), *Handbook of Critical Information Systems Research: Theory and Application*. Cheltenham: Edward Elgar Publishing.

Hancock, P. & Tyler, M. (2007). Un/doing gender and the aesthetics of organizational performance. *Gender, Work and Organization, 14*(6), 512–33.

Haraway, D. (2011). Speculative fabulations for technoculture's generations: Taking care of unexpected country. *Australian Humanities Review, 50* (5), 1–18.

Hebdige, D. (1979). *Subculture: The Meaning of Style*. New York: Methuen.

Hernes, T. (2014). *A Process Theory of Organization*. Oxford: Oxford University Press.

Hjorth, D., & Holt, R. (eds) (2016). *It's entrepreneurship, not enterprise: Ai Weiwei as entrepreneur*. *Journal of Business Venturing Insights*, 5, 50–54.

Hochschild, A. R. (1983). *The Managed Heart: The Commercialism of Human Feeling*. Berkeley, CA: University of California Press.

Holmes, H. (2014). Chameleon hair: How hair's materiality affects its fashionability. *Critical Studies in Fashion & Beauty*, 5(1), 95–110.

Hussenot, A. & Missonier, S. (2016). Encompassing stability and novelty in organization studies: An events-based approach. *Organization Studies*, 37(4), 523–46.

Islam, G. (2015). Organizational Ritual: Rupture, Repetition, and the Institutional Event. In R. Mir ,H. Wilmott & M. Greenwood (eds), *The Handbook of Philosophy and Organization* (pp. 542–9). London: Routledge.

Jordan, G. (2011). *Clear Cut: One Woman's Journey of Life and in the Body*. New York: Lantern Books.

Kaufman, J. C. & Sternberg, R. J. (eds) (2021). *Creativity: An Introduction*. Cambridge: Cambridge University Press.

King, D. & Land, C. (2018). The democratic rejection of democracy: Performative failure and the limits of critical performativity in an organizational change project. *Human Relations*, 71(11), 1535–57.

Korczynski, M. (2003). Communities of coping: Collective emotional labour in service work. *Organization*, 10(1), 55–79.

Küpers, W. (2015). *Phenomenology of the Embodied Organization: The Contribution of Merleau-Ponty for Organizational Studies and Practice*. Basingstoke, UK: Macmillan.

Land, C. (2005). Apomorphine silence: Cutting-up Burroughs' theory of language and control. *Ephemera: Theory and Politics in Organisation*, 5(3), 450–71.

Langley, A. & Tsoukas, H. (eds) (2016). *The SAGE Handbook of Process Organization Studies*. London: Sage.

Latour, B. (2004). Why has critique run out of steam? From matters of fact to matters of concern. *Critical Inquiry*, 30(2), 225–48.

Latour, B. (2013). *An Inquiry into Modes of Existence: An Anthropology of the Moderns*. Cambridge, MA: Harvard University Press.

Latour, B. (2017). *Facing Gaia: Eight Lectures on the New Climatic Regime*. London: John Wiley & Sons.

Learmonth, M., Harding, N., Gond, J. P. & Cabantous, L. (2016). Moving critical performativity forward. *Human Relations*, 69(2), 251–6.

Lorino, P. (2018). *Pragmatism and Organization Studies*. Oxford: Oxford University Press.

Lyotard, J. F. (1984). *The Postmodern Condition: A Report on Knowledge*. Trans. G. Bennington & B. Massumi. Minneapolis: University of Minnesota Press.

Malcolmson, P. (2013). *Me and My Hair: A Social History*. Luton: Andrews UK.

Marres, N. (2016). *Material Participation: Technology, the Environment and Everyday Publics*. Basingstoke, UK: Springer.

Mauksch, S. (2020). Five Ways of Seeing Events (in Anthropology and Organization Studies). In R. Mir & A.-L. Fayard (eds), *The Routledge Companion to Anthropology and Business* (pp. 357–77). London: Routledge.

McMurtrie, R. J. (2010). Bobbing for power: An exploration into the modality of hair. *Visual Communication, 9*(4), 399–424.

McRobbie, A. (2004). Notes on *What Not To Wear* and post-feminist symbolic violence. *The Sociological Review, 52*(2 suppl.), 97–109.

Nickson, D. & Korczynski, M. (2009). Editorial: Aesthetic labour, emotional labour and masculinity. *Gender, Work & Organization, 16*(3), 291–9.

O'Doherty, D. P. (2007). The question of theoretical excess: Folly and fall in theorizing organization. *Organization, 14*(6), 837–67.

O'Doherty, D. P. (2017). *Reconstructing Organization: The Loungification of Society.* London: Palgrave Macmillan.

O'Doherty, D. P. (2020). The Leviathan of rationality: Using film to develop creativity and imagination in management learning and education. *Academy of Management Learning & Education, 19*(3), 366–84.

O'Doherty, D. P. & De Cock, C. (2019). Rethinking politics in organization. www.cbs.dk/en/research/departments-and-centres/department-of-organiza tion/events/rethinking-politics-in-organization (last accessed 12 March 2021).

O'Doherty, D. P., De Cock, C., Rehn, A. & Ashcraft, K. L. (2013). New sites/ sights: Exploring the white spaces of organization. *Organization Studies, 34*(10), 1427–44.

Ouellette, L. (2017). Dream Jobs? The Glamourisation of Beauty Service Work in Media Culture. In *Aesthetic Labour* (pp. 183–98). London: Palgrave Macmillan.

Parker, M. (2000). The sociology of organizations and the organization of sociology: Some reflections on the making of a division of labour. *The Sociological Review, 48*(1), 124–46.

Parker, M. (2013). What is to be done? CMS as a political party. In V. Malin, J. Murphy & M. Siltaoja (eds), *Getting Things Done* (pp. 165–81). Bingley, UK: Emerald Group Publishing.

Pascoe, D. (2001) *Airspaces.* London: Reaktion Books.

Pinchera, V. & Rinallo, D. (2021). Marketplace icon: The fashion show. *Consumption Markets & Culture, 24*(5), 479–91.

Raffoul, F. (2020). *Thinking the Event.* Bloomington, IN: Indiana University Press.

RIBA (Royal Institute of British Architects). (2004). *Manchester: Shaping the City.* London: RIBA Enterprises.

Roach, J. R. (2007). *It.* Ann Arbor: University of Michigan Press.

Rust, D. (2014). 'The Critical Role of Good Hair in Business Leadership'. Available at: https://linkedin.com/pulse/20140225195519-16076441-the-critical-role-of-good-hair-in-business-leadership.

Sandberg, J., Loacker, B. & Alvesson, M. (2015). *Conceptions of Process in Organization and Management.* Oxford: Oxford University Press.

Saraiva, T. (2016). *Fascist Pigs: Technoscientific Organisms and the History of Fascism (Inside Technology).* Cambridge, MA: MIT Press.

Serres, M. (1995). *Angels: A Modern Myth*. Paris: Flammarion.

Shortt, H. (2012). Identityscapes of a hair salon: Work identities and the value of visual methods. *Sociological Research Online, 17*(2), 22.

Shortt, H. (2015). Liminality, space and the importance of 'transitory dwelling places' at work. *Human Relations, 68*(4), 633–58.

Shortt, H. & Warren, S. (2012). Fringe benefits: Valuing the visual in narratives of hairdressers' identities at work. *Visual Studies, 27*(1), 18–34.

Silverman, D. (2021, March). 'Reflections on the Theory of Organizations (1970)'. Paper presented to Now Then: David Silverman's The Theory of Organisations at 50. Available at: https://youtube.com/watch?v=KgxexlVj2OM. Last accessed July 31, 2021.

Skeggs, B. (2005). The making of class and gender through visualizing moral subject formation. *Sociology, 39*(5), 965–82.

Spicer, A., Alvesson, M. & Kärreman, D. (2009). Critical performativity: The unfinished business of critical management studies. *Human Relations, 62*(4), 537–60.

Staincliffe, C. (2002). Northern Quarter. In J. Chlebik, L. Grant, P. Herrmann & I. Lawson (eds), *The Mancunian Way* (pp. 130–9). Manchester: Clinamen Press.

Tarlo, E. (2016). *Entanglement: The Secret Lives of Hair*. London: Oneworld Publications.

Taussig, M. T. (1992). *The Nervous System*. New York: Routledge.

Taussig, M. T. (1999). *Defacement: Public Secrecy and the Labor of the Negative*. Stanford, CA: Stanford University Press.

Tsoukas, H. & Chia, R. (2002). On organizational becoming: Rethinking organizational change. *Organization Science, 13*(5), 567–82.

Warhurst, C., Nickson, D., Witz, A. & Cullen, A. M. (2000). Aesthetic labour in interactive service work: Some case study evidence from the new Glasgow. *Service Industries Journal, 20*, 1–18.

Williams, C. (2003). Sky service: The demands of emotional labour in the airline industry. *Gender, Work & Organization, 10*(5), 513–50.

Witz, A., Warhurst, C. & Nickson, D. (2003). The labour of aesthetics and the aesthetics of organization. *Organization, 10*(1), 33–54.

Wolkowitz, C. (2006). *Bodies at Work*. London: Sage.

Womack, Y. L. (2013). *Afrofuturism: The World of Black Sci-Fi and Fantasy Culture*. Chicago: Chicago Review Press.

Part III

New Ways of Organizing Work, Digitality and the Politics of Time

9 'Working the Time'
Time Self-Management Practices of Remote Workers

Claire Estagnasié

Introduction

The notions of work and time are, in everyday language, implicitly intertwined. Historically, the association between 'work' (the activity which is supposed to happen at the workplace) and 'work time' (schedules which are supposed to be set in advance by the employer) comes from the Industrial Revolution: the worker went 'to work' by physically going to the factory at certain times of the day. Dennis Mumby (2012) used the term 'clock time' to refer to this temporality, which is a relic of nineteenth and early twentieth-century factories, when employees were closely monitored by hours. Ever since then, workers have been renting their labor force by the hour, or by the day, that is, according to the time spent at work. In this context, the distinction between work and private life is obvious, the two spheres being doubly segmented, both by distinct places, but also by different temporalities. Yet, working remotely represents not only a disruption of the traditional spatiotemporal framework of work (Taskin, 2006) but also a qualitative shift from centralized forms of social organization to a more diffuse, fragmented, and emergent set of social relations (Sewell & Taskin, 2015).

Remote work is not new, but Covid-19 has speeded it up (Ozimek, 2020). In fact, the notion of 'teleworking' appeared in the late 1970s. However, the Covid-19 health crisis in 2020 was an opportunity to experiment with it on a large scale, leading to the continuation of certain practices over time, forty years after Alvin Toffler (1981) predicted that progress in personal computing would lead to a generalization of telework for professionals belonging to the category of 'knowledge workers'. Due to its high flexibility, this alternative working arrangement could develop exponentially, or even become the dominant organizational configuration (Erickson & Norlander, 2022; Popovici & Popovici, 2020). Even before the pandemic, this underlying trend was linked to the spread of high-speed and wireless internet which, together with the growing availability of mobile communication and collaboration tools, fostered the emergence of new forms of work characterized by greater flexibility in terms of places, times, and ways of working (Aroles et al., 2019).

In this chapter, I focus on teleworkers who have chosen this way of working precisely to take advantage of the space–time flexibility offered by remote work. Some of them were full-time remote workers, while others worked remotely part-time. It is important to remember that the term 'remote workers' encompasses a plurality of profiles: some 'work from home' while others 'work from anywhere' (Choudhury et al., 2021). In fact, digital nomads define their lifestyle by their mobility and the primacy given to leisure and travel (Bonneau & Aroles, 2021; Cook, 2020; Reichenberger, 2018). However, according to Thompson (2019), telecommuters (who work from home) appear to be the opposite lifestyle figure of digital nomads (who work from anywhere), because digital nomads use the flexibility of their work modality to be mobile and travel, while teleworkers use it to avoid travel and stay at home. Under the umbrella term of 'remote workers', some are employed while others are freelancers, an important distinction since those in the latter category are more likely to have latitude to arrange their work time. Nevertheless, they all have one thing in common: the difficulty in establishing boundaries between the different spheres of life (Cook, 2020; Thompson, 2019). These fragile boundaries are often invoked as a spatial metaphor, as boundaries separating the inside from the outside of organizations is an instrument to control labor (Fleming & Spicer, 2004). In fact, those boundaries can be embodied in the material arrangements of space (Estagnasié et al., 2022); for example, creating an office space for working, with plants and objects on the dining table. But they are also embodied in the choices of temporalities (early mornings, nights, weekends, fragmented and irregular schedules). Of course, digital nomads or freelancers – who may have chosen this lifestyle in order 'to escape the 9 to 5' (Ferriss, 2009) – can adapt their working schedule more freely than employees whose schedules might be set by their organization.

Contextualization

Since the beginning of the twentieth century, the interweaving between time and work has been considered from a social perspective. Max Weber (1905) studied the relationship to work of workers in Germany in order to understand the differences in productivity, and pointed out that social variables (gender, age, religion, etc.) influence the relationship to time. By collaborating in the preparation of a vast survey in Germany of workers in large-scale industry in 1907, Max Weber (2012) created one of the first breakthroughs in the understanding of the relationship between time and work: that working time and performances are not mechanically linked, since multiple external factors (alcohol, marriage, remuneration) or internal factors (fatigue, sleep, motivation) influence the performance of work (Desmarez & Tripier, 2014). A second rupture has come with information and communication technologies (ICT), as workflows can nowadays be detached from the workers' location. In some cases, the work hours performed remotely remain the same as those in the office, but generally, the remote context allows for a dissociation of the work activity from a rigid schedule. We are thus witnessing a fundamental break in the spatiotemporal framework of work which was previously structured around the notions of space and time (Taskin, 2006; Taskin et al., 2017). Work performed on a fixed schedule, at the firm's place (Kalleberg et al., 2000, p. 257) is an idea that no longer reflects the current reality of work. Technological change in a wide range of occupations has effectively changed workers' perceptions of space and time. Once-stable notions of how to conduct oneself in familiar social settings, such as industrial plants, can no longer be taken for granted as the line separating work from other aspects of human experience.

Thus, remote workers are likely to experience tensions between the temporalities of work and personal life. That is why Sewell and Taskin (2015) proposed the concept of *spatiotemporal scaling* which has (1) a physical component, (2) an experiential component, and (3) a temporal component. This concept invites us to take space and time seriously and explore the demands placed on employees who are neither exclusively tied to traditional work arrangements nor exclusively 'at home' but find themselves divided between the personal and professional scales.

Problematization: 'Working the Time' to Dedicate Time to Work

This research is rooted in a context of new ways of working (Ajzen et al., 2015; Aroles et al., 2021a, 2021b; Taskin et al., 2017) and spread of remote work which encourages us to renew our conception of the spatio-temporal frameworks of work. The temporal dimension of remote work has been less explored in the literature (Ancona et al., 2001; Colley et al., 2012; Gherardi & Strati, 1988; Hamilakis & Labanyi, 2008; Holt & Johnsen, 2019) than the spatial one (Clegg & Kornberger, 2006; de Vaujany & Mitev, 2013; Massey, 2005; Tyler & Cohen, 2010; Van Marrewijk & Yanow, 2010), even if there is a growing interest for the importance of time and temporalities in organizational literature (Hernes et al., 2013; Reinecke et al., 2020; Shipp & Jansen, 2021; Winch & Sergeeva, 2021). That is why this chapter aims to contribute to time work as a way of working organizational boundaries. How could we better understand the practices of remote workers in relation to the (re)creation of times dedicated to work?

In this chapter, I adopt a sociomaterial approach to time, which considers that a temporality of work is never simply 'there', as a container in which 'things' happen. On the contrary, time and the people who (inter) act with it, influence and constitute each other. Since the late 1990s, organizational studies have been marked by several shifts, including a (re) turn to materiality (Dale, 2005; Orlikowski, 2000; Pickering, 1995), a processual conception of organization (Chia, 1995; Chia & King, 1998; Van de Ven & Poole, 1995), and a renewed focus on the practices that constitute the frameworks of collective action (Schatzki et al., 2001). Far from opposing each other, these scholarly communities are in dialogue and share common orientations. Thus, the organization is seen as a heterogeneous phenomenon made of actors and artifacts, as a situated phenomenon, in continuous movement, which results from and constrains at the same time the collective action (Hussenot et al., 2016). According to a processual ontology (Bouty, 2017; Hussenot, 2016; Hussenot et al., 2019; Langley et al., 2013; Langley & Tsoukas, 2016), the organization is considered as a perpetual movement constituted by the relations between material and social elements that compose it and are themselves constituted by it. With this in mind, the clock-time orientation is linked to a Western organizational mentality, characterized by a linear, clock-time orientation optimized to enhance efficiency, coordination, and control, whereas processual approaches of temporalities are more associated with Eastern thought (Reinecke & Ansari, 2015). According to this processual thought, Reinecke and Ansari suggested an agentic view of time, when time is used as a cultural resource. In this vein, the two authors presented the concept of *ambitemporality* to explain how organizations accommodate seemingly contradictory temporal orientations. An ambitemporal approach proposes to recognize plural temporalities and explicitly articulate temporal pressures. This concept is thus useful to understand the relationship between organizational temporalities and the worker's private ones.

It is interesting to see that 'work organization' could both refer to the state of the division of labor structure or the action of defining this structure, with an inherent tension and movement between both, that Alter (2003) called 'dyschronies'. In the case of remote work, there could also be dyschronies between the division of labor structure, traditionally based on a 9-to-5 model, and the action of remote workers dealing with their own professional and personal time management. That is why I suggest that remote workers create their workspace by *working the time*. This expression refers to the actions carried out on the initiative of individuals to dedicate time to work – for example, blocking time in a calendar – and is inspired by the concept of 'making time' suggested by Martin Hand (2020). 'Making time' consists of 'everyday adjustment, coping and management of temporal demands' (Hand, 2020, p. 85), for which individuals are responsible, in a context of porosities of work and home (Gregg, 2014). While 'making time' could be applied to all types of activities, *working the time* only applies to work activities. In proposing this concept, I want to emphasize that *working the time* requires additional work on top of the primary work activities. Without these individual practices, the work may simply not take place, or, on the contrary, take up all available time.

To explore this phenomenon, I conducted an exploratory qualitative study in Montreal with seventeen remote workers who were already working remotely before the Covid-19 pandemic. The data has been examined in the light of the sociomateriality literature focussing on organizational practices (Beyes & Steyaert, 2012; Vásquez, 2016), in a context of digitalization (Orlikowski & Scott, 2016). First, I review the concept of temporal structuring and show its application to better situating the *working the time* phenomenon. Then, the research methods are presented followed by an overview of the different practices of remote workers that aim at (re)creating work time. Finally, I will discuss the possible consequences of *working the time*, both at the individual and collective level.

A Different Perspective on Time: Temporal Structuring

There is already an extended literature dealing with the boundaries between professional and personal life among remote workers, whether it is in management (Bourdeau et al., 2019; Eddleston & Mulki, 2017; Mulki et al., 2009; Ollier-Malaterre et al., 2019), in psychology (Gillet et al., 2021; Şentürk et al., 2021; Shirmohammadi et al., 2022; Sullivan, 2012), or in communication (Enel et al., 2019; Estagnasié et al., 2022). There is even a whole research field known as work-family balance literature (Alfanza, 2020; Como et al., 2021; Magni et al., 2020; Ollier-Malaterre, 2009; Ollier-Malaterre et al., 2013; Palumbo, 2020; Spagnoli et al., 2021), also dealing with the specific case of remote workers. Boundaries at/of work are often viewed under the premise of the power-laden nature of spatiality: management control the labor that is done within the workplace (Fleming & Spicer, 2004). Nevertheless, in the case of remote work, we are witnessing a shift in the control of workers from the place of work to the temporalities of work.

That is why the question of temporalities matters so much in remote working. Twenty years ago, Orlikowski and Yates (2002) suggested the notion of *temporal structuring* as a way of understanding and studying time as an enacted phenomenon within organizations. In doing so, they followed the *organizational time* conceptualized by Gherardi and Strati (1988) who consider that time is involved in intra-organizational dynamics in relation to other times. By this concept, the authors refer to times within each individual organization, as opposed to the temporal limits that mark out each aspect of the organization with objective and external units of time (such as the reduction of work time, shift work, time allocation in strategic choices). According to this view, time is not a 'container' anymore (1988, p. 149). Instead, organizational time is a twofold concept, where (1) the internal, particular time of the individual organizational process or event is distinct from objective, external time, and (2) the time involved in intra-organizational dynamics is multifaceted, since it stands in relation to other times, which presumes the plurality of time (Gherardi & Strati, 1988, p. 150).

Orlikowski and Yates's main idea is that through their everyday actions, actors (re)produce a variety of temporal structures which in turn shape the temporal rhythm and form of their ongoing practices. This view is a way to bridge the so-called objective time of 'clock time' (which would exist independently of human actions), and subjective time (the one that is experienced through interpretative processes as events, routines, or cycles). For the authors, a practice-based perspective on time invites us to consider it as constituted by and constituting human actions: time is viewed as realized through people's recurrent practices that (re)produce temporal structures, which are both the medium and outcomes of those practices. It is also considering time in practice, which means time by its use, and not objective (clock time, *chronos*) or subjective time (event time, *kairos*). Consequently, actors enact, explicitly or implicitly, renew or modify temporal structures in their practices. Hussenot et al. (2020) make the same distinction between an objective ontology of time and a subjective ontology of temporalities.

Most management models continue to be optimized for economic efficiency driven by linear 'quantitative' time and clock-based structures, which shapes people's temporal practices, for example, deadlines, inventory systems, or fiscal year (Reinecke & Ansari, 2015). That is why the concept of *temporal structuring* has not only contributed to management literature in general (Ancona et al., 2001; O'Leary & Cummings, 2007), but has also been featured in the literature on work-life boundary management (Rothbard et al., 2005). Time is a fundamental building block of our life as human and social beings, and, by extension, the organization is the organization of time itself (Becker & Messner, 2013).

Time is then inherently social, which implies, according to a sociomaterial lens based on a relational ontology, that time is inherently material too.

The concept of *temporal structuring* has also been used in research focussing on time management (Claessens et al., 2007), sociology (Colley et al., 2012), and organizational studies (Kahrau & Maedche, 2013; Winch & Sergeeva, 2021). For example, Winch and Sergeeva (2021) used this concept to show a narrative perspective on a project and move beyond the binary perspective on objective versus subjective time. Drawing on the organization of a project, they identified three different kinds of temporal work in project organizing: convincing oneself, convincing the team, and convincing stakeholders. On their side, Kahrau and Maedche (2013) identified three main goals pursued by knowledge workers performing individual time management practices: remembering tasks, deciding what to do next, and maintaining a well-organized workplace. They noted fourteen different practices of time management, all of them implying human and non-human agencies. The two authors also found that the practices were highly interrelated, each having an influence on the next, with any change in one practice having an impact on another. In this chapter, we build on this research by proposing a larger sample of respondents, relying on interviews with seventeen remote workers (instead of only five in Kahrau and Maedche's study), who are also knowledge workers, but with different employment modalities (freelancers, employees, entrepreneurs) and different mobility lifestyles (digital nomads, home-based teleworkers, workers in third places). Our study also considers the impact of the pandemic, in a context of rapid digitalization (Barrett & Orlikowski, 2021).

Research Design: Understanding How Remote Workers 'Work the Time'

Between May 2020 and April 2021, I conducted seventeen semi-structured interviews with different types of remote workers (part-time and full-time remote workers in a brick-and-mortar company, employees in full remote companies, full remote CEOs, freelancers, and digital nomads) who consider Montreal (Quebec, Canada) as their home port. All of them worked remotely (at least occasionally) before the pandemic: being remote was an individual choice which was not forced by the company or the health context (although in some cases the pandemic reinforced these working arrangements). The interviews lasted around ninety minutes each and were all recorded and manually transcribed.

They were conducted virtually using the Zoom video conferencing software, except for two, which were conducted at the respondents' home, between the first and second waves of the pandemic. Far from being a disadvantage for the data collection, the remote setting allowed for experimentation with other methods. For example, I asked my respondents to show me around their homes via webcam or to share screenshots of their digital calendars. The context of confinement was conducive to the creation of a bond of trust with me as a researcher, despite the distance, as the respondents were generally enthusiastic about sharing their working conditions and practices. I kept in contact with most of the respondents during the pandemic, and they sometimes updated me if their work practices were impacted by a new event, related or not to the pandemic (childbirth, moving to another place, a new work project, etc.), which allows a better understanding of personal temporal reflexivity (Reinecke & Ansari, 2015). Even though they had all worked remotely before the pandemic, the lockdown impacted their routines. In fact, their remote working experiences were all disrupted by the presence of other people in the household (for example Audrey, Rahul, or Alice), by all collaborators going online (Jeanne or Mark), by the lack of hybridity (Johnny), or by the closure of third places for those who were used to working remotely from there (Rosa, Arthur, or Kathleen). In any case, during the pandemic, the home became a contested space with multiple meanings, and in which competing interests played out. Whereas previously, telecommuters worked from home to have more focus in their tasks (Mark, Audrey, Stephan), Covid-19 highlights the liminal spaces of the home, that is, 'somewhere that is on the "border," a space somewhere between front and back – such as restrooms, hallways, stairs, and corners, are frequently used by workers' (Shortt & Izak, 2020, p. 46) (see Table 9.1).

In terms of analysis, I first performed a manual thematic coding of the data collected in an open and inductive manner, inspired by a grounded theory approach (Glaser & Strauss, 1967). This included the coding of emerging themes linked to the temporalities of their work, but also the practices and lived experiences associated with them. This allowed me to identify a common pattern shared by most of my respondents, who have developed specific practices to arrange the space-time(s) dedicated to work. That means that all of them are expected to be proactive in the (re)creation of a temporality suitable for work: whether it is an implicit requirement of their employer in the case of employees, or an unconsciously integrated responsibility for others.

Table 9.1 *Individuals participating in the study*

	Pseudonym	Age	Occupation	Comments
#1	Jeanne	32	Analyst	Remy's colleague
#2	Remy	25	Computer forensics specialist	Jeanne's colleague and Jean-François' son
#3	Rosa	34	Journalist	Full-time employee but accepts additional freelance work
#4	Mark	32	Project manager	Works in the public sector
#5	Jean-François	55	Product director	Remy's father
#6	Audrey	33	Accounting system consultant	Employee of an officeless company; Stephan's colleague
#7	Stephan	45	Professional services manager	Employee of an officeless company; Audrey's colleague
#8	Arthur	56	General manager	Cofounder of the company
#9	Paloma	28	Scenarist	Freelancer
#10	Charbel	35	Creative director	Works from home; the company has no offices
#11	Rahul	32	Aerospace engineer	Entrepreneur
#12	Kathleen	26	Corporate translator	Digital nomad
#13	Mary	36	Business coach	Entrepreneur; considers herself 'location independent'
#14	Samy	30	Social media manager	Part-time employed worker and self-employed at the same time
#15	Alice	33	Photographer	Freelancer
#16	Charlotte	48	Marketing and sales strategist	Employed in a metallurgic company which offers 'work from anywhere programs' for its white-collar employees
#17	Johnny	50	Visual effects artist	Freelancer

An Overview of the Temporal Practices of Remote Workers

The data analysis identified three main types of temporal practices of remote workers. First, 'blocking time' refers to the practices of segmenting time into 'blocks of time' and/or a fixed schedule. Despite the attempt to separate work time from personal time, remote workers more often find themselves transitioning between these types of activities, which we refer to as 'navigating' practices. Finally, the third type of practice concerns the 'ritualization' of certain types of temporalities through which individuals give meaning to their private and professional time.

Blocking Time

Being able to work from other space-time is a frequent demand among remote workers, especially among digital nomads and freelancers. As all my interviewees chose to work remotely *before* the pandemic, at least on an occasional basis, they are more likely to be favorable, *a priori*, to non-traditional temporalities. Mary, who is a freelance business coach and defines herself as 'location independent', admitted she chose this way of life to escape the famous '9 to 5' evoked in Tim Ferriss' (2009) best-seller, and to manage her time freely.

My main motivation is the freedom to manage my schedule, so that I can leave room in my life for something other than work – be it travel, personal projects, art, or family. Basically, I wanted to be able to travel more often. Also, the traditional corporate world didn't suit me because I work fast, and I hated having to stay from 8 a.m. to 5 p.m. – which in the advertising world was 8 a.m. to 8 p.m. (Mary)[1]

Flexibility and Adjustments   Some teleworkers tried to stick to a fixed schedule, but all our interviewees admit they adjust it according to their energy level, or to the unexpected events of the day. For example, Jean-François, who has been teleworking for twenty years, is usually an early bird, but keeps some flexibility in his schedule.

The hours are not really fixed. I try to start around 7 a.m. in the morning to be able to finish earlier in the afternoon, but if one morning . . . I'm at an age where we get up more crooked than others . . . If I started at 9 a.m., so as not to finish later in the day, I'll take just 15 minutes of lunch, then finish at the same time. (Jean-François)   .

In a society dominated by knowledge work, working from different temporalities often means being connected to work at other times than regular office hours. Of course, it has always been possible to work at times other than traditional office hours; for example, scholars who write late at night or early in the morning (because they don't have any other free time to do so). What is changing nowadays is the continuous access to emails and collaborative platforms, an access made materially possible by smart mobile phones, the use of which is quasi-essential to remote

---

[1] All the interviews were conducted in French or French Quebecois and then freely translated in English for the purpose of this chapter, except the one with Rahul which was directly recorded in English.

workers and increased in the pandemic (Shortt & Izak, 2020). While some teleworkers respect the same working hours as in the office, most respondents choose different temporalities for working remotely. For example, Rahul, an aerospace engineer and entrepreneur, is more efficient in the evening, and works several times a week between 10 p.m. and midnight, when his girlfriend goes to sleep. He admits also working during weekends, around three or four hours a day. Sometimes, he 'gives himself a full day off to recharge'. Rahul needs to 'plan' actively not to work, so he can rest.

Stephan, who has worked remotely since 2007, and has been with an officeless company since 2014, organizes his work tasks according to the times most favorable to his own performance. He concedes that teleworking requires an 'entrepreneurial side', because you are responsible for managing your own time, to 'adapt to your personal performance cycle'.

Away from the Norm ... But Always Referring to It Charbel, a creative director, explains he chooses to work remotely because he feels 'away from the norm', away 'from the classic metro/work/sleep'.

When I work remotely, I feel at a distance from the normal ... To wake up every day, take the subway, the train, or your car, then go to work. At a distance from everyday life. I think that the distance theoretically speaking, it's really at a distance from life, I think from the habit and routine, which is the norm. (Charbel)

While he praises the merits of the choice of remote working temporalities, he works every day from '9 to 5', which surprised me. Because he has internalized the norm, Charbel is inspired by the idea he has of a traditional office work time. That is why he structures his work activities while working remotely, even if he could do differently. Kathleen, who is a corporate translator and digital nomad, also admits working according to traditional office hours, even if she has chosen this way of life for more flexibility.

When I asked them to tell me about yesterday, all participants described yesterday (or another day of their choice) as a succession of events. For example, Audrey, an employee of an officeless company, looked at her electronic agenda and chose to tell me about last Friday. She listed the activities which were written on it, as a 'to do list' (make this call, finish this report, go to that meeting). She was relying on events which were materially scripted in the digital agenda instead of relying on her memory, as her workday was defined by the addition of micro times dedicated to work. Audrey reported her work tasks and her so-called 'social duties' (having lunch with a friend) in the same way. She said she asked for a day off to help her friend who had just given birth to a baby, which she considers to be a 'friendly duty', but she answered the professional calls that day anyway, despite the baby crying in the background. Social 'tasks', whether professional or personal, are managed by blocks of time in an electronic calendar. They are interrelated, or sometimes overlapping, as the Google Calendar function allows it. Within this logic, the next type of practice is the ability to navigate from one 'time block' to another.

Navigating

Audrey is not the only one mixing professional and personal 'tasks' in her agenda. Mary does the same: when I asked her about yesterday, she coldly listed orally what she wrote in her agenda, which was a mix of personal growth activities, work tasks, and personal leisure.

So yesterday . . . 6:30 a.m.: I did my morning routine: meditation, reading, sport. 10 a.m.: I had a call with a client. 12 p.m.: I had another call with a partner to create an online course. 1 p.m.: call with a client again. 3 p.m.: I had a call with a potential freelance writer. Between 4 and 6 p.m.: content writing for social networks. 7 p.m.: end of my workday. (Mary)

What is particularly interesting about Mary's example is that it is not just work that is temporalized, but all her day-to-day activities. A lot of Mary's personal time is dedicated to activities that could increase her performance (sport, reading, meditating, etc.). It is therefore difficult to clarify what she considers to be working or not. The differentiation of times according to their nature is perhaps not even relevant according to this entrepreneur.

Defining What Work Is In fact, for many people working remotely, especially for those who are self-employed, it is not only a question of demarcating work time from private time, but first of determining whether the activity performed represents work or not. Sometimes, this distinction is hard to establish, especially for creative workers (Estagnasié, 2022). Rosa, a journalist, uses the criteria of being paid (or not) to determine if the activity is work or leisure.

I'm really on this quest to balance work with my private time, but it's hard to talk about because my spare time, if you know what I mean, is also writing. If I read a book, is that work? I must be paid extra to know if it is, for example, to write a review afterwards. In fact, work is really the thing that you must do something or else they don't pay you. You really must show that you've done something, so that you'll pay your rent . . . . (Rosa)

It is the same for Alice, who admits that she doesn't 'see the point of getting nothing out of a given time', and at the same time admits that this conception is in tension with her anti-capitalist political convictions.

My free time must be profitable. I don't necessarily mean in financial terms, but it must be used for something. Even when I see friends, I like to feel like I'm having an interesting discussion, that I'm getting something out of it that will feed my creativity. Even if I am convinced that boredom is useful [for creativity] and that I was brought up in this logic, today I have the impression [I take] an approach where I don't have much time. It's a bit contradictory. (Alice)

So, *working the time* would then not only consist of creating time dedicated to work outside the walls of a classical organization, but also in determining what are working activities, non-working activities, and a hybrid of both. This questioning and its implementation are the responsibility of the worker.

Collapsing   Alice confesses that even when she was on vacation in Greece with her lover, she thought about how each moment spent could ultimately be useful for her creative photography work afterwards. Here, we can see there is a temporal tension between work and private time: they are collapsing. There are also 'dead times' within the set work schedules. Considering time as 'dead' or, on the contrary, as time 'put to good use' are other ways of reconfiguring the time/space of work and leisure. In any case, there is always more interconnection than separation between these temporalities.

Audrey only records 'actual' work on her time sheet and does not include the calls she makes for private business. However, she does answer her work calls when she takes a day off to visit her friend who has just given birth. It is the same for Remy, who is afraid that if the projects he has been assigned have taken too long to complete, he would be seen as doing a bad job.

I must report my actual hours working on a tracking tool. I don't cheat, because if it looks like it's taking too long, they'll [the management] think I really suck at my job! (Remy)

In this case, time is part of the internalized control. Rosa has a different conception of it, because as a senior journalist, she has more autonomy in her tasks.

We procrastinate a lot, during the day, we have moments of emptiness, but instead of looking at my screen, I look in detail at what's going on around me, or I feed myself a little bit . . . and that's important I think, for the mind. I've never liked working in an office, within four walls, it's not my thing. I need to get some fresh air, in the alley, maybe come back . . . that's part of the job. (Rosa)

Idealizing Their Time Management   Remote workers tend to be idealistic about how they see the way they manage their working time. Like Mary, Rosa admits navigating between work and private times. She did not want to tell me about the day before, Tuesday, but preferred to tell me about the current day. As we met during the lunch break, she told me about her morning and about what she had planned to do in the afternoon, so in the future! A future which she may consider as a perfect idea of what 'work' should be: efficient, limited in time to allow some free time – but always professional. But in real life, personal and work temporalities often collapse in a messy way.

After our meeting, I have plenty of messages that I'm not looking at: and so, I'm going to respond, on Slack only. And I must read two articles from Lise and [I have] a video to put online, and after that the day will be over, because I finish at 5 p.m. But in real life, I often go downstairs and have a drink with our neighbors who are our buddies. We play with my daughter, but often in the evening when she goes to bed, I take some things back for myself, I check that I haven't forgotten anything. That's why I tell you that a day doesn't really end before 9 p.m. (Rosa)

Rosa and her partner coordinate their time slots to care for their child, return to their work tasks, spend time together, return to emails, chat with the neighbors, and so on. Not only does Rosa navigate all day long between her professional and personal time, but this navigation is so unconsciously integrated that she and her spouse have ritualized it.

Ritualizing

Materialization   Some of the respondents I met tried to use rituals for delimiting barriers between personal and professional times, but in the end, mixed all of them. Jean-François, a remote worker for more than twenty years, wears a hat while working, to show his children he is not available, but often forgets to remove it when he is having dinner. This practice is inherently material (the hat) and social (the practice toward the children) at the same time. Audrey has a hammock and a 'relax' pillow in her home office (but often works on it overnight on her stressful job as a consultant). Charbel likes to be near his plants while working, while Stephan moves places in his home to follow the daylight to send himself 'signals it is time to work'. For all of them, objects or other beings are associated with different temporalities, or at least different practices of temporal arrangements. Food can also do the trick. For example, Remy has placed a small basket of chocolates next to his writing space, and he associates these treats with a sense of success and well-being at work.

It's to congratulate me, it's my motivation: when I'm working on the big days, I'm allowed to take one! (laughing). (Remy)

Mediation   Using media in the ritualization of working time is a strategy employed by the majority of those interviewed. Most respondents admitted connecting to work emails first thing in the morning, as a ritual that tells them that the (work)day is starting.

I wake up early in the morning. I have my phone next to me, and I start by opening emails and checking if I need to get up for something urgent. (Samy)

Since checking email is often the first thing you do in the morning, it loses its symbolic value as the beginning of the working day, since it is the beginning of the day itself.

Before I got out of bed, I started looking at my cell phone . . . I checked my email and answered two work messages . . . and then I took my shower and had my breakfast. (Alice)

In the same way, closing one's laptop is a material and symbolic gesture that can indicate the end of the working day. Same for Remy, who does not check his emails at night – at least not on his laptop. Digital devices could symbolically be used for different tasks than emails. Remy explained that he uses the alarm to remind himself to take a break.

My routine is an alarm that goes off every day of the week at noon to remind me to get up and go for a walk . . . Because sometimes I can get really wrapped up in what I'm doing, I don't see the time going by at all . . . and then I forget to get up, and that's bad for my health. (Remy)

Other media can be used to delineate temporalities. When not working from home, many respondents say they consume media in a ritualized way before and after work. Charlotte says that in her previous job where she worked with people face-to-face, she listened to music in the car on the way to work. Jeanne prefers to listen to podcasts on the subway. When she works from home, she still uses media before starting to work, but in a different way.

In the morning, I listened to news podcasts, and in the evening, I juggled between five types of podcasts. I stopped listening to the news podcast completely since I work from home, but instead I read the newspapers every morning, on their websites. (Jeanne)

Some practices for delimiting work time involve digital objects, whether for checking emails, for disconnecting, or for putting oneself in a work state of mind. Thus, attempting to create a work time involves practice with material and symbolic dimensions simultaneously. Moreover, it implies different agencies, such as objects, different spaces, other people in the household, or other type of beings (some remote workers associate their 'work mode' with the presence of a pet or plants).

Discussion: 'Working the Time' to Work Anytime...

Remote workers seem to be new kinds of sailors. They tend to separate temporalities into 'blocks of time', which are materially scripted on an agenda or an electronic device, then navigate between them, often collapsing them, and finally, try to find their compass by establishing daily rituals. The navigation metaphor is interesting, since according to a relational ontology of organization (Orlikowski, 2010; Orlikowski & Scott, 2008), work is not a fixed entity, neither physical nor temporal, but a process where the material and the social are entangled and in constant redefinition. Consequently, work practices are intrinsically sociomaterial (Feldman & Orlikowski, 2011; Gherardi, 2016), implying human and other-than human agencies (Kahrau & Maedche, 2013). The social and the material of those practices are seen as inextricably linked, all social being material, and all material being social, since the agencies at the basis of these phenomena have become so saturated with each other that the boundaries that once delimited them have dissolved (Orlikowski, 2007). That is why it is not relevant to ask which structuring temporal practices are material, rather than symbolic or embodied, since, by definition, every sociomaterial practice carries all these dimensions. For example, Remy's practice of using chocolate as a reward shows that material, symbolic, and sensitive dimensions are inextricably linked. Remy also set an alarm to remind him to take a break; the sound of the alarm clock is symbolically associated with a new temporality, that of the beginning of rest time. Its practice was conceived, in an ironic way, in opposition to the commonly accepted social function of an alarm clock, that of going to work. It is thus natural in practice that the social and the material intertwine, here by creating thematic temporalities, by *working the time*. Using the same logic, Audrey has a (material) hammock in her office which reminds her that she has chosen to work remotely, and this comes with advantages and (social) consequences. The function of the hammock could only be understood in Audrey's practice of having time to work and time to disconnect from work, even if she often mixes them.

So, matter does time (Barad, 2013), and this materiality appears in the objects of daily organizational life. Whether it is when Mary looks at what has been materially written in her calendar, whether it is with digital technologies (Samy's or Alice's smartphone, or Remy's alarm), presenting material characteristics, or with other objects (cushions, hammocks, hats, etc.) or food, *working the time* has an inherently material dimension.

However, this material aspect is inseparable from the social norms that are associated with it. The digital practices of connection represent a relevant example illustrating which professional norms are associated with connecting to one's professional emails with the material object of the laptop, the smartphone, or the tablet – or not. The representations of work, and more broadly of working time, are symbolic with material and social aspects. Charbel or Kathleen want to escape certain representations associated with work (transport, for example) but have integrated the norms to such an extent that they reproduce, from a distance, the idea they have of a traditional work setting and work schedule. Audrey uses a hammock in her home office, symbolically recreating the practice of vacations, as a foil to the constraint that work represents, even at a distance. In any case, remote workers are all proactive in the (re)creation of temporalities to work, because without it, work would not just happen by itself. The analysis highlighted three different practices of *working the time*, but what is even more relevant is the entanglement between them: blocking time is often interwoven with the practice of ritualization, as it could be a routine to 'block time'. Moreover, there is a part of ritualization that navigates between times (as the way Rosa and her spouse both manage to work while taking care of their child), which was supposed to have previously blocked time for the different temporalities of life.

... But Still into the Clock Time

Like social structures in general (Giddens, 1984), temporal structures simultaneously constrain and enable (Orlikowski & Yates, 2002). With the notion of *temporal structuring*, Orlikowski and Yates emphasize the human role in shaping, as well as being shaped by, time. As noted by these two authors (2002), there is a fundamental dichotomy between objective time (clock time) and a subjective perspective on time, based on experiences and events. By trying to fill in blocks of time in their diaries, or by catching up in the evening on the two hours not worked in the afternoon to pick up the children from school, remote workers still adopt an 'objective' vision of time, based on clock time, even if they think they adopt a subjective one. As shown previously in the example of Mary or Rosa, there is a certain idealization in the way remote workers consider they manage their time. That is why, at the individual level, all the people interviewed seemed to have internalized the norm of time at work (efficient, professional time, a certain number of hours). The only thing that changes is the way in which this time is organized. This is where a practical view of the notion of time as a temporal structuring could be useful. Time at work is still time at work – and it is the one that takes up the most 'space' in their calendar. Even if remote workers freely organize their tasks, they do it in blocks, fitting these blocks into a linear conception of time – that of clock time. As Dennis Mumby (2012) pointed out, 'clock time' originated during the Industrial Revolution. The transition from task time to clock time can be explained by the introduction of hourly rather than piecework wages for workers. Thus, the notion of temporality switched from task time to linear clock time, but this is socially and historically constructed.

A Meta-Work to Create a Time Suitable for Work

In fact, most remote workers, who do not have business hours fixed by the company, need to proactively create spaces-times dedicated to work. In doing so, they are *working the time*, first to manage their work, but second and more importantly to avoid overwork, which could have consequences for their mental health and work/life balance. It recalls the concept of 'meta-work', which, according to Salzman and Palen (2004) is defined as 'the work that enables work'. In a recent article, Aroles et al. (2022) explore the meta-work performed by digital nomads. Although our interviewees are not all digital nomads, the concept of meta-work is useful to understand how their practices aim to produce 'the work of making work go well' (Gerson, 2008, p. 196). Previous research in computer supported cooperative work (CSCW) and in sociology of work had identified three main meta-work practices through the identification of mobilization work (activities performed to assemble the resources required to complete a task), configuration work (activities that make systems operate), and articulation work (the activities required to manage the distributed nature of cooperative work). Aroles et al. (2022) added to it 'transition work', which encapsulates all the different activities needed to deal with work fragmentation across different temporalities and spatialities. In their article, the three authors explain how digital nomads must adapt their schedules to the needs of their clients/collaborators, even if it means working at night due to jetlag. Not only do these workers have to constantly readjust their time to meet the different demands of their different employers, but they remain highly dependent on the timelines imposed by their clients. It is the same for different kinds of remote workers, even those who are employed full-time by a unique company. They are responsible for creating a time suitable for work.

Temporal Tensions

There are inherent tensions between organizational life, linear and clock time (deadlines, projects, etc.), and the reality of life (complex, always emergent, messy), which could be better understood with a processual view of temporalities, as suggested by Reinecke and Ansari (2015) and their concept of *ambitemporality*. As shown in the example of Alice working remotely while on vacation in Greece, or Rosa, who needs to have the feeling of not working while she is in a coffee shop (even if she is doing so), we thus noticed temporal tensions in remote workers' practices. For them, labeling temporalities as 'work' or 'personal time' is difficult. In the 1990s, Nowotny (1992) drew on Martins' (1974) works on 'thematic temporalism' to suggest the existence of 'pluritemporalism', which related to the existence of a plurality of different modes of social time(s) which may exist side by side, and yet are to be distinguished from the time of physics or that of biology. In this view, work and personal time are two types of different social times, as different types of actions may shape them. According to Nowotny (1992, p. 429) pluritemporalism asserts the existence of social time next to physical (or biological) time while posting different 'modes' of time. *Working the time* in remote work thus requires an additional practice to that of blocking time, navigating between times, and ritualizing times, or even an interweaving between the three. Before these practices can be implemented, another 'metapractice' (a practice that enables the other work practices) is needed: that of *labeling times*. Labeling temporalities as being work or personal time, or indeed, having difficulty doing so (like Alice, Rosa, or Mary), is characteristic of the new world of work for remote workers: a quest for a new relationship between work and time, which leads to fragmented times with blurred boundaries, which is subject to tensions for individuals (Aroles et al., 2021b).

With the rise of the remote work phenomenon, we have the feeling that the organization of time (whether work or personal) is freer and task-based, but in the end, the 'created' temporalities end up fitting into the predominantly used clock time at organizational (and society-wide) level. Moreover, remote work is the 'spearhead' of the new ways of working (Ajzen, 2021, p. 207), characterized by an apparent and increased autonomy in the ways of living and working, but also with more surveillance and control based on the subjectivity of workers (de Vaujany et al., 2021). Therefore, at the collective level, following a single concept of time organization – that of clock time – is necessarily part of a political model, that of capitalism, from which it is difficult to deviate even when one wants to do things differently (Del Fa, 2019). Thus, remote workers have an individual responsibility to create adequate time to work, which is an additional meta-work on top of other work tasks. Often, they are tempted to organize this time in a processual way, based on tasks and events, but are inevitably caught up in the social and organizational norm of clock time. This makes meta-work somewhat paradoxical and even more difficult.

Conclusion

Rooting into a processual ontology of time, on sociomaterial literature and an epistemology of practice, this chapter has proposed the concept of *working the time* as a sociomaterial practice of remote workers. Working hours are no longer a given element of the organization, but rather a process constituted by the entanglement of workers' practices, both social and material. Although employers and their own practices are part of this organizational entanglement, *working the time* seems to be mostly carried by workers. *Working the time* would thus be a meta-work making work possible, or more precisely, a type of 'transition work' (Aroles & al., 2022) between temporalities constituting it and being constituted by it. Recognizing the existence of this meta-work calls for an ethical and political awareness on the part of organizations, as they consider this extra work to rest on the shoulders of workers.

Due to its exploratory nature, this research remains limited. Adopting a practice-based perspective involves getting up close and personal with workers' activities: an ethnographic approach would be useful to extend this research when the pandemic context fully allows it. In doing so, future researchers could study the place of the body in these *working the time* practices. Bodies have a center part in contemporaneous organizational studies, maybe more than ever, which is why an affective ethnography drawing on a sociomaterial lens could be an interesting avenue for future research (Gherardi, 2019).

References

Ajzen, M. (2021). From De-materialization to Re-materialization: A Social Dynamics Approach to New Ways of Working. In N. Mitev, J. Aroles, K. A. Stephenson & J. Malaurent (eds), *New Ways of Working: Organizations and Organizing in the Digital Age* (pp. 205–33). London: Palgrave Macmillan.

Ajzen, M., Donis, C. & Taskin, L. (2015). Kaléidoscope des Nouvelles Formes d'Organisation du Travail: L'instrumentalisation stupide d'un idéal collaboratif et démocratique. *Gestion 2000, 32*(3), 125–47.

Alfanza, M. T. (2020). Telecommuting intensity in the context of COVID-19 pandemic: Job performance and work-life balance. *Economics and Business, 35*(1), 107–16.

Alter, N. (2003). Mouvement et dyschronies dans les organisations. *L'Année Sociologique, 53*(2), 489–514.

Ancona, D. G., Okhuysen, G. A. & Perlow, L. A. (2001). Taking time to integrate temporal research. *Academy of Management Review, 26*(4), 512–29.

Aroles, J., Bonneau, C. & Bhankaraully, S. (2022). Conceptualising 'meta-work' in the context of continuous, global mobility: The case of digital nomadism. *Work, Employment and Society.* https://doi.org/10.1177/09500170211069797

Aroles, J., De Vaujany, F-X. & Dale, K. (2021a). *Experiencing the New World of Work*. Cambridge: Cambridge University Press.

Aroles, J., De Vaujany, F-X. & Dale, K. (2021b). *Conclusion: Experiences of Continuity and Change in the New World of Work*. Cambridge: Cambridge University Press.

Aroles, J., Mitev, N. & de Vaujany, F-X. (2019). Mapping themes in the study of new work practices. *New Technology, Work and Employment, 34*(3), 285–99.

Barad, K. (2013). Ma(r)king Time: Material Entanglements and Re-memberings: Cutting Together Apart. In P. R. Carlile, D. Nicolini, A. Langley & H. Tsoukas (eds), *How Matter Matters* (pp. 16–31). Oxford: Oxford University Press.

Barrett, M. & Orlikowski, W. (2021). Scale matters: Doing practice-based studies of contemporary digital phenomena. *MIS Quarterly, 45*(1), 467–72.

Becker, S. D. & Messner, M. (2013). Management control as temporal structuring. *Managing in Dynamic Business Environments*. https://doi.org/10.4337/9781782544531.00015

Beyes, T. & Steyaert, C. (2012). Spacing organization: Non-representational theory and performing organizational space. *Organization, 19*(1), 45–61.

Bonneau, C. & Aroles, J. (2021). *Digital Nomads: A New Form of Leisure Class?* Cambridge: Cambridge University Press.

Bourdeau, S., Ollier-Malaterre, A. & Houlfort, N. (2019).Not all work-life policies are created equal: Career consequences of using enabling versus enclosing work-life policies. *Academy of Management Review, 44*(1), 172–93.

Bouty, I. (2017). Robert Chia: Approches processuelles et pratiques en management, une ontologie alternative. In S. C. Petit (ed.), *Les Grands Auteurs en Management* (pp. 268–80). Caen: EMS Editions.

Chia, R. (1995). From modern to postmodern organizational analysis. *Organization Studies, 16*(4), 579–604.

Chia, R. & King, I. W. (1998). The organizational structuring of novelty. *Organization, 5*(4), 461–78.

Choudhury, P., Foroughi, C. & Larson, B. (2021). Work-from-anywhere: The productivity effects of geographic flexibility. *Strategic Management Journal, 42*(4), 655–83.

Claessens, B. J. C., van Eerde, W., Rutte, C. G. & Roe, R. A. (2007). A review of the time management literature. *Personnel Review, 36*(2), 255–76.

Clegg, S. R. & Kornberger, M. (eds) (2006). *Space, Organizations and Management Theory* (Vol. 17). Copenhagen: Liber & Copenhagen Business School Press.

Colley, H., Henriksson, L., Niemeyer, B. & Seddon, T. (2012). Competing time orders in human service work: Towards a politics of time. *Time & Society, 21*(3), 371–94.

Como, R., Hambley, L. & Domene, J. (2021). An exploration of work-life wellness and remote work during and beyond COVID-19. *Canadian Journal of Career Development, 20*(1), 46–56.

Cook, D. (2020). The freedom trap: Digital nomads and the use of disciplining practices to manage work/leisure boundaries. *Information Technology & Tourism, 22*(3), 355–90.

Dale, K. (2005). Building a social materiality: Spatial and embodied politics in organizational control. *Organization, 12*(5), 649–78.

De Vaujany, F-X., Leclercq-Vandelannoitte, A., Munro, I., Nama, Y. & Holt, R. (2021). Control and surveillance in work practice: Cultivating paradox in 'new' modes of organizing. *Organization Studies, 42*(5), 675–95.

De Vaujany, F-X. & Mitev, N. (2013). Introduction: Space in Organizations and Sociomateriality. In F-X. de Vaujany & N. Mitev (eds), *Materiality and Space: Organizations, Artefacts and Practices* (pp. 1–21). London: Palgrave Macmillan.

Del Fa, S. (2019). Ce que différer veut dire: Absences, présences et processus de différenciation dans deux universités alternatives. (PhD thesis). Montréal: Université du Québec à Montréal.

Desmarez, P. & Tripier, P. (2014). Travail et santé dans la sociologie industrielle de Max Weber. *La nouvelle revue du travail*, 4. https://doi.org/10.4000/nrt.1678

Eddleston, K. A. & Mulki, J. (2017). Toward understanding remote workers' management of work–family boundaries: The complexity of workplace embeddedness. *Group & Organization Management, 42*(3), 346–87.

Enel, L., Millerand, F. & Aurousseau, C. (2019). Comment penser le pouvoir d'agir dans un contexte de travail médiatisé et à distance? *Terminal. Technologie de l'information, culture & société*, 125–6.

Erickson, C. L. & Norlander, P. (2022). How the past of outsourcing and offshoring is the future of post-pandemic remote work: A typology, a model and a review. *Industrial Relations Journal, 53*(1), 71-89.

Estagnasié, C. (2022). 'Nourrir' sa créativité malgré la distance: Le métatravail ambivalent des métiers créatifs à l'ère de la covid-19. *Commposite, 22*(2), 88–121.

Estagnasié, C., Bonneau, C., Vasquez, C. & Vayre, É. (2022). (Re)creating the Inhabited Workspace: Rematerialization Practices of Remote Work. In É. Vayre (ed.), *Digitalization of Work, New Spaces and New Working Times*. London: ISTE.

Feldman, M. S. & Orlikowski, W. J. (2011). Theorizing practice and practicing theory. *Organization Science, 22*(5), 1240–53.

Ferriss, T. (2009). *The 4-Hour Workweek: Escape 9–5, Live Anywhere, and Join the New Rich*. New York: Harmony.

Fleming, P. & Spicer, A. (2004). 'You can checkout anytime, but you can never leave': Spatial boundaries in a high commitment organization. *Human Relations, 57*(1), 75–94.

Gerson, E. (2008). Reach, Bracket, and the Limits of Rationalized Coordination: Some Challenges for CSCW. In M. Ackerman, C. Halverson, T. Erickson & W. Kellogg (eds), *Resources, Co-Evolution and Artifacts* (pp. 193–220). London: Springer.

Gherardi, S. (2016). Sociomateriality in Posthuman Practice Theory. In A. Hui, T. Schatzki & E. Shove (eds), *The Nexus of Practices: Connections, Constellations, Practitioners* (pp. 50–63). London & New York: Routledge.

Gherardi, S. (2019). Theorizing affective ethnography for organization studies. *Organization, 26*(6), 741–60.

Gherardi, S. & Strati, A. (1988). The temporal dimension in organizational studies. *Organization Studies, 9*(2), 149–64.

Giddens, A. (ed.) (1984). Elements of the Theory of Structuration. In *The Constitution of Society: Outline of the Theory of Structure* (pp. 1–40). Berkeley, CA: University of California Press.

Gillet, N., Huyghebaert-Zouaghi, T., Austin, S., Fernet, C. & Morin, A. J. (2021). Remote working: A double-edged sword for workers' personal and professional well-being. *Journal of Management & Organization*, 27(6), 1060–82.

Glaser, B. G. & Strauss, A. L. (1967). *The Discovery of Grounded Theory: Strategies for Qualitative Research*. Chicago: Aldine Publishing Company.

Gregg, M. (2014). Presence Bleed: Performing Professionalism Online. In M. Banks, R. Gill, & S. Taylor (eds), *Theorizing Cultural Work: Labour, Continuity and Change in the Cultural and Creative Industries* (pp. 136–48). London: Routledge.

Hamilakis, Y. & Labanyi, J. (2008). Introduction: Time, materiality, and the work of memory. *History & Memory*, 20(2), 5–17.

Hand, M. (2020). Making Time, Configuring Life: Smartphone Synchronization and Temporal Orchestration. In A. Kaun, C. Pentzold & C. Lohmeier (eds), *Making Time for Digital Lives: Beyond Chronotopia* (pp. 85–102). London: Rowman & Littlefield Publishers.

Hernes, T., Simpson, B. & Soderlund, J. (2013). Managing and temporality. *Scandinavian Journal of Management*, 29(1), 1–6.

Holt, R. & Johnsen, R. (2019). Time and organization studies. *Organization Studies*, 40(10), 1557–72.

Hussenot, A. (2016). Introduction au tournant processuel. In F-X. de Vaujany, A. Hussenot & J. F. Chanlat (eds), *Théories des organisations, nouveaux tournants* (pp. 261–78). Paris: Economica.

Hussenot, A., Bouty, I. & Hernes, T. (2019). Suivre et retranscrire l'organisation à partir des approches processuelles. In L. Garreau & P. Romelaer (eds), *Méthodes de recherche qualitatives innovantes* (pp. 125–44). Paris: Economica.

Hussenot, A., De Vaujany, F-X. & Chanlat, J-F. (2016). Introduction: Changements socio-économiques et théories des organisations. In F-X. de Vaujany, A. Hussenot & J-F. Chanlat (eds), *Théories des organisations: Nouveaux tournants* (pp. 11–21). Paris: Economica.

Hussenot, A., Hernes, T. & Bouty, I. (2020). Studying organization from the perspective of the ontology of temporality. In J. Reinecke, R. Suddaby, A. Langley & H. Tsoukas (eds), *Time, Temporality, and History in Process Organization Studies*, (pp. 50–66). Oxford: Oxford University Press.

Kahrau, F. & Maedche, A. (2013). Knowledge Workers' Time Management as Sociomaterial Practice. ECIS Completed Research. 195. http://aisel.aisnet.org/ecis2013_cr/195

Kalleberg, A. L., Reskin, B. F. & Hudson, K. (2000). Bad jobs in America: Standard and nonstandard employment relations and job quality in the United States. *American Sociological Review*, 65(2), 256–78.

Langley, A. N. N., Smallman, C., Tsoukas, H. & Van de Ven, A. H. (2013). Process studies of change in organization and management: Unveiling temporality, activity, and flow. *Academy of Management Journal*, 56(1), 1–13.

Langley, A. & Tsoukas, H. (2016). *The SAGE Handbook of Process Organization Studies*. Thousand Oaks, CA: Sage.

Magni, F., Tang, G., Manzoni, B. & Caporarello, L. (2020). Can family-to-work enrichment decrease anxiety and benefit daily effectiveness in remote workers? The unlocking effect of work-life balance. OB Plenary Spotlight Rapid Research Plenary (Covid19 and Organizational Behavior), *11, 2021*.

Martins, H. (1974). Time and theory in sociology. In J. Rex (ed.), *Approaches to Sociology* (pp. 246–94). London: Routledge & Kegan Paul.

Massey, D. (2005). *For Space*. Thousand Oaks, CA: Sage.

Mulki, J. P., Bardhi, F., Lassk, F. G. & Nanavaty-Dahl, J. (2009). Set up remote workers to thrive. *MIT Sloan Management Review, 51*(1), 63.

Mumby, D. K. (2012). *Organizational Communication: A Critical Approach*. Sage.

Nowotny, H. (1992). Time and social theory: Towards a social theory of time. *Time & Society, 1*(3), 421–54.

O'Leary, M. B. & Cummings, J. N. (2007). The spatial, temporal, and configurational characteristics of geographic dispersion in teams. *MIS Quarterly, 31*(3), 433–52.

Ollier-Malaterre, A. (2009). Télétravail, horaires flexibles, crèches et projets humanitaires: Quand la nouvelle organisation du travail brouille les frontières. *Personnel*, (499), 76.

Ollier-Malaterre, A., Jacobs, J. A. & Rothbard, N. P. (2019). Technology, work, and family: Digital cultural capital and boundary management. *Annual Review of Sociology, 45*(1), 425–47.

Ollier-Malaterre, A., Valcour, M., Den Dulk, L. & Kossek, E. E. (2013). Theorizing national context to develop comparative work–life research: A review and research agenda. *European Management Journal, 31*(5), 433–47.

Orlikowski, W. J. (2000). Using technology and constituting structures: A practice lens for studying technology in organizations. *Organization Science, 11*(4), 404–28.

Orlikowski, W. J. (2007). Sociomaterial practices: Exploring technology at work. *Organization Studies, 28*(9), 1435–48.

Orlikowski, W. J. (2010). Sociomateriality of organisational life: Considering technology in management research. *Cambridge Journal of Economics, 34*(1).

Orlikowski, W. J. & Scott, S. V. (2008). Sociomateriality: Challenging the separation of technology, work and organization. *Academy of Management Annals, 2*(1), 433–74.

Orlikowski, W. J. & Scott, S. V. (2016). Digital work: A research agenda. In B. Czarniawska (ed.), *A Research Agenda for Management and Organization Studies* (pp. 88–96). Cheltenham: Edward Elgar Publishing.

Orlikowski, W. J. & Yates, J. (2002). It's about time: Temporal structuring in organizations. *Organization Science, 13*(6), 684–700.

Ozimek, A. (2020). The future of remote work. Available at: https://content-static.upwork.com/blog/uploads/sites/6/2020/05/26131624/Upwork_Economi stReport_FWR_052020.pdf.

Palumbo, R. (2020). Let me go to the office! An investigation into the side effects of working from home on work-life balance. *International Journal of Public Sector Management, 33*(6/7), 771–90.

Pickering, A. (1995). *The Mangle of Practice: Time, Agency, and Science*. Chicago: University of Chicago Press.

Popovici, V. & Popovici, A-L. (2020). Remote work revolution: Current opportunities and challenges for organizations. *Ovidius University Annals Economic Sciences Series, 20,* 468–72.

Reichenberger, I. (2018). Digital nomads: A quest for holistic freedom in work and leisure. *Annals of Leisure Research, 21*(3), 364–80.

Reinecke, J. & Ansari, S. (2015). When times collide: Temporal brokerage at the intersection of markets and developments. *Academy of Management Journal, 58* (2), 618–48.

Reinecke, J., Suddaby, R., Langley, A. & Tsoukas, H. (2020). *Time, Temporality, and History in Process Organization Studies.* Oxford: Oxford University Press.

Rothbard, N. P., Phillips, K. W. & Dumas, T. L. (2005). Managing multiple roles: Work-family policies and individuals' desires for segmentation. *Organization Science, 16*(3), 243–58.

Salzman, M. & Palen, L. (2004). The tools we live by: A description of personal support media in work life. *Computer Science Technical Reports CU-CS-981,* 4, 1-10.

Schatzki, T. R., Knorr-Cetina, K. & Von Savigny, E. (2001). *The Practice Turn in Contemporary Theory.* London: Routledge.

Şentürk, E., Sağaltıcı, E., Geniş, B. & Günday Toker, Ö. (2021). Predictors of depression, anxiety and stress among remote workers during the COVID-19 pandemic. *Work, 70*(1), 41–51.

Sewell, G. & Taskin, L. (2015). Out of sight, out of mind in a new world of work? Autonomy, control, and spatiotemporal scaling in telework. *Organization Studies, 36*(11), 1507–29.

Shipp, A. J. & Jansen, K. J. (2021). The 'other' time: A review of the subjective experience of time in organizations. *Academy of Management Annals, 15*(1), 299–334.

Shirmohammadi, M., Au, W. C. & Beigi, M. (2022). Remote work and work-life balance: Lessons learned from the covid-19 pandemic and suggestions for HRD practitioners. *Human Resource Development International, 25*(2), 163–81.

Shortt, H. & Izak, M. (2020). The Contested Home. In M. Parker (ed.), *Life After Covid-19: The Other Side of Crisis* (pp. 43–52). Bristol: Bristol University Press.

Spagnoli, P., Manuti, A., Buono, C. & Ghislieri, C. (2021). The good, the bad and the blend: The strategic role of the 'middle leadership' in work-family/life dynamics during remote working. *Behavioral Sciences, 11*(8), 112.

Sullivan, C. (2012). Remote Working and Work-Life Balance. In N. P. Reilly, M. J. Sirgy & C. A. Gorman (eds), *Work and Quality of Life* (pp. 275–90). Dordrecht: Springer.

Taskin, L. (2006). Télétravail: Les enjeux de la déspatialisation pour le management humain. Revue Interventions économiques. *Papers in Political Economy,* 34.

Taskin, L., Ajzen, M. & Donis, C. (2017). New Ways of Working: From Smart to Shared Power. In *Redefining Management* (pp. 65–79). London: Springer.

Thompson, B. Y. (2019). The Digital Nomad Lifestyle: (Remote) Work/Leisure Balance, Privilege, and Constructed Community. *International Journal of the Sociology of Leisure, 2*(1), 27–42.

Toffler, A. (1981). *The Third Wave.* New York: Bantam Books.

Tyler, M. & Cohen, L. (2010). Spaces that matter: Gender performativity and organizational space. *Organization Studies, 31*(2), 175–98.

Van de Ven, A. H. & Poole, M. S. (1995). Explaining development and change in organizations. *Academy of Management Review, 20*(3), 510–40.

Van Marrewijk, A. & Yanow, D. (2010). Introduction: The Spatial Turn in Organizational Studies. In *Organizational Spaces: Rematerializing the Workaday World*. Cheltenham: Edward Elgar Publishing.

Vásquez, C. (2016). A spatial grammar of organizing: Studying the communicative constitution of organizational spaces. *Communication Research and Practice, 2*(3), 351–77.

Weber, M. (1905). *L'éthique protestante et l'esprit du capitalisme*. Paris: Plon.

Weber, M. (2012). *Sur le travail industriel*. Trans. P-L. van Berg. Belgium: Editions de l'Université de Bruxelles.

Winch, G. M. & Sergeeva, N. (2021). Temporal structuring in project organizing: A narrative perspective. *International Journal of Project Management, 40*(1), 40–51.

10 Temporal Structures of Telework in Public Sector Organizations

Renata Cherém de Araújo Pereira and André Carlos Busanelli De Aquino

Introduction

The recent fast and intense growth of telework has focussed mostly on activities previously performed in offices (rather than external services, such as delivery or sales). When implementing telework transfer, organizational routines move from offices to the domestic setting of home offices, or alternatively to collaborative spaces. It reorganizes work outside organizations, transforming how people organize their tasks and duties during a working day, and introducing tensions between work and daily life. It potentially reorganizes work boundaries, spaces and temporal structures.

Telework is a modality of work that occurs outside the company facilities; for instance at home, and not necessarily during business hours (Claessens et al., 2009; Orhan, 2017). As the work occurs in different spaces and is not constrained by the temporal frame of normal business hours, different elements play a role in coordinating work, such as deadlines and control over the time-log system when working (Kim et al., 2021).

Organizational life is made of temporal structures which organize action, such as reporting performance, frequency of meetings and deadlines for projects. Temporal structures are social constructions of time which bring understanding, coordination and guidance to people in their ordinary life (Orlikowski & Yates, 2002; Reinecke & Ansari, 2015; Rowell et al., 2016) (e.g., rhythms, deadlines and cycles of behavior). Similarly, temporal structures organize life at home. However, the temporal structures of professional routines which originated in organizations may not be compatible with temporal structures at home.

Telework is a partially organized social setting, as the work is transferred to alternative working spaces (Blagoev et al., 2019). Despite new forms of teleworkers emerging – digital nomads, freelancers, digital entrepreneurs – here we focus on the more traditional form of telework, when employees work remotely but are subject to the rules of their employer. In such non-traditional office spaces, organizations establish communication platforms in which there is a temporary interactional setting (Dacin et al., 2019; de Vaujany & Vaast, 2014). An office setting has a specific set of rules or guidelines about "who can participate ... how people shall behave ... ways to monitor others' behavior [and] ... how to issue positive or negative sanctions" (Ahrne & Brunsson, 2019, p. 4). When telework is implemented, new organizing features synchronize employees, projects and tasks through work policies, deadlines, working hours and task delegation. For instance, in a public sector organization, back-office activities (e.g., tax collection registering) may be run by government accountants working from home, connected through a communication platform or information system. The platform and work policies are organizing entities, partly carrying the institutions from the organizational setting or the offices in which the activities were previously executed.

Some positive expectations about telework relate to cost reduction and productivity gains (Aguilera et al., 2016; Bailey, 2019; Caillier, 2012; Kitou & Horvath, 2003; Martinez et al., 2007; Pyöriä, 2011), flexible working hours and spending more time with family members (Aguilera et al., 2016; Baines & Gelder, 2003; Caillier, 2012; Kossek et al., 2015; Martin & MacDonnell, 2012; Peters et al., 2014; Suh & Lee, 2015; Vega et al., 2015; Vihalemm & Harro-Loit, 2019). However, empirical studies have also pointed out the existing pressures on workers living in populated households from mothers caring for their young children and inadequate facilities to single households complaining of the solitude of working alone from home.

In this chapter our aim is to understand how the temporal structures (from office and from home) accommodate workers and what eventual contradictions emerge when the work moves from a regular office to a home office regime. As a telework program or regime is implemented, the temporal structures that previously existed in the office are carried over to home telework policies and practices, but new ones are adopted. These temporal structures may collide with those that exist in household routines. Despite positive expectations regarding telework, as new organizing features are adopted to synchronize employees and projects, some conflicting structures can appear. The possibility of performing tasks remotely may require a certain adjustment to temporal structures, especially if the new work context clashes with already established temporal structures (e.g., sharing computers or desks during business hours, childcare commitments).

This chapter looks at civil servants who have freely opted for remote working at home in a pre-pandemic context. Interviews were conducted with thirty-two civil servants from six different public organizations in Brazil who currently carry out their activities in the teleworking modality. The activities carried out are back-office activities without the need for interaction with citizens or the provision of public services. Our interviewees were playing with two types of temporal structures: dealing with pressures to accommodate the multiple temporal structures from their professional setting and those from their family's routines, such as their children's schooling.

In an inductive approach, we classified the activities performed by teleworkers at home as synchronous and asynchronous, and analyzed how their activities were related to their domestic routines. The analysis showed that there are contradictions in how respondents understand and perceive elements of temporality, such as flexibility, pace, duration and waiting.

The findings of this study indicate that the civil servants interviewed were still conditioned by the temporal structures transferred from work previously performed in person in offices. Domestic telework seems to induce in the civil servants a perception of greater time control, but it also indicates three temporal contradictions: they do not have options as to how to allocate their working hours; they are not able to coordinate their work routine in order to assimilate family responsibilities; and finally, they are deeply driven by the rhythm of their work.

Temporal Structures of Telework

Temporal structures are social constructions about time, about how to coordinate our times and synchronize our daily tasks (e.g., rhythms, deadlines, cycles) (Orlikowski & Yates, 2002; Reinecke & Ansari, 2015; Rowell et al., 2016). As Orlikowski & Yates (2002, p. 686) suggest, people regulate, coordinate and account for their activities "through the temporal structures they recurrently enact." The same happens in organizations where employees and supervisors use temporal structures to coordinate actions (Orlikowski & Yates, 2002; Reinecke & Ansari, 2015; Rowell et al., 2016). Temporal structures shape behavior and actions, constrain agency and also influence how actors interpret and interact with time (Orlikowski & Yates, 2002; Reinecke & Ansari, 2015; Rowell et al., 2016). As these temporal structures are reproduced daily, they are reinforced and legitimated in organizational life. Changes in temporal structures may occur due to organizational innovations, as management tools (just-in-time; risk management), by workarounds and adaptations or by cumulative changes in some practices (new measures of work productivity).

Telework is an innovation in traditional work within company facilities, reinterpreting the traditional conventions of work (Sewell, 2012) and introducing changes in temporal structures. It is a modality of work outside the domain of the traditional time–space of offices operating during working hours. The set of tasks is executed, not within company facilities, but at home (Lee, 1999; Lee & Sawyer, 2010;) and sometimes not during working hours, affecting synchronicity (Orhan, 2017) and imposing coordination elements, such as deadlines (Claessens et al., 2009). With telework, individuals accommodate diverse temporal structures (Sennet, 1998; Tietze & Musson, 2002). Such coordination includes task scheduling, using Gantt charts and synchronizing activities (Barley, 1988; McGrath & Kelly, 1986; Moran, 2015; Orlikowski & Yates, 2002; Shipp & Richardson, 2017). The possibility of working in "virtual offices" means more than "getting things done faster" and "working with people in different locations" (Lee & Sawyer, 2010). It is normal for individuals to work long hours, melting the boundaries of the traditional working hours (8 a.m. to 5 p.m. in Brazil).

However, despite the supposed flexibility of telework, control over an employee's performance and behavior (Brocklehurst, 2001; Seweel & Taskin, 2015), social distance and uncertainty bring stress and physiological illness (Bittman, 2004; Kossek et al., 2015; Neufeld & Fang, 2005; Suh & Lee, 2015; Vihalemm & Harro-Loit, 2019). Studies on telework in public sector organizations (e.g., Dzigbede et al., 2020; Schuster et al., 2020) have discussed the benefits (Caillier, 2012; Eom et al., 2016) but have not considered the transference of temporal structures and the associated tensions.

The displacement of work from space-time allows for a set of tasks to be performed remotely during flexible working hours. Therefore, the positive and negative effects of telework are often associated with aspects of temporality (Lee, 1999; Lee & Sawyer, 2010;) such as waiting time and synchronicity (Orhan, 2017).

Telework offers possibilities for managers to redesign temporal rules and to assign meaning to an activity (Bailey, 2019; Lee & Sawyer, 2010; Van Tienoven, 2019). For instance, waiting for the next step in the work process or for the conclusion of a task by another colleague or team is an undesired aspect, but can be redefined as it is a social construction (Bailey, 2019; Van Tienoven, 2019). Another temporal social construction is the pressure to respond, almost instantly, to organizational demands (Skade et al., 2020). Acceleration of work leads individuals to carry out their professional activities in shorter periods of time, looking for faster achievements and deliverables (Rosa, 2013; Skade et al., 2020).

However, the desynchronization of activities between workers in home offices and their office colleagues does not mean that individuals have more freedom (Blue, 2019), although it supposedly allows greater choice when allocating time to daily activities.

Despite individuals being able to establish their routines and times for work (Tietze & Musson, 2002), the observed acceleration of work is increasingly less coordinated by clock time and calendars, and more attached to subjective time as work activities, memories, traumas, historical changes and technology (Mavrofides & Papageorgiou, 2013; Moran, 2015).

Perhaps, in teleworking, the disconnection between the perception of objective time and subjective time is widened (Vihalemm & Harro-Loit, 2019). When working from home, people's professional and personal experiences can overlap (Vihalemm & Harro-Loit, 2019). Individuals may expect to maintain their previous office working hours at home, at the same time they expect to maintain the division between work time and family time. Alternatively, they may benefit from the flexibility of working hours that imply the end of their previous routines (Sennet, 1998; Tietze & Musson, 2002).

Methods

We conducted interviews with thirty-two civil servants from six different Brazilian public sector organizations, working at home between one and seven days per week (these were not digital nomads and were not located in co-working spaces) (Table 10.1). We focus on back-office jobs in which the teleworkers have no interaction with citizens, only with other civil servants (accountants, legal advisors, analysts). The back-office activities are more suited to telework, as they are considered less problematic for remote coordination (Korte & Wynne, 1996; Olson, 1983; Simmons, 1996). In total we recorded and transcribed 1,104 minutes of interviews.

Those organizations adopted a program or regime of telework before the Covid-19 pandemic. Here we use the term telework regime, meaning a telework program implemented to offer benefits to eligible civil servants as a reward for their good performance in a previous performance evaluation. It applies to civil servants who demonstrate a higher level of individual performance in the telework program. In the public sector organizations analyzed, employees may freely opt for teleworking, as they are eligible for the telework regime, being in tenured job positions and maintaining superior job performance compared to their peers.

Table 10.1 *List of interviewees*

State-owned agencies and secretaries	Job position	Gender	Age (years)	Living with	Telework from	Telework days per week	Interview time (minutes)	Type of activity	#
	Analyst (budget & planning)	Female	52	Alone	Jun 2017	2	28	asynchronous	AS1
	Tax agent	Female	38	Husband and daughter	Mar 2017	3	24	asynchronous	AS2
	Analyst (budget & planning)	Male	35	Wife and son	Jan 2019	2	15	asynchronous	AS3
	Analyst (budget & planning)	Male	48	Wife and son	Jul 2018	3	18	asynchronous	AS4
Sao Paulo State Secretariat of Finance and Planning	Analyst (accounting)	Female	42	Husband	Jan 2018	2	21	asynchronous	AS5
	Analyst (accounting)	Female	39	Husband	Apr 2018	2	28	asynchronous	AS6
	Analyst (accounting)	Female	41	Husband and sons	Apr 2018	2	48	asynchronous	AS7
	Analyst (accounting)	Male	52	Wife and two sons	Aug 2018	2	32	asynchronous	AS8
	Analyst (accounting)	Male	46	Wife and daughter	Mar 2019	3	36	asynchronous	AS9
	Analyst (general affairs)	Female	34	Husband and daughter	Sep 2018	2	39	asynchronous	AS10
	Analyst (general affairs)	Female	38	Husband and sons	Feb 2019	2	33	asynchronous	AS11

Organization	Role	Gender	Age	Household	Date	No.	Age2	Mode	Code
Federal sanitary and phytosanitary agency	Analyst (health surveill.)	Female	37	Husband and sons	Jan 2017	7	36	asynchronous	AS12
	Analyst (health surveill.)	Female	36	Husband	Aug 2017	3	42	asynchronous	AS13
	Analyst (general affairs)	Male	41	Wife and daughter	Feb 2018	3	39	asynchronous	AS14
	Analyst (legal)	Male	34	Father and mother	Mar 2017	3	21	synchronous	SS1
	Analyst (legal)	Male	34	Wife and son	Jun 2017	3	20	synchronous	SS2
Pernambuco State Court of Justice	Analyst (legal)	Male	35	Wife and son	Feb 2018	3	21	synchronous	SS3
	Analyst (legal)	Female	39	Sister	Jan 2017	7	30	synchronous	SS4
	Analyst (legal)	Female	29	Husband and daughter	May 2017	2	25	synchronous	SS5
	Analyst (legal)	Female	28	Mother	Apr 2018	2	22	synchronous	SS6
	Analyst (legal)	Female	35	Husband and two sons	Jan 2017	7	66	synchronous	SS7
	Analyst (legal)	Female	33	Mother and sisters	Aug 2019	2	38	synchronous	SS8
	Analyst (legal)	Female	37	Alone	Jan 2019	1	48	synchronous	SS9
Rondônia State Court of Justice	Analyst (legal)	Female	31	Mother	Jul 2018	1	34	synchronous	SS10
	Analyst (legal)	Female	42	Husband and daughters	Oct 2017	2	41	synchronous	SS11
	Analyst (legal)	Male	31	Wife and daughter	Jun 2018	2	37	synchronous	SS12
	Analyst (legal)	Male	32	Wife and daughter	Aug 2018	2	48	synchronous	SS13
Rondônia Public Defender	Public defender	Female	35	Daughters	Aug 2019	1	45	synchronous	SS14

Table 10.1 (cont.)

State-owned agencies and secretaries	Job position	Gender	Age (years)	Living with	Telework from	Telework days per week	Interview time (minutes)	Type of activity	#
	Analyst (general affairs)	Male	28	Wife	Mar 2018	7	41	*synchronous*	SS15
Federal Public Prosecutor	Analyst (general affairs)	Male	45	Wife and sons	Jan 2018	7	47	*synchronous*	SS16
	Analyst (general affairs)	Male	36	Alone	Mar 2017	7	38	*synchronous*	SS17
	Analyst (general affairs)	Female	43	Mother	Feb 2018	1	43	*synchronous*	SS18

Source: Author's own

These organizations are public bureaus, secretaries, executive agencies or courts of justice. All of them present a bureaucratic or legalistic logic of action, in which there are expectations to comply with legal rules, and a lack of institutionalized meritocracy. There is a resistance to adopt telework by the agencies' senior officers, as their supervision of the employees would be reduced, taking place at a distance. Therefore, the adopted telework from home regime is kept for those with superior job performance; it is a prize for which employees make their best efforts to sustain superior performance, even under a less intensive supervision.

Our protocol focussed on work pace and intensity, flexibility, duration, deadlines and waiting time. Our content analysis coding (Charmaz, 2009) started with temporality elements and evolved to include conflicts in and from temporal structures. The analysis was interrupted when we reached theoretical saturation for the observed temporal structures and associated conflicts. Our inductive approach showed that the routines of our interviewees differ; some are composed mainly of synchronous tasks, others of asynchronous tasks (Table 10.2), and that our interviewees organize such activities differently in their daily working hours.

Synchronous tasks flow, present deadlines, steps and pace, and are determined and enacted by a sequence of connected activities. One task starts when the previous one is concluded, demanding that employees work simultaneously during the day. Asynchronous tasks are executed independently of time coordination, and the employee in charge of it can freely allocate the task in their time schedule, provided they comply with the shared deadline. Some workers strongly segregate professional routines and family duties, but other interviewees allowed both routines to be blended. In the end, we interviewed fourteen employees working at home on asynchronous tasks and eighteen on synchronous tasks.

Table 10.2 *Types of tasks undertaken by our interviewees*

Feature of their routines	Synchronous tasks	Asynchronous tasks
Sequence of tasks	Dependent on previous stages	Not dependent on previous stages
Execution of tasks	Sequential	Parallel
Interaction between individuals	Continuous	Not continuous
Work shifts	Simultaneous	Not simultaneous

Source: Author's own

Temporal Contradictions in Teleworking

The collected evidence revealed that the technological tools used in remote work create new temporal rules, and civil servants develop a perception of greater control over what to do with the time they have: "I am the owner of my time" as one of the respondents stated (Table 10.3).

Teleworking from home can lead to the understanding that one has mastery and autonomy in relation to the time available. For the interviewed employees, remote work allowed them to manage time, a similar finding to the studies that indicate that, through teleworking, individuals create a routine and impose a new work pace (Sennet, 1998; Tietze & Musson, 2002). However, our analysis also indicates contradictions, or nuances of this supposed control over time, pace, routine and waiting. The meanings attributed to time by the respondents carry three contradictions: (1) control over working hours; (2) control of their routine; and (3) control of their work pace. Such contradictions were identified in the respondents' statements, although they were not aware of them.

Table 10.3 presents nuances in the perception of time control by the same employees. Although respondents mention autonomy, control over their time and the possibility of "controlling time," they also mention "urgency," "need for readiness" and "availability for response" as conditions and expectations imposed by the organization. Another relevant aspect of the reports is the presence of objective time, such as chronological time and the calendar, which is expected, especially in synchronous activities.

Table 10.3 *Nuances of time control perception*

Declared control over time	Reduction of control over time
"I own my time"	"... rules imposed on my activity"
"I do my job when I want"	"You are on standby in case an email arrives ... *you can do things at home as long as you keep an eye on your computer*"
"... possibility of driving your own schedule"	"I *have to always be available* in case of an emergency"
"I organize my routine as I want"	"I get in touch *during the weekend or very late at night ...*"
"Possibility of managing your time"	"... creativity sometimes comes at night, [but] *I have to be available during business hours*"

Source: Author's own

Although the civil servants believe that they have more control over their time, they are still unable to dissociate themselves from clock time. Despite a sense of autonomy and expected control over time, they are still attached to clock time, as they respond to expectations of "urgency," "need for readiness" and "availability for response" imposed by the organization: their control over time is actually reduced.

Teleworking is seen as an innovative way of working (Aguilera et al., 2016; Kossek et al., 2015; Seweel & Taskin, 2015; Sewell, 2012) for greater flexibility and time control (Suh & Lee, 2015; Vihalemm & Harro-Loit, 2019), but the reported experiences are still associated with a time that has an objective, quantitative, linear and measurable perspective, as observed in other studies (e.g., Blue, 2019; Clancy, 2013; Lee & Sawyer, 2010; Mavrofides & Papageorgiou, 2013; Moran, 2015; Van Tienoven, 2019).

Even with telecommuting providing the possibility of carrying out tasks at any time of the day, our interviews showed that civil servants teleworking at home end up trying to reproduce at home the routines they used to exercise in the face-to-face work environment of their offices (Table 10.4). Some explanations for this reproduction could be a combination of the following influences: (1) previous office routines have been adapted for working at home, and for general telework frameworks or policies, (2) social norms exist that define how the work "should be done at home," and expectations for how people should behave, organize and perform, including dress codes, (3) the style of direct supervision. Consequently, the old temporal structures are translated to the home office, as the routine developed during business hours.

The employees highlighted that the normative prohibition of integral teleworking is related to the prejudice (in their words) that still exists in relation to remote work. This prejudice also operates a social pressure, which maintains a constant tension due to the fear that the teleworking regime could be canceled, involving the cost of moving back to the office's neighborhood (some families moved to other cities or states as they achieved the home office benefit). Such fear reduces criticism and induces a high level of productivity from teleworkers, despite their skepticism about teleworking.

Finally, the influence of the telework model can also be observed in the work pace. The interviewees described their routines as dependent on whether tasks were synchronous or not with other tasks performed by colleagues, and whether it involved a level of interaction. For synchronous tasks, interaction over a shorter period of time and the dependence on individuals for continuity of the work process ended in a constrained time flexibility. The work pace is determined by the time it takes for the process

Table 10.4 *Translation of routines from the office*

Sources of influence	Quotations on previous organizational structures transferred to home office
Routines and frameworks	"... *you have to be connected synchronously* from 1 p.m. to 7 p.m. Monday to Friday"; "even if I achieve my target/goal, I am stuck within my schedule 1 p.m. to 7 p.m."
Synchronicity	"I have my hands tied ... I conclude a task, I send it to be evaluated, then *I need to wait for the next round.*" (*Synchronous* task) "The task depends only on me; I think it will take me X hours ... I *organize myself* during my working hours *usually at night.*" (*Asynchronous* task)
Social norms	"*Try to do the same thing you did before.* Wake up, get dressed, dress like you're going there."
Supervision	"*[my] boss thinks I'm available at any time*; after all, I'm at home."

Source: Author's own

to come back from colleagues or a supervisor. The waiting time was reported as a negative factor by all synchronous respondents. This aspect reinforces the studies on waiting as something considered "undesirable," or a "waste of time," to be eliminated (Bailey, 2019; Liang, 2019; Rotter, 2016). However, waiting is a neglected factor in organizational studies (Bailey, 2019), as well as by the organizations that design telework regimes.

We observed two relevant aspects in relation to waiting time in synchronous activities. On the one hand, waiting is considered "a waste of time," "when nothing is produced." On the other hand, the civil servants express that it is precisely at this moment of waiting that they "profit from the flexibility of teleworking time," as they are able to take care of personal affairs during the waiting time. Going to the supermarket, to the doctor (SS7; SS9), caring for children (SS9), domestic services (SS2), vocational courses (SS3) and learning new languages (SS2) are actions carried out during these periods. Why, then, is the waiting time so "disliked" and unwanted?

The discomfort with waiting time seems to be a critical issue in telework. A respondent described how he gets anxious about waiting time when working in a synchronous task; or when he lacks the presence of his colleague in the office.

When I was in [the office] in person I could hear the [colleagues] attendance, we shared the office so you could hear, "Look, there's a request for you." Then the person would come to me and say, "You have an emergency request." Then you'd say, "I'm coming." When you are remote working, you are working on a complicated process and every notification [that comes in] you get tense, because you think that it can't take long (your colleague is not there at your side), it can't take two minutes, so after a moment you don't know if you still have time . . . the right word is anguished. But I think it is important to give an answer, to solve a problem. Sometimes everything, not everything, but most [things] are urgent, they have orders of priority. (SS7)

One of the main advantages of digital artifacts in teleworking is the possibility of "real-time communication" at a distance (Mavrofides et al., 2014). Failure to use any digital platform during the "waiting" period generates perceptions of "impotence," "deceleration" and "loss of production," in contrast to face-to-face work, where "waiting" is interpreted as a potential for production.

Asynchronous activities, on the other hand, are not connected to other tasks conducted by other teams, simultaneously or sequentially, or their connections are separated by a duration that may accommodate eventual variations in how much time they use to perform the task. In such cases, public servants are under less pressure to run their activities at home. They perceive that they have greater flexibility to manage their time, as they are able to choose periods of the day to work when they consider themselves more productive. It maintains a work pace that is less subject to external pace-marking elements. The pace may depend more on aspects of their own household routine, family and habits.

However, the pace can still be affected by rules imposed on the teleworking model. For example, it can be slowed down by imposing the day of the week on which the server needs to work in person, or by the normative prohibition of opting for full teleworking (five days a week). In the literature considered, to the best of our knowledge, such factors have largely to date not been identified.

Such dynamics are also reinforced by digital artifacts, such as commercial messaging applications (WhatsApp and email) or the organization's dedicated communication systems. These applications create and maintain an open space for interaction between employees from that division or department. As these spaces are created and maintained on cell phones and computers, the time window remains open for the duration accepted by the user. Respondents identify that they are working from the moment they access virtual work systems. These artifacts are interpreted by professionals in residential teleworking as the "space-time window" in teleworking.

These artifacts also end up accelerating the pace of remote work. Notification systems, audible or visual, set the pace for interaction. However, although the tools speed up communication and the work pace, some respondents report effects such as increased feelings of loneliness: "the disadvantages are that you end up spending a lot of time alone. It goes faster, it does. But nothing compares to the people, right?" (SS4).

Discussion and Conclusions

The telework regime transfers part of the routines out of the office and proposes a redesign of the organizing. With telework emerges new work boundaries, spaces and temporal structures. At the six public sector organizations, the people we talked with believed they would save time not driving to the office and would have more control over their time by working from home. However, our interviews revealed some temporal contradictions and organizational challenges due to multi-temporalities being in place.

First, although they assume they will gain more control over their time, the previous rules and work policies about working hours imposed by the organization remain in place. A shared perception among all interviewees is "I am the owner of my time," as expressed by one of the interviewees. Notwithstanding, the observed teleworkers are unable to detach from the office "clock time," transferred by previous office temporal structures (such as working hours arrangements) to guarantee coordination in synchronous tasks.

Second, they also fail when they assume they can control the work routine. Although they think that being in another physical space (out of office) will give them control over their routines, they end up replicating temporal structures from previous office organizing. They expressed "urgency," "need for readiness" and "availability for response" as expectations imposed by the organization. Temporal structures of deadlines, immediacy, urgency, real time and online presence are impositions that contradict some temporal structures of the family, such as mealtimes and family weekends.

Third, employee performance pressures were intensified with expectations for reducing the response time, putting pressure on workload. Telework temporal structures seem to depend on whether the task is synchronous and connected to other simultaneous tasks. Synchronous tasks demand interaction in a shorter time and depend on individuals for the continuity of the work process, reducing discretion on how to distribute tasks through the working hours. In synchronous tasks, the pre-existing routines from the office are still used to coordinate people in telework regimes as they are connected to other departments in the office.

The pace and intensity of the work can be decelerated, but only temporarily, when a worker needs to wait to start a task preceded by another task (waiting time). It is out of the control of teleworkers. Waiting time was reported by all respondents with synchronous tasks as undesirable and something to be eliminated (Bailey, 2019; Liang, 2019; Rotter, 2016). We observed two aspects in relation to waiting time in synchronous tasks: first, waiting is considered "a waste of time" as "nothing is being produced," but at precisely this temporal window, teleworkers "enjoy the telework time flexibility." Therefore, despite it being a waste of time (according to the office parameters), individuals use it to accommodate the demands of personal daily affairs (going to the supermarket, to the doctor, caring for children, domestic services, learning new languages). It seems that there is a plasticity as temporary spaces emerge, and teleworkers realize they can accommodate other demands.

In asynchronous tasks, teleworkers perceive that they have greater flexibility to manage their time. In such a case, they choose moments of the day when they consider themselves to be more productive, to work. The work pace is less subject to office rules. Teleworkers can better detach their daily dynamics from office dynamics when compared to those working on synchronous tasks. Therefore, the accommodation of professional temporal structures and household routine, family and habits, is more in the control of the employee.

We noticed that the temporal structures from the office can be translated into rules and work policies, but they are also influenced by the style of direct supervision, and by social pressures to legitimize "what should be" efficient and reliable telework in the organization. Such (inadequate) temporal structures prevent greater benefits being derived from teleworking, although its innovative face (Aguilera et al., 2016; Kossek et al., 2015; Seweel & Taskin, 2015; Sewell, 2012; Suh & Lee, 2015; Vihalemm & Harro-Loit, 2019), attachments to clock time and structures of temporal coordination mitigate flexibility. Such rigidity of clock time has been considered in other studies (e.g., Blue, 2019; Clancy, 2013; Lee & Sawyer, 2010; Moran, 2015; Van Tienoven, 2019).

The transference of routines out of offices, promoted by telework, induces changes in temporal structures, requiring reflection on organizational design to potentialize the expected gains from telework regimes.

References

Aguilera, A., Virginie, L., Alain, R. & Lauret, P. (2016). Home-based telework in France: Characteristics, barriers and perspectives. *Transportation Research Part A: Policy and Practice*, 92, 1–11.

Ahrne, G. & Brunsson, N. (eds) (2019), Organization outside Organizations. In *The Abundance of Partial Organization in Social Life*. Cambridge: Cambridge University Press.

Bailey, C. (2019). Waiting in organisations. *Time & Society, 28*(2), 587–612.

Baines, S. & Gelder, U. (2003). What is family friendly about the workplace in the home? *New Technology, Work and Employment, 18*(3), 223–33.

Barley, S. (1988). On Technology, Time, and Social Order: Technologically Induced Change in the Temporal Organization of Radiological Work. In F. A. Dubinskas (ed.), *Making Time: Ethnographies of High-Technology Organizations* (pp. 123–69). Philadelphia: Temple University Press.

Bittman, M. (2004). Parenting and employment. What time-use surveys show. In N. Folbre & M. Bittman (eds), *Family Time: The Social Organization of Care* (pp. 152–70). New York: Routledge.

Blagoev, B., Costas, J. & Kärreman, D. (2019). "We are all herd animals": Community and organizationality in coworking spaces. *Organization, 26*(6), 894–916.

Blue, S. (2019). Institutional rhythms: Combining practice theory and rhythm analysis to conceptualise processes of institutionalisation. *Time & Society, 28* (3), 922–50.

Brocklehurst, M. (2001). Power, identity and new technology homework: Implications for "new forms" of organizing. *Organization Studies, 22*(3), 445–66.

Caillier, J. (2012). The impact of teleworking on work motivation in a US federal government agency. *The American Review of Public Administration, 42*(4), 461–80.

Charmaz, K. (2009). Grounded Theory: Objectivist and Constructivist Methods. In N. Denzin & Y. Lincoln (eds), *Handbook of Qualitative Research* (2nd ed.). Thousand Oaks, CA: Sage.

Claessens, B., Roe, R. & Rutte, C. (2009). Time Management: Logic, Effectiveness and Challenges. In R. A. Roe, M. J. Waller & S. R. Clegg (eds), *Time in Organizational Research*. London & New York: Routledge.

Clancy, C. (2013). The politics of temporality: Autonomy, temporal spaces and resoluteness. *Time and Society, 23*(1), 28–48.

Dacin, T., Zilber, T. B., Tracey, P., Boxenbaum, E., Canniford, R., Dacin, P., Dacin, T., Farny, S., Gray, B., Kibler, E., Putnam, L. L., Shepherd, D. & Svejenova, S. (2019). "Situated institutions: The role of place, space and embeddedness in institutional dynamics." Academy of Management Meeting: Proceedings, 1, first published online on August 1, 2019.

de Vaujany, F-X. & Vaast, E. (2014). If these walls could talk: The mutual construction of organizational spaceand legitimacy. *Organization Science, 25* (3), 713–31.

Dzigbede, K. D., Gehk, S. B. & Willloughby, K. (2020). Disaster resiliency of U.S. local governments: Insights to strengthen local response and recovery from the COVID-19 pandemic. *Public Administration Review, 80*(4), 634–43. https://onlinelibrary.wiley.com/doi/10.1111/puar.13249

Eom, S., Choi, N. & Sung, W. (2016). The use of smart work in government: Empirical analysis of Korean experiences. *Government Information Quarterly, 33* (3), 562–71.

Kim, T., Mullins, L. B. & Yoon, T. (2021). Supervision of telework: A key to organizational performance. *The American Review of Public Administration, 51* (4), 263–77. https://doi.org/10.1177/0275074021992058

Kitou, E. & Horvath, A. (2003). Energy-related emissions from telework. *Environmental Science & Technology*, *37*(16), 3467–75.

Korte, W. & Wynne, R. (1996). Telework: Penetration, Potential and Practice in Europe. Amsterdam: IOS Press Ohmsha.

Kossek, E., Thompson, R. J. & Lautsch, B. A. (2015). Balanced workplace flexibility: Avoiding the traps. *California Management Review*, *57*(4), 5–25.

Lee, H. (1999). Time and information technology: Monochronicity, polychronicity and temporal symmetry. *European Journal of Information Systems*, *8*, 16–26.

Lee, H. & Sawyer, S. (2010). Conceptualizing time, space and computing for work and organizing. *Time and Society*, *19*(3), 293–317.

Liang, C. C. (2019). Enjoyable queuing and waiting time. *Time & Society*, 28(2), 543–66. doi: 10.1177/0961463X17702164.

Martin, B. & MacDonnell, R. (2012). Is telework effective for organizations? A metaanalysis of empirical research on perceptions of telework and organizational outcomes. *Management Research Review*, *35* (7), 602–16.

Martinez, A., Pérez-Pérez, M., De-Luis-Carnicer, P. & Vela-Jiménez, M. J. (2007). Telework, human resource flexibility and firm performance. *New Technology, Work and Employment*, *22*(3), 208–23.

Mavrofides, T. & Papageorgiou, D. (2013). The expansion of ICT: A new framework of inclusion and exclusion from the global realm. *International Journal of Criminology and Sociological Theory*, *6*(1).

Mavrofides, T., Papageorgiou, D., Papadopoulos, T. & Los, A. (2014). ICT and systemic time squeeze: The uncoordinated temporalities of globalization. *Time & Society*, *23*(1), 69–96.

McGrath, J. E. & Kelly, J. R. (1986). *Time and Human Interaction: Toward a Social Psychology of Time*. New York: Guilford Press.

Moran, C. (2015). Time as a social practice. *Time & Society*, *24*(3) 283–303.

Neufeld, D. & Fang, Y. (2005). Individual, social and situational determinants of telecommuter productivity. *Information & Management*, *42*(7), 1037–49.

Olson, M. (1983). Remote office work: Changing work patterns in space and time. *Communications of the ACM*, *26*(3), 182–7.

Orhan, M. A. (2017). When tasks get virtual. *Journal of Management and Innovation*, *3*(2), 1–26.

Orlikowski, W. J. & Yates, J. (2002). It's about time: Temporal structuring in organizations. *Organization Science*, *13*(6), 684–700.

Peters, P., Poutsma, E., Van der Heijden, B., Bakker, A. B. & Thomas, B. (2014). Enjoying new ways to work: An HRM-process approach to study flow. *Human Resource Management*, *53*(2), 271–90.

Pyöriä, P. (2011). Managing telework: Risks, fears and rules. *Management Research Review*, *34*(4), 386–99.

Reinecke, J. & Ansari, S. (2015). When times collide: Temporal brokerage at the intersection of markets and developments. *Academy of Management Journal*, *58* (2), 618–48.

Rosa, H. (2013). *Social Acceleration: A New Theory of Modernity*. New York: Columbia University Press.

Rotter, R. (2016). Waiting in the asylum determination process: Just an empty interlude? *Time & Society*, 25(1), 80–101.

Rowell, C., Gustafsson, R. & Clemente, M. (2016). How institutions matter "in time": The temporal structures of practices and their effects on practice reproduction. *Research in the Sociology of Organizations*, 48A, 303–27.

Shipp, A. J. & Richardson, H. A. (2021). The impact of temporal schemata: Understanding when individuals entrain versus resist or create temporal structure. *Academy of Management Review*, 46(2), 299–319.

Schuster, C., Weitzman, L., Sass Mikkelsen, K., Meyer-Sahling, J., Bersch, K., Fukuyama, F., Paskov, P., Rogger, D., Mistree, D. & Kay, K. (2020). Responding to COVID-19 through surveys of public servants. *Public Administration Reviews*, 80(5), 792–6. http://doi.org/10.1111/puar.13246

Sennett, R. (1998). *The Corrosion of Character: The Personal Consequences of Work in the New Capitalism*. New York: W.W. Norton.

Sewell, G. (2012). Employees, Organizations and Surveillance. In K. Ball, K. D. Haggerty & D. Lyon (eds), *The Handbook of Surveillance Studies* (pp. 303–12). London: Routledge.

Seweel, G. & Taskin, L. (2015). Out of sight, out of mind in a new world of work? Autonomy, control, and spatiotemporal scaling in telework. *Organization Studies*, 36(11), 1507–29.

Simmons, S. (1996). *Flexible Working: A Strategic Guide to Successful Implementation and Operation*. London: Kogan Page.

Skade, L., Stanske, S., Wenzel, M. & Koch, J. (2020). Temporary organizing and acceleration: On the plurality of temporal structures in accelerators. *Tensions and Paradoxes in Temporary Organizing Research in the Sociology of Organizations*, 67, 105–25.

Suh, A. & Lee, J. (2015). Understanding teleworkers' technostress and its influence on job satisfaction. *Internet Research*, 27(1), 140–59.

Tietze, S. & Musson, G. (2002). When "work" meets "home": Temporal flexibility as lived experience. *Time & Society*, 11(2/3), 315–34.

Van Tienoven, T. (2019). A multitude of natural, social and individual time. *Time & Society*, 28(3),971–94.

Vega, R. P., Anderson, A. J. & Kaplan, S. A. (2015). A within-person examination of the effects of telework. *Journal of Business and Psychology*, 30(2), 313–23.

Vihalemm, T. & Harro-Loit, H. (2019). Measuring society's temporal synchronization via days of importance. *Time & Society*, 28(4), 1333–62.

11 Towards a Processual Understanding of Buildings
Temporality, Materiality, and Politics

Jonathan Feddersen, Tor Hernes and Silviya Svejenova

Introduction

To address the role of buildings for organizing, scholars commonly draw on the concept of 'organizational space' (Elsbach & Pratt, 2007; Taylor & Spicer, 2007; Weinfurtner & Seidl, 2019). With some notable exceptions (e.g., de Vaujany & Vaast, 2014; Decker, 2014; Giovannoni & Napier, 2022; Giovannoni & Quattrone, 2018; Jones & Massa, 2013; Petani & Mengis, 2016), studies of organizational space consider buildings mostly through the ways in which their material spaces afford (that is, enable and constrain) organizing in the present or longitudinally over time, in successive presents. Thereby, they conceive of the social and material as inherently entangled in an 'ontological fusion' (Leonardi, 2013), which also reflects the predominant conceptualization in studies of sociomateriality more generally (Orlikowski & Scott, 2008). This conceptualization, we argue, along with others (Beyes & Holt, 2020; de Vaujany et al., 2014; Leonardi, 2013, 2016, 2017), hinders progress towards a temporal, processual understanding of materiality because it fails to appreciate materiality as a process in its own right. Arguably, such appreciation is particularly difficult in the case of buildings:

> [T]he problem with buildings is that they look desperately static. It seems almost impossible to grasp them as movement, as flight, as a series of transformations. Everybody knows – and especially architects, of course – that a building is not a static object but a moving project. (Latour & Yaneva, 2008, p. 80)

To advance a processual understanding of materiality demands an appreciation of how material artifacts (such as material buildings) and social actors form separate processes through time (Hernes, 2004; Hernes et al., 2021; Leonardi, 2016). Material artifacts have their own past and future, or 'temporality' which may entail their interactions with social actors but is not reducible to these interactions (Hernes et al., 2021). This view has socio-material organizational space as a potential outcome, rather than a starting point of analysis, instead directing analytical attention to the encounters of and emerging relations between social actors and material artifacts (Leonardi, 2016). Considering the empirical case of material buildings, prior studies exploring such a view show how buildings attain their own trajectory through time, to become associated with social actors (Giovannoni & Quattrone, 2018; Yaneva, 2009). An implication of these studies is that, to appreciate what buildings 'do', we need to catch buildings in flight – to follow their becoming through time (Latour & Yaneva, 2008).

Our study seeks to trace the flight of BLOX, a new landmark building on Copenhagen's harbour front, inaugurated in May 2018 following twelve years of planning and development. To date, it is the largest investment made by Realdania, a Danish philanthropic association dedicated to improving quality of life through the built environment. Designed by Rem Koolhaas' Office for Metropolitan Architecture (OMA), the building's name reflects its appearance of stacked blocks. Proclaimed 'more than a building' (Realdania, 2018), BLOX provides workspaces for over eighty private, public, and non-profit organizations, and hosts activities and events that connect 'architecture, design, construction and tech with global decision makers, scientists and citizens to explore and develop new sustainable urban solutions' (BLOX, 2019). Alongside its strategic importance for Realdania, the building has been influenced by and has gone on to influence the trajectories of several other organizations. It has supported, among others, the City of Copenhagen's harbour-front regeneration efforts, the Danish Architecture Center's (DAC's) world-leading ambitions, and the Ministry of Business's implementation of a new industry and innovation policy in Denmark.

Drawing on a combined ethnographic and historical case study, we follow organizing processes unfolding between public, private, and philanthropic organizations and the material building. Our theoretical framework distinguishes between three dimensions of the building's 'material temporality' (Hernes et al., 2021): *historicizing the building through time, projecting the building over time,* and *enacting the building in time.* To operationalize these processes, we adopt an event-based approach (Feddersen, 2020; Hernes, 2014, 2022; Hussenot & Missonier, 2016). In the discussion, we argue that 'the building' emerged as a temporarily stabilized organizational outcome of political struggles and negotiations between the enacting, projecting, and historicizing dimensions, connecting encounters between social actors and materiality 'in time' into a distinguishable socio-material trajectory 'over time'.

The first main contribution of our chapter is the addition of the 'historicizing' dimension to the concept of material temporality (Hernes et al., 2021), supplementing the 'epochal' and 'processual' dimension. The second contribution is to show that the organizing effects of material buildings emerges not only from their material durability, but also from their temporal malleability. Adding to previous studies that have explored how buildings' pasts have a bearing on the present (e.g., de Vaujany & Vaast, 2014; Decker, 2014; Giovannoni & Napier, 2022; Giovannoni & Quattrone, 2018; Petani & Mengis, 2016), our study shows how a building may act as an anticipated future event, through its imagined materialization (see also Alimadadi et al., 2021).

Theoretical Framework: Three Dimensions of a Building's Material Temporality

To highlight that materiality is not readily available to organizing, but a process in itself (Leonardi, 2013, 2016), we build on the concept of 'material temporality' (Hernes et al., 2021). Theorizing the temporality of materiality from a 'becoming' perspective, Hernes et al. distinguished between a 'processual' and an 'epochal' dimension.

'Processual temporality' designates the processual, flow-like character of materials in the ongoing present. On the one hand, this dimension may designate processual temporality independent of human actors. Whereas this dimension is central in the case of perishable food products as considered by Hernes et al. (2021), it is less prominent in the case of a relatively more durable building, where it may refer to the ongoing weathering of building materials, for instance. On the other hand, this dimension also captures the ways in which human actors may directly interact with, investigate, use, and transform materials, forming a 'human-substance present' (Hernes, 2014). Most work on socio-materiality (Orlikowski & Scott, 2008) foregrounds this processual aspect. When considering the material becoming of a physical building, the processual dimension of material temporality encompasses, for instance, the interaction of architects with physical models (see, e.g., Comi & Whyte, 2018), the actual construction activity on the building site, and how human actors use and inhabit a building after its completion (see, e.g., Brand, 1994; Cnossen & Bencherki, 2019). This dimension informed what our findings refer to as *enacting the building in time*.

'Epochal temporality' denotes the ways in which actors imagine materiality at other points in time: 'It is labelled "epochal" because it assumes that a state of affairs imagined in the past or future persists for a certain amount of time' (Hernes et al., 2021, p. 4). The epochal temporality of materials emerges from the ways in which human actors imagine materiality by remembering past or projecting and imagining future materialities (Hernes et al., 2021). In the case of the BLOX building, this dimension captures how different actors anticipate the future material building to be consequential for their organizational trajectories, which involves imagining the building at a future point in time. For instance, the epochal dimension refers to the ways in which Realdania's management envisioned the transformation of a plot of land from a past 'wasteland' to a future 'landmark building'. In the context of our study, this dimension informed what we labelled *projecting the building over time*. Projecting the building over time refers to the ways in which actors sought to define the building's role in their future organizational and political ambitions.

Adding to these two dimensions, our analysis revealed a third dimension, which we label *historicizing the building through time*. Historicizing through time involved instances in which actors narrated the building's position and role in its wider urban (spatial, material) and societal context. In our study, historicizing the building through time refers to the ways in which actors referred to the building 'as a whole', and thereby connected – or historicized – the building's past, present, and future. Through historicizing, the building attained duration and continuity through time. According to Heidegger (1927), 'historicity' denotes the history belonging to a specific entity, which it attains through the temporal state of being in time. Following Heidegger, 'historicizing' is the activity of making an entity's historicity meaningful by reconstructing and reconnecting its past, present, and future. Whereas projecting the building over time refers to the ways in which actors in organizations attempt to make the building endogenous to their organizing efforts, historicizing the building through time accentuates how the building attains its own temporality due to and despite such organizing attempts as it acquires its own history. By historicizing, these organizing attempts become endogenous to the building's movement through time. While forming a recognizable temporal shape or pattern, the building's historicity remains open and subject to ongoing revision.

Research Process

This section provides some background on BLOX, as the empirical case of our study, describes our data collection process which combines historical and ethnographic methods, and details our event-based approach to making our theoretical framework amenable to empirical analysis.

Case Description

Our research focuses on BLOX, a new landmark building on Copenhagen's harbour front, financed by Danish philanthropic organization Realdania. At the time of the study, the building had three main tenants (excluding the underground carpark, restaurant, and fitness centre): the Danish Architecture Center (DAC), 'the meeting place for architecture, design and urban culture in Denmark' (Danish Architecture Center, 2020) and organizer of exhibitions and events directed at professional and broader cultural audiences; the Design Society, a foundation that 'coordinates publicly funded efforts for growth in the Danish design and fashion industries' (Design Society, 2020) through its three member organizations; and BLOXHUB, a non-profit association that supports sustainable urban innovation with over 280 member organizations across societal sectors (roughly 70 per cent private, 20 per cent public, and 10 per cent non-profit). BLOXHUB occupied one-and-a-half floors of BLOX and some adjacent historic buildings. It operated a co-working space with over eighty resident-member organizations. Figure 11.1 depicts main funding and co-founding relationships between the main tenant organizations and their financial backers.

In summary, BLOX combines three main functions. First, through DAC's cultural activities, BLOX serves as a cultural venue and

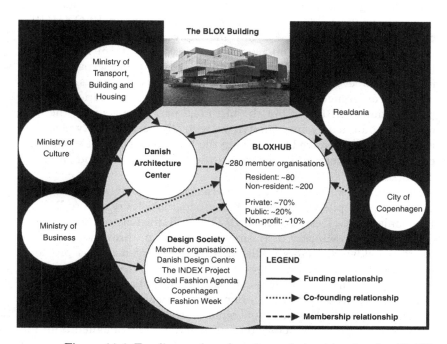

Figure 11.1 Funding and co-founding relationships for the BLOX building's three main tenants

exhibition space, a semi-public building welcoming citizens and tourists (in 2019, it attracted 200,000 visitors). Second, it serves as headquarters for three non-profit organizations, who respectively promote and facilitate interactions around design (Design Society), architecture and urban development (DAC), and sustainable urban innovation (BLOXHUB). Through activities and events hosted by these organizations, the building attracts a steady flow of external professional visitors from Denmark and abroad. Third, through BLOXHUB's co-working space, BLOX provides workspaces for over 800 people from a diverse set of organizations across a variety of sectors.

Data Collection

We collected data from an ethnographic field study, interviews, and archival documents.

The first author conducted a thirty-six-month ethnographic field study from October 2016 to October 2019, a period that covered the opening phase and first full year of BLOX's operations. Throughout the fieldwork, he observed interactions in BLOXHUB's co-working space, engaged in informal conversations with actors who frequented the spaces, and participated in weekly team meetings at DAC and BLOXHUB. Apart from regular meetings, he participated in over 100 events (e.g., innovation workshops, keynotes, start-up pitches, conferences, and panel debates) organized by various tenant organizations of BLOX. For the historical part of our study, the first author conducted twenty interviews with eighteen primary decision makers directly involved in planning the building's concept and development who were affiliated with the main tenant and funding organizations.

In addition, we gathered both internal and publicly available documents. We compiled a database of newspaper articles related to BLOX, Realdania, DAC, Design Society, BLOXHUB, the City of Copenhagen, and Denmark's Ministry of Business. In addition, throughout the first author's fieldwork, actors affiliated with these organizations provided access to BLOX-related strategy documents. Finally, to trace the involvement of the Ministry of Business, the City of Copenhagen, and Realdania over time, we drew on a number of publicly available policy and strategy documents, press releases, annual reports, strategy evaluations, and general assembly protocols. Our archival material complemented both the interview-based historical and ethnography-based contemporary part of our study.

Data Analysis

To translate our theoretical framework for empirical analysis, we adopted an event-based view of organizing (e.g., Feddersen, 2020; Hernes, 2014, 2016; Hernes & Schultz, 2020; Hussenot et al., 2020; Hussenot & Missonier, 2016).

Three main assumptions of an event-based view are particularly relevant for our purposes. First, events are not important in themselves, but may become important through the ways that other events refer to them, either by anticipating them as future events or by remembering them as past events. Through connecting, events come to mutually define each other. Second, even though both social and material actors contribute to the making of events, events are not reducible to these actors and their actions. Rather, actors attain temporal existence through the connecting of events into 'temporal trajectories' (Hernes, 2016). Third, from an event-based view, organizational phenomena can be seen as emerging from 'event formations' (Hernes, 2014) of past, present and future events, which include those events constitutive of actors' trajectories. While most events are 'exemplary' events reflective of ongoing patterns, some come to stand out as 'singular' events (Hernes & Schultz, 2020).

From the event-based view that we pursue in this study, we may conceptualize the becoming of BLOX as the connecting of a set of events into a distinguishable past-present-future trajectory. This event-based view allows us to disentangle analytically the three organizing processes that comprise our theoretical framework. *Historicizing the building through time* refers to the ways in which actors construed the building's own, emergent past-present-future trajectory, treating the building and all that becomes associated with it as an event in itself. *Projecting the building over time* involved the ways in which actors in different organizations made events associated with the building-in-the-making, the present, completed building, or the future building endogenous to their organizational trajectories. This process reflects what Hernes et al. (2021) termed the 'epochal' dimension of material temporality. *Enacting the building in time* refers to the enactment of any present events that involved the building either as an actualized material artifact, imagined future, or remembered past. This process corresponds to the 'processual' dimension of material temporality (Hernes et al., 2021).

Findings

We structure our findings according to the three dimensions of our theoretical framework: *historicizing the building through time, projecting the building over time*, and *enacting the building in time*. We discuss our findings concerning each dimension in two phases. The first phase relates to envisioning and realizing the material building as a future potentiality, while the second phase reports how actors anticipated and enacted the material building as an actuality, during its construction and after the opening. The presentation of our findings follows the sequential order in which we found the three analytical dimensions to interrelate: *Historicizing I, Projecting I, Enacting I, Projecting II, Enacting II, and Historicizing II.* The findings show how each phase built on preliminarily stabilized outcomes of preceding phases. Figure 11.2 offers an empirical model of our findings that summarizes the interplay between these dimensions, showing how they connect encounters between the material temporality of the building and the temporality of social actors into a past-present-future trajectory.

It is important to highlight that all three dimensions were always present, yet that their relative prominence varied over time. Likewise, the order in which the three dimensions came to the fore varied across our study. First, historicizing the wasteland as opportunity provided the ground for projecting a mixed-use cultural building and its eventual materialization. Second, alternative projections re-conceptualized the initial projection of a mixed-use cultural building, so that actors were confronting conflicting future projections. These different potential trajectories were temporarily resolved by historicizing BLOX as a contemporary landmark for sustainable urban development. This different order suggests that historicizing may serve as the ground for or outcome of the interplay between projecting and enacting.

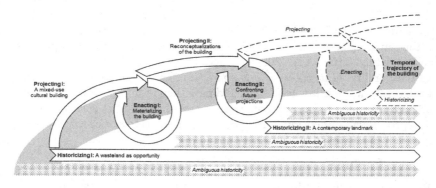

Figure 11.2 Empirical model of the emergence of a building's past-present-future trajectory from the interplay between historicizing, projecting, and enacting

Our model accentuates that construing the building's historicity – that is, its past-present-future trajectory through time – differently, at different points in time, does not imply that these trajectories replace each other. Rather, our findings suggest that different ways of construing the building's temporal trajectory layer on top of one another like sediments, where periods of ambiguous historicity follow periods of a temporarily stabilized historicity.

Historicizing I: A 'Wasteland' as Opportunity

BLOX was built on the 'Brewhouse site', a harbour-front plot in central Copenhagen, named after a brewery that had burned down in the 1960s. Since then, it had served as a parking lot and provisional playground. My sources described the site, among various descriptions, as a 'windswept car park', an 'unattractive dead end', or a 'wasteland', which was surprising, considering its central location, only a few hundred metres from Copenhagen City Hall, the Danish Parliament, and the National Museum of Denmark. Since 1941, seventy-five architectural proposals had been developed for the site, none realized: 'No other building site in Copenhagen has been the topic of so many competition proposals' (Thau, 2018, p. 111). The site was difficult to develop because zoning laws required a building with a cultural function, and because a 'ring road cuts the site into two plots, each plot too small to build an efficient building on' (van Loon & Weiss, 2018, p. 59). In addition, the site's adjacency to historical buildings made it subject to extensive building codes and regulations.

Meanwhile, since the early 1990s, Copenhagen's former industrial waterfront had been subject to a comprehensive revitalization process (see, e.g., Katz & Noring, 2017). The development of the site came into focus as a provoking 'hole' in the urban fabric because the revitalization of the urban spaces around the building plot were already complete. In this way, the potentiality of another attempt to put a building in this specific place and space at this specific time emerged from recently completed and ongoing processes of material and spatial transformation. At the same time, adjacent historical buildings and more recent material transformations as part of the revitalization process were a reality with which any renewed attempt would have to engage. Seen through the historicity dimension, BLOX marks the termination of a series of unsuccessful attempts to build on this plot while completing an urban revitalization process that had lasted for more than twenty years.

Historicizing a building before it is built refers to the way in which a building inserts itself as a potentiality into the evolving material and spatial urban fabric, as well as into ongoing social processes. For the opportunity to materialize (that is, actualize) and attain its own historicity, a building has to take both the past and the future into account. Because material artifacts cannot remember or imagine, it is the challenge of developers and architects to come up with a proposal that connects to the past and future of the material space, place, and its associated social processes. They need to recognize what is timely for the involved actors at a given time in a specific space – what we describe as 'projecting the building over time' – and seize such potential timeliness by connecting their proposals to the pasts and futures of ongoing processes – what we refer to as 'enacting the building in time'. In this view, previous failed attempts to build on the Brewhouse site suggest an inability to historicize building proposals consistently with the historicity of the city and society in which they were to 'take place'. In our temporal view, these proposals were not (made) 'timely'.

Projecting I: A Mixed-use Cultural Building

Our findings reveal how actors in several organizations projected a potential building into this specific place (i.e., the Brewhouse site) to play a role in realizing their respective organizations' future ambitions.

Realdania's shifting philanthropic strategy provided a starting point for BLOX. In its early years, Realdania awarded most of their grants by evaluating unsolicited applications. To gain inspiration for their strategy, Realdania's management team met with US philanthropic organizations, who were pursuing their own strategic priorities, for instance, through major investments in cultural buildings. Several informants referred to 'the Guggenheim museum's opening a few years earlier [in 1997] ... so there was a feeling that landmark buildings ... can raise [the profile of] a town moving forward' (Board member, Realdania). In their strategy, Realdania referred to 'prominent, visible and often capital-intensive projects, which set the course and point the way for others, and which ideally lead to further changes in the context of their realization' (Møller, 2009, p. 199, own translation from Danish). Endowed with the financial means due to strong money markets, Realdania began supporting the construction of several major cultural buildings across Denmark.

The Danish Architecture Center (DAC) (founded in 1986), a cultural institution that Realdania had been supporting and considered a 'natural partner institution ... had it not been already there, we would have had to invent it' (Manager, Realdania), had continuously struggled to secure its future through a solid funding base. Yet, its management was determined to raise its profile and convert it into 'one of the greatest architecture centers in the world' (Manager, DAC). In 2002, a partnership between Realdania and two Danish ministries eventually stabilized DAC's funding base. In addition, the management of Realdania and DAC agreed that DAC's nineteenth-century warehouse exhibition facilities were 'not optimal, at least not for exhibitions of a certain ambition level' (Manager, Realdania), and decided to pursue the construction of a new building for DAC.

At the same time, Realdania's management was considering a move from their 'completely anonymous . . . non-interesting and non-branded' office space (Board member, Realdania) and decided to integrate its own headquarters into the new building for DAC. These coinciding, mutually supportive future projections provided the starting point for the materialization of BLOX. Realdania and DAC combined their organizational projections into a proposal for a building. These projections were mainly concerned with the role that the building could attain in realizing their organizational futures. Projecting the building over time led to the emergence of a mutually agreeable concept for a 'mixed-use cultural building', which provided the grounds on which actors decided to pursue the building's construction – what we term enacting the building in time.

Enacting I: Materializing the Building

Enacting the building in time refers to the concrete activities and practices actors engaged in for the building to materialize. It involves connecting the historicity of a building plot with a fitting building proposal and giving this connection a concrete form by means of architectural design. For a new building to materialize, a developer with the vision and necessary financial means needs to meet an architect capable of articulating this vision in the form of a feasible, mutually agreeable design, which eventually requires municipal approval to obtain a building permit, before eventually materializing through the construction process. As our findings show, these activities involve ongoing negotiation of the building's multiple projections and emergent, fragile historicity.

Determined to build a new exhibition space for DAC that would integrate Realdania's headquarters, the search for a suitable plot soon led to the Brewhouse site: 'we were left with only one site in the central part of Copenhagen' (Manager, Realdania). However, it was not only availability that informed this choice. Realdania's offices were located opposite the Brewhouse site on the other side of the harbour, its view irritating Realdania's management: 'every single day, we looked at that shabby site and thought that we should do something about it' (Manager, Realdania). Informants described how unsuccessful past attempts to develop the plot increased Realdania's determination to 'do something about it':

They [the City of Copenhagen] had this piece of land on the books and nobody showed interest in building on that area because it was damn difficult. Neighbors, complexity, and historical heritage all around ... you could say an area like this can only be successfully developed with an owner like us. (Manager, Realdania)

The manager explained that it was difficult for a private developer to build a commercially viable building, considering the site restrictions, while the municipality did not have the financial means. However, from the manager's perspective, as a philanthropic and therefore non-profit organization, Realdania had the financial means, did not need to worry about commercial viability, and operated on a long-term time horizon.

In March 2006, Realdania launched an architecture competition and acquired the plot in October 2006, conditional on obtaining a building permit. In December 2007, at the peak of the financial boom, Realdania's board approved the project:

A little more than nine months before the big crash in September 2008 ... we decided to spend a hell of a lot of money, 2.5 billion DKK ... If we hadn't done that before the financial crisis, we would never have done it. ... This way, we had already taken the money out of our books. (Board member, Realdania)

To move ahead with the building's materialization, the visual and organizational challenge posed by the Brewhouse site's 'wasteland' was paired with the preliminary concept of a mixed-use cultural building.

The architecture competition brief envisioned a mixed-use cultural building to house DAC's exhibition space and offices, Realdania's offices, commercial lease offices, a restaurant and a café, underground parking, and apartments (as housing was a key concern of Copenhagen's mayor at the time). The project had three main intentions. First, to provide improved facilities for DAC, thereby raising its profile, and to cross-finance these by leasing remaining office space. This goal also lived up to the zoning law requirement for the building to have a cultural function. Second, it had to link city and harbour front, completing the pedestrian walkway along the harbour front, as per the City of Copenhagen's ambitions. Third, in line with Realdania's 'landmark building' strategy, to find a 'highly qualified and internationally renowned architect' to design a 'world class' building with positive ripple effects. Thus, the brief connected references to the site's historicity with organizational projections.

In April 2008, Realdania announced OMA, a Dutch architectural firm of international renown, as the winner of the architecture competition. OMA had proposed embracing the building's envisioned connecting function by leading traffic flows through the building as an "Urban Connector' ... almost an inhabited highway intersection embracing city movement' (van Loon & Weiss, 2018, p. 56). By traversing the ring road, OMA's design mimicked a proposal made fourteen years earlier by Danish architect Henning Larsen. The design also connected the building's different functions, with it looking much like an 'octopus' (Louisiana Channel, 2018) with DAC at its centre, as explained by OMA's lead architect Ellen van Loon, who termed this concept 'contaminating architecture':

The institution could architecturally contaminate the surrounding functions. ... The different building functions would no longer only coexist next to each other, but would constantly react to and be influenced by each other, thus turning the complete building into an architectural centre. (van Loon & Weiss, 2018, p. 55)

DAC's CEO, who was deeply involved in the dialogue with the architects, claimed that this proposal reflected the long-held ideas of OMA's co-founder, Rem Koolhaas:

In Realdania, OMA for the first time encounters a client that is willing to allow the firm to realize the ideas about the building as city that were articulated in Rem Koolhaas's book *Delirious New York* ... That is crucial for understanding why BLOX looks the way it does, but even more importantly, how the building is programmatically organized as a mix of functions that collide and interact. (Martinussen & Weiss, 2018, p. 159)

Realdania's proposed concept of a mixed-use cultural building and OMA's translation into a concrete design connected and balanced the Brewhouse site's place and time in urban historicity with organizational projections in a way that previously unsuccessful proposals had failed to achieve. The material space of the 'wasteland' provoked and afforded crystallization and temporal alignment of different organizational future ambitions into a concrete building project.

However, after announcing the winning proposal, the building permit remained pending for another five years. A series of disputes emanated from the public consultation process concerning the spatial relationship between the new building and the surrounding historical buildings. As OMA's Ellen van Loon put it, the main question was how to position the building vis-à-vis 'the real monuments. ... [P]eople ... considered this building far too modern and far too massive ... so we had to ... [rethink the building's] interaction with heritage to see how we [could] make the building lighter on that side' (Louisiana Channel, 2018). Citizens mobilized the urban fabric's historicity to challenge the new building's material form and spatial position. Such conflicts and delays occur because the design process is only transparent to those directly involved: the architects, developers and municipality, yet largely opaque to citizens and the public. Their evolving vision of the building enacted by actors involved in the design process only superficially surfaces through prelim-inary projections, such as material drawings and renderings in citizen hearings and newspaper reports. After several design modifications, Realdania eventually obtained a building permit and ground was broken in May 2013, over seven years after Realdania had acquired the Brewhouse site.

Projecting II: Re-conceptualizations of the Building

The design and construction of material buildings takes time. Even though the initial concept of a building may have seemed timely when actors conceived of it, this may change over time. The shifting future ambitions of the organizations involved may require an adjustment of the building's future use and constellation of tenants. Such shifts may spring from the observation of changing societal concerns; in our case, the increasing importance of 'sustainability' inspired re-conceptualizations of the building. In addition, other organizations may become aware of the building-in-the-making and try to connect their organizational futures with the building.

Even though Realdania's management had decided to move ahead with the construction of the new building, the financial crisis initially stopped the project as its financial viability came under scrutiny. For a while, it seemed as though the planned building had no organizational, and thus, material future. That Realdania had already written off the project budget safeguarded its continuation. A Realdania manager recalled repeatedly negotiating extensions of their sell-back clause with the municipality: 'any private investor would just have sold the land back, but we have a more long-term perspective'. Being aware of past difficulties in developing the site, the municipality willingly granted these extensions, thereby keeping the material space open and preserving the possibility for the new building to be constructed.

Realdania's altered financial situation and shifting strategic priorities changed Realdania board members' view of the Brewhouse project planned on the former wasteland and 'for a period there was a discussion about whether we could get rid of the area' (Board member). For the Brewhouse project to move forward, the board demanded a rethinking of the building's concept because 'it's absolutely essential if you build such a monstrous building that there is content that reflects the purpose of Realdania' (Board member). Specifically, there were sugges-tions that the building should no longer become Realdania's new headquarters, and the office space for commercial rent should be reconsidered. One board member acknowledged:

We never got into reality before the financial crisis . . . We could no longer justify such an enormous investment and then risk that lawyers, accountants and consulting companies would be in that building. . . . That was also a bit of a mindset shift in the board . . . you can plaster Danish society with a lot of brick and mortar. But, so what? (Board member, Realdania)

This mindset shift also reflected an ongoing shift in Realdania's philanthropic strategy. Realdania's management had become acquainted with the concepts of 'collective impact' (Kania & Kramer, 2011) and 'venture philanthropy' (see Mair & Hehenberger, 2014). Whereas Realdania had previously sought to improve the built environment through direct investments in physical buildings and public spaces, there was a growing conviction that more could be achieved by funding innovation activities (Møller, 2009). The Realdania board tasked the management team with developing a new concept for the building. In an effort to prolong recent activities to stimulate innovation and efficiency in the construction sector, Realdania's management proposed turning the building into a 'house of construction' that would host

all the disciplines from the construction industry – including . . . the developers, the contractors, the urban planners, the building designers, the engineers, . . . all the advisers that work with the built environment – these are the people that we wanted to have inside this . . . huge space that we were creating. (Manager, Realdania)

This nascent idea allowed the board to approve the project's continuation in autumn 2010, along with an additional budget to further develop the idea.

At the same time, while the building was being enacted through planning and – eventually – construction, Realdania's building on the waterfront caught the attention of actors in Denmark's Ministry of Business, who saw a potential role for the building in implementing a new approach to industrial and innovation policy that defined specific priority industries, including 'creative industries and design'. A report presented in February 2013 by a 'growth team' of managers and academics suggested perceiving of 'design' not merely as an industry in itself, but as a 'driver of entrepreneurship and innovation' (senior civil servant, Ministry of Business) in other industries. Aware of Realdania's difficulties with the Brewhouse project and with an increasing focus on innovation, the growth team proposed to move the design-related institutions of the Design Society to the new building, envisioning a 'lighthouse for Danish architecture and design':

We are missing a place in Denmark where international tourists, companies, and business delegations can see the best of Danish architecture and design. . . . The

Brewhouse has the potential to become an international lighthouse that show-cases Danish solutions and competencies in urban development, architecture, and design, and which provides a meeting place for leading entrepreneurs, companies, research institutions, etc. in this field. (Growth team report, February 2013, own translation from Danish)

Just like Realdania, Denmark's Ministry of Business conceived of the building as a tool for realizing future strategic ambitions. Initially, Realdania's management considered it 'ridiculous that the government would interfere in what our new building was going to be used for. That was our first reaction. Then we thought a little deeper about it' (Manager, Realdania). Realdania's management realized that the involvement of the Ministry of Business was in line with the newly adopted collective impact approach and struck an agreement to move the Design Society to the new building. As one informant admitted with a smile, 'the building got slightly hijacked by politics' (senior civil servant, Ministry of Business).

Realdania's management tasked DAC with exploring a joint vision for DAC and the Design Society. The project manager at DAC recalled how the report by the growth team 'was kind of the strange event that sparked everything', broadening the building's scope from architecture and construction to design: 'Can we merge those two focuses? ... I mean, today it makes sense ... [but] back then, it did not seem that meaningful.' DAC suggested transforming the 'house of construction' idea into an 'innovation and growth hub', entailing three main elements: 'export promotion, close relationships between research and business, and public engagement' (project manager, DAC). The hub's primary purpose was facilitating innovation and growth: 'The vision back then was not to make a difference in the world; it was not to promote sustainable development worldwide. ... It was promoting Danish business ... or promoting innovation/efficiency within the building sector' (project manager, DAC).

In autumn 2015, Realdania's management established the hub in the legal form of an association, providing a governance structure for the organizations affiliated with and physically sharing the building. First, Realdania's management convinced the Ministry of Business and the City of Copenhagen to become co-founders of the association, binding them even closer to the building and placing the project on a broader footing, in line with the collective impact approach. Second, through its co-working space, BLOXHUB opened the possibility for organizations not physically located in the building to become associated with BLOX. Third, in the spring of 2016, Realdania's management and the incoming director of

BLOXHUB turned 'innovation and growth' from an end in itself into a means to develop sustainable urban solutions:

The theme acts as an occasion. ... The reason why [BLOXHUB] is not merely a ... plain coworking space is because we are part of something greater. ... The story that is greater is obviously sustainability. The theme allows me to answer all the stakeholders' questions: Why engage? (Hub director, BLOXHUB)

When Realdania, the City of Copenhagen, and the Ministry of Business officially established the BLOXHUB association in June 2016, the Articles of Association reflected this newfound purpose: 'to contribute to sustainable urbanization – on a global scale – through the development of innovative solutions encompassing architecture, design, construction and urban development.'

This section revealed how, as long as actors anticipated the material building as a future object, the building was patient. The future material space invited imaginations and projections, without prompting (or affording) investigations of their eventual compatibility. Despite potential tensions and inconsistencies between their future projections, the anticipated future materiality of the building provided a sense of continuity, so actors felt as if they were part of 'the same project'. Anticipated incongruences between different organizational projections onto the BLOX building led to the establishment of BLOXHUB as a new organization and governance structure.

Enacting II: Confronting Future Projections

In the beginning of May 2018, BLOX opened its doors to the public. After the opening of BLOX, actors from the different tenant organizations found themselves thrown together in the same space, along with their respective future projections. Co-location in the material building resulted in hitherto concealed tensions surfacing between different organizational projections, which had emerged from two main dynamics.

First, tenant organizations saw themselves confronted with aspirations, purposes, and tenants that had not been part of the future concept for the building at the time they had decided to join the project. For example, while initial plans designated DAC as the new building's main tenant, it had become one among others. Rather than being a means for DAC to become a 'world-leading' architecture centre, the building had become more prominent than DAC itself. In consequence, DAC struggled not to be overshadowed by the activities of other tenants. The struggle became physically manifest when, a few months after the building opened, DAC's management successfully lobbied Realdania for permission to mount a 'DAC' logo on the façade and install a huge screen facing the square in front of BLOX to create awareness for its exhibitions and events.

Second, the future aspirations of organizations had evolved over time and present aspirations differed from those that had previously motivated organizations to become involved with the BLOX project. For example, shortly before BLOX opened, Realdania's CEO made the following statement in an interview with a major Danish newspaper: 'Would we have done it today? Hardly. Will we do something of this size again? Not in my time, not even if I was 20 years younger' (cited in Benner, 2018, own translation from Danish). At the time, this statement left the first author of this chapter puzzled. Why would the CEO denounce the biggest investment Realdania had ever made before BLOX had even opened its doors to the public? As our historical analysis later revealed, the decision to construct a landmark building had resulted from fundamentally differ-ent strategic premises than those Realdania had come to adopt over time; however, the philanthropic organization remained bound by previously agreed commitments.

These tensions indicate how the material building not only afforded the projection and realization of organizational futures but also deflected and redirected organizational futures. Through the material building, previ-ously unrelated organizations now had to account for each other in their respective ongoing activities in the present, as well as in their future-oriented strategies. We observed two divergent responses to this situation.

Some actors expressed a desire to settle the tensions emerging from the co-existing use concepts of and ambitions associated with the building and define which of the main tenant organizations would engage in which kind of tasks and activities. This view comes to the fore in the following statement:

Now, of course both Realdania and the government . . . say: So what is it actually that we have here? Now comes the next step, how can we optimize, tune that? . . . my hope is that they understand that it's kind of a big ship that they have created together. It's not so important who . . . is on board, but how the machinery is working on that ship. What does it offer society? (Manager, DAC)

Roughly a year after the building's inauguration, Realdania compiled a list of all activities and programmes run by BLOX's main tenants. Likewise, representatives from DAC, the Design Society, and BLOXHUB met for regular strategy and coordination meetings, and launched several joint activities. These constituted attempts to create a closed, defined future that consolidated the co-existing concepts and assigned clearly circumscribed roles to the different tenant organizations in the future enactment of the building. Put differently, these activities sought to homogenize future projections in the present. However, as we observed actors being unable to make explicit and to account for their respective past-present-future trajectories, these attempts proved largely unsuccessful.

Instead of resolving present tensions, actors engaged in the production of additional, novel futures. These futures were much more vague, and hence more readily mutually agreeable than the diverse past, now co-existing future projections. Indeed, some actors suggested that the ambiguity of aspirations was necessary for the functioning of BLOX: 'You can never say ... "Ok, now we can celebrate and it's over." It has to be an evolving ecosystem all the time' (Manager, Design Society). This stance was clear in the unabated launch of new programmes and initiatives after the opening of the building. This ongoing search for the 'next' also came to the fore in the explanation of several interviewees that sustainability, as the core of the building's proclaimed concept, was becoming 'mainstream' and was increasingly considered a 'hygiene factor rather than a strategic differentiator'. For example, a BLOXHUB board member expressed this view:

We really had some interesting discussions about sustainability on the BLOXHUB board. ... is it the core purpose or is it the current standard ... I think we ended up putting it in the right place rather than making it, 'We are here for sustainability'. It became a broader purpose, focusing on 'city development'. And of course, it has to be sustainable, and it has to be digital, and in three years' time it has to be something else.

This statement suggests the importance of the ongoing production of novel future projections, which afford an ongoing reconceptualization of BLOX, and allow the building and its hosted organizations to stay relevant and contemporary.

Historicizing II: A Contemporary Landmark

After Realdania as developer and OMA as architects obtained a building permit, historicizing continued in anticipation of the eventual completion of BLOX, and particularly after the building's opening, once BLOX had become a 'material fact'. BLOX gradually attained its own historicity, emancipating itself from the historicity of the urban fabric that had given rise to the potentiality of a building in *that* material space. From being a mere proposal in space and time, the building materialized. The emergent historicity of BLOX became evident to both tenants and other stakeholders, as well as us as researchers, for instance, by obtaining an address, making its way into tourist guidebooks, and getting its own stop for tourist boats. At the same time, multiple actors claimed interpretive dominance over the building's historicity, and over how it would fold into urban and societal historicity.

As owner and developer of the building, Realdania took a leading role in attempting to shape the historicity of the building by constructing an overarching identity and narrative. In August 2015, Realdania framed the building's aesthetic identity by naming it 'BLOX'. According to Realdania's press release, 'The name BLOX matches the form and function of the distinctive building: architecturally, because the structure is built up as a number of blocks, staggered on top of each other; content wise, because BLOX will house many different functions, which, like blocks, build upon and support each other' (Realdania, 2015, own translation from Danish). However, due to tensions between the future ambitions that different organizations had projected onto the building, the ways in which the space's 'many different functions ... build upon and support each other' remained far from obvious.

The establishment of BLOXHUB became another way of historicizing the BLOX building. Struggles with conceptualizing the building in light of a growing number of tenants and purposes eventually resulted in the establishment of the BLOXHUB association as a new organization that provided a governance structure to the different tenants and as a way for non-resident organizations to become associated with the building. While encompassing the building's purposes as stated in previous concepts, BLOXHUB subsumed them under 'sustainable urban development' as its overarching purpose. This purpose mirrored an ongoing shift in Realdania's strategic focus. As a board member acknowledged, Realdania was 'a little late in terms of making sustainability a clear foundation of our values and our strategies'. However, following a change in the philanthropic organization's executive management in 2013, sustainability had increasingly become a central focus. In line with this shift, Realdania's management elevated the contribution to sustainable urban development to become the purpose of the entire building: 'not only is BLOXHUB speaking exactly to that agenda ... the whole building is speaking exactly to that agenda' (Manager, Realdania).

When Realdania reframed the building's principle purpose as contributing to sustainable urban development, BLOX became 'more than a building' (Realdania, 2018), or, in the words of Realdania's chief philanthropy officer, 'a contemporary landmark, not only for Copenhagen but for sustainable urban development' (Skovbro & Weiss, 2018, p. 147). From its inception in 2006, BLOX was aesthetically always intended to become a landmark building, yet it was only in 2016, two years before its opening, that the actors involved settled on what it was going to be a landmark for – that is, its symbolic meaning. The claim that BLOX was a landmark for sustainable urban development had become possible to make because Copenhagen as a city had itself become an icon of sustainable urban development during the years of the building's development and construction. BLOX both supported and benefitted from the city's successful urban regeneration, having its symbolic meaning legitimated.

Other actors contested Realdania's claims concerning the benefits of BLOX for urban and societal development. For instance, actors working for other initiatives and programmes trying to facilitate innovation in the field of sustainable urban development feared that BLOX would stifle the requisite heterogeneity and niches for new ideas to emerge by attracting public and private resources and attention. Moreover, the building faced negative reviews from national and international architectural critics. For instance, in the UK, the *Guardian* newspaper called BLOX 'a missed opportunity for Denmark' and claimed 'the building exudes the off-putting sense of a generic corporate office block' (Wainwright, 2018), while a Danish newspaper called the building a 'monster' (Ifversen, 2018). Confronted with this criticism during a public event, a Realdania manager shrugged his shoulders and responded that he was not surprised: 'the building was designed with future generations in mind – it still has to function 100 years from now'. Seemingly, the manager was well aware of the building's evolving historicity.

Discussion: Materiality, Temporality, and Politics

Our findings followed the creation of BLOX along three dimensions: *historicizing the building through time, projecting the building over time* ('epochal' dimension; Hernes et al., 2021), and *enacting the building in time* ('processual' dimension; Hernes et al., 2021). We summarized the interplay between these three dimensions in our empirical model (Figure 11.2).

The first main contribution of our chapter is the addition of the 'historicizing' dimension to the concept of material temporality (Hernes et al., 2021), supplementing the 'epochal' and 'processual' dimension. Analytically, we showed how we might conceptualize the building-as-temporal trajectory that emerges between social actors' temporalities and the temporality of the material building. From an organizational perspective, this trajectory *is* 'the building' as a temporarily stabilized outcome. Rather than becoming lastingly entangled, as most extant research on socio-materiality assumes (see, e.g., Orlikowski & Scott,

2008), social actors and the material building each pursue their trajectory through time, with the socio-material trajectory of the building emerging as a third trajectory between them. The 'historicizing' dimension captures how this socio-material trajectory takes shape by drawing connections between past, present, and future encounters between social and material actors.

Holding the three dimensions analytically separate revealed the different kinds of encounters between the material temporality of the building and the temporality of social actors. In this section, we focus on their interplay and the political struggles and negotiations that unfolded between them and through which they entangled, which have 'a shape, trajectory, and force of [their] own' (Geertz, 1973, p. 316). Our findings show how the building emerged from, gave rise to, and temporarily resolved or suspended such political struggles.

First, the building itself emerged from political struggles. The historicity of the urban space (the Brewhouse site), the place (Copenhagen, Denmark), and associated social processes (e.g., urban revitalization) gave rise to a spatio-temporal opening in the urban fabric that provided the potential for a new building on the Copenhagen harbour front. DAC and Realdania combined their organizational future projections into a building proposal. Through timely enactment of their socio-material proposal, these actors seized the opening in the urban fabric.

Second, the building gave rise to new political struggles by bringing together new constellations of actors. During construction, other actors projected their futures onto the building. Once social actors encountered each other inside the material building, tensions surfaced between their respective, simultaneously present future projections.

Third, the building temporarily resolved or suspended such political struggles. On the one hand, the material building temporarily resolved political struggles by affording initially stable conceptualizations and associated constellations of actors, such as the establishment of BLOXHUB as a governance mechanism. On the other hand, unable to settle these tensions permanently, actors continued projecting novel futures. In this way, the building's 'patient' materiality allowed for the suspension of political struggles, pushing them into an ill-defined future. These observations resonate with Slavich et al.'s (2020) study of the legitimization of a novel category, in which 'a process of taking stock of the meanings generated' (Slavich et al., 2020, p. 283) succeeded periods of intense controversy. In our case, BLOX attained its own trajectory through an ongoing back and forth between enacting and projecting, thereby wrenching its existence from the urban fabric and staying airborne.

The second main contribution of our chapter is to show that the organizing effects of material buildings emerge not only from their material durability, but also from their temporal malleability. Several previous studies have explored how buildings' pasts have a bearing on the present (e.g., de Vaujany & Vaast, 2014; Decker, 2014; Giovannoni & Napier, 2022; Giovannoni & Quattrone, 2018; Petani & Mengis, 2016). In contrast, our study shows how a building may act as an anticipated future event, through its imagined materialization (see also Alimadadi et al., 2021).

Beyond the case of material buildings, the temporal view of socio-materiality pursued in this chapter opens new perspectives on the critiqued 'ontological fusion' (Leonardi, 2013) often assumed by studies of socio-materiality (Orlikowski & Scott, 2008). Following social actors and material artifacts as distinct processes, our study shows how they both constantly resist their entanglement, pursuing through time their own evolving past-present-future trajectory. Instead, we found actors engaging in projecting and historicizing, representing attempts to articulate, imagine and eventually enact social and material trajectories together. To leverage this insight in future studies, researchers may direct their analysis to the respective past, present, and future of social and material actors before investigating their various encounters in time and the connection between these encounters – what we analysed as the connecting of events. This approach turns on whether or not, and, if so, how, these encounters result in a socio-material trajectory through time to become empirical questions.

Implications for a Temporal Understanding of Affordances

As an afterthought, our study may also have implications for a temporal understanding of affordances. Central for studies of socio-materiality, the concept of affordances denotes the possibilities for action that emerge in the encounter between materiality and human actors (e.g., Blagoev et al., 2018; Leonardi, 2017; Orlikowski & Scott, 2008). Extant conceptualizations of the concept of affordance have seldom engaged with the temporal dimension yet have analytically focussed on encounters between human actors and materiality in the present. The past played a role in these present encounters in terms of material inscriptions and the experience of human actors guiding interaction with material objects.

Adding to this focus on the present and past, our study suggests that materiality may afford *before* it has materialized, through anticipation, which affects in turn what it affords *after* it has materialized, as actors' respective anticipations continue to linger and may reveal unanticipated inconsistencies that give rise to tensions and demand ongoing negotiation. Affording before actually materializing, as a material potentiality, provides a temporal understanding of the 'materiality of absence' (Giovannoni & Quattrone, 2018). Extending from a relational view of affordances (Leonardi, 2017), we propose a temporally relational view of affordances. The latter view takes into account that both social actors and materiality have their own temporality, so that affordances may emerge in the present between a social actor's past and a material object's projected future, for example. The event-based analytical approach we pursued in this chapter may provide a way for future studies to explore such a temporally relational view of affordances.

References

Alimadadi, S., Davies, A., & Tell, F. (2021). A palace fit for the future: Desirability in temporal work. *Strategic Organization, 20*(1), 20–50. Advance online publication. https://doi.org/10.1177/14761270211012021

Benner, T. (2018, April 28). Realdania: Vi havde ikke bygget Blox i dag. *Politiken.* https://politiken.dk/kultur/arkitektur/art6474412/Realdania-Vi-havde-ikke-bygget-Blox-i-dag

Beyes, T. & Holt, R. (2020). The topographical imagination: Space and organization theory. *Organization Theory.* Advance online publication. https://doi.org/10.1177/2631787720913880

Blagoev, B., Felten, S., & Kahn, R. (2018). The career of a catalogue: Organizational memory, materiality and the dual nature of the past at the British Museum (1970–Today). *Organization Studies, 39*(12), 1757–83. https://doi.org/10.1177/0170840618789189

BLOX. (2019). About BLOX. www.blox.dk/english/about-blox/

Brand, S. (1994). *How Buildings Learn: What Happens after They're Built.* New York: Viking Press.

Cnossen, B. & Bencherki, N. (2019). The role of space in the emergence and endurance of organizing: How independent workers and material assemblages constitute organizations. *Human Relations, 72*(6), 1057–80. https://doi.org/10.1177/0018726718794265

Comi, A. & Whyte, J. (2018). Future making and visual artefacts: An ethnographic study of a design project. *Organization Studies, 39*(8), 1055–83. https://doi.org/10.1177/0170840617717094

Danish Architecture Center. (2020). About us. https://dac.dk/en/about/

de Vaujany, F-X. , Mitev, N., Laniray, P., & Vaast, E. (eds.) (2014). *Materiality and Time: Historical Perspectives on Organizations, Artefacts and Practices.* Basingstoke, UK & New York: Palgrave Macmillan.

de Vaujany, F-X. & Vaast, E. (2014). If these walls could talk: The mutual construction of organizational space and legitimacy. *Organization Science, 25* (3), 713–31. https://doi.org/10.1287/orsc.2013.0858

Decker, S. (2014). Solid intentions: An archival ethnography of corporate architecture and organizational remembering. *Organization, 21*(4), 514–42. https://doi.org/10.1177/1350508414527252

Design Society. (2020). *Design Society.* https://designsociety.dk/english/

Elsbach, K. D. & Pratt, M. G. (2007). The physical environment in organizations. *The Academy of Management Annals, 1*(1), 181–224. https://doi.org/10.1080/078559809

Feddersen, J. (2020). The Temporal Emergence of Social Relations: An Event-based Perspective of Organising (PhD thesis). Copenhagen Business School. https://research.cbs.dk/en/publications/the-temporal-emergence-of-social-relations-an-event-based-perspec

Geertz, C. (1973). *The Interpretation of Cultures: Selected Essays.* New York: Basic Books.

Giovannoni, E. & Napier, C. J. (2022). Multimodality and the messy object: Exploring how rhetoric and materiality engage. *Organization Studies.* Advance online publication. https://doi.org/10.1177/01708406221089598

Giovannoni, E. & Quattrone, P. (2018). The materiality of absence: Organizing and the case of the incomplete cathedral. *Organization Studies, 39*(7), 849–71. https://doi.org/10.1177/0170840617708005

Heidegger, M. (1927). *Being and Time.* Oxford: Blackwell Publishers.

Hernes, T. (2004). *The Spatial Construction of Organization.* Amsterdam & Philadelphia: John Benjamin.

Hernes, T. (2014). *A Process Theory of Organization.* Oxford: Oxford University Press.

Hernes, T. (2016). Process as the Becoming of Temporal Trajectory. In A. Langley & H. Tsoukas (eds.), *The SAGE Handbook of Process Organization Studies* (pp. 601–7). London: Sage. https://doi.org/10.4135/9781473957954.n38

Hernes, T. (2022). *Organization and Time.* Oxford: Oxford University Press.

Hernes, T., Feddersen, J., & Schultz, M. (2021). Material temporality: How materiality 'does' time in food organizing. *Organization Studies, 42*(2), 351–71. https://doi.org/10.1177/0170840620909974

Hernes, T. & Schultz, M. (2020). Translating the distant into the present: How actors address distant past and future events through situated activity. *Organization Theory.* Advance online publication. https://doi.org/10.1177/2631787719900999

Hussenot, A., Hernes, T., & Bouty, I. (2020). Studying Organization from the Perspective of the Ontology of Temporality: Introducing the Events-Based Approach. In J. Reinecke, R. Suddaby, A. Langley, & H. Tsoukas (eds.), *Time, Temporality, and History in Process Organization Studies.* Oxford: Oxford University Press. https://doi.org/10.1093/oso/9780198870715.003.0005

Hussenot, A. & Missonier, S. (2016). Encompassing stability and novelty in organization studies: An events-based approach. *Organization Studies, 37*(4), 523–46. https://doi.org/10.1177/0170840615604497

Ifversen, K. R. S. (2018, April 25). Skal fremme interessen for arkitektur: Blox er blevet et misfoster. *Politiken.* https://politiken.dk/kultur/arkitektur/art6469098/Blox-er-blevet-et-misfoster

Jones, C. & Massa, F. G. (2013). From novel practice to consecrated exemplar: Unity temple as a case of institutional evangelizing. *Organization Studies*, *34*(8), 1099–136. https://doi.org/10.1177/0170840613492073

Kania, J. & Kramer, M. (2011). Collective impact. *Stanford Social Innovation Review*, *11*(1), 36–41.

Katz, B. & Noring, L. (2017). *The Copenhagen City and Port Development Corporation: A Model for Regenerating Cities*. Washington, DC: The Brookings Institution.

Latour, B. & Yaneva, A. (2008). Give Me a Gun and I Will Make All Buildings Move: An ANT's View of Architecture. In U. Staub & R. Geiser (eds.), *Explorations in Architecture: Teaching, Design, Research* (pp. 80–9). Basel: Birkhäuser.

Leonardi, P. M. (2013). Theoretical foundations for the study of sociomateriality. *Information and Organization*, *23*(2), 59–76. https://doi.org/10.1016/j.infoandorg.2013.02.002

Leonardi, P. M. (2016). Materiality as an Organizing Process: Toward a Process Metaphysics for Material Artifacts. In A. Langley & H. Tsoukas (eds.), *The SAGE Handbook of Process Organization Studies* (pp. 529–42). London:Sage. https://doi.org/10.4135/9781473957954.n1

Leonardi, P. M. (2017). Methodological Guidelines for the Study of Materiality and Affordances. In R. Mir & S. Jain (eds.), *The Routledge Companion to Qualitative Research in Organization Studies* (pp. 279–90). New York: Routledge. https://doi.org/10.4324/9781315686103.ch15

Louisiana Channel. (2018, May 2). Ellen van Loon interview: Contaminating architecture. https://vimeo.com/267581418

Mair, J. & Hehenberger, L. (2014). Front-stage and backstage convening: The transition from opposition to mutualistic coexistence in organizational philanthropy. *Academy of Management Journal*, *57*(4), 1174–200.

Martinussen, K. & Weiss, K. L. (2018). Towards the Architecture Centre of the 21st Century. In K. L. Weiss (ed.), *BLOX* (pp. 154–60). Copenhagen: Realdania.

Møller, J. N. (2009). *Penge til husene*. Copenhagen: Realdania.

Orlikowski, W. J. & Scott, S. V. (2008). Sociomateriality: Challenging the separation of technology, work and organization. *The Academy of Management Annals*, *2*(1), 433–74. https://doi.org/10.1080/19416520802211644

Petani, F. J. & Mengis, J. (2016). In search of lost space: The process of space planning through remembering and history. *Organization*, *23*(1), 71–89. https://doi.org/10.1177/1350508415605102

Realdania (2015). Bryghusprojektet bliver til BLOX (Press release). https://realdania.dk/projekter/blox/nyheder/bryghusprojektet-bliver-til-blox

Realdania (ed.) (2018). *BLOX: Denmark's World of Architecture, Design and New Ideas*. Realdania. https://blox.dk/media/1363/blox-pixie-book.pdf

Skovbro, A. & Weiss, K. L. (2018). *BLOX from the Inside Out*. In K. L. Weiss (ed.), *BLOX* (pp. 145–53). Copenhagen: Realdania.

Slavich, B., Svejenova, S., Opazo, M. P. & Patriotta, G. (2020). Politics of meaning in categorizing innovation: How chefs advanced molecular gastronomy by resisting the label. *Organization Studies*, *41*(2), 267–90. https://doi.org/10.1177/0170840619835268

Taylor, S. & Spicer, A. (2007). Time for space: A narrative review of research on organizational spaces. *International Journal of Management Reviews*, 9(4), 325–46. https://doi.org/10.1111/j.1468-2370.2007.00214.x

Thau, C. (2018). Near and Far in the City: The Building as Urban Nerve Centre. In K. L. Weiss (ed.), *BLOX* (pp. 97–112). Copenhagen: Realdania.

van Loon, E. & Weiss, K. L. (2018). City in a Box. In K. L. Weiss (ed.), *BLOX* (pp. 49–64). Copenhagen: Realdania.

Wainwright, O. (2018, May 1). Urban jumble: The building that wants to upset the calm of Copenhagen. *The Guardian*. https://theguardian.com/artanddesign/2018/may/01/blox-danish-architecture-centre-copenhagen

Weinfurtner, T. & Seidl, D. (2019). Towards a spatial perspective: An integrative review of research on organisational space. *Scandinavian Journal of Management*, 35(2). https://doi.org/10.1016/j.scaman.2018.02.003

Yaneva, A. (2009). *The Making of a Building: A Pragmatist Approach to Architecture*. Oxford & New York: Peter Lang.

12 The Temporality of Entrepreneurship
How Entrepreneurs Blend Memories and Projections in the Ongoing Present of New Venture Creations

Christian Garmann Johnsen

Introduction

In 2017 RZC Investment, owned by two Walmart heirs, acquired Rapha, founded by Simon Mottram, for £200 million. Over the previous two decades, Rapha had established itself as a fashionable, high-end cycling apparel company offering direct-to-consumer deliveries through online stores and selected shops. Having left his accountancy career in the early 1990s, Mottram wanted to create a line of apparel that crystalized the essence of cycling. Aspiring to start his own company, he began tinkering with various business plans, all of which he declared to be 'totally rubbish'.[1] Still, from 1999 onwards, his frustration with the available kits drove him to play seriously with the idea of starting a cycling apparel company: his thinking was, 'someone could do this better'.[2]

Initially, Mottram had no elaborate plans for growing a business. Instead, he spent countless hours 'thinking about why I like cycling',[3] using a scrapbook to record his thoughts and solidify his ideas. Eventually, he arrived at what he considered lay at the heart of cycling, expressing this spirit in the motto ultimately used in Rapha's original marketing campaign: *ex duris gloria* (glory through suffering). Having experience in brand management, Mottram named his company after the Saint-Raphaël cycling team of the 1950s and 1960s. He thus aimed to create a brand of cycling apparel that reflected what cycling is all about: pushing yourself beyond your comfort zone.

Having invested in no prototypes of the clothes he wanted to sell, Mottram had initial difficulty attracting investors. However, he eventually managed to raise £140,000, mostly from friends and family, using the funds to establish Rapha in 2004. He hired two people to help with the

---

[1] https://cyclingtips.com/2020/03/from-the-top-podcast-building-rapha/
[2] https://99u.adobe.com/articles/7087/simon-mottram-on-passion-obsession-why-your-brand-should-take-sides
[3] https://cyclingtips.com/2020/03/from-the-top-podcast-building-rapha/

company: a graphic designer, Luke, to help develop products and the website, and Claire, who took care of the administration and consumer relations. (He and Luke later disagreed about Luke's status, with Luke seeing himself as a co-founder, but Mottram considering him an employee.) To launch the company, Mottram decided to host an exhibition entitled the 'King of Pain' at a London art gallery, where he displayed vintage products he had bought to celebrate cycling legends like Eddy Merckx and Fausto Coppi.

At the exhibition, visitors could watch the stages of the Tour de France, which was illegally broadcast on a gallery wall every day. Although frustration with the look and quality of cycling kits had spurred Mottram to found Rapha, he also recognized that cycling was a somewhat esoteric sport and hoped the exhibition would spark interest in it. The first Rapha collection ranged from a cycling jersey to a T-shirt and cap, all of which were intended to be sold at the exhibition but did not arrive in time. These early events kicked off the journey that would eventually make Rapha an iconic cycling apparel brand. With its combination of retro appeal to classic road cycling and the use of new technologically advanced fabrics, Rapha has managed to create clothing that matches the functionality of other high-end brands but also evokes the history of the sport and its iconic fashion.

Mottram's story of Rapha's evolution from scrapbook ideas to a company today featuring over 200 products serves as a reminder that we cannot understand entrepreneurship without considering how the process of creating a new venture unfolds in time (Dimov, 2020; Johnsen & Holt, 2021; Lévesque & Stephan, 2020; McMullen & Dimov, 2013; Wadhwani et al., 2020; Wood et al., 2021). Entrepreneurship is the process of bringing something into being that did not exist before – a new mode of production, product or service, a change from nothing to something. Indeed, how a venture goes from conception to a business is a journey that takes place in time (McMullen & Dimov, 2013), often meted into discrete pockets of time – a period of formulating a new venture idea, of combining resources to establish a company and then of engaging with market actors. However, rather than progressing in a chronological sequence, entrepreneurship often involves recursive patterns: failed attempts provide the basis for experimenting with new resource combinations, in turn possibly sparking new ideas (Dimov & Pistrui, 2020). Over time, entrepreneurs must continuously revise and amend their initial venture ideas in light of the feedback received from other market participants, such as consumers and competitors (Chiles et al., 2010). Similarly, an initial plan for a new business might be discarded during the entrepreneurial journey, even as a new plan takes shape.

As Mottram shares Rapha's story for a cycling magazine interview in 2020, it becomes apparent how time does not follow a linear trajectory of one event after another, such as an idea that develops along a timeline into a business. In fact, we come to recognize that Mottram is telling the story retrospectively, plotting the previous experiences that lead to Rapha's eventual success. As Dimov (2011) remarks, however, reading the entrepreneurial journey backwards differs from reading it forwards. As entrepreneurs venture into the future, they might imagine how consumers can benefit from a product or service currently unavailable to them. Yet, at the moment of imagining, the envisioned future is uncertain, with no guarantee that their visions will be realized (McMullen & Shepherd, 2006). However, when their visions prove right, entrepreneurs can, as Mottram does, relate how there was a 'gap in the market'[4] or untapped market demand that their business was able to exploit. Still, such claims can only be made once a business is established. Only in hindsight can Mottram share the experience of building his company. Indeed, he tells the story in the context of how we in the present can recall the past, a temporal distance that allows Mottram to reflect on his achievements but also his mistakes and the lessons he learned from them. In this way, the past, being more than simply what has taken place, becomes a repertoire of stories open to interpretations that influence not only how the present is experienced, but also how the future is projected (Wadhwani et al., 2020).

This goes to show how the temporality of entrepreneurship is multi-layered (Lévesque & Stephan, 2020): there is no 'one' time of entrepreneurship, but rather many layers of time expressed in the way entrepreneurship unfolds. Here, time relates to how entrepreneurs recall memories of the past in the present, and how these memories serve to project the future (Wood et al., 2021). On the other hand, time in entrepreneurship also unfolds sequentially: something happens and then something else happens (McKelvie et al., 2020). Entrepreneurs often fail because of their unmaterialized projections, an outcome that might even threaten their credibility (Garud et al., 2014). So, how can we make sense of the temporality of entrepreneurship? In this chapter, I set out to explore the different temporal layers involved in entrepreneurship, drawing insights from the philosophy of time and showing their value in helping us to think about entrepreneurship. I will focus on two ways time relates to entrepreneurship: the first being entrepreneurship as a journey or process, and the second as actions that take

---

[4] https://99u.adobe.com/articles/7087/simon-mottram-on-passion-obsession-why-your-brand-should-take-sides

place in time. Although these two aspects of entrepreneurship are inter-related, they must nevertheless be understood against the backdrop of different categories of time.

What Is Time?

Thinking about time requires a conceptual discussion. According to Schatzki (2006, p. 155), a key distinction can be made between chrono-logical time ('time of the world') and phenomenological time ('time of experience'). Chronological time refers to time as a 'linear succession of instances' (Ricœur, 1980, p. 170) and originates from Aristotle's concep-tion of time as 'a number of motions in respect to "before" and "after"' (Aristotle & McKeon, 2001, p. 292). Basically, for Aristotle, time is change, because we can only capture it by registering how things change from one state to another: the movement from 'before' something hap-pens to 'after' it has taken place constitutes time. This is why McTaggert (1908, p. 459) insists that we can only recognize time by recognizing change taking place in the world. A never-changing universe would be timeless by virtue of the fact that no point of reference existed to distin-guish an earlier state of affairs (before) from a later one (after). Thus, we can say that one event came before another because the two are distin-guishable, and, likewise, we can say something has remained the same because something else changed.

Chronological time can be portrayed as an 'arrow' (Ricœur, 1980) consisting of distinct instances (t1, t2, t3, t4 and so on) that can be measured and numerically represented with instruments, such as clocks or calendars. Each numeric instance is ordered in a sequence of 'before-now-after' (Schatzki, 2006, p. 171) each other (e.g., the *now* t2 becomes *after* t1, but *before* t3), and the moving interval between these instances constitutes time. As such, the 'now' moves along the arrow. Being object-ive and measurable, time as conceived by Aristotle is often considered 'time of the world'. However, according to Ricœur, the Aristotelean definition of time pivots on the 'mind's ability to distinguish two end points and an interval' (1985, p. 15). Once we understand this notion of before and after points and the movement between them as the interval, then we can grasp time. Aristotle's theory of time, Ricœur argues, pre-supposes that the mind can make distinctions between before, now and after, but without making this supposition explicit (1985, p. 16). But do we, in fact, experience time in this way?

This idea of chronological time underlies Bergson's attempt to grasp the experience of time as *duration*. For Bergson, chronological time tends to reduce time to geometrical space. Hence, with chronological time, instances are plotted on a timeline equivalent to the way that geometrical space allows objects to be placed side by side on a diagram. However, this reduction of time to space fundamentally discounts the experience of movement, which Bergson insists numeric representations cannot capture. To illustrate his argument, Bergson (2001, p. 103) invites us to consider a point A that moves along a line. If this point possessed self-consciousness, Bergson notes, then A would 'feel itself change, since it moves' (2001, p. 103). However, this feeling is not tantamount to the line on which the point moves. In fact, point A might take an elevated perspective so it can see the line from above and thus trace the movement's trajectory. The line thus becomes visible to A because it takes the outside perspective, but the inward experience of movement differs because the experience of movement is what Bergson terms '*durée*', or 'duration', meaning a 'succession of qualitative changes' (2001, p. 104).

In this experience of duration, each instance of time cannot be divided into points on a line without betraying its qualitative nature. This renders the ongoing experience of movement not a line of discrete instances but an array of changes that continuously 'permeate one another' (Bergson, 2001, p. 104). As Schatzki notes, duration is therefore a 'succession in the flow of consciousness' (2006, p. 163). This process of succession is not segmented, but rather involves the 'melting of states of consciousness into one another' (Bergson, 2001, p. 107). This experience of time as duration cannot be conceptually grasped, but only intuitively understood (Schatzki, 2006). Herein lies the difference between chronological time and Bergson's concept of durée: whereas the lived time of durée is a qualitative multiplicity in which the flux of experience unfolds, chronological time, in its usual sense of clock time, is a quantitative representation of points on a trajectory.

Time, Process and Entrepreneurship

Dimov and Pistrui (2020) use Bergson's reflection of time as duration to ponder the perspectives involved in entrepreneurship. From an outside perspective, we might trace the journey of building a new venture as a process comprised of distinct steps, instances and phases. For example, entrepreneurship can be considered a process that starts with creating a new venture idea, then performing entrepreneurial action and interacting with the market (Davidsson, 2015; Kier & McMullen, 2018; Vogel, 2017). Each step can be captured by creating a chronology. A new venture idea is a 'mental image of a particular group of customers benefiting from using a particular product or service' (Dimov, 2007, p. 566). However, entrepreneurship requires more than simply imagining a new market offering; entrepreneurs must also acquire resources, make an effort and invest time to realize an idea in practice (Foss & Klein, 2020). The process of turning a venture idea into an actual business entails entrepreneurial action (McMullen & Shepherd, 2006). Such action consists of the activities that enable the creation of a new venture, such as attracting investors and making contracts with suppliers and distributors. What is more, entrepreneurs need to interact with the market in which they intend to sell their products or service.

Although the relationship between a new venture idea and entrepreneurial action is often considered a linear progression that involves converting a cognitive outline for a new venture into a tangible business that can flourish on the market, the two are also connected in a recursive pattern that unfolds in time (Dimov & Pistrui, 2020). Entrepreneurs striving to create profitable business models must make continual adjustments between their venture idea (e.g., that a new market offering can benefit consumers) and their actual efforts (e.g., creating a business, but to uncertain ends). The founder of a new venture might, for example, be able to draw on prior experiences and knowledge that foster the pursuit of a profitable business model. In turn, however, a venture idea might motivate an action to be taken, but the consequence of that action might lead to the venture idea being revised.

Davidsson and Gruenhagen (2021) distinguish between two process views on entrepreneurship. The first considers entrepreneurship 'a directional and temporal journey towards a goal' (Davidsson & Gruenhagen, 2021, p. 23). By this account, regarding entrepreneurship as a temporal process that evolves towards the creation of a new venture tends to make us organize all instances that took place in the process as a natural sequence leading to a distinct outcome. As such, in the case of Rapha, we can retrospectively see Mottram's every act as an event on a timeline that culminated in the establishment of a company he could sell for £200 million. Yet process has another meaning: 'a journey through qualitative changes in content' (Davidsson and Gruenhagen, 2021, p. 23). This is the meaning of process that resonates with Dimov and Pistrui's (2020) reading of Bergson.

Although an outside perspective allows us to organize the entrepreneurial process into a sequence of formulating a new venture idea, performing actions and interacting with the market, Dimov and Pistrui (2020) note that this is not how the process is experienced within entrepreneurs themselves, who are instead exposed to successive impressions. Here, they can be seen 'as tracing a journey in which sometimes the only constant is their evolving intent' (Dimov & Pistrui, 2020, p. 269). Mottram's narrative can be structured to align with the first meaning of the process, but also reveals traces of other experiences of time associated with the second meaning. For example, one of Rapha's first products, a performance merino-wool cycling jersey, remains a top seller. Planning to launch Rapha through his first exhibition 'Kings of Pain', Mottram had intended to have the product ready in time for the opening. However, in the time leading up to the launch, Mottram recalls the following incident:

I tried to make it [the Classic Jersey] in the UK and this factory in Nottingham, and the guy called me up and said, 'I'm not going to send them tomorrow.' And I said, 'Well, why not?' He said, 'Well, because you've done 15 prototypes, and it's never right and you won't accept it. It's got to fit. I'm not going to get to the sort of quality you want. I'm not going to risk running my machines through the night and using the raw materials and paying for them for you to say "no".' I said, 'Well, listen mate, I've just invested a huge amount of money in a launch, or for me it was a huge amount of money. If they don't have sleeves, I don't care. You know, just, I need to have products.' And he just said 'no'. So, I walked downstairs to this little room we had where Luke and Claire were, and I said, 'I've got a bit of a problem guys. We're not going to have the classic jersey for the launch.' But as it happened, it didn't matter. We'd done enough to establish the brand. I went to Paris and bought lots of vintage stuff to sell instead, and we sold some of that.[5]

These experiences of stress and anticipation, worries and hopes, cannot be reduced to a linear sequence. Time in this instance is more than a series of events falling one after the other on a line. Each moment carries anticipation and worries about what the future will bring, but also reflections on the past. When a person is stressed and worried, time goes swiftly, but unease and anxiety can make time stand still (Johnsen, 2016). In the above incident, Mottram was not paralyzed; he decided to drop his aim to have the Classic Jersey ready for the launch and to sell vintage cycling products purchased in France instead. How can we understand the way entrepreneurs act in time? While Bergson lets us see the flow of time, Heidegger allows us to explore the temporality of entrepreneurial activities.

Phenomenological Time and Entrepreneurship

As we have seen, chronological time organizes instances in the sequence of *before-now-after*. In this equation, the before is assumed to be what has passed and the future what is yet to be. However, as Augustine (1960) observes, this poses a dilemma (Ricœur, 1985): if the past has ceased to exist, while the future has yet to happen, does time have any existence? Does it make sense to say that time has any reality at all? To solve this

---

[5] https://cyclingtips.com/2020/03/from-the-top-podcast-building-rapha/

conundrum, Augustine (1960) acknowledges that we can experience the past in the present by evoking memories and imagine the future by making projections. Thus, phenomenological time, which derives from Augustine (1960), refers to the experience of the 'past-present-future'. From a phenomenological perspective, as Ricœur (1980) explains, time is therefore experienced as a dynamic interplay between past memories, the perception of the present and expectations for the future.

According to chronological time, the before-now-after constitutes a sequential order. However, Heidegger maintains that this is not how humans temporally orient themselves in the world. As humans, we primarily relate to time as the way in which we project possibilities for the way we can be in the future. As such, *dasein* – the German word for 'being there', or presence – is, as Heidegger notes, 'constantly ahead of itself' (1962, p. 386). Heidegger bases his critique of the ordinary understanding of time on the three temporal markers of past, present and future. As we have seen, chronological time creates a sequential timeline, but for Heidegger, this is an abstraction from our primary relation to time. Activity, Heidegger insists, characterizes the human condition: above all, humans engage, act and dwell in the world. As we do so, our engagement is temporarily constituted, but not chronologically, because when engaging in the world, we are typically ahead of ourselves, our focus being on what we want to do. For example, when I enter a room, my attention is usually not on the present – that is, the instant of crossing the threshold – but rather on what I want to do once I am in the room, for example, talk to a specific person or find a seat.

Heidegger describes this future temporal orientation of humans in the form of 'not yet' (1962, p. 186): being in the world is a constant gliding towards what has 'not yet' taken place or what we have 'not yet' become. At the same time, being in a situation where this focus can occur only happens on the basis of the past: I am here as the result of what has already taken place. Moreover, my existence is always taking place as an engagement with things in the present here-and-now. According to Heidegger, human existence therefore has the coinciding temporal character of projection ('ahead-of-itself'), facticity ('being-already-in') and falling ('being-alongside') (1962, p. 293). Heidegger makes clear that being ahead-of-itself is 'grounded in the future', being-already-in assumes the form of 'having been', which relates to the past, whereas being-alongside is enabled by 'making present' (1962, p. 375). Temporality, for Heidegger, thus consists of a unity between having been, making present and ahead-of-itself (1962, p. 374), with projection being the way we can understand ourselves as possibilities for being. However, such possibilities, Heidegger notes, cannot simply be reduced to available choices, as existence itself creates possibilities for being. As Schatzki explains, projection is 'putting possible ways of being before oneself' (2006, p. 171). This makes any activity not only a choice but also a way of becoming: what I do signifies a way of life.

As Ricœur (1980) explains, in Heidegger's thinking, projection, facticity and falling replace the ordinary temporal markers of past, present and future. Hence, as Mulhall notes, it is a 'distinctly human capacity to be at once ahead, behind and alongside oneself' (2013, p. 161). Any human activity is futural, its being directed at what should be achieved is past, since one is situated within a historically produced context of possibilities, and is present, because the activity occurs alongside others that are here-and-now (Gilbert-Walsh, 2010, p. 179). In fact, time 'temporalizes itself in its being *lived* through temporally' (Scott, 2006, p. 184, original emphasis), which is to say that it is through human activity that the temporal aspects of past, present and future become visible. Heidegger reserves the term 'time' to talk about the ordinary conception of a 'pure sequence of "nows", without beginning and without end' (1962, p. 377), whereas 'temporality' refers to the way that the structure of having been, making present and ahead-of-itself constitutes human existence.

For Heidegger, humans can existentially assume three temporal aspects in different ways. Here, Heidegger distinguishes between an authentic and inauthentic way of relating to the future, well aware that humans remain situated within a historical context that conditions the space for action. Culture is inherited from the past, which stretches beyond the finite temporal horizon of birth and death. According to Heidegger, this cultural heritage opens possibilities, because humans can actively repeat the past in the present in order to make future projections. Hence, humans are cast into a world structured by cultural conditions, yet these conditions not only constrain the scope for action but also contain resources, templates and patterns in which humans can find possibilities for actions. Repetition, Heidegger (1962, p. 437) continues, refers to the way in which the past becomes actualized in the present in order to pave the way for future ways of being (Ricœur, 1980, p. 182). As Schrag suggests, for Heidegger, repetition is the 'handing-over and appropriation of possibilities' (1970, p. 289), making repetition an oscillation between the past and the future. Hence, repetition allows the past to enable possibilities in the future, but also for the past to be understood in light of how the future is projected.

For Heidegger, the concept of anticipatory resolution captures an authentic relation to the future. Anticipation, he states, consists of an awareness of the possibilities that remain available, whereas resolution involves commitment to these possibilities. Hence, anticipatory resolution is a way of being in which humans commit to a way of life enabled by the possibilities that lie within the specific situation in which they dwell. Heidegger therefore calls this resolution the 'authentic coming-towards-itself' (1962, p. 388). Because humans are existentially defined as a possibility, the coming towards does not segmentate a static state (e.g., who one really is), but rather opens up possibilities for ways of being (e.g., what one can become). Herein lies freedom, according to Heidegger, as humans free themselves from 'them' (what one should do) and instead actively assume a way of being. The counterpoint to anticipation is expectation. When one expects something, one is merely passively 'awaiting' (Heidegger, 1962, p. 386) something happening. This expectation takes the form of a preoccupation with the present – what Heidegger calls the 'feasible, urgent, or indispensable in our everyday business' (1962, p. 386). As we are absorbed by current affairs, we relate to the future by focussing on resolving immediate concerns. Unlike expectation and its preoccupation with the present, however, anticipation is an active projection of the future. With projection, humans can seek out the possibilities beyond present occupations and decide to commit to a way of life enabled by these possibilities, thereby 'projecting itself upon whichever possibility best releases its capacity for genuine individuality' (Mulhall, 2013, p. 165).

The Temporality of Entrepreneurial Opportunities

Inspired by Heidegger, we can rethink the role of time in entrepreneurship. Hence, with Heidegger, it is possible to explore time not only as an external factor (e.g., the entrepreneurial journey unfolds in time), but also explore how the activities undertaken by entrepreneurs are temporally structured. Drawing on Heidegger, Popp and Holt (2013) suggest that entrepreneurial endeavours do not radically depart from the present, but rather occur on the basis of existing practices that open up new ways of being. As such, entrepreneurs are attentive not only to prevalent practices of the past, but also to how an 'anomaly' in the present, as Spinosa et al. (1997) put it, clears a pathway for new ways of being in the future. For Spinosa et al. (1997), an anomaly is a problem in everyday life to which entrepreneurs can respond by changing a style of life. Thus, as Spinosa et al. maintain, entrepreneurs 'start with a disharmony between their understanding of what they do and what in fact they do' (1997, p. 193). On this basis, they find ways to reflect on what have previously been 'passed-over possibilities' (1997, p. 67) in the social fabric of society. Thus, Popp and Holt write: 'working imaginatively and with a set of practices and styles, alert to anomalies that suggest but do not determine opportunities, entrepreneurs envision ways in which the world around them might be re-shaped' (2013, p. 20).

Consequently, Popp and Holt contend that entrepreneurship involves what Heidegger calls the process of 'making present', understood as 'allowing of what is not yet present to come forward' (2013, p. 20). Spinosa et al. (1997) assert that entrepreneurship involves 'history making', suggesting that entrepreneurs change social practices by remaining sensible to an anomaly. They illustrate this point by citing King C. Gillette's development of the disposable razor blade. After having to shave with a dull straight razor, Gillette asked himself whether men could shave in a more convenient fashion. He further wondered whether men could attain 'different relations to things in general' (Spinosa et al., 1997, p. 42) and thus be willing to give up their 'masculine rituals' of learning to shave from their fathers. Following this line of thought, Gillette was able to invent a razor blade that could be discarded once it had served its purpose.

If we return to Mottram's story of Rapha, the temporal dimensions of making this new venture present come into focus. Rapha was not a radical invention – a break with the past or a departure from the present that led into a new future. Instead, Rapha is a repetition of cultural resources, a revival of the cultural heritage of cycling, with a nostalgic appeal to its classic heroes. Cycling as a professional sport emerged in tandem with modernity, its development reflecting the tremendous efficiency machines had gained from the advent of modern technologies. Indeed, cycling was yet another area designed to demonstrate how the merger of man and machine could push the human potential (Oosterhuis, 2016). For Mottram, this cultural heritage was a possibility, but not one he passively assumed. Instead, he actively repeated the cultural heritage of cycling in Rapha's blending of classic design with modern fabric technologies. In this way, Rapha is a repetition that rearticulates the past in the present, thus creating possibilities in the future. The anomaly in Mottram's case was the way cycling apparel had lost touch with its classic design, a lapse that afforded him an opportunity to start a business.

The prevalence of opportunity as the dominant construct in entrepreneurship research forms the backdrop for Popp and Holt's Heideggerian view of entrepreneurship. Typically, opportunities are considered discrepancies between market supply and demand that entrepreneurs can exploit. Hence, as Shane and Venkataraman put it, opportunities are 'those situations in which new goods, services, raw materials, and organizing methods can be introduced and sold at a greater than their cost of production' (2000, p. 220). Kirzner (1997) maintains that such opportunities occur because markets have 'errors', stressing that 'opportunities are created by earlier entrepreneurial errors which have resulted in short-ages, surplus, misallocated resources' (1997, p. 70). Yet, as Dimov (2020) notes, such an opportunity view not only abstracts from entrepreneurial practices, but also loses force because the objective existence of an opportunity can only be inferred after the profits are earned. Consider, for example, an entrepreneur who invests in some more-valuable-than-expected resources, thus realizing a windfall. In this instance, the entrepreneur is able 'to "see" future prices more correctly than others see them', according to Kirzner (2009, p. 148). Yet, only once the entrepreneur has profitably sold the resources can this opportunity be said to have existed in the first place (Klein, 2008). Had the entrepreneur failed to turn a profit, then clearly no price discrepancy existed. What is more, the very presence of an opportunity cannot be established, as its existence cannot be analytically demonstrated (Dimov, 2020).

Much of the literature on opportunities has revolved around determining whether entrepreneurial opportunities are created or discovered (Alvarez & Barney, 2007). Those taking the discovery view argue that opportunities objectively exist in the market as latent consumer demands that entrepreneurs can discover and exploit by introducing new products, services or production means (Ramoglou & Tsang, 2016). In contrast, the creation view assumes that entrepreneurs can subjectively imagine new ventures that they then realize through their efforts. Suddaby et al. illustrate this approach with the example of Steve Jobs, who created the iPhone not by locating a gap in the market, but rather by launching 'a product that consumers did not even realize they wanted' (2015, p. 3). Yet, as Alvarez and Barney note, it is possible to 'describe the actions of a particular entrepreneur in both "discovery" and "creation" terms', since the two approaches lack 'empirical content' (2007, p. 12). For instance, one could say that Mottram discovered a lack of quality cycling apparel that appealed to classic design, but still had to create an exhibition that would attract consumers' attention. This example demonstrates how entrepreneurship requires both the presence of a context and the use of imagination and deliberate efforts (Crawford et al., 2016; Ramoglou & Gartner, 2022). For Alvarez and Barney (2007), discovery and the creation views do not differ in their empirical applications, but rather in how entrepreneurs are able to adopt either approach in practice.

According to McKelvie et al. (2020), an analytic focus on time is often the missing link in discussions of entrepreneurial opportunities. Opportunities are considered static misalignments in the market, but the dynamics between supply and demand changes over time are often overlooked, as are the subjective perceptions of the entrepreneur. McKelvie et al. (2020) focus on the 'passage of (clock) time' to study the dynamic interplay between objective market conditions and the entrepreneur's subjective perceptions. This allows them to explore how entrepreneurial actions spring from subjective beliefs about market conditions at one point in time, but also how later market feedback allows entrepreneurs to learn from their mistakes, acquire new information and update their beliefs.

Beyond Subjective and Objective Time in Entrepreneurship

A shift in analytic focus from chronological time to phenomenological time allows us to look not only beyond both the creation versus discovery dualism, but also the distinction between objective and subjective time. According to Heidegger, humans are not primarily in the world as subjects perceiving objects, a way of being that assumes a difference between inner sensations and external things. Rather, humans are characterized by their practical engagement. Temporality is therefore neither objective nor subjective. It is more than objective, as it enables humans to engage with objects. Similarly, temporality is more than subjective, because it allows for experience. To consider 'opportunity' within such a perspective is therefore to draw attention to entrepreneurs' practical engagement in social settings. Dimov (2020) takes this approach by considering how the 'entrepreneurial process starts with an individual vision and ends with a social entity' (p. 342). Rather than seeing opportunity as an abstract market discrepancy, Dimov associates it with its everyday meaning of 'a situation in which it is possible to do something' (2020, p. 343). This experience of 'making present some new state of the world' (Popp & Holt, 2013, p. 25) is precisely what Heidegger's thinking on temporality allows us to illuminate. Entrepreneurship is the process of bringing something into existence, and one can only capture this process by exploring how the activities entrepreneurs undertake involve a blend of past, present and future.

Offering an alternative to both the Kirznerian entrepreneur who discovers market errors and the Schumpeterian entrepreneur who disrupts established market orders, Chiles et al. (2010) draw on the work of Shackle to propose a radical subjectivist view of entrepreneurship. Entrepreneurs, they contend, 'actively engage the human mind to creative subjective mental images of possible future actions and outcomes, and to select the scenario they deem most desirable' (Chiles et al., 2010, p. 143). As such, this view assumes that thinking precedes action: entrepreneurs can imagine and calculate what they consider the most appropriate course of action for reaching their objectives. For example, entrepreneurs must assess when things should be done, in what order and with what results (Wood et al., 2021). Because other market participants also base their decisions on subjective projections and continuously revise their plans as new information comes in, the market process is characterized by uncertainty. Resources are constantly combined and recombined even as consumer preferences continually change and evolve, which forestalls the future from ever being a ready-made reality just waiting to arrive. Rather, 'the economic world is unknowable in principle because it is yet to be created and discovered' (Svetlova, 2021, p. 993). In such a world of 'unknown unknowns' (Foss & Klein, 2012, p. 85), uncertainty prevails because unforeseeable change always occurs (Townsend et al., 2018). This was Knight's basic insight: 'the fundamental uncertainty of economic life are the errors in predicting the future' (2005/1921, p. 259).

Although the radical subjectivist view aptly discerns how entrepreneurs act in the present by imagining the future, it nevertheless continues to draw a clear line between subjective imagination and objective conditions: entrepreneurs hold subjective beliefs about the future – an imaginary of a venture yet to be created – but surrounded by objective conditions, including potential consumers, technologies and available resources. Such a reliance on the distinction between subjective imagination and objective conditions leads to a duplicated reality: potential consumers are simultaneously subjectively imagined in the entrepreneur's mind and objectively exist as agents in the market. Converging rather than distinguishing these subjective and objective realities, however, is a condition for new venture creations: successful entrepreneurs launch a market offering on the basis of a projected demand that actually matches consumer preferences.

Gartner et al. challenge the assumption that entrepreneurship necessarily begins with a conscious business plan by asserting that 'acting precedes thinking' (1992, p. 18). For example, an entrepreneur might begin by interacting with potential consumers, thus enabling the entrepreneur to act 'as if' (Gartner et al., 1992) a business exists. Sarasvathy calls such entrepreneurial efforts a process of 'worldmaking': the entrepreneur can 'co-create new worlds and new futures' (2021, p. 8) by involving stakeholders in developing the venture. To take such an approach, the entrepreneur does not have to imagine potential consumers, as those consumer relations can be built on the basis of the means used to create a business. Faced with uncertainty, entrepreneurs can design their ventures to meet the predicted demands without having first to envisage future market conditions. Instead, they can start with the means available to them, such as the given resources, established networks and the knowledge possessed (Sarasvathy, 2001). On this basis, entrepreneurs can delve directly into action by setting up a new venture.

The temporality of entrepreneurial actions becomes visible once we recognize that past, present and future determine actions in the ongoing process of human activities. Subjective beliefs and motives do not exist 'before' the action takes place in the 'now' that creates results 'after'. Rather, as Schatzki (2006) argues citing Heidegger (1962), actions are determined in the moment they are performed. Hence, Schatzki suggests, 'it is with the performance of action that the actor's reasons for action become determinate' (2006, p. 161), and what determines the action is the configuration between the past, present and the future. Thus, an action is temporarily structured: it is at once evoked on the basis of the past, takes place in a present context and is directed at the future. For example, Mottram's efforts to stage an exhibition for his launch of Rapha was past, present and future all at once. In other words, the event could only take place on the basis of the past, namely Mottram's aspirations and his connection to cycling history; it was present because it took place within a specific context; and it was directed at the future, its being aimed to create a new venture. Similarly, Schatzki (2006) notes, the action is situated in world time: actions took place here-and-now and produced results in the future. In this light, the various temporal layers of entrepreneurship come into view.

Conclusion

As this chapter has shown, there are multiple temporal layers of entrepreneurship. How do we capture these layers? According to Ricœur (1980), narratives can present a storyline organized around a plot and thus trace the entrepreneurial journey while also remaining attentive to entrepreneurial experiences (Garud & Giuliani, 2013; Johnsen & Holt, 2021). However, the narratives portraying entrepreneurship are often heroic: an entrepreneur conquers the market with an innovative product that outcompetes those of established players. However, Brattström and Wennberg (2022) expose the prejudices entrenched in entrepreneurial storytelling, such as the tendency to ascribe a new venture's success exclusively to its founder's heroic actions. This overshadows the numerous others involved in creating ventures as well as the multiple factors that must fall into place for a new venture to succeed. Portraying Mottram as the sole inventor of Rapha risks precisely such an oversight. However, Brattström and Wennberg (2022) do not suggest dropping storytelling, but rather call for new stories of entrepreneurship that acknowledge 'the everyday struggles and obstacles faced by entrepreneurs, in both favored and unfavored institutional contexts' (2022, p. 14). It is within these struggles that the temporality of entrepreneurship becomes visible: entrepreneurship takes place in a flow of time that involves considering past, present and future at one and the same time.

References

Alvarez, S. A. & Barney, J. B. (2007). Discovery and creation: Alternative theories of entrepreneurial action. *Strategic Entrepreneurship Journal*, *1*(1–2), 11–26. https://doi.org/10.1002/sej.4

Aristotle & McKeon, R. (2001). *The Basic Works of Aristotle*. Modern Library.

Augustine (1960). *The Confessions of St. Augustine*. New York: Image Books.

Bergson, H. (2001). *Time and Free Will: An Essay on the Immediate Data of Consciousness*. New York: Dover Publications.

Brattström, A. & Wennberg, K. (2022). The entrepreneurial story and its implications for research. *Entrepreneurship Theory and Practice*, *46*(6), 1443–68. https://doi.org/10.1177/10422587211053802

Chiles, T. H., Vultee, D. M., Gupta, V. K., Greening, D. W. & Tuggle, C. S. (2010). The philosophical foundations of a radical Austrian approach to entrepreneurship. *Journal of Management Inquiry*, *19*(2), 138–64. https://doi .org/10.1177/1056492609337833

Crawford, G. C., Dimov, D. & McKelvey, B. (2016). Realism, empiricism, and fetishism in the study of entrepreneurship. *Journal of Management Inquiry*, *25* (2), 168–70. https://doi.org/10.1177/1056492615601506

Davidsson, P. (2015). Entrepreneurial opportunities and the entrepreneurship nexus: A re-conceptualization. *Journal of Business Venturing*, *30*(5), 674–95. https://doi.org/10.1016/j.jbusvent.2015.01.002

Davidsson, P. & Gruenhagen, J. H. (2021). Fulfilling the process promise: A review and agenda for new venture creation process research. *Entrepreneurship Theory and Practice*, *45*(5), 1083–118. https://doi.org/10.1177 /1042258720930991

Dimov, D. (2007). From opportunity insight to opportunity intention: The importance of person–situation learning match. *Entrepreneurship Theory and Practice*, *31*(4), 561–83. https://doi.org/10.1111/j.1540-6520 .2007.00188.x

Dimov, D. (2011). Grappling with the unbearable elusiveness of entrepreneurial opportunities. *Entrepreneurship Theory and Practice*, *35*(1), 57–81. https://doi .org/10.1111/j.1540-6520.2010.00423.x

Dimov, D. (2020). Opportunities, language, and time. *Academy of Management Perspectives*, *34*(3), 333–51. https://doi.org/10.5465/amp.2017.0135

Dimov, D. & Pistrui, J. (2020). Recursive and discursive model of and for entrepreneurial action. *European Management Review*, *17*(1), 267–77. https:// doi.org/10.1111/emre.12360

Foss, N. J. & Klein, P. G. (2012). *Organizing Entrepreneurial Judgment: A New Approach to the Firm*. Cambridge: Cambridge University Press. https://doi.org /10.1017/CBO9781139021173

Foss, N. J. & Klein, P. G. (2020). Entrepreneurial opportunities: Who needs them? *Academy of Management Perspectives*, *34*(3), 366–77. https://doi.org/10 .5465/amp.2017.0181

Gartner, W. B., Bird, B. J. & Starr, J. A. (1992). Acting as if: Differentiating entrepreneurial from organizational behavior. *Entrepreneurship Theory and Practice*, *16*(3), 13–32. https://doi.org/10.1177/104225879201600302

Garud, R. & Giuliani, A. P. (2013). A narrative perspective on entrepreneurial opportunities. *Academy of Management Review, 38*(1), 157–60. https://doi.org /10.5465/amr.2012.0055

Garud, R., Schildt, H. A. & Lant, T. K. (2014). Entrepreneurial storytelling, future expectations, and the paradox of legitimacy. *Organization Science, 25*(5), 1479–92. https://doi.org/10.1287/orsc.2014.0915

Gilbert-Walsh, J. (2010). Revisiting the concept of time: Archaic perplexity in Bergson and Heidegger. *Human Studies, 33*(2–3), 173–90. https://doi.org/10 .1007/s10746-010-9158-5

Heidegger, M. (1962). *Being and Time*. Oxford: Blackwell.

Johnsen, C. G. & Holt, R. (2021). Narrating the facets of time in entrepreneurial action. *Entrepreneurship Theory and Practice*, OnlineFirst. https://doi.org/10 .1177/10422587211038107

Johnsen, R. (2016). Boredom and organization studies. *Organization Studies, 37* (10), 1403–15. https://doi.org/10.1177/0170840616640849

Kier, A. S. & McMullen, J. S. (2018). Entrepreneurial imaginativeness in new venture ideation. *Academy of Management Journal, 61*(6), 2265–95. https://doi .org/10.5465/amj.2017.0395

Kirzner, I. M. (1997). Entrepreneurial discovery and the competitive market process: An Austrian approach. *Journal of Economic Literature, 35*(1), 60–85.

Kirzner, I. M. (2009). The alert and creative entrepreneur: A clarification. *Small Business Economics, 32*, 145–52. https://doi.org/10.1007/s11187-008-9153-7

Klein, P. G. (2008). Opportunity discovery, entrepreneurial action, and economic organization. *Strategic Entrepreneurship Journal, 2*(3), 175–90. http s://doi.org/10.1002/sej.50

Knight, F. H. (2005/1921). *Risk, Uncertainty and Profit*. New York: Cosimo Classics.

Lévesque, M. & Stephan, U. (2020). It's time we talk about time in entrepreneurship. *Entrepreneurship Theory and Practice, 44*(2), 163–84. https:// doi.org/10.1177/1042258719839711

McKelvie, A., Wiklund, J., McMullen, J. & Palubinskas, A. (2020). A dynamic model of entrepreneurial opportunity: Integrating Kirzner's and Mises's approaches to entrepreneurial action. *Quarterly Journal of Austrian Economics, 23*(3–4), 499–541. https://doi.org/10.35297/qjae.010078

McMullen, J. S. & Dimov, D. (2013). Time and the entrepreneurial journey: The problems and promise of studying entrepreneurship as a. *Journal of Management Studies, 50*(8), 1481–512. https://doi.org/10.1111/joms.12049

McMullen, J. S. & Shepherd, D. A. (2006). Entrepreneurial action and the role of uncertainty in the theory of the entrepreneur. *Academy of Management Review, 31*(1), 132–52. https://doi.org/10.5465/amr.2006.19379628

McTaggart, J. E. (1908). The unreality of time. *Mind, 17*(68), 457–74.

Mulhall, S. (2013). *The Routledge Guidebook to Heidegger's Being and Time*. London & New York: Routledge.

Oosterhuis, H. (2016) Cycling, modernity and national culture. *Social History, 41* (3), 233–48. DOI: 10.1080/03071022.2016.1180897

Popp, A. & Holt, R. (2013). The presence of entrepreneurial opportunity. *Business History*, 55(1), 9–28. https://doi.org/10.1080/00076791.2012.687539

Ramoglou, S. & Gartner, W. B. (2022). A historical intervention in the "opportunity wars": Forgotten scholarship, the discovery/creation disruption, and moving forward by looking backward. *Entrepreneurship Theory and Practice*, OnlineFirst. https://doi.org/10.1177/10422587211069310

Ramoglou, S. & Tsang, E. W. K. (2016). A realist perspective of entrepreneurship: Opportunities as propensities. *Academy of Management Review*, 41(3), 410–34. https://doi.org/10.5465/amr.2014.0281

Ricœur, P. (1980). Narrative time. *Critical Inquiry*, 7(1), 169–90.

Ricœur, P. (1985). *Time and Narrative* (Vol. 3). Chicago: University of Chicago Press.

Sarasvathy, S. D. (2001). Causation and effectuation: Toward a theoretical shift from economic inevitability to entrepreneurial contingency. *Academy of Management Review*, 26(2), 243–63. https://doi.org/10.5465/amr.2001.4378020

Sarasvathy, S. D. (2021). Even-if: Sufficient, yet unnecessary conditions for worldmaking. *Organization Theory*, 2(2). https://doi.org/10.1177/26317877211005785

Schatzki, T. R. (2006). The time of activity. *Continental Philosophy Review*, 39(2), 155–82. https://doi.org/10.1007/s11007-006-9026-1

Schrag, C. O. (1970). Heidegger on repetition and historical understanding. *Philosophy East and West*, 20(3), 287–95.

Scott, D. (2006). The 'concept of time' and the 'being of the clock': Bergson, Einstein, Heidegger, and the interrogation of the temporality of modernism. *Continental Philosophy Review*, 39(2), 183–213. https://doi.org/10.1007/s11007-006-9023-4

Shane, S. & Venkataraman, S. (2000). The promise of entrepreneurship as a field of research. *Academy of Management Review*, 25(1), 217–26. https://doi.org/10.5465/amr.2000.2791611

Spinosa, C., Flores, F. & Dreyfus, H. L. (1997). *Disclosing New Worlds: Entrepreneurship, Democratic Action, and the Cultivation of Solidarity*. Cambridge, MA: MIT Press.

Suddaby, R., Bruton, G. D. & Si, S. X. (2015). Entrepreneurship through a qualitative lens: Insights on the construction and/or discovery of entrepreneurial opportunity. *Journal of Business Venturing*, 30(1), 1–10. https://doi.org/10.1016/j.jbusvent.2014.09.003

Svetlova, E. (2021). On the relevance of Knight, Keynes and Shackle for unawareness research. *Cambridge Journal of Economics*, 45(5), 989–1007. https://doi.org/10.1093/cje/beab033

Townsend, D. M., Hunt, R. A., McMullen, J. S. & Sarasvathy, S. D. (2018). Uncertainty, knowledge problems, and entrepreneurial action. *Academy of Management Annals*, 12(2), 659–87. https://doi.org/10.5465/annals.2016.0109

Vogel, P. (2017). From venture idea to venture opportunity. *Entrepreneurship Theory and Practice*, 41(6), 943–71. https://doi.org/10.1111/etap.12234

Wadhwani, R. D., Kirsch, D., Welter, F., Gartner, W. B. & Jones, G. G. (2020). Context, time, and change: Historical approaches to entrepreneurship research. *Strategic Entrepreneurship Journal, 14*(1), 3–19. https://doi.org/10.1002/sej.1346

Wood, M. S., Bakker, R. M. & Fisher, G. (2021). Back to the future: A time-calibrated theory of entrepreneurial action. *Academy of Management Review, 46*(1), 147–71. https://doi.org/10.5465/amr.2018.0060

13 Management as Dramatic Events
Intense Decentred Organizing (IDO)

François-Xavier de Vaujany and Elen Riot

Introduction

Long before the pandemic, the world of work appeared to be a shared loneliness. More and more, we all "work alone together" (Turkle, 2011; Spinuzzi, 2012). Managers, employees, freelancers, entrepreneurs: all workers are gradually transformed into individuals continuously assembled and de-assembled by projects, platforms and ephemeral modes of organizations (Aroles et al., 2019; de Vaujany et al., 2021; Fayard, 2021). The Covid-19 pandemic and the recent generalization of remote work has made this trend stronger and more visible. Today, connectivity prevails over commonality.

Nonetheless, organizing still requires some sort of 'organization', at least a whole integrative scheme likely to hold the (lasting) value sold to customers and citizens. The more unstable a group of people and objects involved in collective activity are, the more there is a need for a minimal shared repertoire of routines, capabilities and infrastructures that it can draw on to become agentive. These 'organizational commons' require maintenance and continuity. What holds things together is repetition and confirmation. But the growing explosion of the time-space unity of work (and modes of consumption) has deeply endangered this process. The usual embodied modes of co-learning – the traditional onsite acculturation of workers – does not happen anymore (de Vaujany & Aroles, 2019). Contemporary modes of organizing have neither the time (shorter direct interactions and higher turnover in many industries) nor the place (many organizations have become non-places) to build togetherness and shared repertoires through traditional co-presence. So, how do we cultivate the organizational commons necessary for collective activity and its (dis)continuities? We argue here that new ways of working and organizing require intense shared moments (as they become rare, they need to be more intense) but also more intense differential past and future events likely to challenge each other, to prehend each other to become the kind of clusters constitutive of the organizational commons described here.[1] In the former case, recurrent time-space unity or shared narratives need to be continuously (re)built. In the latter case, work events need to be intense enough to challenge other events from their past or to challenge past events through the anticipation of their becoming. Events are productive differences (see Deleuze, 1969; Zourabichvili; 2012; Beck & Gleyzon, 2016) that gather harmoniously other events on the way to a collective activity (without any integration). In both directions, organizing requires more and more a dramatization and theatricalization in the sense that these accelerated, dense moments put aside the rest of the world in the process of their happening. The moment is so luminous that everything around it is dark. Collective work experience becomes close to an intense theatre experience. According to Peter Brook (1995),

Essentially, (theatre) is life, but it is life in a more concentrated form, more compressed in time and space .... In the writing or in the playing, there is a spark, the small flame that lights up and gives an intensity to that compressed, distilled moment. ... The spark is what matters and the spark is rarely there. This shows to what extent the theatrical form is frighteningly fragile and demanding, for this small spark of life must be present each and every second. (pp. 11–12)

The theatrical situation is intense because of its fragility and openness. Today, management cultivates this fragility both in (rare) common time and in the decentred life, which is becoming the new rule.

We propose to explore here the vocabulary, concepts and spacing of theatre as a new way to build a pre-subjective togetherness based on intense moments together 'now' or intense moments created, revisited or amplified in the past or in the future.

First, we will come back to the transformation of work and organizing itself. We will explore it both historically and metaphysically. Then, we will gather elements of theatre literature, either on the history of theatrical space, the narratives of dramatization or more philosophical elements borrowed from Deleuze, linked to the concept of intensity. At this stage, we will describe our theoretical perspective focussed on Intense Decentred Organizing (IDO).

---

[1] As pointed out by Juhlin and Holt, 2021, taking into account our "sensory imperative" may involve disturbing both traditional and emergent forms of work and hierarchies of knowledge just as they are becoming the new norm.

On Modern Organizational Phenomena: The Time-Space Unity of Work and the Hidden Gaze

Time and Space Modes of Organizing: An Historical Perspective

Modes of organization can be described historically or metaphysically.

Historically, collective activity was first artisanal, family and community-based before becoming industrial, societal and inter-individual (with the "modernity" of the Enlightenment).

From the *Compania* of the Renaissance to factories and then to firms (see Hatchuel & Glise, 2003 or de Vaujany, 2010), work collectives became increasingly attached to a "legal person". A firm can take different legal forms, bringing together individuals bound to it by an employment contract.

In a firm, the collective activity is 'localized'. It 'takes place' somewhere; it is 'emplaced'. After a long pre-modern period during which distinctions between private life and professional life were non-existent, when everything was community, guild or corporation (see Kieser, 1989), the end of the Middle Ages and the period of the Enlightenment were a time of huge expansion and dislocation. Private and professional spaces became more and more distinct, moving further away from each other. If silk weaving took place in private apartments (e.g., for the "soyeux" in Lyon), if peasants worked at the doorstep of their cottage, if merchants had their home next to or within their shop, the massive development of large cities and networks of communication has expanded and accentuated differences in the same movement. In the middle, "third places" (inns, restaurants, libraries, etc.) multiplied in societies that were soon concerned with the "leisure" of their individual-citizens (see Oldenburg & Brissett, 1982).

Spatially, real institutions (labour law, business, scientific management, etc.) emplace individualities. Everyone has a well-defined working day. Time (now gauged by unmarked mechanical clocks) is measurable and measured, and increasingly standardized across the capitalist planet (Birth, 2012). In the factory, in the workshop, in the design offices, everyone has their place. From that place, there is a limited horizon. But the worker knows that they can be seen by the foreman, the middle manager and some managerial devices themselves involved in more or less regular movements within workspaces. More than anything, production, or 'output' is measured and therefore made visible. The performance and its continuity nail a worker to the spot. Taken onto the assembly line and assigned to an often arbitrarily chosen role, the worker is attached to a job the value of which escapes him/her. To get through it, it is often better to cultivate a form of detachment from the work and perhaps, to show solidarity with others caught in the same situation.

The design office and offices in general are not left out. Here, everyone also has their place. Everything happens here – it is fixed and anchored in the heavy materiality of the workspace. The worker has just arrived at his/her workstation. He/she feels at regular intervals the boss's gaze on a present or future viewing (which can now be recorded and viewed later or viewed invisibly from afar). Furthermore, since the end of the nineteenth century, the chain of command has become endless. The boss is less and less the last link in the chain of power of an industrial family with a long history. They are more and more a management professional without property, simply 'mandated' to command. And behind them, the shareholders, an informed and attentive mass, command the commander. Large-sized firms (Chandler, 1993) with managerial hierarchies (Whyte, 1956(2013)) and changing plans (Jackall, 1988), located in different parts of the world, inform the designs of buildings, offices and furniture (Giedion, 2009; Riot, 2019).

In the 1990s, the spatial and temporal unity of modes of organization gradually broke up (Hatchuel & Glise, 2003; Cummings et al., 2017). Workers are moving away from the "I go to work every day on a fixed schedule" pattern. The heavy tools and spaces of industrial work are giving way to the mobility, lightness and fluidity of digital work. Even in service spaces such as hotels and airports, discrete areas are at once everywhere and nowhere (Cederström & Spicer, 2015). No longer do people have an instituted, pre-assigned place in a productive space waiting to be occupied. The modes of organization now constitute open spaces, flexible offices, co-working spaces and bosses with no office (Aroles et al., 2019; de Vaujany et al., 2021; Orel et al., 2021). Everything has moved towards projects, flexible organizations, nomadic work, lean management, connectivity. The explosion of the binary logics of the Cold War period, the development of strategies of full outsourcing (everything can be outsourced, from the information system to the management of human resources), the emergence of increasingly open access (the Internet) and the platformization of economies, marks a profound break in the functional organization and its unique time-space (de Vaujany, 2022). Finally, the logic of Plan, Organize, Command, Control, Coordinate formalized by Henri Fayol (1916) was part of a very clear Euclidean space where time-space is fully integrated and where ultimately time is only a spatialization, a change of coordinates in space. This space is being replaced by a Riemannian space and spacing (Deleuze, 1966, 1985) in which things and, most of all, events can be close and can emphasize endogenously a sense of neighbourhood, but the distance between neighbourhoods of events is itself undeterminable (Sewell & Taskin, 2015). Only closeness makes sense, as long as we have the capacity to co-exist in an interior (Sloterdijk, 2013). Away from an immediate neighbourhood, the position and localization of what is close or far is unknowable.

The Covid-19 pandemic has accelerated and made visible in the same movement an older trend: the explosion of the time-space of work and the new managerial challenge of the plurality of times of work (Nowotny, 1992; Alter, 2003). This multiplicity of (often) dyschronic managerial events must be integrated (Alter, 2003; de Vaujany, 2006; Reinecke & Ansari, 2015) or harmonized (Lorino, 2018; de Vaujany 2022).[2] Ephemeral time-space unities (we all find ourselves from time to time in the same meeting room and the same Zoom loop) and common narratives sometimes make it possible to maintain a strength in these ever more decentralized ways of working, consuming and living (see Alter, 2003). In other logics, a certain management can on the contrary play with these productive differences and seek harmony rather than "unity" or "integration" (Lorino & Mourey, 2013; Lorino, 2018; de Vaujany, 2022). This "pragmatist" management (Lorino, 2018), concerned with cultivating productive "gaps" (Jullien, 2012) and "productive differences" (de Vaujany, 2022) presupposes a distinct, more continuous relationship with experimentation.

Temporality and Spatiality: The Metaphysical Way

For the previous historical logic articulating different and above all, successive presents, the metaphysical track substitutes a more profoundly temporal vision. It denounces an ontological error of management. The organization has not become more procedural on its merits. It always has been. This is the central message of process-based approaches: collective activity is only becoming, processes and events. Organizations have no exteriority and pre-existence to activity (Chia, 2003; Lorino, 2018). As Whitehead (1929(1978)) puts it, "everything flows" and managerial roles, procedures and boundaries come to existence and matter as part of a process of becoming.

---

[2] Of course, the pragmatist perspectives described by Lorino and Mourey (2013), Lorino (2018) or de Vaujany (2022) have a metaphysical dimension. Temporality is always plural. Here, we anticipate the next section and what could be also (and mostly) seen as a cosmological move, a change in eventfulness regimes itself (a more open encounter of pasts and future events in a connected world).

If everything is becoming, then temporality is primordial. In what happens, a 'now' makes it possible to establish one or more 'here'. The event expresses and materializes volumes and places, and "emplaces" future activities (Wahl, 1932). The ultimate reality of the organizational world (and of the world in general) is permanent change, the great continuity of discontinuities, the endless reopening of presents.

So what is the problem? Are managers and management systems wrong? Are they out of step with their own reality? Sort of. As Chia (2003) clearly explains when returning to Whitehead (1938(1968)), our relationship to the world is caught up in hyper-spatial conceptions. Our daily language, our habitual mediations, are 'representationalist'. We strive to represent an outside world. We strive to link these representations as closely as possible to an external reality. The world is supposed to be a gigantic Euclidean space within which localizable, 'placed' events occur at an objective distance from each other. But as proponents of process thinking show (for a general presentation see in particular Helin et al., 2014), the events and processes of the world produce their own topology in their occurrence. Events attach and emplace. Places have meaning and coordinates only within their production.

The challenge is then to de-linearize the world and its history, to most of all think about collective activity with a new language and new mediations showing its processuality and its future. Paradoxically, we may need to cultivate a new eventfulness or new regimes of eventfulness. We need to become procedural in our ways of thinking and in managerial mediations. Unlike the previous historical perspective (or a certain historical vision), the organization is no longer an evolving entity whose phases of development will be distinguished. It is the type of dominant processes of a present. The cosmological changes themselves, the new modes of production of the world and its eventfulness, must be the heart of the reflection. But how to describe this organizational metaphysics with a new language, with new images, with new mediations in continuity with the stated future? How to single out the present of management and modes of organization without emplacing it at the end of an evolving, simple, straight and unique line?

Existing attempts insist on different aspects of this question in terms of decision: they mention process as opposed to planning (Chia & Holt, 2009), or different forms of knowledge for action beyond calculative rationality (Chia & Holt, 2008) or on Dionysian and Apollonian opposite styles in relation to strategic design and choice (Holt, 2018). To complement this attempt, our focus here is rather on co-presence and collective action.

In the next part, we propose to take a detour through theatre and the genealogy of modern staging and then its explosion and decentring both visually, narratively and materially in some forms of experimental or improvised theatricalization. Although it takes place in an informal way, this process is quite different from that described by Turner (1990) and Goffman (2021(1959)) and in that it corresponds to a deliberate extra effort fulfilling a collective need of staging and framing interactions rather than the everyday course of actions that are spontaneously dramaturgic as illustrated by Schein (1992), among others. We can hypothesize that just as there is a history of theatre as an art, there is a history and different styles of managerial dramatization, namely the conscious use of staging action as a managerial technique. This dramatization of the theatrical world offers a unique opportunity to processually describe the temporalities and spatialities of our intense modes of organizing.

The Managerialization of Theatre and the Theatricalization of Work and Management: In Search of a New Intensity

Theatre has a long and fascinating history dating back to ancient Greece (see in particular Folco & Boisson, 2010; Pavis, 2011; Folco, 2013; Martin, 2021). Here, in order to build our argument, we will start from a more recent period and present: that of farce theatre and a little further, from classical theatre in the seventeenth and eighteenth centuries. Throughout this history of theatre, we can see how the infinite nuances of meaning of play and game go beyond what interactions in organization studies have so far offered us. As a complement to "systems of enabling conventions, in the sense of ground rules for a game, the provisions of a traffic code, or the syntax of a language" (Goffman, 1983, p. 5) for interactions, theatre offers the vast possibilities of imagination and expressive styles that delve into all realms, from the fantastic and oneiric to the hyperbolic and absurd.

The farce theatre was a street theatre in the Middle Ages. It had an ephemeral place in the public space. It set up a temporary scene. The game was noisy, hard work. One had to capture the attention of passers-by with a performance that held nothing back. Everything was cartoonish. Actors had to entertain and make people laugh. The use of these free scripts instead of previously written plays remained even in the times of Shakespeare (Palfrey & Stern, 2000) and Sheridan (Stern, 2007).

Classical theatre and the Italian theatre stage (Brown, 2001) corresponded to a return to the etymological meaning of theatre, namely the *theatron* of the Greeks, a "place from which one looks" (Loraux, 1999; Carter, 2011). In the classical period, the theatre was a closed place while being relatively undefined. In the 'basket' of the theatre, anything from 500 to 700 people followed the play, all standing. Some arrived very tipsy. Fights, thefts and even rapes were not uncommon. Women rarely attended and were sometimes dressed as men to avoid being molested. Everybody had to jostle for the best place. Sometimes, circles and conversations formed at the expense of plot and actors. In the upper sections, there might be stands, which allowed aristocrats some distance, to both see and be seen.

For the lucky ones, it was also possible to be seated on the stage, close to the actors and visible to everyone. The notion of stage was then very porous, as was ultimately the distinction between the space of actors and that of spectators. The marquis might be seated next to the actors, who were looking for the right word. In the middle, the actors were not really acting. They were declaiming (Banham & Brandon, 1995). Behind them, a painted perspective often suggested a line of flight. There was very little furniture and only a few objects on the stage. Decor was not really significant; it was strictly decorative. Actors played on a background decor, but not *with* the decor. The light did not cut anything. It was diffused in the room and imperfect on the stage (Kennedy, 2010). Finally, the actors' voices, postures, gestures and costumes 'replaced' a very ephemeral scenic space. At that time, it probably required a lot of audacity and courage from the actors. The basic rule was that of "unity"; in particular, that of space and time (Wiles & Dymkowski, 2012). In the French plays (Forestier, 2016), the piece should have a single frame and unfold linearly over a single beat.

The authors organized their play and the actors owned – possessed – their role (the French comedian Rachel played the young leads well beyond her fifties). Technical support was very limited.

Interestingly, there was an indistinguishability between the stage and the room, the spectators and the actors, while striving to put the play on. Intensity was both on stage and in the room, in the basket of the theatre. In this logic, the public had to be there. It had to accompany the rhythm of the piece with its applause, its laughter, its breathing.

In the nineteenth century, the figure of the director appeared and made secondary the presence of the author. The director created, animated and managed the stage space. The theatre began to rely on a manager and on technical teams with increasingly differentiated roles (Brook, 1995, 1996).

By then, the atmosphere had become essential. First, at the end of the eighteenth century and for a good part of the nineteenth, the large chandelier in the room was left lighted, reinforcing indiscernibility. On stage, the 'limelight' lighted the faces from below, forcing the game, making the 'faces fatter'. The orchestra was a ground-breaking addition for the public – a U-shape was created, making everyone visible. In the basket, chairs were installed. But the border between the room and the stage remained diffuse. Actors sought the public's applause, which punctuated and accentuated the show. Actors had to speak very loudly. Dramatization was not just in the play but also in the relationship.

The decisive break occurred at the end of the nineteenth century with a switch to new scenic animation modes. With André Antoine and his famous *Talks on Staging* (*Causeries sur la mise en scène*) (1999(1903)), the function of director became institutionalized and the technical functions of the theatre became professionalized. From then, the sets actively participated in theatrical creation. They were no longer a simple perspective and illustration of the text. They 'played' the play, with the actors playing with them. Each act – each scene – was an event with depth; multiple events answering each other, more than a perspective with a single vanishing point, never to be broken.

For the actors, this modern phase was a revolution. They no longer declaimed or played by convention: they acted. They were reconciled with Shakespeare's and Molière's invitation for more natural games (Abirached, 2011). The whole body of actors became engaged on the stage. For actors, it was even possible to turn their back on the audience. A fourth (imaginary) wall had to 'close' the scenic space (and in doing so, enclose a spectator in a way indistinguishable to him-/herself).

Now, theatre turned off the light in the room. Everyone was seated, the body at rest, silent, passive, except to applaud (in a more exceptional way). The whole scene was reworked, with increasing amounts of electric lighting, the placement of which fixed the points of attention before becoming diffused to multiply the events and give more depth to the scene.

Finally, after being often indistinguishable for the duration of the play, the spectator disappears into the theatrical arrangements (Mitchell, 2008; Ledger, 2019), no longer aware of their own passivity. They are caught up in the experience on the stage, the drama, the acceleration and deceleration of the play (Warner, 2014; Janssens & Steyaert, 2020), the events on stage which cover the whole basket and expand to fill the theatre.

We can present the transformations of scenic experiences in a table (see Table 13.1).

Of course, the parallel with the history of work and the modalities of organizing already described is striking. Management has professionalized over recent centuries. Its time-space (and that of work at large) continues to explode. Paradoxically, consumers and workers are both more passive (covered by the scene, or part of a managerial 'scene') and are also expected to be co-productive in the very process of the consumption of what they buy and pay for, with opportunities for subjectivation, care, resistance and emancipation quite rare.

Table 13.1 *Evolution of modes of theatricalization*

	Medieval theatre	Classic theatre	Modern theatre	Contemporary theatre
Type of theatre	Face theatre; fairgrounds theatre	Classic theatre, Shakespeare, French tragedy and Comedy	Italian theatre, realism (broadening space and time unity)	Modern theatre, broadening or forgetting the Western tradition of the stage and its unity of time and space.
Relationship between stage and room	The show takes place in a public space	There is absolute continuity between the stage and the room (marquis on the stage and the public standing in the room)	Relative continuity: a very visible frontier settles	Radical rupture between the stage and the room. The room is simply erased. The stage is visually extended and covers the whole space of the theatre. Sometimes, the public is invited to co-produce the show and what could appear as the room is also erased. Time-space unity is broken.
Presence of a gaze	A very collective gaze	A relational, cross-gaze, aware of itself	The room is lighted. All gazes meet and cross each other subtly. Gazes are distributed throughout the room	The lights are off. A unique gaze is assumed, even if angles are multiplied. Subjectivation is still expected. But the depth of field and inter-eventfulness (far from the principle of a vanishing point) imposes itself gradually.

Intense Decentred Organizing: The New Way for a Connected Management?

How to reveal the metaphysical richness of management and contemporary modes of organization? How to describe their temporalities and their spatialities? The theatre and the art of the theatre offers possibilities well identified by Gilles Deleuze, notably in his famous *Parlers* (*Pourparlers*) (Flore, 2013).[3]

Deleuze was often very critical of the theatre, which he reproached for its excessive sense of mimesis, of an imitation at the heart of a 'representation'; precisely the kind of practices and vocabulary he wanted to get rid of. And yet, it did not escape him that the theatre had a rich past and a future far removed from that of performance alone. Beyond (e.g., with Beckett) he also gradually realized that theatre was or could be highly experimental and productive.

Deleuze claims that Francis Bacon's art, with its bodies as figures, and spaces as "round areas", exists in the zone of indiscernibility, a parallel to the plane of immanence which also artistically follows lines of flight in "the act of fleeing or eluding" (Deleuze, 2003). He makes similar comments about Camelo Bene's work as a stage director and author: "What is interesting is never the manner in which one begins or ends. The interest lies in the middle, that which occurs in the middle ... where becoming, movement, speed, excess" take place (Bene & Deleuze, 1979, p. 95). In his visual and dramaturgic reflection on game and play, Deleuze seems to oppose two types of arts: one that creates a golden cage and one that is open to life as he understands it; a plateau of sorts.

Interested in the dramatization of images and in images, Deleuze rather suggests a passage from the 'scene' of a plot to the 'plateau' of events. Images respond to each other. They produce their temporalities in between the productive differences of their rhythms, speeds and most of all, intensities. The plateau of event in the present is the procedural, co-productive reality of the organization. It always has been. It is also the process veiled and made invisible by several management presents. If the great invention of modernity is the permanent 'gaze' (see Chia, 2003), the great orchestration of our time is in the pre-assignment of an 'I' (and a 'game'?) to this gaze.

Director-managers and orchestration processes are more 'naturalized' than ever. The room is forgotten. It is continuously observed beyond the time-space of the room (the meeting, the corporate seminar, the co-working space event, etc.), but through mediations such as Enterprise

---

[3] On the issue of the relationship between Deleuze and the theatre, see Chevallier (2015).

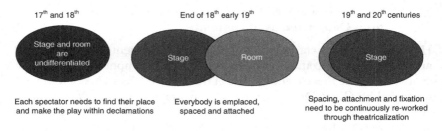

Figure 13.1 The historical relationship between stage and room images

Resource Planning (ERP), big data, social networks or search engines re-casting a Euclidean, integrated, 'global' space (see de Vaujany, 2022). The imageries of rooms and stages keep transforming themselves (see Figure 13.1) as pointed out by both Deleuze (1969, 1985) and Brook (1995, 1996) in the case of the art theatre.

In contemporary framework, everyone paradoxically becomes a classic actor or actress. The scenic space of the manager and the entrepreneur become their body, their gestures and their faces. All express the most essential images (Turkle, 2011). On Instagram, as in the co-working space, in the client's meeting room as in the open space of its project teams, in its square of the Zoom meeting as on the kitchen table used for telecommuting. One has to mobilize one's whole body to space out a micro-workplace and fix ephemeral bubbles. Sometimes attentional, sometimes presentational or even mediating, these bubbles are exactly those of the classic actor.

They are the area, the point of attention of the actor and his/her spectators (customers, collaborators, citizens, etc.). They are the ongoing event. They show the children that the parents are working. "She's not the same, not as usual." Behind her helmet, she listens to a meeting, not music. His face, his gesture, his posture in the dining room or his office are not the same. It's her. His style of gesture. And at the same time, it's different. There is an unusual tension in this gesture, repeated a thousand times, running the hand through the hair. Employees and managers must feel a specific atmosphere in this place that is too smooth or carries too much of a co-working atmosphere for us to differentiate. And of course, the bubble is a mediator: it allows collective activity in the midst of an increasingly ontologically decentralized management.

Strangely, the issue of attentional, bodily and technical fixation is more important than before. In the space of the stage, the actor knows this well. they have to anchor themselves. They must expand themselves in space through their gestures and movements. Objects and decor are not around them. They are also spaced by their occurrence and their co-mobilization in the movements of the piece. Everything is taken up by multiple vanishing lines, the meeting of which produces events and a depth of more than one perspective. In this process, the game must envelop the spectator's concentration; follow the breath of this invisible room for him as for herself. And for everyone, it must produce this ephemeral but sufficiently durable bubble in order to lead the experience towards a denouement or rather, an opening to be explored by an imagination. In this ultimate time-space, subjectivation can explode, form and express itself. At the great closure of classical pieces, modernity and, above all, post-modernity found openings – events pointing to new possibilities of subjectivation.[4]

Both the director and the manager obviously have important responsibilities in this experience. Their roles are now unowned. They have a life and an autonomous future. They have their own way. The author always sees their work more or less escape them. It is only becoming in the adaptation, the pre-registrations and even, sometimes, the improvisations. Parts are repeated. Calibrated. The actors express themselves, give their opinion and make suggestions. Then the first arrives, anxious, waiting. The 'representations' follow one another, all identical and different at the same time. Anyone who has ever had the chance to attend the same play several times has no doubt realized this. With the same actors, a new gesture can reconfigure everything. A slower gait. An unexpected laugh (also creating a form of complicity with the room). A more committed and playful face. A truncated or enriched replica. And more obviously, the change of a single actor changes the entire universe of the play. All the nuances between gestures and roles are rearranged by a new image.

Finally, with Deleuze, it is tempting to move from the onto-epistemology of the 'stage' to that of the 'plateau' (see Deleuze & Guattari, 1980). The scene always induces and presupposes the viewer as a (passive) gazer. But contemporary management has multiplied the gazes, decentring the activity of meaning and perception. It has removed the vanishing points. Everything perceives and builds in the same movement. As the noisy spectators of the theatre in the seventeenth and eighteenth centuries could co-constitute an axis-less spectacle, management processes build their accommodating patchwork. And the actor declaiming against the backdrop of a simple 'perspective' decor was ultimately very atmospheric. Pre-modern theatricalization was already

---

[4] On this issue, the managerialization of work is certainly different to that of many companies today.

a plateau rather than a stage. In the same shared present, multiple temporalities were spread out and could at any moment become a spectacle (a fight, applause coming from a particular group, an impromptu arrival or departure, a particular declamation performance at some point in the room). The differences in intensity of the events at work in the room could rearrange the place and its future without giving it a particular outline, without placing something precise on the edge of these dark walls. The very boundaries of the *theatron* were ultimately porous with the neighbourhood's atmosphere and drinking spots.

Today, everything is done with images taken in the same depth, a usual temporality of pasts and futures (de Vaujany, 2022). And yet, in many ways, our present work also includes another stage: that of modern theatre in which our experience is primary. Workers enter into the experience of the stage before anything else. The stage encroaches entirely on the room, placed in darkness and silence; that is to say, nowhere. Workers have to wait for the end of the play or for rare moments of complicity during which the fourth wall (it cannot be otherwise) is very briefly cracked before being quickly resealed. In the (digital or physical) room, everyone has their pre-assigned seat. They are an 'I' in their place (also a social place in the assembly). Invited to manifest themselves, they do so without being able to develop their space. In the dark and surrounded by a necessary silence, nothing temporalizes, nothing spaces. The actors and the whole set have to constantly space and re-space: through narration, rhythms, phrasing, they must also temporalize. In short, like managers and management systems, they must co-produce a world in which value finds its (very temporary) legitimate place.

In the contemporary transformations of management, the processes must also temporalize and emplace. They must, in turn, forget the fourth wall of their world (a permeable wall, listening to the breath of the room but not too much, a wall above all to summon the room into its world). The product, the service, the entrepreneurial project must find a clear place in the world. On this path, the classic plateau is more than ever a possibility. 'Placed' without already being a subjectivity, the 'I' can potentially always find the entire surface of the stage. He/she can dive into social networks or onto Google, and find the theatres, the play, its content, its comments, its stolen extracts from all angles, the neighbourhood around it, the good restaurants to eat in before or after. The spectator-consumer can subtly leave the room with his/her fingers. They can, using thought, project themselves onto their next point of fixation. They can do this without even realizing how much this coming fixation is accompanied by the technique. They can also stay in the dark and not be a spectator. Just a stream. That of indistinctly theatrical and managerial arrangements making the spectacle of a lifetime.

Theatrical modes of organization today explore various forms of 'spect-action'. Improvisation theatre, stand-up in conversation with a small audience, experimental theatre brought up to date, street happenings partially scripted and embellished from conversations with the crowd and their reactions. In the public space of the street, actors can point out remote events and places in the space of the city. They can bring up past imagery and walk along historical buildings and historical vestiges. Everything at hand is likely to become a past or future event actors can play with. Openness of the situation in the public space (anything can happen, anybody can contribute) increases the intensity of what is lived and what is projected from the past or in the future. Because they have to play with the public, actors have to fluidly improvise and build the fluid modalities of their improvising, a fuzzy, open and flexible shared repertoire of answers to the public.

A recent French play ('Dernier coup de ciseaux',[5] a play for a child audience) attended by one of the authors epitomizes this. Actors engage with the audience to identify the murder of an old lady. At some point during the show the light is switched on. Suddenly, the spectators become actors, and the room is full of potential surprises that are intense levers for the play. During the break, the inspector leading the inquiry went in the main corridor of the theatre to meet people and to hear their questions. At the end, people voted to identify the murderer, which activates both open scenarized interactions and improvisations. The show was an intense experience for most people present, who will certainly remember it.

Since the 1960s, theatre has reinvented itself as a highly open, fluid and intense stage or dispersed set of past and future narrative events. It is no longer the 'place from which one looks'. It is the activity producing multiple places and events and multiple neighbourhoods of gazes with rare and always ephemeral coincidences. It perfectly embodies the new modes of organization without a centre but with subtle common connections that vary in its patchwork of processes. There are no more endings, only the vanishing lines of an ever more visual text. Theatricalization involves a set of dramatic events more or less clustered together. The process of organizing of theatre and play becomes the temporal node constitutive of this dramatization.

Are the new time-spaces of management ultimately something else? It remains for the citizen spect-actors to actively construct the subjectivities that can put them at the heart of more democratic adventures. It is up to each and every one to be the great director of the profound event of their subjectivity.

[5] https://theatredesmathurins.com/spectacle/494/dernier-coup-de-ciseaux

Conclusion: New Work Settings as the New 'Carpets' of a Theatrical World of Management?

In our [theatrical] work we often use a carpet as a rehearsal zone, with a very clear purpose: off the carpet, the actor is in daily life, he can do what he wants – waste his energy, engage in movements that don't express anything in particular, scratch his head, fall asleep … But as soon as he finds himself on the carpet, he is under the obligation of having a clear intention, of being intensely alive, simply because an audience is watching. (Brook, 1995, pp. 12–13)

New ways of working could become such a new spatio-temporal liminality. But this intensity can also become devastating if one moves from a metaphysical or historical stance to a more psychological one. Burnout, identity loss and stress can be part of this new common way of life. In this way, non-intense moments could become as important as the IDO emphasized here. They could give to them a depth. They could become an interesting hiatus, processual chiasms.

Intense Decentred Organizing needs the quietness, loneliness, unboundedness and openness of other moments. In and with these other times, true emancipation and resistance can happen creating true selves and constituting better managers, but also, and most of all, true citizens.

References

Abirached, R. (2011). *Le théâtre français du XXe siècle: histoire, textes choisis, mises en scène/sous la direction de Robert Abirached* (p. 1). Paris: Éditions L'avant-scène théâtre.

Alter, N. (2003). Mouvement et dyschronies dans les organisations. *L'Année sociologique, 53*(2), 489–514.

Antoine, A. (1999(1903)). Causerie sur la mise en scene. In J-P. Sarrazac & P. Marcerou (eds), *Antoine: l'invention de la mise en scène* (pp. 106–20). Arles: Actes Sud-Papiers.

Aroles, J., Mitev, N. & de Vaujany, F-X. (2019). Mapping themes in the study of new work practices. *New Technology, Work and Employment, 34*(3), 285–99.

Banham, M. & Brandon, J. R. (eds) (1995). *The Cambridge Guide to Theatre*. London: Cambridge University Press.

Beck, C. & Gleyzon, F. X. (2016). Deleuze and the event(s). *Journal for Cultural Research, 20*(4), 329–33.

Bene, C. & Deleuze, G. (1979). *Superpositions*. Paris: Editions de Minuit.

Birth, K. (2012). *Objects of Time: How Things Shape Temporality*. New York: Springer.

Brook, P. (1995). The Slyness of Boredom. In *There Are No Secrets: Thoughts on Acting and Theatre*. London: Methuen Drama.

Brook, P. (1996). *The Empty Space: A Book about the Theatre: Deadly, Holy, Rough, Immediate.* London: Simon and Schuster.

Brown, J. R. (ed.) (2001). *The Oxford Illustrated History of Theatre* (Vol. 1). Oxford: Oxford Illustrated History.

Carter, D. M. (ed.) (2011). *Why Athens? A Reappraisal of Tragic Politics.* Oxford: Oxford University Press.

Cederström, C. & Spicer, A. (2015). *The Wellness Syndrome.* London: John Wiley & Sons.

Chandler Jr., A. D. (1993). *The Visible Hand.* Boston, MA: Harvard University Press.

Chevallier J-F. (2015). *Deleuze et le théâtre, Rompre avec la representation.* Paris: Editions des Solitaires Intempestifs.

Chia, R. (2003). Ontology: Organization as World-making. In R. Westwood & S. Clegg, (eds), *Debating Organization: Point/Counterpoint in Organization Studies* (pp. 98–113). Oxford: Blackwell Publishing.

Chia, R. C. & Holt, R. (2008). On managerial knowledge. *Management Learning,* 39(2), 141–58.

Chia, R. C. & Holt, R. (2009). *Strategy Without Design: The Silent Efficacy of Indirect Action.* London: Cambridge University Press.

Cummings, S., Bridgman, T., Hassard, J. & Rowlinson, M. (2017). *A New History of Management.* London: Cambridge University Press.

Deleuze, G. (1966). *Le bergsonisme.* Paris: PUF.

Deleuze, G. (1969, 1995). *Difference and Repetition.* New York: Columbia University Press.

Deleuze, G. (1985). *Cinéma 2. L'Image-Temps.* Paris: Les Éditions de Minuit.

Deleuze, G. (2003). *Francis Bacon: The Logic of Sensation.* London: Continuum.

Deleuze, G. & Guattari, F. (1980). *Mille plateaux.* Paris: Les Editions de Minuit.

De Vaujany, F.X. (2006). Between eternity and actualization: the co-evolution of the fields of communication in the Vatican. *Communications of the AIS, 18,* 355–391.

de Vaujany, F-X. (2010). A new perspective on the genealogy of collective action through the history of religious organizations. *Management & Organizational History,* 5(1), 65–78.

de Vaujany, F-X. (2022). *Apocalypse managériale,* Paris: Editions Les Belles Lettres.

de Vaujany, F-X. & Aroles, J. (2019). Nothing happened, something happened: Silence in a makerspace. *Management Learning,* 50(2), 208–25.

de Vaujany, F-X., Leclercq-Vandelannoitte, A., Munro, I., Nama, Y. & Holt, R. (2021). Control and surveillance in work practice: Cultivating paradox in 'new' modes of organizing. *Organization Studies,* 42(5), 675–95.

Fayard, A. L. (2021). Notes on the meaning of work: Labor, work, and action in the 21st century. *Journal of Management Inquiry,* 30(2), 207–20.

Fayol, H. (1916). *Administration industrielle et générale.* Paris: Dunod.

Flore, G-M. (2013). Pourparlers sur le théâtre. In F. Bourlez & L. Vinciguerra (eds), *Pourparlers, entre art et philosophie. Images et langages chez Gilles Deleuze*

(p. 31–46). Reims: ESAD-EPURE, Éditions et Presses Universitaires de Reims.

Folco, A. (2013). *La querelle sur les origines de la mise en scène et les enjeux mémoriels autour de la figure d'André Antoine*. Paris: Revue d'Histoire du Théâtre numérique.

Folco, A. & Boisson, B. (2010). *La mise en scène théâtrale de 1800 à nos jours* (p. 271). Paris: PUF.

Forestier, G. (2016). *La tragédie française-2e éd: Règles classiques, passions tragiques*. Paris: Armand Colin.

Giedion, S. (2009). *Space, Time and Architecture: The Growth of a New Tradition*. Boston, MA: Harvard University Press.

Goffman, E. (1983). The interaction order. *American Sociological Review*, *48*, 1–17.

Goffman, E. (2021(1959)). *The Presentation of Self in Everyday Life*. New York: Anchor Books.

Hatchuel, A. & Glise, H. (2003). Rebuilding Management: A Historical Perspective. In N. Adler, A. B. Shani & A. Styhre (eds), *Collaborative Research in Organisations: Foundations for Learning, Change and Theoretical Development*. Thousand Oaks, CA: Sage.

Helin, J., Hernes, T., Hjorth, D. & Holt, R. (eds) (2014). *The Oxford Handbook of Process Philosophy and Organization Studies*. Oxford: Oxford University Press.

Holt, R. (2018). *Judgment and Strategy*. Oxford: Oxford University Press.

Jackall, R. (1988). *Moral Mazes: The World of Corporate Managers*. New York & Oxford: Oxford University Press.

Janssens, M. & Steyaert, C. (2020). The site of diversalizing: The accomplishment of inclusion in intergenerational dance. *Journal of Management Studies*, *57*(6), 1143–73.

Juhlin, C. & Holt, R. (2021). The sensory imperative. *Management Learning*. doi:10.1177/13505076211062220

Jullien, F. (2012). L'écart et l'entre. Ou comment penser l'altérité. Working Papers Series n°3, FMSH-WP-2012–03, février 2012. Available at: https://halshs.archives-ouvertes.fr/halshs-00677232/document

Kennedy, D. (ed.) (2010). *The Oxford Companion to Theatre and Performance*. Oxford: Oxford University Press.

Kieser, A. (1989). Organizational, institutional, and societal evolution: Medieval craft guilds and the genesis of formal organizations. *Administrative Science Quarterly*, *34*(4), 540–64.

Ledger, A. J. (2019). *The Director and Directing: Craft, Process and Aesthetic in Contemporary Theatre*. London: Springer.

Loraux, N. (1999). *La voix endeuillée: essai sur la tragédie grecque*. Paris: FeniXX.

Lorino, P. (2018). *Pragmatism and Organization Studies*. Oxford: Oxford University Press.

Lorino, P. & Mourey, D. (2013). The experience of time in the inter-organizing inquiry: A present thickened by dialog and situations. *Scandinavian Journal of Management*, *29*(1), 48–62.

Martin, R. (2021). Histoire et épistémologie de la notion de mise en scène. *Pratiques* [online], 191–2. Available at: http://journals.openedition.org/pratiques/11254

Mitchell, K. (2008). *The Director's Craft: A Handbook for the Theatre*. London: Routledge.

Nowotny, H. (1992). Time and social theory: Towards a social theory of time. *Time & Society*, *1*(3), 421–54.

Oldenburg, R. & Brissett, D. (1982). The third place. *Qualitative Sociology*, *5*(4), 265–84.

Orel, M., Dvoulety, O. & Ratten, V. (2021). *The Flexible Workplace*. Switzerland: Springer Nature. https://doi.org/10.1007/978-3-030-62167-4

Palfrey, S. & Stern, T. (2000). *Shakespeare in Parts*. Oxford: Oxford University Press.

Pavis, P. (2011). *La mise en scène contemporaine: origines, tendances, perspectives*. Paris: Armand Colin.

Reinecke, J. & Ansari, S. (2015). When times collide: Temporal brokerage at the intersection of markets and developments. *Academy of Management Journal*, *58* (2), 618–48.

Riot, E. (2019). Patterns of intention: Oberkampf and Knoll as Schumpeterian entrepreneurs. *Entrepreneurship & Regional Development*, *31*(7–8), 623–51.

Schein, E. H. (1992). How can organizations learn faster? The problem of entering the Green Room. MIT Working Papers. Available at: https://sloanre view.mit.edu/article/how-can-organizations-learn-faster-the-challenge-of-entering-the-green-room/

Sewell, G. & Taskin, L. (2015). Out of sight, out of mind in a new world of work? Autonomy, control, and spatiotemporal scaling in telework. *Organization Studies*, *36*(11), 1507–29.

Sloterdijk, P. (2013). *In the World Interior of Capital: Towards a Philosophical Theory of Globalization*. London: Polity.

Spinuzzi, C. (2012). Working alone together: Coworking as emergent collaborative activity. *Journal of Business and Technical Communication*, *26*(4), 399–441.

Stern, T. (2007). *Rehearsal from Shakespeare to Sheridan*. Oxford: Oxford University Press.

Turkle, S. (2011). *Alone Together: Why We Expect More from Technology and Less from Each Other*. New York: Basic Books.

Turner, V. W. (1990). *By Means of Performance: Intercultural Studies of Theatre and Ritual*. Cambridge: Cambridge University Press.

Wahl, J. (1932). *Vers le concret*. Paris: Editions Vrin.

Warner, V. S. (2014). Borderless dramaturgy in dance theatre. In M. Romanska (eds), *The Routledge Companion to Dramaturgy* (pp. 382–7). London: Routledge.

Whitehead, A. N. (1929, 1978). *Process and Reality. An Essay in Cosmology*. New York: The Free Press.

Whitehead, A. N. (1938, 1968). *Modes of Thought*. London: Simon and Schuster.

Whyte, W. H. (1956, 2013). *The Organization Man*. Chicago: University of Pennsylvania Press.

Wiles, D. & Dymkowski, C. (eds) (2012). *The Cambridge Companion to Theatre History*. Cambridge: Cambridge University Press.

Zourabichvili, F. (2012). *Deleuze: A Philosophy of the Event: Together with the Vocabulary of Deleuze*. Edinburgh: Edinburgh University Press.

Part IV

History and Duration: Making Things Last, Enduring Politics and Organizing

14 Times *Alla Turca E Franga*
Conceptions of Time and the Materiality of the Late-Ottoman Clock Towers

Deniz Tunçalp

Introduction

Time is the progression through moments into the future and the passing of the present towards the past. In contrast, temporality means being time-bound. The understanding of time is necessarily temporal, spatial, and, therefore, not universal. It is a typical construct of socio-technical structuration (Adam, 1990, 2004; Glennie & Thrift, 1996, 2005, 2009). It is also central to social inquiry, as every social phenomenon is essentially temporal and, therefore, conditional and relational. Consequently, time-related artifacts and practices are multilayered and path-dependent. How one values, measures, records, and uses time depends on respective societies.

The invention of the mechanical clock changed ideas about time (Bradbury & Collette, 2009). The Industrial Revolution and the rise of modernity have further transformed the social and organizational understanding of time. The increasing weight of time-based employment over work-based employment has increased the widespread need for an awareness of clock time (Thompson, 1967). The modernization of industrialized countries and the efforts of non-industrialized others to catch up have propagated a more "homogeneous, empty," (Benjamin, 1968, pp. 261, 264) singular, linear, and synchronous time in the West and mainly diffused with modernity. However, it matured with multilateral, covert, or explicit negotiations between various actors, societies, and civilizations. Extant literature mainly analyzes the institutionalization of time and the temporal order across the world from a modern and Western point of view (Holt & Johnsen, 2019). This perspective reduces complex, contested, multiple realities into a dichotomous, binary opposition. It reduces the modern understanding of time to a linear, homogenous, and Western construct. In contrast, other conceptualizations are circular, organic, and inherently Oriental (Delanty, 1995; Hamann, 2016).

While these binary conceptions may attempt to legitimize Western colonialism as developmental and progressive (e.g., Gilley, 2017), these views also provide simplistic worldviews that are insufficient for grasping the inherent dialectic complexities (Makdisi, 2002) of social construction and change over time across different locations. Various studies have strived to understand how time and temporal order have been established and changed across cultures and societies (Munn, 1992; Howell, 2003; Callizo-Romero et al., 2020). However, few studies have explored how non-industrialized countries moved to time-based modernization, especially outside their power centers.

This study explores the materiality of clock towers to understand how temporal order was collectively constructed and changed in the Ottoman Empire. Clock towers are monumental holders of clocks as time-structuring devices for the public. The study focusses on the clock towers constructed in the late nineteenth century outside İstanbul, the imperial center. The study controlled contextual variabilities by selecting a particular construction period and geography while analyzing and comparing different clock towers as case studies. Specifically, the study focussed on the materiality of clock towers constructed during Sultan Abdülhamid II's reign between 1876 and 1909. As early modernization efforts characterize this interval, it represents a critical period to study. In this period, the government introduced various novel institutions such as the first constitution, the first parliament, formal elections, and educational institutions, such as universities, to Ottoman society. Different initiatives built over 100 clock towers in the Ottoman Empire during this period. Therefore, reading how temporal order was established and changed from clock towers is particularly interesting. Studying changes in temporal order outside the capital city is also remarkable as the usual explanations for institutional changes in the temporal order of societies, namely the state, travel infrastructure (e.g., trains, ferries), and industrial employment, were less influential in these locations.

Clock towers as monumental time measurement and synchronicity-creating devices present a wealth of empirical data. In performing their analysis, this study takes a microhistorical perspective (Hargadon & Wadhwani, 2022) with a critical realist (CR) lens (Collier, 1994; Archer, 1995; Bhaskar, 1998, 2008, 2013, 2016). From a philosophical and methodological angle, microhistory provides "a microtemporal frame suited for an empirically grounded study ... in time and a macrotemporal frame accounting for processes of continuity and change in social structures over time" (Hargadon & Wadhwani, 2022, p. 1). At the same time, CR pushes the subjective-objective divide in social and organizational analysis to provide an alternative to radical-constructivist and realist-positivist perspectives. CR holds a realist but not a positivist ontology and a constructivist but not subjectivist epistemology (Collier, 1994), potentially bringing a relatively fresh perspective to understanding time and temporal understanding. The explanatory practice of most historical sociologists is also in line with critical realism (Steinmetz, 1998).

Unfortunately, many of the clock towers built in this period were ruined. Some of these towers no longer exist due to political, environmental, or technical reasons. There are places where governors, earthquakes, fires, and mechanical breakdowns have destroyed the clock towers. For example, while not in the initial sample, the Jerusalem clock tower is a compelling case. In Jerusalem, the city elite had donated finances to construct the clock tower on the ancient city walls. The tower quickly became "the pride of the city" as a significant symbol of civic identity (Hashkafa, 1907; cited in Wishnitzer, 2010). In 1922, the British governor of the city destroyed the clock tower, despite the protests of locals and elites' petitions (Fuchs & Gilbert, 2001).

The study has limited its analysis to those clock towers that exist today within the national borders of Turkey. It includes clock towers in this geography that have been ruined but have enough data with pictures and archival records. The study has mainly focussed on the independent clock towers, which were not annexes of another building and had no additional side functionality but were built and used entirely as clock towers. The study has covered all twenty-four clock towers following the above criteria and collected primary and secondary data about them. In addition, the study has developed case studies of three 'exceptional typical' clock towers, namely Kastamonu, Çorum, and İzmir Clock Towers, for in-depth analysis.

Our results followed the path-dependent and sociopolitical understanding of time. From a non-industrialized and non-Western historical context, the study illustrated how clock towers materialize to gain and maintain power and display authority. These monumental artifacts were not primarily linked to any functional reasons for timekeeping at the beginning, except for learning how much time remains until the next praying session. Many of these towers were in the town or city centers, side-by-side with prominent mosques. There are also a few instances where the clock towers were built on the outskirts of cities and towns, over hills and slopes, without a mosque. Mosques had been traditionally responsible for timekeeping and the announcement of time information to the public through calls for prayers five times a day. Most clock towers also look similar to minarets or churches, probably due to available architectural practices at the time.

The analysis of the Ottoman clock towers examined the continuity, change, and multiplicity in the Ottoman temporal understanding. It also emphasized how temporal understanding and modern artifacts had hybridized during this period. Clock towers materialized evidence of this hybridization. They were originally the products of the Western notions of timekeeping (Alla Franga). However, the Ottoman state had used them to keep and promote the Ottoman time system (Alla Turca). However, the clocks had to be adjusted daily to follow the Alla Turca time. Some towers also included multiple clocks or clock dials that may have simultaneously indicated both time systems to the public (Alla Turca e Franga[1]). "Alla Turca" and "Alla Franca/Franga" are common musical and cultural adjectives borrowed from the Italian language and used in the Ottoman Empire to represent the traditional and the French/European/modern styles. This chapter uses these terms to indicate the hybrid and mixed materiality of the Ottoman clock towers.

The study also provided an opportunity to focus on the role of the periphery and non-state actors in developing a broadly defined Ottoman modernity and emphasized the importance of local actors and contexts in managing institutional changes. It also indicated that time arrangements could be mapped and colonized by states/elites for social control and change (Adib & Emiljanowicz, 2019). The results indicate that local governors and sub-governors with other members of the local elite were politically central to the diffusion and propagation of the clock towers. Therefore, it was not solely the Sultan who ordered the diffusion of the modern time discipline. The local elites were also actively involved in the diffusion of modernity. Some local elites also competed to build clock towers to grab the Sultan's interest in their town, making these buildings symbolically more than just a clock tower.

The results suggest that the coexistence and hybridization of the old and new have helped with the appropriation of clock towers. However, the bells in most clock towers have resembled and reminded locals of churches, creating some struggles between different religious groups. With or without bells, these clock towers were primarily icons of the state authority, involving local governors and sub-governors and the economically wealthy local elite as sponsors. The results also reflect the multifaceted understanding of time in the Ottoman Empire's and partly in today's Turkey. For example, even Turkey's most formal business circles readily permit ten-minute latencies for meeting times, possibly following the legacy of similar praying time allowances.

---

[1] The author is grateful to Wishnitzer (2015) for the "Alla Turca" inspiration.

The following section reviews time and timekeeping in different cultures and societies. It also describes Islamic practices of timekeeping and Ottoman society, with a brief history of clocks and clock towers. The chapter then goes on to cover the methodology and results, including four comparative case studies and discussions, before concluding.

Evolution of Time and Temporal Understanding in Societies

Researchers have usually held the Industrial Revolution, railways, and telegraph networks responsible for the emergence of modern time arrangements that involved countries using standardized times worldwide. In 1884, an international timekeeping system started to evolve with the International Meridian Conference in Washington, D.C. Representatives from the Ottoman Empire had also attended the conference and declared that Alla Turca and Alla Franga times would coexist in the country (Wishnitzer, 2015, p. 151).

Standardization of time across countries was a complex process combined with daylight savings rules and the countries' shared calendars (Ogle, 2015). Governments saw this unification as an opportunity to build unified and powerful states. Previously, cities and towns used different time alignments according to their local geographical experience with the sun. Countries' particular focus on centralizing their people and their time-based authority leveraged how the overall process of unification progressed (Ogle, 2015). Countries walked at different speeds towards time unification and aligning their time according to Greenwich Mean Time (GMT), completing the global process in the mid-twentieth century. These differences in pace were due to countries' contextual political and economic conditions, where colonial/imperial states had little control (Ogle, 2015, p. 75–98).

Despite the dialectical and comprehensive nature of how time and temporal understanding have changed, the grand narrative of time studies assumes time perceptions with a binary opposition between the East and the West. According to this literature, time perception has taken a relatively organic, holistic, and cumulative understanding in Eastern societies. The first comprehensive, water-powered clock was developed in China, which shows time with the movements of stellar objects without dividing time into equal pieces or giving time measures. This clock helped people to relate to time holistically (Gimpel, 1988). The literature also claims that Western societies understand time as more mechanical and manipulative (e.g., Mumford, 1934). The latter used clocks rather than time display and measurement devices to control and schedule activities.

Table 14.1 *Clock towers built 1876–1909 in Anatolia outside Istanbul (n=24)*

Location	Year opened	Donors/architect	City center	Near mosque	Minaret form	Inscription	Fountain	Chime
Adana	1882	Abidin Paşa & Hacı Yünus Ağa	+	-	-	-	-	+
Ankara	1884	Sırrı Paşa & Hacı Süleyman Refik	+	-	-	+	-	+
Antalya	1908	-	+	-	-	-	-	+
Balıkesir	F:1827 R:1901	Restored: Governor Ömer Ali Bey	+	-	-	+	-	+
Bilecik	1907	Governor Musa Kazım Bey	-	-	-	+	-	-
Bolu	1882	-	-	-	-	-	-	-
Gerede								
Bolu Mudurnu	F:1891 R:1905	-	-	-	-	-	-	-
Bursa Tophane	F:1876 R:1905	Restored: Reşid Mümtaz Paşa & Mehmet Emin Bey	+	-	-	-	-	+
Çanakkale	1896	Governor Cemil Paşa	+	-	-	+	+	+
Çankırı	1901	Sub-Governor Hacı Efe	+	+	+	-	-	+
Çorum	1894	Yedisekiz Hasan Paşa	+	-	+	+	-	+
Çorum Sungurlu	1891	Sub-Governor Edib Bey, Arch: Yozgatlı Şakir Usta	+	+	-	-	-	+
Elazığ Maden	1898	Governor Halid Bey	+	-	-	+	-	-
Eskişehir Sivrihisar	1900	Sub-Governor Mahmut Bey & Sub-Governor Yüzügüllü Hacı Mehmet	-	-	-	-	-	+

Location	Year	Description						
İzmir	1901	Kıbrıslı Kamil Paşa+ Bahriye Mirlivası Said Paşa & Sub-Governor Eşref Paşa, Arch: Raymond Péré	+	+	+	-	+	+
İzmit Kocaeli	1902	Musa Kazım, Archs: Vedat Tek, Mihran Azaryan	+	-	+	+	+	+
Kastamonu	1885	Abdurrahman Nureddin Paşa	-	-	-	-	-	+
Kayseri	1907	Governor Haydar Bey, Arch: Tavlusunlu Salih Usta	+	+	-	-	-	+
Muğla	1885	Hacı Süleyman Efendi, Arch: Rum Filivari Usta	+	+	-	+	+	+
Samsun Vezirköprü	1908	Governor Reşit Akif Paşa & Kaim Makam Ahmet Reşit Efendi	+	-	+	+	-	+
Samsun Ladik	1889	Sub-Governor Reşit Bey	+	-	+	-	-	-
Tarsus Mersin	1893	Sub-Governor Ziya Bey	+	+	+	-	-	-
Tokat	1902	Governor Bekir Paşa & Sub-Governor Enver Bey	+	+	+	+	-	-
Yozgat	1908	Tevfikizade Ahmed Bey, Arch: Şakir Usta	+	-	-	-	+	+

In contrast to the simplistic approaches, this chapter argues that the actual variations of time conceptualizations have a wider variety across different periods and societies. It examines particular clock towers' materiality in the late-Ottoman Empire.

Methodology

As described earlier in the introduction, this study examined the clock towers built during the same period across the Ottoman Empire, which still exist within Turkey's borders, with a microhistorical approach while adopting a critical realist lens.

Microhistories of Late-Ottoman Clock Towers

Microhistory, as a historical tradition, was developed primarily in Italy (Ginzburg & Poni,1991, 1979) in response to the French "Annales" school (Levi, 1991). Annales historians propose a holistic history analysis, whereas microhistorians argue that this leads to missing critical, small-scale phenomena. Therefore, they perform historical analysis on a smaller scale (Lepore, 2001) around an event, collective, family, or object (Darnton, 2004). They ask "big questions in small places" (Joyner, 1999, p. 1) to resolve meaning structures behind a single item or an occasion. Thus, they relate historical data with its context (Beaudry, 1995, p. 4).

The study has focussed on the independent clock towers that are not annexed to another building and that have no additional functionality. These clock towers have been built and used entirely as separate and stand-alone clock towers. The study has identified 24 single, independent, entirely dedicated clock towers with these criteria (See Table 14.1) from a larger pool of 102 clock towers.

This study mainly used secondary data about these clock towers. These sources are Turkish Archives Directorate for Ottoman Archives (DABOA-Devlet Arşivleri Başkanlığı Osmanlı Arşivi), books and encyclopedias (Acun, 1994, 2011; Cansever, 2009; Wishnitzer, 2015), related masters theses and doctoral dissertations (Köker, 2002; Duymaz, 2003; Birol, 2005; Güntan, 2007; Wishnitzer, 2009; Üçsu, 2011; Altınışık, 2012; Singer, 2013), and academic papers and other relevant literature (Şapolyo, 1969; Acun, 1991, 1992; Tanyeli, 1998, 1999; Cengizkan 1999, 2002; Kreiser, 2006; Gürbüz, 2009; Uluengin, 2010; Üçsu, 2017). The author also visited these clock towers for primary data collection and observation over three years, between 2017 and 2020. During these visits, the researcher also tapped into local stories and ephemera and recorded the positioning relative to the closest historical mosque constructed before the clock tower. The study has identified three 'exceptional typical' (Lepore, 2001, p. 131; Chin, 2011) cases among these twenty-four clock towers to develop Kastamonu, Çorum, and İzmir clock towers as case studies. In selecting the microhistorical case studies, the study has used the norms described in Chin (2011) to broaden the case study approach to expand case studies' generalizability: the case should identify an interesting behavioral or situational similarity (coherence), support, or contradict a relevant macro-level concept, information or expectation, contribute to the macro-level meanings or invite readers to think in novel ways, identify interesting interrelationships between different micro-level occasions or situations, invite us to ask new questions, and involve necessary detail to relate micro-level behaviors and motivations and macro-level logic (Chin, 2011, p. 356).

Critical Realism on Time and Temporal Understanding

The study adopted a critical realist lens to uncover the reality of time and timekeeping in Ottoman society, going beyond the empirical and actual domains around the clock towers. Critical realism, as a philosophical, theoretical, and methodological approach, originated from the philosophy of Roy Bhaskar (e.g., Bhaskar, 2008, 2013, 2016). It explains how the world fits together, combining transcendental realism with critical naturalism. According to this perspective, reality exists independent of people's perceptions or language. Subjective interpretations influence how humans understand and experience reality. Critical realism is an empirical project due to its strong commitment to realism and extensive efforts to refine/explore its philosophical details and key concepts. It also offers a philosophy and a shared vocabulary for developing a more comprehensive understanding of time and temporality.

Critical realism is not simply concerned about the natural world and our knowledge of it. However, it has a deep, three-layered ontology: the real, the actual, and the empirical. The real involves existing things, objects, structures, and causal mechanisms. On the other hand, the actual includes events that occur as a subset of the real. Lastly, the empirical only involves the events and objects that people have experienced and therefore is a subset of the actual (Bhaskar, 2008). Thus, every phenomenon is naturally layered and has emergent properties. Critical realism considers these layers as laminated and distinct layers when developing explanations. They are dependent upon but irreducible to their constituents (Bhaskar, 2008).

Critical realism has a constructivist epistemology. However, it is not subjectivist. According to this view, people generate knowledge and meaning from their experiences. However, discourses available to us mediate the knowledge about reality. Therefore, knowledge is not entirely discursive because the knowledge of an external 'reality' is possible. After all, external reality exists independent of texts or discourses (unlike strong social constructionism). This view lets us know about objective reality (unlike weak social constructionism). For example, does patriarchy only exist when and where there are related discourses? One should separate people's beliefs from the corresponding reality; otherwise, this leads to another form of 'thin' explanation (Edwards et al., 2014, p. 6). Objectivity and truthfulness claims have negative consequences, as science is political; truth claims may only represent the current orthodoxy within a scientific community. They are vulnerable to different circumstances and interests. However, neither is it always an Orwellian hegemony generated through dominance. Science can also provide a better understanding of the world. Critical realism offers a sophisticated vocabulary and may generate novel perspectives for traditionally ahistorical frameworks adopted in organization theory and management. Critical realism methodology provides tools and means to distinguish social structures and generative mechanisms for structural changes over time.

In CR, the structure and the agency are codependent on each other's formation, continuation, and development. They are different emergent entities with different properties and powers. According to this view, humans are reflexive, whereas the structures are enduring. Analytical dualism can separate the structure and the agency. Their interplay provides examinations of the structuring and restructuring of social institutions. As structure and agency operate diachronically through time, structure predates the action(s) that transform it (Archer, 1995). Therefore, actors are born into existing structures where structural elaborations post-date those actions.

In its treatment of time, critical realism works with retroduction that focusses on causal mechanisms and conditions and explains why things happen and appear the way they do. Retroduction focusses on "the manifest phenomena of social life, as conceptualized in the experience of the social agents concerned, to the essential relations that necessitate them" (Bhaskar, 1979, p. 32). It is "a means of inference which involves imagining a model of a mechanism that, if it were real, would account for the phenomenon in question" (Bhaskar, 2016, p. 79). It is about generalizing the fundamental structures, causal powers, and mechanisms that act 'transfactually.' These mechanisms exist independent of events and observations. This perspective is unlike inductive inference, which seeks inferences from empirical regularities. Therefore, CR researchers avoid simplified models/theories that favor complex histories/narratives. They may derive causes of an event in time from the retroduction of later events as structures are enduring generative mechanisms.

According to critical realism, structural formation (morphogenesis) is also temporal (Archer & Morgan, 2020). The reality is historical, following structural conditioning, social interaction, and structural elaboration steps. From this perspective, breaking time into phases is critical because causal explanations involve where an event or a structural property comes over time (diachronically), not simply how it works now (synchronically).

Late-Ottoman Clock Towers' Sociohistorical Materiality

Were the Ottoman clock towers symbols of a continuous or discontinuous change in temporal understanding in Ottoman societies? Sultan Abdülhamid II issued an imperial order, "İrade-i Seniyye," that instructed provinces to build clock towers to celebrate the twenty-fifth anniversary of his rise to the throne in 1900–1901 (Uluçay, 1941, p. 22–3). While some of the towers constructed during his reign coincided with these years, very few documents from the Ottoman Archives tied these towers' construction with İrade-i Seniyye. Clock towers constructed in this period seem more like a local response. In their relationship with the empire's center, they responded to what was changing in the empire and what local notables wanted.

In the Ottoman Empire, dedicated 'muvakkit' (time measurer) experts used precise techniques to determine the time for prayers. A muvakkit works in a muvakkithane (time room), usually located near, or at, the central mosques of cities and towns, to determine the times for prayer from astronomical observations (Aydüz, 1995, 1999, 2004a, 2004b; Kumbasar, 2008; Dayioğlu, 2010). In Istanbul, the empire's capital, sixty-nine muvakkithanes were registered, showing that time estimation is an essential and widespread task (Ünver, 1975, 1980). However, not all cities and towns could maintain multiple muvakkithanes to determine times for their purposes. In many cities, clock towers became modern muvakkithanes for the public. In some cities, clock towers were built side-by-side with the central mosque, sometimes like another minaret. They complemented mosques' task of announcing/identifying time information to the public.

Islamic practices rely greatly on time measurements like daily prayers, Hajj, fasting, and religious festivals. Ottoman people used multiple timing conventions, called "Ezani" and "Zevali" times. Prayers announced over minarets (ezan) not only call the Muslim public to pray but also announce the "Ezani" time.

Ezani times are also named "Alla Turca" or "gurûbî" (sunset) time. This convention was the official time system of the Ottoman Empire. In this system, days begin and end at sunset and are divided into twenty-four -hour parts. Daytime starts with the sunrise, finishes with the sunset, and is divided into twelve pieces. On the other hand, the night-time is divided into twelve pieces, making temporal differences between the day and the night slots in different seasons. Therefore, mechanical clocks needed a manual reset every day. According to this scheme, muvakkits determine each praying time with the following criteria:

- The morning praying is before the sunrise, as it finishes before the sun appears on the horizon.
- The noon praying is when the shadow of a stick perpendicular to the horizon and the ground (the perpendicular stick) starts getting longer.
- The afternoon praying is the time between when the perpendicular stick's shadow is the smallest and the stick size (early time). The perpendicular stick's shadow is its smallest size + twice the stick size (second time).
- The night praying is after the sun sets completely, representing the start of a new day.
- The sleep-time praying is when an ordinary eye cannot differentiate between two objects in black and white that stand next to each other outside.

The above description of the criteria for determining praying times shows that exact timing is possible only for noon and afternoon prayers to some degree. There is approximately a ten-minute tolerance when one misses these time windows for praying.

By the second half of the nineteenth century, the 'seasonal' hours had standardized into two sets of sixty-minute hours measured from sunset, as the 'official' Alla Turca system. In this way, they avoided seasonal changing length problems. The standardization attempt was most effective in government services and transportation, mainly influencing the empire's center, Istanbul, and other essential power centers.

Therefore, in Ottoman society, timings were never exact; they were open to negotiation. Time is not a mechanical, deterministic, and exact reference. However, it is a socially negotiated, continuous, and ongoing contract. There was an average variance in timings within different ranges, and people considered time to be relatively smooth and continuous.

'Zevali' times came from the Hellenic legacy of the geography and transposed into the mean time, European time, or Alla Franga time. Local mean time depended on the length of a mean solar day (averaged to correct the variations coming from the Earth's rotation) divided into twenty-four hours for a specific location on Earth. Towards the end of Sultan Abulhamid II's reign, after the Young Turk Revolution in 1908, the Ottoman government decided to use only Alla Franga hours in the government and military. However, the clock towers have run with either or both clock systems for many years since the construction of the empire's first clock tower in the sixteenth century (Karač & Žunić, 2018, p. 77; Alihodzic, 2019, p. 2).

Sultan Abdülhamid II and the Ottoman Modernization

Sultan Abdülhamid II is one of the most critical and controversial figures of the late-Ottoman period. The main political and historical discussion has been about whether he was the ruthless 'Red Sultan' who forcefully stopped separatist rebels in different parts of the country or the 'great Khan' who reformed the foundations of the Ottoman state to solve the problems of a fracturing empire. He lived between 1842 and 1918 and ruled the Ottoman Empire, also named 'Devlet-i Aliyye' (the Grand State), between 1876 and 1909. He worked with twenty grand viziers (prime ministers), appointing them to the position twenty-eight times with some serving terms as short as three days.

In his early period, he accepted the establishment of the Ottoman Parliament and the Ottoman Empire's first constitution in 1876. The main reason was to prevent foreign interference via different ethnic and political groups with enhanced participation and civil rights. However, after suppressing the Bulgarian uprising (May 1876) and taking back control over Serbia and Montenegro, he dismissed parliament in March 1877. After a disastrous war with Russia, he suspended the constitution in February 1878 (Berkes, 1978).

However, constitutional reforms and modernization efforts continued. The Sultan's policy aimed to centralize and partly liberalize the empire to tie different nationalities and geographies to strengthen its sovereignty. His objective was to respond to the European powers, which were provoking the Christian population of the empire. He pursued a pan-Islamist policy to control the people and connect with other Muslims outside the empire, creating difficulties for the European empires in their Muslim colonies (Berkes, 1978).

During his period, Muslim communities worldwide financed the construction of the Hejaz Railway from Damascus to Medina with donations. The train line opened in 1908, short of 400 km to Medina. In addition, around the same period, commercial permits were given to Germany for the construction and management of the Baghdad Railway in 1899, which became operational in 1903. The state established the University of Istanbul in 1900 and other educational and professional institutions during his time. In addition, Istanbul Asia, Istanbul Europe, and Damascus train stations were built during this period.

Heavy police intelligence and tight press censorship characterized Sultan Abdülhamid II's last thirty years. Despite this tight control, France occupied Tunisia in 1881 and Britain occupied Egypt in 1882. However, the Ottoman military suppressed the Armenian uprising between 1894 and 1896. The army also won the Greek–Ottoman war with a clear victory in 1897. While he restored the constitution after the Young Turks' coup in 1908, he was replaced by an uprising in Istanbul in April 1909, ending his reign.

The following sections present case studies of three clock towers in Kastamonu, Çorum, and İzmir for an in-depth analysis.

Kastamonu Clock Tower: A Tower in Exile

Kastamonu clock tower was built in 1885 on top of the 'Sarayüstü' hill overlooking the city administration building at the center (See Figure 14.1) long before the order of the Sultan. The tower was 12 m

Figure 14.1 Kastamonu clock tower

tall and made of yellow and green stones, standing on a 5.90 x 5.90 m square foundation. Its clock was imported from Strasbourg and had 'Brunberger' branding, having a single quadrant in 1.60 m diameter with Arabic numerals. The tower has two floors. The first floor has a clock, and the second has a bell. The top of the tower is enclosed with a pyramidal roof. The clock is barely visible from the city center for reading time information. However, it is likely that people can hear the tower bell throughout the city. The tower's form is rectangular, with a bell, symbolically reminiscent of a church. There are stories that the Muslim community did not like the building when it was constructed.

Kastamonu was a sizable city and the center of the *sanjak* (administrative divisions of a *vilayet* (province) run by a *mutesarriff* appointed directly by the Sultan). In 1870, 159,858 Muslim, 2,557 Orthodox, and 59 Gregorian men brought the male population to 162,474. In 1892 records, the population of men and women was reported as 178,076 Muslim men, 175,157 Muslim women, 4,608 non-Muslim men, and 4,421 non-Muslim women, totalling a population of 362,262 people.

The construction of the clock tower had been ordered and sponsored by Abdurrahman Nureddin Paşa (General) (See Figure 14.2), who was the province's governor from 1882 to 1891, having been previously appointed grand vizier in 1882. However, the Sultan dismissed him after two months and eleven days due to their disagreement on the Egypt policy. Prior to this position, the Paşa had been the *mutesarriff* of Shumen (Bulgaria), Varna (Bulgaria), and Niš (Serbia) sanjaks. He was the governor of Prizren in 1872 (Kosovo), Tuna in 1873 (Balkans), Ankara in 1875, Bagdad in 1875 (Iraq), Diyarbakır in 1877, and Bagdad again from 1878 to 1880.

Figure 14.2 Prime actors of the three clock towers' construction

People called the clock tower 'the tower in exile' as it stood outside the city on a hill. The story goes that the Sultan exiled the clock from Istanbul as it frequently malfunctioned. However, there have been no reports of the clock malfunctioning since its opening at Kastamonu. As the clock requires charging and aligning every twenty-four hours, the locals interpreted it as a malfunction. Another story was more personal: "a pregnant female servant of the Sultan's harem got afraid of the bell ringing and lost the Sultan's baby." While these stories vary, the ex-grand vizier Abdurrahman Paşa seemed to be the inspiration for them, as he was a governor in 'exile.'

Abdurrahman Paşa was a good governor. He supported modernization efforts by renewing the infrastructure and creating educational establishments, such as the Kastamonu high school. He also renovated İnebolu town's city plan after a major fire. After gaining the Kastamonu governorship, he became the governor of the larger Aydın and Edirne units and worked in the Ministry of Justice from 1895 to 1907. The Sultan again offered him the grand vizier position in 1901, which he rejected. In 1908, the Sultan invited him to become grand vizier for the second time. Paşa agreed on the condition he had complete authority over his decisions. Instead of giving this authority, the Sultan appointed Mehmet Said Paşa to the grand vizier position for the seventh time. He was in position for just fourteen days.

The Kastamonu Clock tower has been operational without significant interruption for more than 137 years. The neighboring park and café serve visitors who have a view of the city over the hill.

Çorum: Lobbying for a Clock Tower

The Çorum clock tower was constructed between 1894 and 1896, near Hamid Mosque (from the sixteenth century) and the Grand Mosque (from the fourteenth century) in the city center. It is 27.5 m tall, having a minaret-like, circular yellow sandstone structure over an octagonal basis standing 3.9 m on each side. The tower is topped with a rectangular bell tower (see Figure 14.3). It stands on an octagonal foundation with clock quadrants in four directions with Roman numerals (but IIII for four). Mustafa Şemil Pak, the Chief Clock Artisan of the Sultan, produced the clock. The bell has the signature of the Zildjian family from İstanbul, famous for producing bells and cymbals. While records say the bell was ordered for this project, local people say it was from an Istanbul church. The hangers of the bell engraved onto it eight human faces.

The prominent figure in the construction of the Çorum Clock Tower was the 'Seven Eight' Hasan Paşa (see Figure 14.2). The clock tower was

Figure 14.3 Çorum clock tower

his gift to his hometown. On the clock tower, the following dedication is readable:

> The great khan of the time, the generous Abdülhamid Khan
> One of his valuable Paşas, the unique and only Hasan Paşa
> He devoted all his time to doing good deeds.
> May he be successful in his ambitions, every moment, dear God
> This Clock Tower is one of his outstanding gifts.
> It was made abundantly; he revived this city
> History was written on his door at a blessed time
> Look, it was the grace of Hasan Paşa who made this great clock.

Hasan Paşa's nickname was 'Seven Eight' due to his illiteracy. Therefore, his signature is constructed of the two most simple words in Arabic letters: 7 8 (٧٨). At the time, Hasan Paşa was an Ottoman marshal general. He had begun his military career as a private and had come to Istanbul. He fought in the Russian war, where the army promoted him due to his successful service. Later, he was assigned to protect a group going to Mecca for Hajj. On their way back to Istanbul, he saved their lives in a ship accident and was later promoted to lieutenant level.

When Abdülhamid II became Sultan, Hasan was promoted to commander of the guards of Beşiktaş district, covering Yıldız, Dolmabahçe,

Çırağan, and Feriyye Palaces. On 20 May 1878, Ali Suavi, previously the library manager of the Yildiz Palace and the manager of the Galatasaray high school, organized a coup attempt to attack Çırağan Palace with 150 people to replace the Sultan. Paşa defended the Sultan and killed the coup organizer, making him famous and promoting him to paşa (military general) status.

Çorum is in the central-southern part of the Black Sea region towards central Anatolia. In the 1893 census, 24,551 Muslim men, 23,830 Muslim women, 415 non-Muslim men, and 261 non-Muslim women were registered in Çorum, making a total population of 49,057 people. As these numbers illustrate, Çorum was smaller than a city before the clock tower was built and was not a *sanjak*.

As Hasan Paşa became famous, prominent people from Çorum established a committee of representatives to visit him in Istanbul, asking him to help them develop Çorum. Hasan Paşa asked the delegates what infrastructure they needed. The committee considered bringing the Kızılırmak river's water for providing irrigation and powering water mills, educating children in nearby cities with scholarships, or bringing a railway route to Çorum. Each idea was met with resistance from some members of the group. In the end, instead of these ideas, they asked for a clock tower. They heard the Ottoman state was building clock towers in central cities of sanjaks. They demanded Hasan Paşa help Çorum become a sanjak, entitling them to a clock tower and other state investments. Supporting this cause, Hasan Paşa strongly lobbied for making Çorum a sanjak.

In 1894 Çorum had upgraded, adding nearby İskilip, Osmancık, and Sungurlu towns administratively to Çorum. The construction of the clock tower started in 1894, after Çorum received sanjak status, and finished in 1896. The stones were extracted locally from Kavşut village near Sungurlu (Cansever, 2009, p. 80). Sungurlu was larger than Çorum at that time and already had a clock tower that had opened in 1891. However, Çorum won sanjak status with its new clock tower, and the influence of Hasan Paşa and Sungurlu became secondary in the region.

Other cities also copied the Çorum clock tower. For example, during the Russian invasion of north-east Anatolia in 1916, many people from the Bayburt province temporarily migrated to Çorum. When they returned home, they built a near replica of the Çorum clock tower. They opened it on the first anniversary of the Turkish Republic on October 29, 1924. Çorum clock tower had significant restorations in 1976 and 2006. However, the stones used in these renovations made the structure weaker due to problems in the materials selected (Cansever, 2009, p. 80).

Izmir Clock Tower

İzmir clock tower, as an icon and as a building, is the prime symbol of the city (see Figure 14.4). It was opened in 1901 at the Konak Square near the seashore, in front of the Governor's Hall (Konak), near the small Konak mosque built in the eighteenth century. The clock tower is 25 m tall. The building has a minaret form like many other clock towers in the sample. However, indicating the orientalist tendencies of the architect Raymond Péré, it has a North African/Maghreb minaret form rather than following a typical Ottoman mosque. Local rumors suggested the clock was a gift from Kaiser Wilhelm II to the Sultan.

Mehmet Kamil Paşa was appointed to Izmir as a governor 'in exile' in 1895, after being a grand vizier in Istanbul for the second time for only

Figure 14.4 İzmir clock tower

thirty-five days between October 3 and November 7. He was born in Cyprus in 1832 and served in different positions in the Ottoman state, including as grand vizier for the first time between 1885 and 1891. After his second service, the Sultan sent Kamil Paşa to İzmir to distance him from the capital and weaken his political influence. While Kamil Paşa was in a kind of exile, the Sultan appointed his son Said Bey as his adjutant in İstanbul. Kamil Paşa started the construction of the İzmir Clock Tower in such a political climate to improve his appeal and his relationship with the Sultan.

On August 1, 1900, Governor Kamil Paşa organized a meeting in İzmir with regional administrators, officers, and notable local elite to plan how İzmir would celebrate the Sultan's twenty-fifth anniversary. The group had decided to build a monument with the status and prestige of İzmir. Local newspapers announced the decision the next day: "The government attempted to create a work on behalf of our city, as a memory of worship and loyalty" (Yetkin, 2001). The group announced the decision: "This work, which will be created in our city on the occasion of the twenty-fifth anniversary of the accession to the throne, is a very artistic fountain with a clock tower visible from all four sides, which will be built on a marble-paved floor near his highness' military barracks." The group also appointed a standing committee to oversee the project: Abdülkadir Paşa (member of the city council), Eşref Paşa (city mayor), Şevket Beyefendi (military district governor), Arabyan Karabet Efendi (notable tradesman), Sarrafin Efendi (notable tradesman), and Baranofski Efendi (city public works chief engineer) (Yetkin, 2001).

On August 14, 1900, the committee met with the architect, Raymond Péré, who presented an Arabic-style monument project with a fountain and a clock tower. The committee approved the project and decided to conduct the foundation-laying ceremony on September 1, 1900, on the twenty-fourth anniversary of Abdülhamid II's accession and the official celebrations (Yetkin, 2001). Before the ceremony, Kamil Paşa (governor), Ferik Osman Paşa (army commander), Safiyuddin Bey (accountant), Eşref Paşa (mayor), and Servet Paşa (brigadier general) with engineers and other servants decided on the exact location of the monument and started the excavation of the foundation. The newspaper reporting this event also reported that the project had already spent 793 Ottoman lira (Yetkin, 2001). Before the ceremony, the committee also decided to create, decorate, and illuminate a 7.58 m wooden model of the monument near the construction site. The construction ceremony took place as planned with the participation of the city administration, representatives of religious communities of the city, and a ceremony battalion. The İzmir mufti performed a public prayer in Arabic that wished Sultan

Abdülhamid II victory and success, and sacrificed livestock for God's mercy. Kamil Paşa made a speech, and the band of İzmir Industrial School played 'Islamic and national' music. The celebrations continued over the city center, around the city administration building at night. Thousands of people attended the celebrations, where the municipality played music and served sweets, confectionery, and lemonade. As a result, this celebration has become one of the most significant events in the history of İzmir up until that time (Cansever, 2009, p. 140).

After the ceremony, construction began quickly. The total money spent on the project reached 1,412 Ottoman lira in October 1900. In order to speed up the project and ensure it finished on time, before the intended opening celebrations on September 1, 1901, the construction project was transferred to the architect Raymond Péré's company on January 30, 1901, with a tender of an additional 1,700 Ottoman lira (Yetkin, 2001).

The clock tower stands on an 81 m^2 octagonal area with a cross-shaped marble foundation. Four sides of the octagonal shape include four fountains with three faucets over a ceremonial canopy of marble over an altar, covered with smaller arched domes. The base and tower walls are also made of marble, carrying the overall structure, and cut stone blocks. Some of the columns and column heads were made from dark green and cherry-colored marble. The structural elements were aligned and tied with copper rivets without any cement or lime but primed using a solder made of brimstone and river sand (Yetkin, 2001).

The tower's stairs are also part of the structural system that continues the tower on the outside. The tower's surface between the fountains had included the Sultan's tughra (signature). The tower had four floors and was 25 m tall, carrying four clocks on the tower's four sides. The tower's top floor is slimmer than the rest, finished with a metal top. This floor also includes the tower bell which has not worked for many years. There is no record of how long the bell worked. While the clock tower resembles a North African minaret, it was also a combination of the fountains of Şadırvanaltı mosque (opened in 1636) (Baykara, 1974, p. 47; Sözen, 1975, pp. 310–12; Acun, 1994, p. 26) and the multi-floored galleries of St. Fotini church in İzmir (built in the seventeenth century) (Baykara, 1974, p. 52; Acun, 1994, p. 26) (see Figure 14.5).

The marbles for the clock tower body were extracted from Sarayköy in Denizli and cost 190 kuruş (lira cents) per square meter. For the colorful decoration of the clock tower, the construction project had ordered 20 cherry and 20 green marble blocks from Marseilles, France, at 100 francs per square meter, arriving at İzmir port on June 17, 1901. As the cost of the tower exceeded the budget, the governor's office created a public support campaign and collected 1,052 Ottoman lira from donations.

Figure 14.5 St. Fotini church and a section of Şadırvanaltı mosque

Governors Kamil Paşa, Abdülkadir Paşa, Tatyos Efendi, İstefan Efendi, and Arabyan Karabet Efendi had donated to the campaign with 50 Ottoman lira each (Yetkin, 2001). Other notables of the city, such as Hakim Emin Efendi, Mayor Eşref Paşa, Yemişçi Tahir Efendi, Evliyazade Refik Bey, Caferizade Şamlı Sait Efendi, Sarrafim Efendi, Atıf Efendi, Pirinççi Fehmi Efendi, Şemi Bey, Tevfik Nevzat Efendi, and Simon Simonaki Efendi donated to the campaign with 5–20 Ottoman lira. These donations were also published in the local newspapers to invite the public to donate (Yetkin, 2001).

The construction committee had also decided to build a silver clock tower model with jewelry ornaments and present it to Sultan Abdülhamid II. While some local newspapers claimed this model cost 375 Ottoman lira, other local newspapers claimed it cost three times that. The silver-made, ruby, emerald, and diamond ornamented, gold-threaded model was a replica at 90 cm high. The model was developed in Istanbul by Zingulli Usta and included four functional Swiss watches on four sides of the tower (Yetkin, 2001). The model's inscription read: "Built as the object of the presentation of the clock tower with fountains, built in the city of İzmir to remember the twenty-fifth anniversary of the accession of his majesty to the throne 1901." After building the model in İstanbul, it was brought to Izmir to receive the approval of Kamil Paşa. Then, the approved model was transported back to Istanbul and presented to the Sultan in March 1901 by the Mayor Eşref Paşa and Said Bey, the son of Kamil Paşa and the personal adjutant of the Sultan. For this purpose, Kamil Paşa submitted their application on March 23, 1901, to the chief clerk of the House of the Sultan to ask for the Sultan's permission to bring the model, which was granted. However, they could only present the model to the chief clerk on behalf of the Sultan (Yetkin, 2001).

In April 1901, the rough construction of the clock tower finished. The pipes and other fittings brought gas to torches and oil lamps to illuminate the building at different levels at night and on special occasions. Also, infrastructure to bring water to the clock tower's fountains had started. Construction was mostly completed in August 1901. However, the clock was not there yet. The clock tower was missing a gas machine to illuminate the building at night. The gold threads of the fountain's small domes, copper protection of the tower stairs, and some colored ornaments were also not finished. However, the committee decided to complete these missing elements after the opening ceremony, having written a letter to the city governor's office. The clock tower opened on September 1, 1901, as planned with a grand, day-long ceremony, albeit without a functioning clock. The ceremony continued with the military and industry school bands playing 'national and Islamic' songs near the clock tower and the city administration building. The celebration continued at the city administration building into the night with free food and desserts while Salamon Elgaze Efendi sang traditional songs with his fine instrument orchestra (Yetkin, 2001).

The clock tower has remained mostly operational since its opening in 1901. On July 23, 1908, after the Young Turk Revolution, Sultan Abdülhamid II had to accept the reopening of parliament. Some of Sultan Abdülhamid II's protesters celebrated the revolution at Konak Square. They even attempted to destroy the tower (Yetkin, 2001). However, other people participating in the revolution celebrations stopped this attempt. After the Ottoman Empire, a law passed in the Turkish parliament on June 15, 1927, banning the use of sultan tughras in public. Following that, tughras representing the signature of Sultan Abdülhamid II on the clock tower were scraped off and replaced with a crescent and a star representing the Turkish flag. In a major earthquake in 1974, the tower's top floor collapsed, causing the clocks to malfunction for two years.

Discussion

Studies about the late-Ottoman period and its push towards modernity are usually reductionist. Therefore, they miss the dialectical complexities of the eclectic communities in the Ottoman Empire. This chapter focussed on the Ottoman clock towers built in the same period outside Istanbul, the capital. The study results argued continuity with earlier time-related and architectural practices, translating and hybridizing the new and the old.

In the empirical domain, besides other observations, the study identified (1) a pattern in location choices and (2) the daily maintenance of clocks to sustain Alla Turca time (see Table 14.2). Clock tower location choices seem to symbolize their complementarity with the mosques as new muvakkithanes or near city administration buildings symbolizing the Sultan and the Ottoman state. The 'exile' towers built over hills and slopes, mostly on the outskirts of the cities and towns, still provide visibility and public control.

While few of the clock towers were constructed under the Sultan's orders, initiators, sponsors, and supporters of these clock towers were local. These towers were not mere imports; they were not essential

Table 14.2 *A critical realist view of the clock towers' stratified reality*

Empirical Domain Perceptions, experiences, observations	Locations near mosques symbolize a new muvakkithane function. Locations near city administration buildings symbolize the Sultan and the state. Locations over hills and slopes for visibility and control. Daily maintenance of clocks to maintain Alla Turca time.
Actual Domain Observed and unobserved events	Multiple clock arrangements show both Alla Turca and Alla Franga times. Minaret, church, or hybrid architectural forms. Pragmatism towards clock towers and bells. Some Muslim communities resisted bell towers as they resemble churches.
Real Domain Structures and mechanisms that generate events	Temporal integration of diverse communities. Political contests of the local elites. Symbolic reunification of the Ottoman Empire with clock towers and time. Islamic philanthropic traditions.

carriers of the Western notions of time. Instead, the Ottoman communities were diffused and appropriated a novel understanding of time under local elite and related power structures. Clock towers diffused into Ottoman land during this period as part of the initiatives by the elite of the state and the Sultan (Uluengin, 2010). However, the construction of these clock towers was not significantly different from the charity donation of a fountain or a mosque by the Sultan or one of the prominent paşas in their attempt to achieve power by showcasing themselves to the public and the Sultan, and as part of the Islamic philanthropic traditions, part of the real domain (Birol, 2005; Kreiser, 2006; Wishnitzer, 2010).

The clock towers symbolized the dominant power of the Sultan. The Ottoman elite entered power contests to attract and maintain his attention and goodwill with these towers (Yetkin, 2001; Kreiser, 2006; Wishnitzer, 2010). Typically, provincial governors constructed clock towers and performed ceremonies (e.g., DABOA, Y.EE.KP. 13/1210; DABOA, DH.MKT. 462/60; DABOA, DH.MKT. 1174/42). In addition to the governors, the local elite (e.g., DABOA, DH.MKT. 340/41) and some regular citizens (e.g., DABOA, DH.MKT. 1207/93) constructed, participated in, or supported the construction of the clock towers. Some of these people received recognition or even imperial badges for their commitment and loyal service.

In the actual domain, the study diagnosed (1) multiple clock arrangements in some clock towers as they either show Alla Turca time or both Alla Turca and Alla Franga times, (2) their minaret, church, or hybrid architectural forms, and (3) the friction in some Muslim communities to reject bells, as they make clock towers resemble churches (see Table 14.2). The daily maintenance was due to the difference between the Alla Turca and European times in the actual domain. These daily alignments most probably work for the realignment of the clock to meet the local conventions in the actual domain. Clock towers' physical forms followed previous architectural practices, copying churches and mosques. Many of them resembled a circular minaret form (e.g., Samsun Vezirköprü). Some were rectangular-shaped, resembling church forms (e.g., Kastamonu). A few were hybrids of both (e.g., Çorum and İzmir). Most of these towers had bells, emphasizing the similarity with churches. Some districts have no reports of social friction or hostile response from the Muslim community, whereas in others, bells were deactivated or partly silenced in response to demands of the local Muslim people.

In their diffusion and translation, these towers assumed religious functions and acted as a complement to mosques. While these clocks run with European time-alignment basics (Alla Franga), local experts adjust them daily to meet the Ottoman clock conventions (Alla Turca). Several towers also use multiple clock machinery or dials to indicate both times side-by-side. Clock towers were not mere symbols of the secular European time. Ottoman state and society used the two time systems pragmatically. The binary oppositions that idealize clock towers either as an embodiment of secularism or agents of Islamic state hegemony cannot fully comprehend or reflect the local conditions during that period. What is essentially religious or non-religious, Western or Eastern had been intertwined and hybridized in the daily lives of Ottoman subjects. Clock towers were also ticking pragmatically, both Alla Turca and Alla Franga hours on their multiple faces next to significant mosques of the town or city with a minaret-like material form. These clock towers were eclectic and hybridized, imported from Europe but adjusted to the local context and became part of the local traditions.

They were *Alla Turca* and *Alla Franga*, traditional and modern, religious and secular, patrimonial and civic, all simultaneously; they were indicative of the multiplicity of valid cultural alternatives available to contemporaries and, even more important, of the fluidity of the boundaries of those alternatives. If anything, Ottoman clock towers reflected the pragmatic eclecticism adopted by Ottoman elites in their attempts to pave their way to the future. (Wishnitzer, 2010, p. 539)

Islamic opposition to clock towers was not about time measurement or alignment; instead, it was about the bells and their symbolic attachment to churches (Atabaki, 2007). Abdülhamid II actively promoted clock towers, as neither these monuments nor the mean time system was anti-Islamic.

In the real domain, the widespread adoption of clock towers occurred with the Ottoman state's administrative support, together with the 'irade-i seniyye' of the Sultan. It was seen as a symbol of the state's modernization and the empire's reunification. The clock towers carry symbolism and the increasing synchronicity of timing conventions for the temporal integration of diverse communities in the empire. In different ways, the Sultan and the state administration were trying to control different parts of the empire, fighting for independence. Clock towers, without any functional requirement, seem like a symbolic reunification of the different communities of the empire for the Sultan and political leverage for the governors and the local elite.

Unfortunately, many clock towers of the same era were destroyed or faced major mechanical failures. Due to the lack of data on destroyed clock towers, the study could not analyze whether clock towers in any form or location survived in a better condition. However, the limited or lack of contextual appropriation might be why respective communities could not demand the protection of these monumental buildings. With state-led modernization, clock towers were imported and diffused as an official practice and became a tool of daily political competition between public and military officials.

As these examples illustrate, it took more of a gradual approach, attempting to reach a reconciliation with Western cultures and institutions that would allow maintenance and the survival of a fracturing empire. After the revolution and the establishment of the Turkish Republic, the state dismissed the Alla Turca time. Later, the Turkish Republic adopted the European time conventions, representing a revolutionary discontinuity.

Conclusion

Alternative time conceptions can exist, combine, and transform autonomously. During Abdülhamid II's reign, Ottoman clock towers were symbols of continuous and hybridized changes in the temporal understanding of 'polychronous' Ottoman societies. In the literature, researchers usually correlate the diffusion of mechanical clocks and clock towers with the availability of time-based employment schemes and the alignment of train schedules. However, most people in Ottoman society were not in time-based employment schemes. Therefore, clock towers have only represented a new way to learn the time left until the next praying time and relate to the traditional "Ezani" time. The diffusion and translation of timekeeping-related institutions may relate to different generative mechanisms of various modern contexts.

As Ottoman clock towers illustrate, the diffusion of monumental clock towers has resulted chiefly from a set of political relations, almost without any public need for the knowledge of current times. The stories of historical clock towers and their material resemblance and coexistence with the neighboring mosques offer a way to observe the complex multiplicity. It is also an excellent way to dissect how institutional changes compete, conflict, and coexist with symbols and artifacts of pre-existing institutional order.

References

Acun, H. (1991). Az Tanınan Anadolu Saat Kuleleri. *Kültür ve Sanat, 3*(9), 9.

Acun, H. (1992). Az Bilinen Saat Kulelerimiz. *İlgi, 68*(1), 28–31.

Acun, H. (1994). *Anadolu Saat Kuleleri*. Ankara: Atatürk Kültür, Dil, ve Tarih Yüksek Kurumu Atatürk Kültür Merkezi Yayınları.

Acun, H. (2011). *Osmanlı İmparatorluğu Saat Kuleleri*. Ankara: Atatürk Kültür Merkezi Yayınları.

Adam, B. (1990). *Time and Social Theory.* Oxford: Polity Press.

Adam, B. (2004). *Time.* Cambridge: Polity Press.

Adib & Emiljanowicz, P. (2019). Colonial time in tension: Decolonizing temporal imaginaries. *Time & Society, 28*(3), 1221–38.

Alihodzic, R. (2019). Clock towers from the Ottoman period in the territory of today's Montenegro. *METU Journal of the Faculty of Architecture, 36*(2), 1–28. DOI: 10.4305/METU.JFA.2019.2.6

Altınışık, I. U. (2012). *Osmanlı'da Zaman-Mekan Kavrayışının Değişimi ve Mimarlık, T.C. Yıldız Teknik Üniversitesi Fen Bilimleri Enstitüsü Yayınlanmamış Doktora Tezi.* İstanbul: Yıldız Technical University.

Archer, M. S. (1995). *Realist Social Theory: The Morphogenetic Approach.* Cambridge: Cambridge University Press.

Archer, M. S. & Morgan, J. (2020). Contributions to realist social theory: An interview with Margaret S. Archer. *Journal of Critical Realism, 19*(2), 179–200. DOI: 10.1080/14767430.2020.1732760

Atabaki, T. (2007). Time, Labour-Discipline and Modernization in Turkey and Iran: Some Comparative Remarks. In T. Atabaki (ed.), *The State and the Subaltern: Modernization, Society and the State in Turkey and Iran* (pp. 1–17). New York: I. B. Tauris.

Aydüz, S. (1995). Osmanlı Devleti'nde Müneccimbaşılık. In F. Günergun (ed.), *Osmanlı Bilimi Araştırmaları* (pp. 159–207). İstanbul: İstanbul Üniversitesi Yayınları.

Aydüz, S. (1999). Osmanlı Devleti'nde Küçük Gözlemevleri: Muvakkithaneler. In G. Eren (ed.), *Osmanlı Ansiklopedisi, Vol. VIII* (pp. 664–75). Osmanlı, Ankara: Yeni Türkiye.

Aydüz, S. (2004a). Osmanlı astronomi müesseseleri. *Türkiye Araştırmaları Literatür Dergisi, 2*(4), 411–54.

Aydüz, S. (2004b). İstanbul'da zamanın nabzını tutan mekânlar muvakkithaneler. *İstanbul, 51*(4), 92–7.

Baykara, T. (1974). *İzmir Şehri ve Tarihi.* İzmir: Ege Üniversitesi Matbaası.

Beaudry, M. C. (1995). Introduction: Ethnography in Retrospect. In M. Ellin D'Agostino, M. Winer, E. Prine, & E. Casella (eds), *The Written and the Wrought: Complementary Sources in Historical Archaeology* (pp. 1–15). Kroeber Anthropological Society Papers 79. Department of Anthropology. Berkeley, CA: University of California.

Benjamin, W (1968). Theses on the philosophy of history. In:Walter Benjamin: Illuminations:*Essays and Reflections,* trans. H Zohn, ed. and intro. H Arendt. New York: Schocken Books.

Berkes, N. (1978). *Türkiye'de Cagdaslasma* [Modernization in Turkey]. Istanbul: Dogu-Batı Yayınları.

Bhaskar, R. (1979). *The Possibility of Naturalism: A Philosophical Critique of The Contemporary Human Sciences.* Atlantic Highlands, NJ: Humanities Press.

Bhaskar, R. (1998). Philosophy and Scientific Realism. In M. Archer, R. Bhaskar, A. Collier, T. Lawson, & A. Norrie (eds), *Critical Realism: Essential Readings* (pp. 16–47). London: Routledge.

Bhaskar, R. (2008). *A Realist Theory of Science* (2nd ed.). Abingdon, UK: Routledge.

Bhaskar, R. (2013). *The Possibility of Naturalism: A Philosophical Critique of the Contemporary Human Sciences*. London: Routledge.

Bhaskar, R. (2016). *Enlightened Common Sense: The Philosophy of Critical Realism*. London: Routledge.

Birol, N. (2005). Managing the time of the bureaucrat in the late nineteenth century Ottoman administration (MA thesis) (pp. 50–4). İstanbul: Bogaziçi University.

Bradbury, N. M. & Collette, C. P. (2009). Changing times: The mechanical clock in late medieval literature. *The Chaucer Review*, *43*(4), 351–75.

Callizo-Romero, C., Tutnjević, S., Pandza, M., Ouellet, M., Kranjec, A., Ilić, S., Gu, Y., Göksun, T., Chahboun, S., Casasanto, D., & Santiago, J. (2020). Temporal focus and time spatialization across cultures. *Psychonomic Bulletin & Review 27*, 1247–58. https://doi.org/10.3758/s13423-020-01760-5

Cansever, M. (2009). *Türkiye'nin Kültür Mirası 100 Saat Kulesi*. İstanbul: NTV Yayınları.

Cengizkan, A. (1999). *Saat Kuleleri ve Kamusal Mekan* (pp. 96–103). İstanbul: Arredamento.

Cengizkan, A. (2002). *Modernin Saati: 20.nci Yüzyılda Modernleşme ve Demokratikleşme Pratiğinde Mimarlar, Kamusal Mekan ve Konut Mimarlığı* (p. 240). Boyut yayıncılık: Mimarlar Derneği.

Chin, C. (2011). Margins and monsters: How some micro cases lead to macro claims. *History and Theory*, *50*(3), 341–57.

Collier, A. (1994). *Critical Realism: An Introduction to Roy Bhaskar's Philosophy*. London: Verso.

DABOA (Devlet Arşivleri Başkanlığı Osmanlı Arşivi), DH.MKT. (Dahiliye Nezâreti Mektubî Kalemi) 340/41, Tarsus'un Frenklus karyesi hanedanından Feyzullah Ağa'nın saat kulesi inşa edip, içine Avrupa'dan saat getirmesinden dolayı Mecidi Nişan ile taltifi. 08.08.1312 (04.02.1895).

DABOA (Devlet Arşivleri Başkanlığı Osmanlı Arşivi), DH.MKT. (Dahiliye Nezâreti Mektubî Kalemi) 462/60, Bereketli Nahiyesi'nde müceddeden inşa edilen saat kulesinin açılışının yapıldığının Sadaret'e arzı. 21.12.1319 (13.03.1902).

DABOA (Devlet Arşivleri Başkanlığı Osmanlı Arşivi), DH.MKT. (Dahiliye Nezâreti Mektubî Kalemi) 1174/42, Kudüs'te ahali-i İslamiye'den toplanan iane ile ezani saate ayarlı bir saat kulesi inşa edilerek hizmete sokulduğu. 24–03–1325 (07.05.1907).

DABOA (Devlet Arşivleri Başkanlığı Osmanlı Arşivi), DH.MKT. (Dahiliye Nezâreti Mektubî Kalemi) 1207/93, Saat kulesi inşasına ücretsiz nezaretle hizmet ve sadakat gösteren teba-yı Devlet-i Aliye'den Pavkal Mina Efendi'nin dördüncü rütbeden Mecidi Nişanı'yla taltifi talebi. 01.09.1325 (08.10.1907).

DABOA (Devlet Arşivleri Başkanlığı Osmanlı Arşivi), Y.EE.KP. (Yıldız Sadrazam Kamil Paşa Evrakı) 13/1210, Sultan II. Abdülhamid'in tahta çıkışının 25. Senesi münasabetiyle İzmir şehrinde yapılmakta olan şadırvanlı saat kulesi için gümüşten yapılmış süslü bir modelinin gönderildiğine dâir. 02.12.1318 (23.03.1901).

DABOA (Devlet Arşivleri Başkanlığı Osmanlı Arşivi), Y.PRK.UM (Yıldız Perakende Evrakı- Umum Vilayetler Tahrirâtı) 80/69, Kudüs'de ezani saati bildirir bir saat kulesi yapıldığı. 21.9.1325 (27.10.1907).

Darnton, R. (2004). It happened one night. *New York Review of Books 24*(June), 60–4.

Dayioğlu, S. (2010). *Osmanlı'da Zaman Belirleme Mekânları İstanbul Muvakkithaneleri.* İstanbul: Kültür A. Ş.

Delanty, G. (1995). The limits and possibilities of a European identity: A critique of cultural essentialism. *Philosophy & Social Criticism, 21*(4), 15–36.

Duymaz, A. Ş. (2003). II. Abdülhamid Dönemi İmar Faaliyetleri (Türkiye Örnekleri) (PhD dissertation). Isparta: Süleyman Demirel University.

Edwards, P. K., O'Mahoney, J., & Vincent, S. (eds) (2014). *Studying Organizations Using Critical Realism: A Practical Guide.* Oxford: Oxford University Press.

Fuchs, R. & Gilbert, H. (2001). A Colonial Portrait of Jerusalem: British Architecture in Mandate Era Palestine. In N. Alsayyad (ed.), *Hybrid Urbanism: On the Identity Discourse and the Built Environment* (pp. 89–91). Westport, CT: Praeger.

Gilley, B. (2017). The case for colonialism. *Third World Quarterly, 38*(10), 1.

Gimpel, J. (1988). *The Medieval Machine: The Industrial Revolution of the Middle Ages.* London: Pimlico.

Ginzburg, C. & Poni, C. (1979). Il nome e il come: Scambio ineguale e mercato storiografico. *Quaderni Storici, 40*, 1–10.

Ginzburg, C. & Poni, C. (1991). The Name and the Game: Unequal Exchange and the Historiographic Marketplace. In E. Muir & G. Ruggiero (eds), *Microhistory and the Lost Peoples of Europe* (pp. 1–10). Baltimore, MD: Johns Hopkins University Press.

Glennie, P. D. & Thrift, N. J. (1996). Reworking E. P. Thompson's "Time, work discipline and industrial capitalism". *Time and Society, 5*(3), 275–300.

Glennie, P. D. & Thrift, N. J. (2005). Revolutions in the Times: Clocks and the Temporal Structures of Everyday Life. In D. Livingston & C. W. J. Withers (eds), *Geography and Revolutions* (pp. 160–98). Chicago: University of Chicago Press.

Glennie, P. D. & Thrift, N. J. (2009). *Shaping the Day: A History of Timekeeping in England and Wales 1300–1800.* Oxford: Oxford University Press.

Güntan, Ç. (2007). II. Abdülhamit Döneminde İmparatorluk İmajının Kamu Yapıları Aracılığı İle Osmanlı Kentine Yansıtılması (Unpublished thesis). İstanbul: Yıldız Technical University.

Gürbüz, Ş. (2009). *Saat Kulelerinin Varlığı ve Yokluğu Üzerine* (pp. 133–49). Derleyen, İstanbul: YKY, Zamanın Görünen Yüzü Saatler.

Hamann, B. E. (2016). How to chronologize with a hammer, or, the myth of homogeneous, empty time. *HAU: Journal of Ethnographic Theory, 6*(1), 261–92.

Hargadon, A. B. & Wadhwani, R. D. (2022). Theorizing with microhistory. *Academy of Management Review* (in press). https://doi.org/10.5465/amr.2019.0176

Hashkafa (1907, August 30). This Week ("השבוע" or "ha-Shavu'a"), *93*, 2 (in Hebrew).

Holt, R. & Johnsen, R. (2019). Time and organization studies. *Organization Studies, 40*(10), 1557–72.

Howell, S. (2003). Time Past, Time Present, Time Future: Contrasting Temporal Values in Two Southeast Asian Societies. In *Contemporary Futures* (pp. 136–49). London: Routledge.

Joyner, C. W. (1999). *Shared Traditions: Southern History and Folk Culture.* Urbana: University of Illinois.

Karač, Z. & Žunić, A. (2018). *Islamic Architecture and Art in Croatia.* Faculty of Architecture. Zagreb: University of Zagreb.

Köker, N. P. (2002). Time and Modernity in Turkish Context: Clock Towers, Squares and Public Sphere in the Case of Yozgat (Unpublished thesis). Department of Architecture. Ankara: Middle East Technical University.

Kreiser, K. (2006). Ottoman Clock Towers: A Preliminary Survey and Some General Remarks on Construction Dates, Sponsors, Locations and Functions. In H. Eren, M. Kaçar, & Z. Durukal (eds), *Essays in Honour of Ekmeleddin İhsanoğlu, Volume I, Societies, Cultures, Sciences: A Collection of Articles* (pp. 543–56). İstanbul: IRCICA Research Centre for Islamic History, Art and Culture.

Kumbasar, Z. (2008). Osmanlı Dönemi İstanbul Muvakkithaneleri (MA thesis). İstanbul: Yıldız Teknik Üniversitesi.

Lepore, J. (2001). Historians who love too much: Reflections on microhistory and biography. *The Journal of American History 88*(1), 129–44.

Levi, G. (1991). On Microhistory. In P. Burke (ed.), *New Perspectives on Historical Writing* (pp. 93–113). Cambridge: Polity Press.

Makdisi, U. (2002). Ottoman orientalism. *The American Historical Review, 107* (3), 768–96.

Mumford, L. (1934). *Technics and Civilization* (pp. 14–15). London: Routledge.

Munn, N. D. (1992). The cultural anthropology of time: A critical essay. *Annual Review of Anthropology, 21*(1), 93–123.

Ogle, V. (2015). *The Global Transformation of Time.* Cambridge, MA: Harvard University Press.

Şapolyo, E. B. (1969). Saat Kulelerimiz. *Önasya, 4*(44), 10–11.

Singer, S. R. (2013). Clock towers, blended modernity, and the emergence of Ottoman time (PhD dissertation). Bloomington, IN: Indiana University.

Sözen, M. (ed.) (1975). *Türk Mimarisinin Gelişimi ve Mimar Sinan.* İstanbul: Türkiye İş Bankası Yayınları.

Steinmetz, G. (1998). Critical realism and historical sociology. A review article. *Comparative Studies in Society and History, 40*(1), 170–86.

Tanyeli, U. (1998). İslam dünyasında modern zaman bilincinin doğuşu ve mekânsal kavrayış sorunsalı. In C. C. Davidson (ed.), *Anytime Konferansı Bildiriler Kitabı* (pp. 166–76). Ankara: Mimarlar Derneği.

Tanyeli, U. (1999). The emergence of modern time consciousness in the Islamic world and the problematics of spatial perception. In C. C. Davidson (ed.), *Anytime* (pp. 162–70). Cambridge, MA: MIT Press.

Thompson, E. P. (1967). Time, work discipline and industrial capitalism: Past and Present, *38*(1), 56–97.

Üçsu, K. (2011). Osmanlı İstanbul'unda Zamanı Belirlemek İçin Kullanılan Araçlar, Mekânlar ve İlgili Uzmanlar (Unpublished thesis). Institute of Social Sciences. İstanbul: Istanbul University.

Üçsu, K. (2017). Witnesses of the time: A survey of clock rooms, clock towers and façade clocks in Istanbul in the Ottoman era. *Rubrica Contemporanea, 6*(12), 43–60.

Uluçay, M. Ç. (1941). *Manisa'daki Sarây-ı Âmire ve Şehzadeler Türbesi.* İstanbul: CHP Manisa Halkevi Yayınları.

Uluengin, B. (2010). Secularizing Anatolia tick by tick: Clock towers in the Ottoman Empire and the Turkish Republic. *International Journal of Middle East Studies, 42*(1), 17–36.

Ünver, S. (1975). Osmanlı Türkleri İlim Tarihinde Muvakkithaneler. In *Atatürk Konferansları 1971–1972* (pp. 217–59). Ankara: Türk Tarih Kurumu.

Ünver, S. (1980). İstanbul Muvakkithaneleri Vazifelerinin İlmî ve Kültürel Değerleri Üzerine. In M. Dizer (ed.), *International Symposium on the Observatories in Islam, 19–23 September 1977)* (pp. 45–51). Istanbul: Millî Eğitim Basımevi.

Yetkin, S. (2001). *Kentsel bir Sembolün Doğuşu: İzmir Saat Kulesi.* İzmir, Turkey: İzmir Büyükşehir Belediyesi.

Wishnitzer, A. (2009). The Transformation of Ottoman Temporal Culture during the "Long Nineteenth Century" (PhD dissertation). Tel Aviv-Yafo: Tel Aviv University.

Wishnitzer, A. (2010). A comment on Mehmet Bengü Uluengin, "Secularizing Anatolia tick by tick: Clock towers in the Ottoman Empire and the Turkish Republic" (IJMES 42 [2010]: 17–36). *International Journal of Middle East Studies, 42*(3), 537–40.

Wishnitzer, A. (2015). *Reading Clocks, Alla Turca.* Chicago: University of Chicago Press.

15 Temporality and Institutional Maintenance
The Role of Reactivation Work on Material Artefacts

Amélie Boutinot, Sylvain Colombero and Hélène Delacour

Introduction

In the Japanese city of Ise, the Grand Shrine Shinto temple (*Ise Jingū*) is known for housing the Imperial "mirror" relic and, particularly, for its unique construction. Since AD 660 this holy sanctuary has been rebuilt every twenty years in an identical manner. This ancestral tradition guarantees purity (Hladik, 2008) and prevents the institution it instantiates from ever fading away, meaning that it is maintained over time. In a different context, Jones and Massa (2013) studied the case of the Unity Temple designed in 1908 by the architect Frank Lloyd Wright. Due to the revolutionary use of materials for this building, the Unity Temple faced different challenges, enduring decades of oblivion before experiencing a rebirth. This renewed interest provided support for this modern architecture institution and a desire to maintain it.

These two examples illustrate how the maintenance of institutions that are instantiated by a material artefact can express the issue of temporality in different ways. Temporality is understood here in a broad sense, that is, how time, which is a key meta-dimension of management (Chen & Miller, 2011), is instantiated in organizational and institutional life through a process of temporal structuring (Orlikowski & Yates, 2002). As such, temporality provides a "powerful way to view organizational phenomena" (Ancona et al., 2001, p. 660) as well as the institutional phenomena. Institutions can be considered temporal and their material instantiations can undergo and be challenged by the pressures of time, decay and damage, among others (e.g., Boutinot & Delacour, 2022; Colombero & Boxenbaum, 2019; Jones et al., 2019; Jones & Massa, 2013). Reciprocally, working on a material instantiation can anchor or make the associated institution malleable or flexible, as "material forms can also serve to adapt ideas to specific contexts and purposes" (de Vaujany et al., 2019, p. 379). De facto, while studying its materiality, we can discuss the

329

ontology of the institution in regard to its temporality, and thus the question of its maintenance (cf. de Vaujany & Mitev, 2016).

However, previous studies view in different ways the relationship between temporality, the maintenance of institutions and their instantiating material artefacts. Some scholars argue that, if material artefacts vanish then the institution which they are associated with also vanishes. For example, Lawrence et al. (2013) underlined that the natural test of time, which can lead to decay or lack of preservation of the instantiating material artefact, can change the meanings associated with the artefact and, by extension, lead to the gradual erosion of the institution itself. As such, an institution can be deinstitutionalized. Other institutional scholars argue that institutions never completely die and can be maintained while being "dormant" (Tucker, 2006), that is, less present in the public debate and "not taken to bear on the present" (Zerubavel, 1995, p. 224). In addition to considering that memory can shape institutions and help their maintenance (e.g., Ocasio et al., 2016), Dacin and Dacin (2008) advance the idea of dormancy by highlighting that practices rarely disappear completely. Therefore, as long as they do not vanish completely, the institution they are associated with can come back to life after months, years or even decades of dormancy.

This latter idea leaves room for a deeper investigation of the relationship between temporality, institutions and their maintenance with regard to the material artefacts that instantiate them. To investigate this, we need to address two research gaps in the literature. First, we believe that the literature on institutional maintenance, that is, "the purposive action of individuals and organizations" to maintain institutions (Lawrence & Suddaby, 2006, p. 215), has, to date, overlooked the issue of temporality. As previous scholars have called for, we need to elaborate a finer understanding of temporal dynamics (Granqvist & Gustafsson, 2016; Lawrence et al., 2001). Second, and linked to the previous idea, we believe it is necessary to further unpack the "black box" of the maintenance of institutions through their material artefacts, as illustrated by the examples cited above. Indeed, the institutional maintenance literature has paid little attention to the role of material artefacts in this process (e.g., Blanc & Huault, 2014; Colombero & Boxenbaum, 2019), focussing instead on verbal discourse, as discourse and rhetoric are viewed as playing a great role in such a process (e.g. Bitektine & Haack, 2015; Patriotta et al., 2011; Quinn-Trank & Washington, 2009) or their associated practices (Dacin et al., 2010). Better understanding of the role that material artefacts play in institutional maintenance would enable us to reveal the issue of temporality in this process. We support the idea that, as well as focussing on the institution under consideration, institutional maintenance should also focus on the material artefact that instantiates it.

To address these two complementary gaps, this chapter is structured as follows. First, we aim to extend our understanding of institutional maintenance by underlining how temporality is addressed in the current literature. We show that the issue has never been explicitly tackled in debates about institutional maintenance and that existing studies focus primarily on practices. We then highlight a recent turn to the material approach. Second, to deepen our understanding of this material approach, we focus on material artefacts, which are considered "remnants", that is, the traces that remain of something that once existed (Oxford University Dictionary, cited in Dacin & Dacin, 2008, p. 350) and examine their role in the maintenance over time of the institutions they instantiate. In doing so, we introduce the concept of "reactivation work", which we define as an institutional work performed on material artefacts, on different temporal perspectives, to enable atemporal institutional maintenance.

The Different Temporal Perspectives in Institutional Maintenance

Although the current literature on institutional maintenance does not directly tackle the issue of temporality, fine-grained analysis of it allows us to distinguish two main approaches to how institutional maintenance deals with the issue of temporality. The first, and main, approach focusses on the role of practices in the institutional maintenance process. The second, and more recent, approach considers a different level of analysis, that is, the role of material artefacts in instantiating an institution. Before detailing these two approaches and how they illuminate the issue of temporality in the institutional maintenance process, we present how institutions can be viewed as temporal structures.

Institutions as Temporal Structures

First introduced by Orlikowski and Yates (2002) and then developed by Granqvist and Gustaffson (2016), organizations – and by extension institutions – can be viewed as temporal structures. Temporal structuring offers an alternative perspective to the two main and opposing perspectives of time which have long dominated the social sciences: clock time versus event time (Orlikowski & Yates, 2002). On the one hand, time is viewed as objective, in an absolute and exogeneous manner, that is, that which exists independently of human action (e.g., Clark, 1990).

Following this dominant perspective in western culture (Ancona et al., 2001), time acts as a constraint to actors who must adapt to it as they cannot change it. This clock time perspective, which echoes the Greek term *Chronos*, has only one interpretation (Orlikowski & Yates, 2002). By emphasizing measurement and linear succession, time is seen as a scarce resource that must be managed.

On the other hand, some scholars consider time to be subjective, that is, socially constructed by human actions (Adam, 1990; Glucksmann, 1998). Time is "experienced through the interpretive processes of people who create meaningful temporal notions such as events, cycles, routines, and rites of passage" (Orlikowski & Yates, 2002, p. 689). Event time tends to repeat and be cyclical (Ancona et al., 2001). Recalling the Greek term *Kairos*, event time refers to the duration of an event.

Lying between these two opposite perspectives, which consider time either as objective or subjective, (i.e., clock versus event time), Orlikowski and Yates (2002, p. 686) developed a third perspective of time which "is centered on people's recurrent practices that shape (and are shaped by) a set of temporal structures". Or "people in organizations experience time through the shared temporal structures", such as timing norms or the use of a quarterly financial cycle, they enact recurrently in their everyday practices (2002, p. 686). Through temporal structuring, actors implicitly or explicitly draw on existing repertoires of temporal structures and thereby (re)produce (and occasionally change) temporal orientations (2002, p. 686). By focussing on the role actors play in bridging these opposite perspectives of time, they open avenues for a new conceptualization of temporal conditions and their effects on institutional processes such as the maintenance process.

Temporality through the Lens of the Practice Approach in Institutional Maintenance

Referring explicitly and implicitly to institutions as temporal structures, the current literature observes and explores different temporal patterns through the lens of practices and institutional work in the institutional maintenance process.

Temporal Sequence: Daily Versus Annual While multiple temporal orientations often coexist and compete (Ancona et al., 2001), some studies focus on the short-term, day-to-day temporal orientation in the institutional maintenance process. Institutional maintenance is mainly studied as routine work which leads to the reproduction of a worldview (Zilber, 2009), whereby maintenance work can be expressed through the repetition of stories of everyday routines and practices (Townley, 1997; Zilber, 2009). Studies in this tradition show how institutions are maintained through daily actions and practices which correct all the minor changes that take place to preserve the status quo (Herepath & Kitchener, 2016), as in the study of the Cambridge boat team by Lok and de Rond (2013).

At the end of the continuum of this temporal pattern, the long-term or annual basis has also attracted attention by revealing the role of timing norms. Developed by Barbara Lawrence, timing norms refer to what "people experience as shared, expected patterns of paced activity" (quoted in Ancona et al., 2001, p. 648). Timing norms such as rituals provide a temporal framework for structuring practices and activities over long periods and for reproducing them in an identical manner in order to maintain an institution. An example of the role of timing norms in institutional maintenance is the study by Dacin and colleagues (2010) of formal dining at Cambridge University. They highlighted that it was necessary to retain formal dining every academic year to preserve the stable environment of the "formal hall" or "high table", along with other specific and traditional rituals, in order to maintain the institution of the British class system. Timing norms can also occur through the reproduction of contested practices to maintain an institution. Indeed, in their study of the elite French schools, Raynard et al. (2021) underlined the durability and resilience of the business schools' recruitment practices, while facing criticism for being elitist and undemocratic. Such "meta-routines" (2021, p. 7) are reproduced annually, thereby sustaining maintenance over time instead of change.

Urgency of Time: Potential Versus Real Challenge   Another temporal pattern observed in the current literature is based on the distinction between potential and real challenge and threat, highlighting the role of the urgency of time in maintaining or restoring an institution. While the previous temporal orientation (daily versus annual) suggests the need for stable environments to support the identical reproduction of practices on a daily basis or following fixed and regular annual timing norms, the environment can also be more complex and turbulent, posing a potential or real challenge to maintenance of the institution.

When the institution is challenged and may be disrupted, actors can take purposeful action to respond and avoid institutional change. For instance, in their study of the United Kingdom's National Health service, Currie et al. (2013) showed that elite medical professionals employed various types of institutional maintenance work (Lawrence & Suddaby, 2006) to uphold their status which had been threatened by a plan to create new roles. This unexpected situation required them to be creative and committed to respond rapidly and defend their interests. Similar action was highlighted in the study by Wright et al. (2017) of an emergency department.

The threat of change is not the only condition which creates the urgency of time. When a challenge arises and disrupts institutional arrangements, actors can also engage in repair work. In their study, Micelotta & Washington (2013) showed how Italian professions performed maintenance work to reverse change and re-establish the previous institutional arrangements and, thus, the status quo. The aim was first to restore the status quo to impede change from happening and in so doing, it allows the preservation of the institutional arrangements (Quinn-Trank & Washington, 2009).

The above examples highlight a continuum of efforts and activities following different temporal patterns – from the short term (daily) to the long term (annual) – which are needed to deal with the urgency of time, whether the challenge is potential or actual. Taken together, this approach examines what actors actually do at the practice level, and how, in so doing, they shape the temporal structures that shape them, thereby maintaining the institution under consideration. This practice approach also reveals the inherent malleability of even well-established temporal structures and suggests that consideration of temporality in the institutional maintenance process requires study of time in use.

Temporality through the Lens of the Material Approach in Institutional Maintenance

While these previous studies are insightful in adopting the practices approach to understand the different temporalities involved in institutional maintenance, there is little research on the role that material artefacts play in this process. Indeed, materiality is acknowledged as important for producing and reproducing institutions (Pinch, 2008) – "the materials artifacts [being] important 'tools' for the institutional work of actors" (Greenwood et al., 2017, p. 15). As such, a recent stream of research has emerged around this issue (Monteiro & Nicolini, 2015; Zilber, 2011). This focus on materiality, and more specifically on material artefacts, is of great importance as it provides another and promising approach for tackling the issues of institutional maintenance and temporality, as we detail further in the second part of this chapter.

In line with the recent "turn to things" in the social sciences (Boxenbaum et al., 2018) and the growing interest in materiality (Pinch, 2008), research on institutional maintenance starts to consider a specific type of material artefact: buildings. Buildings are "strong material anchors" (Monteiro & Nicolini, 2015, p. 4), but they are not just symbols of an institution (Lawrence & Dover, 2015). As lasting material artefacts, buildings are more likely to "give structure to social institutions [and] persistence to behavioral patterns" (Gieryn, 2002, p. 35). Studies therefore acknowledge that they help to shape institutions, and several demonstrate their role in institutional maintenance (Colombero & Boxenbaum, 2019; Jones & Massa, 2013; Siebert et al., 2017). More precisely, the few studies on buildings as material artefacts and on institutional maintenance show how temporality is taken into account in this process, even if the issue is not at the core of these studies. As is the case for the practice approach, the material approach allows us to identify distinct temporal patterns regarding the periodicity of work, the wear and tear over time as the trade-off between past, present and future orientation.

Periodicity of Work: Regular Versus Episodic   The first temporal pattern refers to time lags, that is, the periodicity of efforts to make buildings support institutional maintenance. Two main periodicities of work, regular or episodic, can be observed in the literature. The two examples cited in the introduction illustrate this distinction. On the one hand, to preserve the institution and buildings which instantiate it, the periodicity for preservation work to be undertaken can be decided in advance. This periodicity can be annual or longer term, as in the case of the Grand Shrine Shinto temple, which has been rebuilt in an identical manner every twenty years since its construction (Hladik, 2008). For the Japanese, the "new" temple is identical to the "old" one, both in its materials and the heritage value it embodies. In contrast, in their study of the Unity Temple church, Jones and Massa (2013) underlined decades of silence and a lack of effort, before maintenance of the temple took place. For them, identification is necessary to inspire institutional maintenance work and support.

Whatever the time lags, research anchored in this approach highlights the need to preserve buildings so that they are identical to the original, as in the case of the Advocates Library, a status symbol in the maintenance of the Scottish advocate profession (Siebert et al., 2017). As they are fixed, material artefacts such as buildings consolidate institutions and facilitate their maintenance over time through their stabilizing effect (e.g., Jones & Massa, 2013; Lawrence & Dover, 2015; Siebert et al., 2017).

Wear and Tear Over Time   Another temporal pattern is linked to the wear and tear associated with the passage of time. Rather than considering the systematic preservation of buildings so that they become fixed, a less developed, and opposite, approach focusses on material artefacts that are decaying or lacking preservation. When there is no desire to take care of a material artefact, the building or material artefact is gradually eroded due to the effects of time (e.g., wear and tear, natural damage, etc.). By deteriorating and eroding material artefacts, their support to an institution can be questionable and even challenge the institution itself or lead to institutional change. For example, McDonnell (2010) illustrates how the deterioration of AIDS prevention posters which can be partially torn down or covered by other advertisements, no longer conveys the message of prevention. To prevent such change taking place, a material artefact can be allowed to become endangered, and can even be demolished (Jones et al., 2019; Jones & Massa, 2013).

Trade-off between Past, Present and Future   Lying between the regular preservation of buildings, to help them to become fixed, and the accepted decay and deterioration, which poses a challenge and threat to the institution they instantiate, is a third option which involves a trade-off between the past, present and future. This recalls the different types of agency highlighted by Emirbayer and Mische (1998). In their study on institutional maintenance of the Architectural Heritage institution in France and Denmark, Colombero and Boxenbaum (2019) revealed the potential for adaptations to buildings facing material decay or erosion. They suggested three forms of "authentication work", ranging from the identical replacement of damaged materials (past orientation) to the use of new components (present orientation), suggesting that buildings can be renovated to become something very different to the original (future orientation). In line with Gieryn (2002, p. 35), Colombero and Boxenbaum (2019) acknowledged that buildings can be "objects of (re) interpretation, narration and representation" while enabling the maintenance of the institution. As such, by mixing and combining the different temporal orientations between past, present and future, they suggest a promising way to deal with temporality and maintenance.

In a similar manner, in their study of the Parisian metro entrances designed by Guimard which instantiate the Belle Epoque institution, Boutinot and Delacour (2022) underlined the need for adaptations to buildings in the face of an evolving environment, thereby contributing to the maintenance of an institution. While acknowledging the role of preservation work (past orientation), they also considered the role of voluntary damage work (present orientation) to make the institution more discrete and thus less rejected. In addition, they examined the role of transferability work (between past and present) in giving historical value to this material artefact by moving some of the entrances to other cultural locations.

In this section, we underlined how material artefacts can be fruitful avenues of research for addressing the issue of temporality in institutional maintenance. Based on that, we now develop an alternative approach to studying the major role played by material artefacts in maintaining institutions.

Reactivation Work on Material Artefacts in Institutional Maintenance

Some institutional scholars believe that if material artefacts in the form of buildings which instantiate an institution vanish, then the institution also vanishes (e.g., Lawrence et al., 2013; McDonnell, 2010). We consider a more complex relationship. In line with other institutional scholars, we suggest that institutions can be maintained over time while being dormant (Tucker, 2006; Zerubavel, 1995). To support this idea, we consider material artefacts as remnants (Dacin & Dacin, 2008) which can be brought back to life through what we call reactivation work. Reactivation work is a specific type of institutional maintenance work carried out on material artefacts with the aim of maintaining a dormant institution. In revealing this concept, we illuminate, in a promising way, the issue of temporality in institutional maintenance and even suggest the potential everlasting nature of institutions.

Material Artefacts as Remnants

To deepen our understanding of the significant role material artefacts play in this process, we focus on artefacts built years or even decades ago. These old buildings can suffer from erosion, decay and damage. As such, they can either pose a challenge to institutional maintenance (Lawrence et al., 2013; McDonnell, 2010) or present an opportunity for it if they are considered remnants.

In their article on the tradition of the Aggie Bonfire at Texas A&M University, Dacin and Dacin (2008) suggested that practices and institutions rarely disappear altogether and can remain through remnants, understood as a "small remaining quantity and/or a surviving trace/vestige of something that once existed" (Oxford University Dictionary, cited in Dacin & Dacin, 2008, p. 350). Although the authors used the example of practices, remnants can also be stories, memories, rituals or material artefacts, which is the case in our study.

This is important as material artefacts can instantiate institutions. Indeed, material artefacts can be modified, physically or socially, through interactions with actors. They can incorporate different ideas and instantiate different social beliefs (Orlikowski, 1992). Because the nature of artefacts is socially constructed in terms of their contextual factors and actors' collective interpretations (Bijker et al., 1987), they primarily act as "physical scaffolding" or as concrete mediators between actors and the institution they represent (Orlikowski, 2006). Furthermore, as they also "embody both technical and symbolic elements" (Suchman, 2003, p. 99), they become a reflection of the institution (Gagliardi, 1990) and act as an institutional vehicle (Scott, 2003).

If these material artefacts which instantiate an institution suffer erosion, decay or damage, they can "leave behind an institutional remnant which forms the raw material for the emergence of a new [institution] or re-emergence" of an institution (Dacin & Dacin, 2008, p. 328). As long as such remnants remain, the institution continues to exist but is considered to be dormant (Tucker, 2006; Zerubavel, 1995). Although the remnants concept is promising, it is unclear how institutions re-emerge after years or decades of dormancy. Considering material artefacts as remnants could be a stimulating area of research, as their existence in terms of aesthetics and meanings can be considered to be atemporal. Indeed, they may, for example, need contemporary tools to understand and translate them into more contemporaneous periods. This would require what we call reactivation work to help institutions experiencing dormancy to re-emerge (Tucker, 2006; Zerubavel, 1995).

Reactivation Work to Material Artefacts

Reactivation work can be considered a type of institutional maintenance work (Lawrence & Suddaby, 2006). We gave it this label as we believe it addresses how actors act on a remnant to bring the dormant institution back to life in more contemporaneous times. More precisely, we define it as institutional work performed on material artefacts with the aim of maintaining an institution which has been dormant for years or decades. Below, we detail the dimensions of this work and the forms it can take (conservative or progressive) and discuss the implications of this re-emergence of institutions, that is, their atemporal maintenance.

The Material and Socio-cognitive Dimensions of Reactivation Work   As an institutional work, reactivation work relies on both material and socio-cognitive dimensions. On the material side, reactivation work is what is done to an artefact to enable it to continue to fit with an evolving environment. This entails repairing and preserving it, for example, through protection of the artefact by official organizations, ensuring it does not suffer too much damage or decay, and is not aesthetically banished. Because of the important nature of material artefacts in the durability of institutional ideas (Blanc & Huault, 2014; Monteiro & Nicolini, 2015), the question of the materialization of an institution is central, particularly when actors try to maintain the institution while playing with its material components. As such, by acting on the material dimension, reactivation work creates the necessary match between a dormant institution, its material artefact, considered as a remnant, and the evolving environment.

On the socio-cognitive side, in parallel, reactivation work requires actors to redesign a frame either for "interpret[ing] the [previous] act of translation" (Boxenbaum, 2006, p. 940) or, as we argue, to design a new one and make the material remnant fit with its associated institutional meanings (cf. Boutinot & Delacour, 2022; Colombero & Boxenbaum, 2019). Adapting Goffman's (1974, p. 21) concept of the "schemata of interpretation", the frame is primarily a socio-cognitive construction by actors to help them better comprehend and predict the environment they must comply with (Snow et al., 1986). This frame helps them to interpret institutional ideas by suggesting symbolic ways to respond to given contextual challenges (Campbell, 2005) and to inform what they can legitimately implement (Elliott et al., 1998). Because framing "is a dynamic and evolving process" (Benford & Snow, 2000, p. 614), a frame can thus be transformed and circulated through translation or editing processes, over time and space (Czarniawska-Joerges, 1990; Sahlin & Wedlin, 2008; Suárez 2007).

Based on its material and socio-cognitive dimensions, reactivation work is rooted in the debate about temporality and institutional maintenance as it addresses past, present and future orientations, both for the material artefact and the institution it instantiates. More specifically, we believe this work can follow a conservative approach, that is, reactivating the artefact as it was originally designed in terms of material and/or meanings, or a progressive approach, that is, reactivating the artefact with material and/or socio-cognitive modifications to make it fit with more contemporaneous times and/or give it future orientations. Choosing one orientation or the other calls for debate, as illustrated below.

Conservative Reactivation Work   Conservative reactivation work is linked to actors who ensure that material artefacts and institutions are maintained in similar ways over time. This reactivation work can be carried out in a conservative way to highlight what the material artefact first instantiated. An example of this is the introduction of the iconic Wallace fountains at the beginning of 2022 in the permanent collection of the Carnavalet museum in Paris, dedicated to Parisian history. Richard Wallace tackled the water shortages that Paris experienced after the Prussian wars and, thus, helped (poor) Parisians to get access to free, drinkable water in the nineteenth century (Perreau, 2009). After having almost completely disappeared from the Parisian streets, they were museumized to showcase and explain to the audiences their original function.

Such conservative reactivation work can also be seen in contemporary adjustments to listed buildings where the original function has been retained and where an adaptive re-use, or "the process of changing a building's function to accommodate the changing needs of its users" (Rathmann, 1998, p. 58), is neither expected nor desired. According to the Council of Europe (1985), listed buildings are protected because they represent artistic styles or historical periods that are deemed to have symbolic and/or artistic value for the nation state. Examples include the French cathedrals from Reims to Paris or privately owned, modern housing from Le Corbusier for example. This protection can even lead to the general public being given close access to buildings to preserve them, as is the case with the natural "building" of the Lascaux caves in the Dordogne region of France, which is famous for its palaeolithic cave paintings.

Conservative reactivation work is thus grounded in the interpretation that associated actors have about the given material artefact. The last contemporary adjustments to the French Panthéon illustrate this point. In terms of heritage-respect, it would have been acceptable to replace the catholic cross at the top of the building with a French flag, as one was historically installed during the reign of Louis-Philippe. But in 2015, institutional actors decided not to make such a change. Instead, they chose to keep the catholic cross, as the building was a church dedicated to Sainte-Geneviève, the patron of Paris. They did not promote the lay Republic Temple where the French "Grands Hommes" are buried, with a flag on its top.

Progressive Reactivation Work   The previous section suggested that a material artefact which is considered to be remnant can be reactivated by preserving its original purpose through the use of previously used or contemporary materials. However, a different temporal orientation can be chosen, resulting in what we call progressive reactivation work. Using "materials available in the present" (Schultz & Hernes, 2013, p. 1), actors can carry out institutional work "by reinterpreting the past, responding differently to present concerns, and envisioning the future in innovative ways" (Kaplan & Orlikowski, 2013, p. 991). For example, the reopening of the Parisian Grand Magasin *La Samaritaine* in 2021, after it had been closed for sixteen years, is a relevant illustration of progressive reactivation work. While the planning application was initially rejected – and protection societies won the legal battle to keep the building exactly in its original form – the French Council of State gave its approval for the original stone façade to be transformed with a more modern glass façade. However, although its function as a department store was preserved, the customers it targeted extended beyond the people of Paris to the national and international elite. In this way, the *Genius Loci*, called the "spirit of the place" by Norberg-Schulz (1980), evolved as a result of the progressive reactivation work to make the building fit its current environment. In this case, the prestige of the building, that is, of its socio-cognitive dimension and the type of items being sold, which are far removed from the store's historic slogan "you can find everything at the Samaritaine" needed to be combined to fit the modern-day environment.

In parallel, progressive reactivation work can also support modern changes without changing the *Genius Loci* of the buildings under consideration. To illustrate this point, we refer to the oldest primary school in Denmark, Sølvgade Skole. From 2009 to 2012, architects built a new extension to this listed building, which had long served as the architectural model for schools subsequently being built in Copenhagen. Taking inspiration from the form and colors of the surroundings, the aim was to accommodate contemporary requirements, such as the expanding student roll, and the need to accommodate space for extracurricular activities, such as sports facilities, while respecting the original school building. By achieving this, the historical importance of the school, which "never gives up" (Siemsen, 1997) has been anchored. As the lead architect stated: "the idea was to create a building that speaks the language of children – colourful and musical, while at the same time ensuring that the building respects its historical surroundings" (Colombero, 2015, p. 106).

The temporal orientation of reactivation work is ubiquitous and can provoke debate and controversy among actors. Such debates in the Architectural Heritage institution can be illustrated by the question of the reconstruction of the arrow at the Saint-Denis Basilica, France, which was dismantled in the middle of the nineteenth century. Although its stones have been stored and labelled to facilitate its reconstruction, there was a major controversy in 2015 between the French academic Erick Orsenna and French Heritage curator Olivier Poisson. As the former was pro-reconstruction, he was of the view that it could be "an incredible way to teach French history and introduce discussion about national pride and identity", while the latter, who was against reconstruction, argued that "the past is dead and we do not have to re-do what our predecessors decided to dismantle, the disappearance of the arrow being part of the Basilica history" (quoted in Leblanc, 2015). Seven years later, there are still opposing views about this, even though the decision to build the controversial arrow has been taken.

Whatever temporal orientation actors choose – whether conservative or progressive – we argue that a dormant institution can be reawakened as a result of reactivation work and its agency on materiality. Although we align with the suggestion by Dacin and Dacin (2008) that material artefacts can act as remnants, we refine understanding of this by highlighting how reactivation work can be applied and its implications for institutional maintenance. Like archaeologists, who try to state the archaeologicity of the artefacts they discover, that is, contextualize, interpret and legitimate them using contemporary tools and practices (Djindjian, 2011; Schnapp et al., 2020), institutional actors can use material artefacts as remnants to interpret or re-interpret their material and socio-cognitive dimensions and, in the end, reactivate institutions and maintain them over time.

Conclusion: Towards an Atemporal Institutional Maintenance

To conclude, this chapter first reviewed how temporality is addressed in institutional maintenance. Focussing on the level of the material artefact, we then introduced the concept of reactivation work as an alternative way to consider this process. We believe this can offer new paths for exploring the life of institutions and, more specifically, their possible atemporal nature.

First, very few studies discuss the possibility that institutions can come to an end. For example, Oliver (1991) considered the deinstitutionalization of practices rather than the actual end of institutions. Similarly, some studies argue that institutions can die if their material instantiations suffer too much damage (e.g., McDonnell, 2010; Lawrence et al., 2013). We believe that these studies address the dormancy of institutions rather than their concrete deinstitutionalization. In introducing the concept of reactivation work, we seek to illuminate, in a promising way, the issue of temporality in institutional maintenance. By considering that dormant institutions can be reactivated over time because their material artefacts are remnants, we suggest that: (1) they never really die and (2) their maintenance can be atemporal. If we consider that institutions can be maintained over time, as defined by Lawrence and Suddaby (2006), the disruption of institutions seems to be rare in the case of dormant institutions. Indeed, reactivation work questions whether they radically disappear.

Second, we suggest a new type of institutional maintenance work: reactivation work, which can take account of the past, present and future. By highlighting various temporal orientations, by distinguishing between conservative and progressive reactivation work, we believe we offer an alternative angle for addressing temporality for institutional maintenance. However, there is one exception to this that should be noted. Some material artefacts can exist and remain over time, even if damaged or partially destroyed. In such cases, reactivation work is not necessary as these material artefacts were initially built to last forever and to carry their associated meanings over time. This is what Riegl labelled a "monument" as it is "a work created by the hand of man and built for the specific purpose to keep always present and alive in the consciousness of future generations the memory of such action or such a purpose (or combinations of one and the other)" (Riegl, [1903]2001, p. 43). For example, whereas a war memorial has been constructed with the aim of commemorating a war, the house of a major general who shone on the battlefield has not been built with the intention that it should last over time. Following that essential definition, the "monument" is a deliberate construction whose destiny was a priori defined and, as such, does not require reactivation work.

To conclude and to extend the reactivation work concept in relation to the temporality issue, further research on the timing of this reactivation work may be required. Empirical data would support the extent to which such institutional work must be designed at the "right time" (Reay et al., 2006) or when actors need to open a "window of opportunity" (Granqvist & Gustafsson, 2016). The challenge of finding the correct timing requires a deep understanding of the evolution of the institutional environment; for example, people's tastes or behaviors, practical life and practices are markers that need to be understood to enable a given material instantiation to be reactivated in a relevant way, so that the dormant institution can be legitimately brought back to life. Indeed, it could be interesting to study if there exists a temporality between conservative and progressive reactivation works. With regard to the example of the Lascaux caves, the first initiative involved conservative reactivation work to protect the caves from potential damage inflicted by tourists. However, twenty years after the original caves closed, a different reactivation work, this time a progressive one, was undertaken when it was decided to build Lascaux 2, a perfect and contemporary replica of the original Lascaux caves and prehistoric paintings. To conclude, we extended our understanding of institutional maintenance by taking a closer look at material artefacts, their reactivation work and how this provides new insights on the issue of temporality. We hope that the thoughts offered here will enrich the institutional debate.

References

Adam, B. (1990). *Time and Social Theory*. Philadelphia: Temple University Press.

Ancona, D. G., Goodman, P. S., Lawrence, B. S. & Tushman, M. L. (2001). Time: A new research lens. *Academy of Management Review*, *26*(4), 645–63.

Benford, R. D. & Snow, D. A. (2000). Framing processes and social movements: An overview and assessment. *Annual Review of Sociology*, *26*, 611–39.

Bijker, W. E., Hughes, T. & Pinch, T. (1987). *The Social Construction of Technological Systems: New Directions in the Sociology and History of Technology*. Cambridge, MA: MIT Press.

Bitektine, A. & Haack, P. (2015). The "macro" and the "micro" of legitimacy: Toward a multilevel theory of the legitimacy process. *Academy of Management Review*, *40*(1), 49–75.

Blanc, A. & Huault, I. (2014). Against the digital revolution? Institutional maintenance and artefacts within the French recorded music industry. *Technological Forecasting and Social Change*, *83*, 10–23.

Boutinot, A. & Delacour, H. (2022). How the malleability of material artefacts contributes to institutional maintenance: The Guimard Metropolitan Railway entrances, 1914–2000. *Organization Studies*, *43*(12), 1967–89.

Boxenbaum, E. (2006). Lost in translation. The making of Danish diversity management. *American Behavioural Scientist*, *49*(7), 939–48.

Boxenbaum, E., Jones, C., Meyer, R. E. & Svejenova, S. (2018). Towards an articulation of the material and visual turn in Organization Studies. *Organization Studies*, *39*(5–6), 597–616.

Campbell, J. L. (2005). Where Do We Stand? Common Mechanisms in Organizations and Social Movements Research. In G. F. Davis, D. McAdam, W. R. Scott & M. N. Zald (eds), *Social Movements and Organization Theory* (pp. 41–68). Cambridge: Cambridge University Press.

Chen, M. J. & Miller, D. (2011). The relational perspective as a business mindset: Managerial implications for East and West. *Academy of Management Perspectives*, *25*(3), 6–18.

Clark, R. K. (1990). *Scheduling Dependent Real-Time Activities*. Pittsburg, PN: Carnegie Mellon University.

Colombero, S. (2015). Instantiating through collective bricolage: The case of the Listed Buildings Institution (PhD Thesis 2015ENMP0033). Paris: Mines ParisTech & Copenhagen: Copenhagen Business School.

Colombero, S. & Boxenbaum, E. (2019). Authentication as institutional maintenance work. *Journal of Management Studies*, *56*(2), 408–40.

Council of Europe. (1985). The Grenada Convention. Convention for the Protection of the Architectural Heritage of Europe. Available at: https://coe.int/en/web/conventions/full-list/-/conventions/treaty/121

Currie, G., Lockett, A., Finn, R., Martin, G. & Waring, J. (2013). Institutional work to maintain professional power: Recreating the model of medical professionalism. *Organization Studies, 33*(7), 937–62.

Czarniawska-Joerges, B. (1990). *Merchants of Meaning: Management Consulting in the Swedish Public Sector*. Berlin: de Gruyter.

Dacin, T. & Dacin, P. (2008). Traditions as Institutionalized Practice: Implication for Deinstitutionalization. In R. Greenwood, C. Oliver, R. Suddaby & K. Sahlin (eds), *The Sage Handbook of Organizational Institutionalism* (pp. 327–51). London: Sage.

Dacin, T., Munir, K. & Tracey, P. (2010). Formal dining at Cambridge colleges: Linking ritual performance and institutional maintenance. *Academy of Management Journal, 53*(6), 1393–418.

de Vaujany, F-X., Adrot, A., Boxenbaum, E. & Leca, B. (2019). Conclusion: Ontological Reflections on the Role of Materiality in Institutional Inquiry. In F-X. de Vaujany, A. Adrot, E. Boxenbaum & B. Leca (eds), *Materiality in Institutions: Spaces, Embodiment and Technology in Management and Organization* (pp. 379–82). London: Palgrave Macmillan.

de Vaujany, F-X. & Mitev, N. (2016). Introduction au tournant matériel en théories des organisations. In F-X. de Vaujany, A. Hussenot & J-F. Chanlat (eds), *Théories des Organisation: Nouveaux Tournants*. Paris: Economica.

Djindjian, F. (2011). *Manuel d'archéologie. Méthodes, objets et concepts*. Paris: Armand Colin.

Elliott, C. S., Hayward, D. M. & Canon, S. (1998). Institutional framing: Some experimental evidence. *Journal of Economic Behavior & Organization, 35*(4), 455–64.

Emirbayer, M. & Mische, A. (1998). What is agency? *American Journal of Sociology, 103*(4), 962–1023.

Gagliardi, P. (1990). Artifacts as Pathways and Remains of Organizational Life. In P. Gagliardi (ed.), *Symbols and Artifacts: Views of the Corporate Landscape* (pp. 3–38). New York: Walter de Gruyter.

Gieryn, T. F. (2002). What buildings do. *Theory and Society, 31*(1), 35–74.

Glucksmann, M. A. (1998). What a difference a day makes: A theoretical and historical exploration of temporality and gender. *Sociology, 32*(2), 239–58.

Goffman, E. (1974). *Frame Analysis*. Cambridge, MA: Harvard University Press.

Granqvist, N. & Gustafsson, R. (2016). Temporal institutional work. *Academy of Management Journal, 59*(3), 1009–35.

Greenwood, R., Oliver, C., Lawrence, T. & Meyer, R. E. (2017). Introduction: Into the Fourth Decade. In R. Greenwood, C. Oliver, T. Lawrence & R. E. Meyer (eds), *The SAGE Handbook of Organizational Institutionalism* (2nd ed., pp. 1–24). London: Sage.

Herepath, A. & Kitchener, M. (2016). When small bandages fail: The field-level repair of severe and protracted institutional breaches. *Organization Studies, 37* (8), 1113–39.

Hladik, M. (2008). *Traces et fragments dans l'esthétique japonaise*. Paris: Mardaga.

Jones, C., Lee, J. Y. & Lee, T. (2019). Institutionalizing Place: Materiality and Meaning in Boston's North End. In P. Haack, J. Sieweke & L. Wessel (eds),

Microfoundations of Institutions. Research in the Sociology of Organizations, Vol. 65B (pp. 211–39). Bingley, UK: Emerald Group Publishing.

Jones, C. & Massa, F. G. (2013). From novel practice to consecrated exemplar: Unity Temple as a case of institutional evangelizing. *Organization Studies, 34* (8), 1099–136.

Kaplan, S. & Orlikowski, W. J. (2013). Temporal work in strategy making. *Organization Science, 24*(4), 965–95.

Lawrence, T. B. & Dover, G. (2015). Place and institutional work: Creating housing for the hard-to-house. *Administrative Science Quarterly, 60*(3), 371–410.

Lawrence, T. B., Leca, B. & Zilber, T. B. (2013). Institutional work: Current research, new directions and overlooked issues. *Organization Studies, 34*(8), 1023–33.

Lawrence, T. B. & Suddaby, R. (2006). Institutions and Institutional Work. In A. Langley & H. Tsoukas (eds), *The Sage Handbook of Process Organization Studies* (pp. 215–54). Thousand Oaks, CA: Sage.

Lawrence, T. B., Winn, M. I. & Jennings, P. D. (2001). The temporal dynamics of institutionalization. *Academy of Management Review, 26*(4), 624–44.

Leblanc, S. (2015). Faut-il reconstruire la flèche de la basilique de Saint-Denis? *20 Minutes,* 2878, 12.

Lok, J. & De Rond, M. (2013). On the plasticity of institutions: Containing and restoring practice breakdowns at the Cambridge University Boat Club. *Academy of Management Journal, 56*(1), 185–207.

McDonnell, T. E. (2010). Cultural objects as objects: Materiality, urban space, and the interpretation of AIDS campaigns in Accra, Ghana. *American Journal of Sociology, 115*(6), 1800–52.

Micelotta, E. R. & Washington, M. (2013). Institutions and maintenance: The repair work of Italian professions. *Organization Studies, 34*(8), 1137–70.

Monteiro, P. & Nicolini, D. (2015). Recovering materiality in institutional work: Prizes as an assemblage of human and material entities. *Journal of Management Inquiry, 24*(1), 61–81.

Norberg-Schulz, C. (1980). *Genius Loci. Towards a Phenomenology of Architecture.* New York: Rizzoli International Publications.

Ocasio, W. C., Mauskapf, M. & Steele, C. (2016). History, society and institutions: The role of collective memory in the emergence and evolution of societal logics. *Academy of Management Review, 41*(4), 676–99.

Oliver, C. (1991). Strategic responses to institutional processes. *Academy of Management Review, 16*(1), 145–79.

Orlikowski, W. (1992). The duality of technology: Rethinking the concept of technology in organizations. *Organization Science, 3*(3), 398–427.

Orlikowski, W. (2006). Material knowing: The scaffolding of human knowledgeability. *European Journal of Information Systems, 15*(5), 460–6.

Orlikowski, W. J. & Yates, J. (2002). It's about time: Temporal structuring in organizations. *Organization Science, 13*(6), 684–700.

Patriotta, G., Gond, J. P. & Schultz, F. (2011). Controversies, orders of worth, and public justifications. *Journal of Management Studies, 48*(8), 1804–36.

Perreau L. (2009). *La fortune de Richard Wallace.* Paris: JC Lattès.

Pinch, T. (2008). Technology and institutions: Living in a material world. *Theory and Society*, *37*(5), 461–83.

Quinn-Trank, C. Q. & Washington, M. (2009). Maintaining an Institution in a Contested Organizational Field: The Work of the AACSB and Its Constituents. In T. B. Lawrence, R. Suddaby & B. Leca (eds), *Institutional Work: Actors and Agency in Institutional Studies of Organizations* (pp. 236–61). Cambridge, MA: Cambridge University Press.

Rathmann, K. (1998). *Sustainable Architecture Module: Recycling and Reuse of Building Materials*. Ann Arbor, MI: National Pollution Prevention Center for Higher Education.

Raynard, M., Kodeih, F. & Greenwood, R. (2021). Proudly elitist and undemocratic? The distributed maintenance of contested practices. *Organization Studies*, *42*(1), 7–33.

Reay, T., Golden-Biddle, K. & Germann, K. (2006). Legitimizing a new role: Small wins and microprocesses of change. *Academy of Management Journal*, *49*(5), 977–98.

Riegl, A. ([1903]2001). *Le culte moderne des monuments: Son essence et sa genèse (2001)*. Paris: Seuil.

Sahlin, K. & Wedlin, L. (2008). Circulating ideas: Imitation, translation and editing. In R. Greenwood, C. Oliver, R. Suddaby & K. Sahlin (eds), *The Sage Handbook of Organizational Institutionalism* (pp. 218–42). London: Sage.

Schnapp, A., Lehoërff, A., Giligny, F. & Demoule, J. P. (2020). *Guide des méthodes de l'archéologie*. Paris: La Découverte.

Schultz, M. & Hernes, T. (2013). A temporal perspective on organizational identity. *Organization Science*, *24*(1), 1–21.

Scott, W. R. (2003). Institutional carriers: Reviewing modes of transporting ideas over time and space and considering their consequences. *Industrial and Corporate Change*, *12*(4), 879–94.

Siebert, S., Wilson, F. & Hamilton, J. R. A. (2017). "Devils may sit here": The role of enchantment in institutional maintenance. *Academy of Management Journal*, *60*(4), 1607–32.

Siemsen, J. (1997). *Sølvgades Skole 150 år i 1997: Tekster og billeder omkring skolen der aldrip gi'rop – især fra de sidste 50 år*. København: Sølvgades Skole Publications.

Snow, D. A., Rochford, E. B. Jr., Worden, S. K. & Benford, R. D. (1986). Frame alignment processes, micromobilization, and movement participation. *American Sociological Review*, *51*(4), 464–81.

Suárez, D. (2007). Education professionals and the construction of human rights education. *Comparative Education Review*, *51*(1), 48–70.

Suchman, M. C. (2003). The contract as social artifact. *Law & Society Review*, *37*(1), 91–142.

Townley, B. (1997). The institutional logic of performance appraisal. *Organization Studies*, *18*(2), 261–85.

Tucker, S. (2006). Cyclical institutions: The case of midwifery care in Ontario, 1800–2005. Working paper. Kingston, Canada: Queen's University.

Wright, A. L., Zammuto, R. F. & Liesch, P. W. (2017). Maintaining the values of a profession: Institutional work and moral emotions in the emergency department. *Academy of Management Journal, 60*(1), 200–37.

Zerubavel, Y. (1995). *Recovered Roots: Collective Memory and the Making of Israeli National Tradition.* Chicago: University of Chicago Press.

Zilber, T. B. (2009). Institutional Maintenance as Narrative Acts. In T. B. Lawrence, R. Suddaby & B. Leca (eds), *Institutional Work: Actors and Agency in Institutional Studies of Organizations* (pp. 205–35). Cambridge, MA: Cambridge University Press.

Zilber, T. B. (2011). Institutional multiplicity in practice: A tale of two high-tech conferences in Israel. *Organization Science, 22*(6), 1539–59.

16   A Time for Justice?

Reflecting on the Many Facets of Time
and Temporality in Justice Service Provision

Marco Velicogna

Introduction

This chapter explores the concept of time in the delivery of justice by
courts and justice systems, reflecting on its multiple dimensions, roles and
functions. It also reflects on the changes that are taking place as the
balance of justice values shifts, and new technologies are introduced.

Time has a key role in judicial proceedings. According to Article 6(1)
European Convention on Human Rights (ECHR), "In the determination
of his [/her] civil rights and obligations . . ., everyone is entitled to a fair
and public hearing within a reasonable time by an independent and
impartial tribunal established by law". Therefore, time and timeliness of
judicial procedures are, first and foremost, a human right. However, what
is a reasonable time? In its decisions, the European Court of Human
Rights identified several factors that provide a guide for the assessment of
timeliness of the procedure: the complexity of the case, the applicant's
conduct and the conduct of the judicial authorities (ECHR, 2020).

Judicial procedures are regulated by laws and norms that define the
possible actions to be undertaken, how such actions should be performed,
by whom, and their timeframe. In this context, failure to act "in accord-
ance [with] the formal rules, or by [not] using the prescribed material
objects in the prescribed ways, has consequences". (Velicogna, 2014,
p. 198). A typical consequence of failing to follow the requirements is
that the act is not legally valid and, therefore, would need to be renewed or
considered null and void for the judicial procedure.

Building on the notion of temporal structuring proposed by Orlikowski
and Yates (2002), the chapter investigates how people, material artefacts
and legal rules defining procedures and their legal performativity contribute to orienting ongoing activities and shaping temporal structures and
their evolution trajectories. In doing this, it addresses a gap in the existing
literature by exploring the effects on time structures and structuring

deriving from the interaction and intertwining of legal and technological performative requirements.

With a solid empirical focus, the chapter examines the material, social and legal elements of time-structuring practices in judicial proceedings, looking at two key events – the filing of a case and the court hearing – and at two objects of time – the court case register and the case file. It also describes the emergence of new temporal structures as paper files and their exchanges are digitised, and remote hearings replace courtroom hearings.

Furthermore, the chapter explores the emergence of a new perspective on time and its related time structures. This new perspective does not substitute the pre-existing one(s) but is simultaneously experienced and enacted. As a result of increasing attention to the managerial and organisational dimensions of courts' activities, the court case temporality is not just that of the single procedure in relation to its time requirements from a legal perspective. It is also increasingly considered from an aggregated viewpoint, with the emergence of new concepts such as disposition time, reasonable timeframe and case weighting, which do not focus on the legal performativity of the single procedure but on the aggregated performance of the system in the (time) management of cases.

The chapter focusses on the Italian case as the primary source of examples. However, it provides comparative references taken from other justice systems to highlight differences in rules, practices and socio-material tools for defining, recording and managing time in and of judicial proceedings.

Theoretical Framework

Time and temporality are one of the central preoccupations in social and organisational life and Management and Organisation Studies. The potential of information and communication technologies (ICT) to decouple action from space and time, and the development of new patterns of working such as "'just in time' manufacture, 'flexible' work, 'zero-hours' contracts, 'hot desking', [and] tele-homeworking" (Glucksmann, 1998, p. 241) have brought up a re-problematisation of time in the academic, managerial and political debate (see, for example, Whipp et al., 2002; Brannen, 2005; Osborne, 2011, Adam, 2013). The Covid-19 pandemic has further increased this trend, radically shifting the balance between physical and remote communications within even the most traditional organisations, bringing about a new 'normality' (Canguilhem, 1991) characterised by synchronous events spanning different time zones, the collapse of time requirements for physical attendance and the blurring of borders between work and personal time.

Temporal Structuring

In a 2002 article, Orlikowski and Yates proposed the notion of temporal structuring as an alternative perspective to overcome the fundamental dichotomy between objective and subjective perspectives on time which characterise social sciences and organisational studies discourse (Taylor, 1911; Thompson, 1967; Zerubavel, 1985; Adam, 2002, 2013; Blyton et al., 2017), where the "Newtonian assumption of time as abstract, absolute, unitary, invariant, linear, mechanical, and quantitative" (Orlikowski & Yates, 2002, p. 685) often associated with *clock* time is put in contraposition to the subjective, heterogeneous and discontinuous *event* time (Zerubavel, 1982; Adam, 2013; de Vaujany et al., 2014), where time is the "product of the norms, beliefs, and customs of individuals and groups" (Orlikowski & Yates, 2002, p. 685), and "perceived and handled by collectivities" (Zerubavel, 1985, p. xii) in a multiplicity of ways. In the notion of temporal structuring, time "is neither objective nor subjective, but ... enacted within organisations" (Yates, 2014, p. 17). Integrating the notion of social practices derived from authors such as Suchman, Lave and Hutchins who "explore the embodied, embedded, and material aspects of human agency in constituting particular social order ... with that of enacted structures drawn from the theory of structuration" (Orlikowski & Yates, 2002, p. 685), Orlikowski and Yates suggest the meaningfulness of looking at how, "through their everyday action, actors produce and reproduce a variety of temporal structures which in turn shape the temporal rhythm and form of their ongoing practices" (2002, p. 684). This approach allows for the exploration of how people, material artefacts and legal rules defining procedures and their legal performativity contribute to orient ongoing activities and to the shaping of temporal structures and their evolution trajectories.

Regulation by Technology

The attention of academic research has been mainly given to the social and material components of temporal structures and structuring and the relation between rules and materiality (Lanzara et al., 2015). In this context, de Vaujany et al., building on two examples presented by Latour (1992) of unquestionable rules delegated to technological artefacts with different enforcement capabilities (the speedbump and the car seatbelt alarm), adding a further one (questionable rules provided by a GPS speed alert), suggest three ways in which humans experience and make sense of their "relationship with materially embodied rules" (de Vaujany et al., 2015, p. 12). Regulations can therefore be enforced through physical control, ICT-based control or a negotiated ICT-based control. "Regulation is enforced through the physical obtrusiveness of the speedbump; or mediated by the software activating several sensory devices; or, in the third case, negotiated and reflexively explored in a dialogue/debate between humans who have different stakes. These situations imply specific ways of making sense of the relationships between artefacts and rules" (2015, p. 14).

Regulation by Law and Legal Performativity

The justice domain, which provides the setting for the analysis of this chapter, presents an additional element: the legal performativity of the actions carried out within the judicial proceedings. According to Hildebrandt, in "our understanding of law we should discriminate between legal rules that are preconditional for – constitutive of – certain legal actions or legal facts, and rules that regulate existing actions or facts" (2008, p. 172). While the action is still being performed as a car exceeds the speed limit, in the case of constitutive rules, the action is not performed.

The legal performativity linked to the respect of the procedural rules thus results in a qualitatively different form of enforcement compared to the socio-technical ones, offering the opportunity to address a potential gap in the temporal structuring literature, which typically focussed on those. The idea is that there is a need for increased and more explicit attention to the legal framework and its impact on the performativity of time-related activities and the "temporal structuring that organisational actors engage in as they go about their everyday activities" (Orlikowski & Yates, 2002, p. 696).

The chapter explores the interaction between temporal structures and legal norms, defining the rhythm and forms of judicial procedures from a practice-based perspective. Procedural laws prescribe how the justice system is to function to provide justice: "For scholars and theorists, such as Hart and Kelsen, ... it may be said that a legal system is largely reducible to a system of regulative, reinforcive, or other rules". (Summers, 2006, p. 4). Within this system, material objects and their functions are defined, their use authorised and prescribed, creating form and features, purpose and function.

Modification of temporal structures is not solely associated with the change in the material artefacts through which time is measured and recorded or in the shift in the ongoing practices "where people (re)produce (and occasionally change) temporal structures to orient their ongoing activities" (Orlikowski & Yates, 2002, p. 685). The specific features of the justice domain allow for the exploration of temporal structures and their structuring process in organisations where the performativity of human and non-human action is strongly associated with the normative component. Therefore, it provides the perfect setup to study how legal norms and their implementation contribute to the temporal and social structures, intended as "both the medium and the outcome of people's recurrent practices" (Orlikowski & Yates, 2002, p. 685).

A New Perspective on Time Structuring: Practicing between and of Legal and Technological Regulative Regimes

Both material objects (paper-based and digital technologies) and laws provide a space of action for human actors in their experiencing of time, enabling and constraining the possibility of their defining temporal structures. As human activity is increasingly enacted through material objects, ICT infrastructures, technical standards and software codes, the regulatory functions of these components add to, complement or displace traditional legal norms and procedural rules (Contini & Lanzara, 2009b). As a result, temporal structures are increasingly determined through the "switch and . . . communication between two distinct regimes of regulation and between two different sets of work practices – law-driven and ICT-driven" (Lanzara, 2009a, p. 33).

These regulative regimes, the legal and the technological, can be defined as two different "system[s] of forces that shape human agency both in the direct way of embodying functionalities that engrave particular courses of action and in the rather unobtrusive fashion of shaping perceptions and preferences, forming skills and professional rules" (Kallinikos, 2009, p. 70). Both these systems "engage 'normativity' but they constitute distinct modes of regulation, and operate in different ways (Hildebrandt, 2008)" (Contini & Mohr, 2014, p. 58). Technology performativity is judged by its capability to produce the expected outcomes, while legal performativity is judged deontologically, separating the legal from the illegal (Contini & Mohr, 2014). Considering the interaction and overlap of these two regulative regimes, results are therefore paramount for understanding the dynamics of change in temporal structures, and how they are constituted through ongoing practices and enacted through increasingly complex *techno-legal assemblages* (Lanzara, 2009b; Velicogna & Contini, 2009), which need to strike difficult balances to avoid solutions which technically work but are not legal or are legal but do not work.

The Time and Temporal Elements in the Court Case

Civil, criminal and administrative judicial procedures vary widely depending on national legal traditions. However, in each, cases are typically organised in phases, and each phase has a variable duration but begins and ends with specific events. In this chapter, I focus on two moments of the judicial case, which allow investigating time, temporality and the socio-material elements that define, measure and record them: the filing of the case, and its service, the court hearing. Humans, material artefacts for time-keeping and legal rules regulating action and its legal performativity combine in a temporal structure and define judicial proceedings and their results.

Time in the Filing of a Court Case

The filing of the case is a constitutive element of the judicial proceedings, which determines its beginning by bringing a claim to the court's attention. Typically, the claim must be filed within a determined time from the event which generates the claim. While in certain jurisdictions the filing must be done physically, by bringing the claim and supporting documents to the court, in other cases, alternative means are available, such as postal services. This may influence the moment in which the claim is considered filed. Given the importance of this moment, as it is relevant both for the filing terms and for measuring the time of the next steps, it is typically registered through multiple means. If the case is filed in paper format, usually a court clerk receives the claim form and attached documents at the front desk, proceeding with a formal check followed by time and date stamping and the certification of the event by signing the document. Furthermore, the clerk issues a time-stamped receipt of the event and proceeds to record the event on the court register. The payment of court fees is another event that is time-bound to the case filing. According to the rules applicable in the jurisdiction, it may take place at the moment of the claim or prior to it, with the onus on the party to demonstrate the payment has been made, or, if it takes place afterwards, that it is temporally linked to the filing of the case. Using Money Claim Online in the UK, for example, the claimant pays by credit or debit card when filing a claim.[1] In Austria, given the complexity of determining the court fee, the court calculates it after the filing and charges it directly to the bank account provided. Failure to pay at the required time may have varying effects, ranging from monetary sanctions to the non-acceptance of the filing.

---

[1] https://gov.uk/make-court-claim-for-money/court-fees

Depending on the national rules, the claimant may have to serve the defendant, informing the other party that the case will be filed or has been filed. In other cases, the court may oversee the service after the claimant has filed the claim. The service of the claim is a fundamental element, and if not properly carried out, may determine the claim's nullity. Several temporal elements are part of the service of documents and have a great relevance to the result of the claim. In Italy, for example, traditionally, the service of a writ of summons in a civil procedure is carried out by the claimant through a bailiff before filing the claim with the court. Accordingly, the party (or their lawyer) goes to the bailiff's office and provides the document(s) to be served. The time of the event is recorded, and a time-stamped receipt is generated. The bailiff will then attempt to serve the document to the defendant. The documents must be served to the defendant in person to ensure that they are properly informed and can exercise their right of defence. If the notification fails, the bailiff records the time of the failure and must proceed with alternative measures, the purpose of which is to balance the right of the defendant to be properly notified with the right of the claimant to a speedy trial.

The performativity of the service is linked to a series of actions carried out by humans (the delivery of the documents, the identification of the addressee, the signature of the receipt) and physical objects (the documents, the watch to verify the time of delivery, the paper receipt, the stamp for recording the time, the pen to sign and certify the event). The result is not just the delivery of the documents but also the recording, certification and generation of temporal evidences of the various moments of the event, which can be used in the following phases of the procedure. Once the document is served, a receipt of the service is sent back to the claimant, who can then proceed to file the claim, attaching to it the service receipt.

Some justice systems may allow different methods of service. Depending on the method, different time events may be relevant. In the UK, if the claimant is in charge of serving the claim form, they must, as a general rule, complete the steps required for the particular "method of service chosen, before 12.00 midnight on the calendar day four months after the date of issue of the claim form".[2] Table 16.1 shows the detail the claimant has to certify within twenty-one days of service to the court, according to UK civil procedure rules in the cases in which the claimant serves the claim form, in relation to the method of service.[3]

---

[2] https://justice.gov.uk/courts/procedure-rules/civil/rules/part07
[3] https://justice.gov.uk/courts/procedure-rules/civil/rules/part06#6.1

Table 16.1 *Methods and date of service in the UK*

Method of service	Details to be certified
1 Personal service	Date of personal service
2 First class post, document exchange or other service which provides for delivery on the next business day	Date of posting, or leaving with, delivering to or collection by the relevant service provider
3 Delivery of document to or leaving it at a permitted place	Date when the document was delivered to or left at the permitted place
4 Fax	Date of completion of the transmission
5 Other electronic method	Date of sending the email or other electronic transmission
6 Alternative method or place	As required by the court

Source: https://justice.gov.uk

Typically, the procedural norms set time limits to provide sufficient time for the defendant to prepare a defence. As EU Regulation (EC) No 1393/ 2007 on the service in the Member States of judicial and extrajudicial documents in civil or commercial matters (service of documents), states, "the material date for the purposes of service varies from one . . . State to another".

The writ of summons itself includes additional time elements. In Italy, it includes, for example, the day of the first hearing and the invite to the defendant to answer twenty days before such hearing (reduced to ten days in specific cases). In the answer, the defendant addresses the dispute on the merits, and presents their defences and any counterclaims. Furthermore, between the day of notification and the first hearing should be a minimum number of days, which can be reduced at the request of the parties. In the UK, the defendant must be informed of the time period for filing a defence.[4]

Time in a Court Hearing

The court hearing is the second event of the court case I will analyse to explore its temporal dimensions. Depending on procedural rules and the nature of the case, a court case may have one, several, or no court hearings. While a judge may have several hearings in one day, a hearing may require several days in complex cases.

Hearings are events that bring together the judge, the parties and/or their representatives, witnesses and evidence in the same place – and

---

[4] https://www.justice.gov.uk/courts/procedure-rules/civil/rules

within the same time slot – to be discussed, to provide the judge with the information needed to reach a fair decision.

A first element to be considered when looking at hearings is their scheduling. The scheduling depends on several factors, such as the hearing days of the court, which follow a calendar logic, and the terms of the case, which may provide for a minimum gap of a certain number of days from a previous event to allow the parties to prepare. It also depends on the availability of the judge, which depends on their workload and annual leave. When a hearing date is set or modified, the date must be communicated to the parties. Postponements may be requested by the parties or determined by the availability of the judge and subject to time requirements to allow the parties to have sufficient time to organise themselves and attend the hearing. Not attending the hearing by one or both parties may have various effects, ranging from the postponement of the hearing to a later date, to the extinguishment, discontinuation or settlement of the case.

The time within the hearing day has different features from the court and party perspectives. The hearing typically takes place between other case hearings for the judge and court personnel. For the external actors, the temporal dimension of the hearing is quite different. Travelling to court, accessing the court building and navigating it to reach the hearing room may take some time. While lawyers and other regular participants may have pre-existing knowledge and dedicated access channels, each step is time consuming for the parties dealing with their first case in court and requires adequate time allocation. Accessing the court building itself and passing the security checks may, for example, require unallocated time, depending on external factors such as the presence of long queues. Once inside and having reached the hearing room, the party can then discover that the hour scheduled for the beginning of the hearing is merely indicative, and many hours may pass before it begins.

Once the hearing begins, time is recorded, and events are ordered in a timely manner. Events include the formal announcement of the beginning of the hearing, the identification of the parties, the taking of the oath and swearing in of witnesses, and defining the timing of follow-up events, including follow-up hearings. The judge may issue court orders, pronounce a decision at the end of the hearing or decide on the matter straight away in chambers. Within the hearing, the order of presentation of the evidence plays a key role. Parties against whom the evidence is presented must have the opportunity to oppose its admission or present pieces of evidence contrary to it. Procedural rules typically define or provide the judge with the power to define the temporal terms for presenting the evidence.

The events taking place during the hearing are typically recorded (in writing, or via audio or audio-video) by a court clerk in the hearing minutes. Such minutes may then be dated and signed by both the clerk and the judge. Specific attention is given to the temporal elements of the hearing (beginning, end, chronological order of the activities carried out). All these elements become part of the case file (see below).

As previously mentioned, the decision can be oral, as the judge reads the judgment at the end of the hearing or written, having been drafted after the sentence. For example, in the Italian court case, after the parties have provided their concluding arguments, the first instance monocratic judge can read the judgment and their reasons. In this case, after the minutes that include the judgment are signed by the judge, the decision is considered published and must be immediately submitted to the Court Registry (Art 281.6 of the Italian Code of Civil Procedure). As an alternative, the judge may allow the parties to exchange further replies within a thirty-day limit and then submit the sentence to the Court Registry within another thirty days (Art 281.6 of the Italian Code of Civil Procedure). The court clerk certifies the event recording the submission with the date and their signature on the sentence.

Objects of Time: The Case Registers and the Case Files

Several socio-material objects play a key role in the definition and recording of time in judicial proceedings. Some, such as the inscription and certification of event dates through time stamps and wet-ink signatures have been introduced in the previous section. The next section will focus on two of these objects: the case registers and the case files.

The case registers and case files fulfil various roles: they keep track of all relevant documentation and communication exchanges and ensure the respect of procedures and timeframe reviews, as well as recording the official time and the regularity of the many procedural events that intertwine to constitute the judicial proceeding.

The Court Registers

Courts typically have several registers dedicated to keeping track of specific activities carried out within the court, including, for example, the register of civil litigation cases; the register of criminal cases; the register of the cases assigned to each section; the chronological and alphabetical register of the cases assigned to each section; the register of the hearings for each judge, keeping track of the cases dealt with in each hearing; the chronological register of measures and other original documents; the repertory register of deeds subject to registration; the register of positions conferred and remuneration paid to technical consultants. The registers' form, functions, creation, use and maintenance are typically defined by law. Figure 16.1 provides an example of a paper register where key events of the proceeding are registered and procedural events are described and dated. Each line, which spans two half-pages, corresponds to a case, with the columns used to identify the case (register number) and register and date the various events that characterise it. As the case is filed with the court, the court clerk registers the case in the court register, attributing to it a chronological register number. This number will be used to identify the case, the case file and the document related to it. According to regulations, cases should generally be registered immediately after the filing has been accepted. However, empirical research has shown that even extended delays may occur, especially in overworked and understaffed courts.

An important aspect of registers is that they are time-bound objects, the legal performativity of which is linked not just to their physical form and to the legal provision regulating their material form and use, but also to sets of activities that need to be performed within the appropriate time-frame to ensure they can be trusted to record accurately the procedural events. In Italy, for example, before being put into use, a court register must be numbered (chronologically positioning each register book in relation to the previous and following one and uniquely identifying it) and signed on each half-sheet by the president of the court or by a judge delegated by him. Furthermore, the number of half-sheets making up the register must be noted in all letters in the last half-sheet. In this way, the court provides the means to verify the future 'completeness' of the material artefact with its composition at the time it is put in use. As one physical book may not be adequate for the organisational needs of a large court

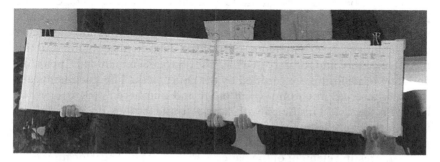

Figure 16.1 Court case register

with a heavy caseload, procedures are put in place for the division of a register in multiple volumes. This allows court clerks to work in parallel on the same register. The case register is not kept by the judges, but by the court clerks, who keep track of and certify the activities carried out, registering the cases and each of the main events relating to them in chronological order, as they take place. In this way, the registers provide a crystallization of the events, and therefore their content cannot be altered once it has been inscribed. Deletion must be done by adding a note indicating the deletion to preserve the deleted part.

Over time, these tools have evolved from paper-based technologies to digital ones. Some of the changes in the socio-material nature of the case registers will be investigated in the next section.

The Case File

After the filing of a case and its registration in the court register, the court clerk proceeds with the creation of the case file. The case file initially includes the claim form and attached documents, such as the proof of service, if carried out, by the party before the filing. Afterwards, the hearing notes, the judge's acts and orders, proof of notifications carried out by the court during the proceeding and all acts carried out by the judge, the court clerk, documents provided by the parties and a copy of the final decision are typically added. Therefore, the case file includes all elements that, from a formal and substantial perspective, can be considered for the decision on the case, up to the decision itself. In a way, the case file is a means to bind to a physical object all legally relevant elements of the case as they take place, allowing for the verification at any point in time during the proceeding and after its end that all legal requirements (including the temporal ones) have been met.

As previously mentioned, the court file is numbered with the court register number under which the case has been registered. The cover of the file typically includes a large amount of information, such as the court, section and judge to whom it has been assigned, the parties and their legal representatives. It also includes a list of the documents contained in the file, their nature and the date in which they have been included. Inclusion and date of inclusion are certified by the court clerk. The documents are typically inserted in chronological order and numbered progressively in line with the list. This helps with access to the various documents and verifies the completeness of the case file at any point throughout the proceeding or after it has ended.

An interesting element of the paper case file is its physical location over the time of the proceeding. The file is typically kept in the judge's clerk's office, grouped accordingly by the case status and next event (i.e. by hearing date) unless the judge needs to study it or in case of a hearing, when the case file is moved to the hearing room.

In addition to the functions performed within the judicial proceedings, court registers and files have also been shown to have a historical function as "sources for . . . social and economic history" (Reilly, 1987, p. 155; see also Sobers-Khan, 2014).

Shifting Materiality and Practices of Time with the Digitisation of Judicial Proceedings

Electronic Court Registers and Files as an Occasion for Temporal Structuring in Asynchronous Working Practices

Paper has been progressively abandoned in courts in favour of digital tools, starting with the introduction of electronic court registers. Electronic court registers allow for multiple actors to work on the registration and consultation of cases simultaneously, automatic reuse of previously entered data and automation of part of the activities carried out by the court clerks (Fabri & Langbroek, 2000; Contini & Fabri, 2003; Velicogna, 2007). Electronic case files and electronic communication have also been increasingly adopted (Cerillo & Fabra, 2009; Contini & Lanzara, 2009a, 2014; Reiling, 2010; Velicogna et al., 2011, 2013; Velicogna, 2021).

Digitisation has required the development of technological tools but also of the legal framework which defines and authorises their use and the respect of the fundamental values and principles driving the justice system's functioning. As Fabri pointed out, "The challenge in applying ICT to the judiciary is to increase effectiveness, efficiency, transparency, and standardisation of processes, but without impinging on the judiciary's basic and fundamental values in a democratic context, such as access to justice, independence and impartiality of judges, fair trial in reasonable time, [and] quality of judgements" (2021).

Where time is concerned, this process of digitisation has resulted in a shift from human "time-keeping activities" (Birth, 2012, p. 7) to (software) artefacts which independently keep track of the time of events and certify them, enabling the assessment of their legal performativity. For example, when a case is filed electronically, the filing time is not ascertained and recorded by the court clerk when he or she receives the document from the party at the court front office. The e-filing system generates and saves the time-evidences required by the procedural rules. Figure 16.2 provides an example of the Italian e-Justice infrastructure used for the Civil Trial On-Line.

Overall architecture

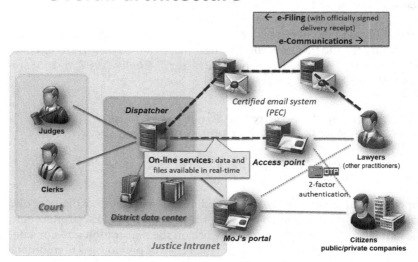

Figure 16.2 Italian e-Justice infrastructure, based on a .ppt provided by Borsari in 2022 (drafted in 2014) and Borsari (2020)

This complex assemblage involving a number of independent organisations and artefacts allows for the e-filing (and legal electronic communication) through a certified email system (Carnevali & Resca, 2014). The system generates evidences (with time stamps) which track the progress of the certified email from the sender outbox to its certified email provider, to the judicial administration infrastructure, to the court inbox and to the moment the document is accepted by the court clerk (and therefore becomes visible to the counterparty). While all these events are tracked and recorded, in the Italian case, the law defines the time the email reaches the court inbox as the time of filing. This technological development also allows for a change in the social (and legal) understanding of time. It also shows how such a change, while linked to the possibilities allowed by the material and legal components, can be influenced by the initiative of the people involved in its development/drafting or use/interpretation. The evolution of temporal structures is not linear; it may depend, for example, on the capability of a group of users to bring up the normative change required for a shift after a new technological system has been deployed. When the new e-Justice system was initially introduced in Italy, the end of the day for the e-filing was considered the time the court front office closed (14:00). Any document received after that time was labelled as filed the following day. This allowed for the existing temporal structure to remain, which was accepted and adopted by all members of the community. At the same time, changes in media and technology "exerts a generative role, being a source of ontological openness and variation" (de Vaujany et al., 2015, p. 23). The potential for the new technology to allow a change in the temporal structure was not lost on some of the practitioners who argued for change. Being a legal domain, the possibility for those involved to "choose otherwise" (Giddens, 1993) could not be immediately enacted. The legal performativity of the actions carried out required a respect for the existing legal rules. It was only after an intense debate that the Italian Law 90/2014 was introduced, 'moving' the end of the day to midnight.

A check that has been introduced in the electronic transmission of documents to the court is the verification of the role and status of the certified email sender through an electronic register of certified emails managed by the Ministry of Justice (ReGIndE, which for the lawyers is constantly updated by their Bar Association). The system, therefore, can automatically check if the lawyer is authorised to practice at the moment the case is filed. This of course opens up the issue of the frequency and delays in the updating of such databases, on which the actions of the people involved may depend.

With its introduction, the Civil Trial On-Line system replaces both the court registers and the case files. The electronic case file is generated at the moment of filing, and the metadata of the electronic activities and of the exchanged documents automatically fill the electronic court register. An e-service portal allows the just-in-time consultation of the electronic court register and the electronic case file documents. The system uses a strong authentication mechanism that identifies the person accessing the system and checks their status.

To provide an idea of the quantitative dimensions involved, between July 2014 (when the system became mandatory) and December 2019, over 50 million acts were e-filed (30 million from external users and 20 million from judges); over 95 million e-communications and notifications were sent from the courts to professionals from 2013; and court registers and files were accessed around 10 million times per day at the beginning of 2020 (Borsari, 2020).

All these elements contributed to the redesign of temporal practices of the parties involved in the judicial proceedings. While some of these changes have been intentional, others have been unexpected side effects. For example, a lawyer can now file a case from any location which has resulted in the end of queueing at the court front office. While a functional aspect to the beginning of a judicial procedure, the queueing also provided a space and time for young practitioners to socialise and familiarise themselves with the court buildings and their rules.

Judges and court clerks have the opportunity to look at court cases and organise them through multiple time variables such as from the most recently filed to the oldest, or vice-versa, or in relation to the 'nearness' of a past or future event, such as the next hearing. At the same time, they are also subject to the prompts generated by the system, which orient their actions to temporal priorities and events inscribed in the software.

The introduction of electronic case registers and file exchange systems has resulted in the automation of some of the practices of the paper procedure and an increasingly reduced relevance of the physical location of the artefacts and people participating in the judicial process. Digital interfaces contribute to shaping the reorganisation of temporal *sensemaking* (Weick, 1995) and structures of the human actors involved in judicial proceedings, for example, through the automatic recording, certification and selective presentation to the human actor of temporal events, and through the creation of new habits based on the emergent temporally structuring properties of the digital systems.

Remote Hearings as an Occasion of Temporal Structuring in Synchronous Communication in Times of Emergency

A widespread change in the management of cases has concerned electronic court hearings, particularly as an emergency response to the Covid-19 pandemic. Before Covid-19, the digitisation of hearings focussed mainly on including technological artefacts in the hearing room. The objectives of these initiatives included improving the presentation of evidence and the recording of the hearings. From the study of these experiences (Lanzara & Patriotta, 2001; Lanzara, 2009a), it was observed that "the specific features of visual medium influence the agency of judicial actors (specifically the judges) and the logic of judicial decisions" (Lanzara, 2015, p. 201). The different media "allow and support different representations of the same event or sequence of events" (Lanzara, 2015, p. 202), thereby contributing to the reconfiguration of temporal structures, the re-conceptualisation of temporal events and the understanding of time.

Remote hearings carried out through videoconferencing tools have radically changed not only the spatial dimensions of the hearings but also their temporal structure. At the same time, until the Covid-19 pandemic and the emergency measures that restricted people's mobility, they have been residual and carried out through complex dedicated infrastructures typically installed in controlled environments, such as courtrooms and prisons. These older systems were designed in an attempt to mimic courtroom features, including, for example, true-to-life video connections to reduce the 'distortion' introduced by the use of the new technology. The remote hearings carried out during the Covid-19 pandemic completely revolutionised things by introducing standard applications developed for general use and not adapted to the justice systems' specific needs. Given the emergency and their specificities, different justice systems adopted different approaches to authorising and regulating the use of these tools (Velicogna, 2021).

Many of the features of the new tools did not fit into the traditional ways of conducting a hearing. The application of established rules and practices was disturbed in multiple ways, raising questions of how the new tools could adequately be integrated. The problems faced were many, from the failure of existing practices of identification, to the impossibility of being sure of the 'presence' of the various actors or their ability to follow the conversation when not checking their status, to the uncertainty over the image the judge was projecting. Systems proved to be prone to technical breakdowns, the origins of which could not always be traced, including network issues and software version compatibility issues (see, for example, Sanders, 2021).

The structure and meaning provided by the physical layout of the court and courtroom, which "subtly influence the work practices, the reasoning strategies, [and] the representations of the actors" (Lanzara, 2015, p. 202), were not reproduced in the new medium. Judges, for example, discovered that the behaviour and dress code expected from the participants in the courtrooms could not be guaranteed or that interruptions from young family members could not be avoided. Another discovery was that the communication in the videoconference setup is articulated differently. The perception and visibility of the other actors, and of their behaviours and actions, are different. This resulted in the reduction of the judges' competencies which are medium-specific. The digitally mediated reality judges interact with does not correspond to the "unconscious and conscious anticipations and assumptions" (Weick, 1995, p. 4) that shape the judge's understanding of the context in which he/she is operating. The visibility of facial expressions, tone of voice, body language, the capability to understand if a person is present in the courtroom or has suddenly disappeared as the result of a connectivity issue are just some of the examples of this discrepancy. The new reality may suddenly and unexpectedly become more "puzzling, troubling and uncertain" (Weick, 1995, p. 9), rendering existing practices inadequate and sense-making (Weick, 1995) more problematic.

With time, new practical knowledge and more stability and understanding of the properties of the interactions in the new medium were generated. This also resulted in the establishment of new rules and redefined attendance in terms of temporal and spatial participation in the hearings, and the introduction of practical solutions, such as pre-hearing testing checks and waiting rooms to reduce interruptions and temporal mismatches.

Changing Perspective on Time: From Case Procedural Time to Case Management

From Single Case to Cases: Measuring Time Differently

The increasing number of court cases, the shrinking resources and the diffusion of public management ideas led, from the 1990s, to increasing attention to the temporal length of cases.

While from a traditional legal perspective, time has been considered from the single judicial procedure perspective in terms of respect of the procedural temporal terms by the parties, and more recently on the individual cases which exceed a reasonable time, increasing attention is being given to the length of judicial proceedings from a managerial (Peckham, 1981) and organisational perspective (Fabri & Langbroek, 2000; Ng, 2007). This has led to the definition of concepts and tools that allow different ways of measuring and representing time. The shift from paper-based technologies to digital ones for the recording of time has contributed to this change, enabling the collection, aggregation and analysis of information which has not previously been recorded. This has not been a linear process and has required – and still requires – great effort to define relevant temporal events and their duration. The issue becomes even greater when a comparison between different justice systems is attempted (see, for example, on the difficulty of comparing EU Member States' judicial data, Velicogna, 2013; Onțanu et al., 2017; Onțanu & Velicogna, 2021).

Beginning with an annual count of the number of incoming, resolved and pending cases which could 'easily' be done using paper register data, a number of other temporal indicators have been developed. The Disposition Time, for example, was introduced by the European Commission for the Efficiency of Justice of the Council of Europe (CEPEJ-CoE) in the 2000s to estimate "the number of days necessary for a pending case to be solved in court" (CEPEJ, 2015, p. 14) by dividing the number of pending cases at the end of a solar year of reference, by the number of cases resolved during the same year. Compared to the average length of proceedings, which is calculated based on the actual length of judicial proceedings, it provided two advantages. It can be easily calculated using data available to all the Council of Europe Member States, as it is consistent with the recording of time on paper registers, and it is not dependent on the definition of the time a case begins and ends, which may vary significantly from one Member State justice system to another.

Shifting Meanings and Practices of Time

In parallel to the definition of new measures of time to monitor and assess the capability of courts and justice systems to deal with cases in a reasonable timeframe, an increased emphasis was put on the use of such data to improve the management of cases. As a result, the role of the judge as a third party, supervising the interactions between claimant and defendant and assessing the evidence and arguments they provide in support of their claims, was challenged. The judge and the court are increasingly asked to monitor the flow of cases and to manage them more actively. Case "management involves the entire set of actions that a court takes to monitor and control the progress of cases, from initiation through trial or other initial disposition to the completion of all post-disposition court work, to make sure that justice is done promptly" (Steelman et al., 2000 p. xi). Basic case management methods and techniques adopted by courts "include (a) early court intervention and continuous court control over case progress, (b) differentiated case management (DCM), (c) realistic schedules and meaningful pretrial court events, (d) credible trial dates, (e) management of trials, and (f) management of court events after initial disposition" (Steelman et al., 2000, p. 3). While some of these initiatives require changes in procedural laws, other have been introduced by the courts, often through open dialogue with the key stakeholders involved. This is linked to the recognition that "changes in case processing speed . . . necessarily require changes in the attitudes and practices of all members of a legal community" (Church et al., 1978, p. 82).

In Search of New Concepts to Talk About (and Act on) Time

Discussions between academics, practitioners and justice institutions, driven by the need to find measures of time more suitable for active monitoring and management of cases, has led to the development of new definitions for the timing of cases, such as timeframe, backlog and case weighting. *Timeframe* for example, has been defined by the Commission for the Efficiency of Justice of the Council of Europe as a period of time within which a certain number or percentage of cases have to be resolved, taking into consideration the age of the pending cases. Timeframes are a managerial tool, which can be set by central authorities (e.g. Judicial Council, Supreme Court, Ministry of Justice, Parliament) and/or by courts. Timeframes should not be confused with procedural deadlines or time limits, which refer to single cases. (CEPEJ, 2016, p. 2)

Backlog, which was initially often confused with the number of pending cases, has also now been defined by CEPEJ as "the number or percentage of pending cases not resolved within an established Timeframe". Furthermore, in order to assess the human resources (judges and administrative personnel) needed to meet the demand for justice within a reasonable timeframe, the concept of case weighting was introduced. *Case weighting* is related to the complexity of the cases and the weight refers to the time required to finalise a case. "The proceedings that have occurred in an office in a given period of time are then multiplied by a 'complexity factor' (i.e. weight), the result of which gives an indication of the time needed for the judge, or for the office, to resolve them" (Fabri, 2022, p. 2).

Emerging Temporal Structure Practices

This new perspective on the time of procedures has resulted in a multiplicity of time-related initiatives to act on these new concepts, collecting and analysing the required data and using it. For example, Austria carried out a major time study in 2008/2009, which led to the development of a case-weighting system, Personalanforderungsrechnung II, "to calculate the number of judges and prosecutors required to manage the demand of justice (incoming cases) in reasonable time and to allocate them to the different courts in line with the principle of immovability of judges" (CEPEJ, 2020, p. 18). The Netherlands has developed a model to finance courts in which the budget is negotiated considering the average time (and cost) judges and legal assistants require to dispose of cases for various categories of claims (Dijkstra et al., 2017, pp. 261–2).

The different perspectives on 'time' have also resulted in a shift in the understanding of the factors affecting the timeliness of justice. The "case volume, court structure, resources, and rules of procedure may not be the sole or most important factors explaining the pace of litigation" (Steelman & Fabri, 2008, p. 4). This requires a shift in the role of the court, from a passive to a more active one. If "a court must actively control the progress of cases from initiation to conclusion" (Steelman & Fabri, 2008, p. 5), the increasing role e-justice artefacts play in tracking time, raising attention of impending time limits (e.g. through alert mechanisms) and enforcing procedural deadlines, seems to be a constitutive component of the process. In this perspective, case registers, case files, electronic communications and the judicial databases which collect an increasing volume of data on court cases "are not merely tools that shape individual cognition, but are artefacts that play a central role in intersubjectively shared cognitive processes" (Birth, 2012, p. 12).

Conclusions

In this chapter, I have attempted to show the centrality of time in the court organisation process and how material objects and legal rules contribute to defining the temporal structuring of judicial case-related activities. Time-watching, timekeeping, time-recording and time-certifying are part of the very fabric of judicial proceedings, often determining the legal performativity of the actions being carried out and the results of the judicial decision. The legal time of the case, and the procedural elements through which it is constructed are instrumental in ensuring that the judicial procedure respects the fundamental values it is built upon and which it serves. The actions and material components which create the legal time of the case contribute to the legitimisation of the justice systems, of the courts and of the judges, affecting the parties' perception of the fairness of the procedures and shaping their "willingness to defer to the decisions made by legal authorities" (Tyler, 2003, p. 292).

Beginning with the description of the practice of two events – the filing of the case and the court hearing – I showed how actors, tools and legal rules combine to shape and be shaped by multiple temporal structures. These temporal structures nest event-based and clock-based components. The calendar of the hearings, for example, is defined through fixed clock-based deadlines, "reified in fixed chronological times" (Orlikowski & Yates, 2002, p. 694), such as the time for replies, which is subject to the actors requesting postponements, but also depends on other factors which follow different temporal logics, such as court hearing days, judge workload and court opening hours. Through a combination of these temporal elements, and of their material, legal and human components, the time of the hearing is organised and enacted in practice. The case hearings also allow for the interrelation and overlapping of the linear perspective of the parties in the cases, where the hearing is a moment in a continuum that runs from the filing to the judicial decision, to the cyclic perspective of the hearing days of the judge and the court.

Observing two key 'objects of time' that record but are also a part of the construction of the judicial case – the case register and the case file – allows us to delve into the role of these material objects, their materiality and their time-bound nature. Their creation and modification occur according to strict rules designed to bind the temporality of the events of the case to the material objects through human actions. The legal time of events is thus 'frozen' through the certification of its inscription by the court clerks.

The analysis of the shift from paper-based communication and recording systems to digital ones allows the exploration of "the influence of communication technology on the timing of processes" (Yates, 2014, p. 19). The justice context allows for the observation of the relationships between technology, legal provisions, practice and organising when this shift takes place. With all its advantages in terms of reducing workload and human error, digitisation brings the increasing complexity and opaqueness of the systems to which the tasks are delegated. These systems are complex *assemblages* (Lanzara, 2009b; Velicogna & Contini, 2009) of technical, legal and organisational components, visible to the end-users only in the form of their interfaces. The time of the certification of the filing of a case is performed 'somewhere' on a server situated in a complex sequence of servers and networks owned by different organisations, between the computer of the claimant and the computer of the court clerk on the basis of a functionality inscribed in the software by developers implementing an interpretation of the legal prescriptions. This raises the risk of "undetectable software errors or 'glitches' that [elude human awareness and control and that can] have potentially disruptive consequences" (Contini & Lanzara, 2018).

The experience of remote hearings allows for further exploring the relation between material objects, space, legal rules and time. It shows "how technology remediates [(Bolter & Grusin, 1999)] practices, influencing their structures and meanings" (de Vaujany et al., 2015, p. 23) in a highly regulated environment, where legal procedural requirements play a significant role in the remediation and in the "object's representations that can be built" (2015) in the new media.

A relevant notion that emerges from the chapter descriptions is that of the legal time of the case. The construction of the legally valid temporality of the case, the only one that can be considered in a judicial decision, is done through a complex recording and certification involving humans, material artefacts and highly regulated procedures. The time recorded thus becomes the legal time on which the legal performativity of the actions carried out and of the events of the case are dependent. While 'objective' measures of time, such as clocks and calendars, are used to measure it, differences between the measures provided by these objects and the one certified in the proceeding can only be challenged according to specific procedures and within specific time limits. If not correctly challenged within defined time limits, the legally certified remain the legally binding ones. The increasing digitisation of procedures and recording and certification of time events has shifted many of the activities from the human actors to the legally defined and regulated software-based systems. It is increasingly from them and from the interpretation of the rules inscribed in them, and no other systems and interpretations, that the recording of the legally valid time depends.

Legal time structures and the material objects and practices used to enact them powerfully shape the judicial process and its results. Nevertheless, the growing attention to the length of judicial proceedings has resulted in creating an alternative, separate and distinct way of looking at time and temporality in justice service provision. The new temporal structures emerging as a consequence of this change do not substitute the existing ones but are increasingly contributing, with their complementary and sometimes contradictory nature, to redefining the understanding of time, its management and the temporal organisation of judicial proceedings. New material and conceptual instruments are being developed to allow the observation of this new temporality and its management. Concepts such as disposition time, timeframe, backlog and case weight have been developed, and ways to collect, analyse and act upon such data have been devised.

The concept of temporal structuring has allowed for the exploration of the multiplicity of the temporal dimension that characterises the justice service domain, reflecting on the complex interrelation that material, social and legal components have in the understanding, experiencing and enacting of time. In its analysis of this concept, this chapter contributes to understanding the notion, exploring the less considered aspect of legal rules and legal performativity and how it combines with all other components in shaping how actors engage with their organisational practices and enact temporal structures.

References

Adam, B. (2002). Perceptions of Time. In *Companion Encyclopedia of Anthropology* (2nd ed., pp. 537–60). London: Routledge.

Adam, B. (2013). *Timewatch: The Social Analysis of Time*. Cambridge: John Wiley & Sons.

Birth, K. (2012). *Objects of Time: How Things Shape Temporality*. New York: Palgrave Macmillan.

Blyton, P., Hassard, J., Hill, S. & Starkey, K. (2017). *Time, Work and Organisation*. London: Routledge.

Bolter, J. D. & Grusin, R. (1999). *Remediation: Understanding New Media*. Cambridge: MIT Press.

Borsari, G. (2020). E-Justice in Italy. National Conference on Technology in the Justice Sector. Kingston, Jamaica, 27–29 February.

Brannen, J. (2005). Time and the negotiation of work–family boundaries: Autonomy or illusion? *Time & Society, 14*(1), 113–31.

Canguilhem, G. (1991). *The Normal and the Pathological.* New York: Zone Books.

Carnevali, D. & Resca, A. (2014). Pushing at the Edge of Maximum Manageable Complexity: The Case of "Trial Online" in Italy. In F. Contini & G. F. Lanzara (eds), The Circulation of Agency in e-Justice (pp. 161–83). Dordrecht: Springer.

CEPEJ (2015). Study on Council of Europe Member States Appeal and Supreme Courts' Lengths of Proceedings Edition 2015 (2006–2012 data). CEPEJ Studies No. 17. Strasbourg: Council of Europe.

CEPEJ (2016). Towards European Timeframes for Judicial Proceedings – Implementation Guide (p. 5). Strasbourg: Council of Europe.

CEPEJ (2020). Case Weighting in Judicial Systems – CEPEJ Studies No. 28. Strasbourg: Council of Europe.

Cerillo, C. & Fabra, P. (2009). E-Justice: Information and Communication Technologies in the Court System. Hershey, PA: IGI-Global.

Church, T., Carlson, A., Lee, J. L. & Tan, T. (1978). *Justice Delayed: The Pace of Litigation in Urban Trial Courts.* Williamsburg, VA: National Center for State Courts.

Contini, F. & Fabri, M. (eds) (2003). *Judicial Electronic Data Interchange in Europe: Applications, Policies and Trends.* Bologna: Lo scarabeo.

Contini, F. & Lanzara, G. F. (eds) (2009a). *ICT and Innovation in the Public Sector.* London: Palgrave Macmillan.

Contini, F. & Lanzara, G. F. (2009b). Introduction. In *ICT and Innovation in the Public Sector.* London: Palgrave Macmillan.

Contini, F. & Lanzara, G. F. (eds) (2014). *The Circulation of Agency in E-Justice. Interoperability and Infrastructures for European Transborder Judicial Proceedings* Berlin: Springer.

Contini, F. & Lanzara, G. F. (2018). The elusive mediation between law and technology. Undetectable errors in ICT–based judicial proceedings. In P. Branco, N. Hosen, M. Leone & R. Mohr (eds), *Tools of Meaning* (pp. 39–66). Rome: Aracne.

Contini, F. & Mohr, R. (2014). How the Law Can Make It Simple: Easing the Circulation of Agency in e-Justice. In *The Circulation of Agency in E-Justice* (pp. 53–79). Dordrecht: Springer.

de Vaujany, F-X., Mitev, N., Laniray, P. & Vaast, E. (eds) (2014). *Materiality and Time: Historical Perspectives on Organisations, Artefacts and Practices.* London: Palgrave Macmillan.

de Vaujany, F-X., Mitev, N., Lanzara, G. F. & Mukherjee, A. (2015). Introduction: Making Sense of Rules and Materiality: The New Challenge for Management and Organization Studies? In *Materiality, Rules and Regulation* (pp. 1–29). London: Palgrave Macmillan.

Dijkstra, R. I., Langbroek, P. M., Bozorg Zadeh, K. & Türk, Z. (2017). The Evaluation and Development of the Quality of Justice in the Netherlands. In F. Contini (ed.), *Handle with Care: Assessing and Designing Methods for Evaluation and Development of the Quality of Justice* (pp. 227–76). Bologna: IRSIG-CNR.

ECHR (2020). Guide on Article 6 of the Convention – Right to a Fair Trial (criminal limb). Strasbourg: Council of Europe.

Fabri, M. (2021). Will COVID-19 accelerate implementation of ICT in courts? *International Journal for Court Administration*, *12*(2), 1–13.

Fabri, M. (2022). Judicial proceedings cannot only be counted, they must be weighted: The situation in the European judiciaries (unpublished manuscript). Bologna: IGSG-CNR.

Fabri, M. & Langbroek, P. M. (eds) (2000). *The Challenge of Change for Judicial Systems: Developing a Public Administration Perspective*. Amsterdam: IOS Press.

Giddens, A. (1993). *New Rules of Sociological Method: A Positive Critique of Interpretative Sociologies* (2nd ed.). Stanford, CA: Stanford University Press.

Glucksmann, M. A. (1998). "What a difference a day makes": A theoretical and historical exploration of temporality and gender. *Sociology*, *32*(2), 239–58.

Hildebrandt, M. (2008). Legal and technological normativity: More (and less) than twin sisters. *Techné: Research in Philosophy and Technology*, *12*(3), 169–83.

Kallinikos, J. (2009). The Regulative Regime of Technology. In *ICT and Innovation in the Public Sector* (pp. 66–87). London: Palgrave Macmillan.

Lanzara, G. F. (2009a). Reshaping practice across media: Material mediation, medium specificity and practical knowledge in judicial work. *Organisation Studies*, *30*(12), 1369–90.

Lanzara, G. F. (2009b). Building Digital Institutions: ICT and the Rise of Assemblages in Government. In *ICT and Innovation in the Public Sector* (pp. 9–48). London: Palgrave Macmillan.

Lanzara, G. F. (2015). How Technology Remediates Practice: Objects, Rules, and New Media. In *Materiality, Rules and Regulation* (pp. 195–220). London: Palgrave Macmillan.

Lanzara, G. F., de Vaujany, F-X., Mitev, N. & Mukherjee, A. (eds) (2015). Materiality, Rules and Regulation: New Trends in Management and Organisation Studies. London: Palgrave Macmillan.

Lanzara, G. F. & Patriotta, G. (2001). Technology and the courtroom: An inquiry into knowledge making in organisations. *Journal of Management Studies*, *38*(7), 94–171.

Latour, B. (1992). Where are the Missing Masses? The Sociology of a few Mundane Artifacts. In W. E. Bijker & J. Law (eds), *Shaping Technology/Building Society: Studies in Sociotechnical Change* (pp. 225–58). Cambridge, MA: MIT Press.

Ng, G. Y. (2007). *Quality of Judicial Organisation and Checks and Balances*. Utrecht: Utrecht University.

Onțanu, E. A. & Velicogna, M. (2021). The challenge of comparing EU Member States judicial data. *Oñati Socio-Legal Series*, *11*(2), 446–80.

Onțanu, E. A., Velicogna, M. & Contini, F. (2017). How many cases: Assessing the comparability of EU judicial datasets. *Comparative Law Review*, *8*(2), 1–39.

Orlikowski, W. J. & Yates, J. (2002). It's about time: Temporal structuring in organisations. *Organisation Science*, *13*(6), 684–700.

Osborne, P. (2011). *The Politics of Time: Modernity and Avant-Garde*. London: Verso Books.

Peckham, R. F. (1981). The federal judge as a case manager: The new role in guiding a case from filing to disposition. *California Law Review*, *69*(3), 770–85.

Reiling, D. (2010). *Technology for Justice: How Information Technology Can Support Judicial Reform*. Leiden: Leiden University Press.

Reilly, J. A. (1987). Sharīʿa court registers and land tenure around nineteenth-century Damascus. *Review of Middle East Studies, 21*(2), 155–69.

Sanders, A. (2021). Video-hearings in Europe before, during and after the COVID-19 pandemic. *International Journal for Court Administration, 12*(2), 1–21.

Sobers-Khan, N. (2014). Slaves without Shackles: Forced Labour and Manumission in the Galata Court Registers 1560–1572. Berlin: Klaus Schwarz Verlag GmbH.

Steelman, D. C. & Fabri, M. (2008). Can an Italian court use the American approach to delay reduction? *Justice System Journal, 29*(1), 1–23.

Steelman, D. C., Goerdt, J. & McMillan, J. E. (2000). *Caseflow Management: The Heart of Court Management in the New Millennium* (pp. 137–43). Williamsburg, VA: National Center for State Courts.

Summers, R. S. (2006). *Form and Function in a Legal System: A General Study.* Cambridge: Cambridge University Press.

Taylor, F. W. (1911). *The Principles of Scientific Management.* New York: Harper and Brothers Publishers.

Thompson, E. P. (1967). Time, work-discipline, and industrial capitalism. *Past & Present, 38*(1), 56–97.

Tyler, T. R. (2003). Procedural justice, legitimacy, and the effective rule of law. *Crime and Justice, 30,* 283–357.

Velicogna, M. (2007). Justice systems and ICT: What can be learned from Europe? *Utrecht Law Review, 3*(1), 129–47.

Velicogna, M. (2013). The EU Justice Scoreboard and the challenge of investigating the functioning of EU justice systems and their impact on the economy of the Member States. Paper presented at the SISP Conference.

Velicogna, M. (2014). Legal, material, spatial and temporal dimensions in EU Cross-Border e-Justice procedures. OAP proceedings.

Velicogna, M. (2021). Cross-border civil litigation in the EU: What can we learn from COVID-19 emergency national e-Justice experiences? *European Quarterly of Political Attitudes and Mentalities, 10*(2), 1–25.

Velicogna, M. & Contini, F. (2009). Assemblage-in-the-Making: Developing the e-Services for the Justice of the Peace Office in Italy. In *ICT and Innovation in the Public Sector* (pp. 211–43). London: Palgrave Macmillan.

Velicogna, M., Errera, A. & Derlange, S. (2011). e-Justice in France: The e-Barreau experience. *Utrecht Law Review, 7*(1), 163–87.

Velicogna, M., Errera, A. & Derlange, S. (2013). Building e-justice in Continental Europe: The TéléRecours experience in France. *Utrecht Law Review, 9*(1), 38–59.

Weick, K. E. (1995). *Sensemaking in Organizations.* Thousand Oaks, CA: Sage Publications.

Whipp, R., Adam, B. & Sabelis, I. (eds) (2002). Making Time: Time and Management in Modern Organisations. Oxford: Oxford University Press.

Yates, J. (2014). Time, History, and Materiality. In *Materiality and Time* (pp. 17–32). London: Palgrave Macmillan.

Zerubavel, E. (1982). The standardisation of time: A sociohistorical perspective. *American Journal of Sociology, 88*(1), 1–23.

Zerubavel, E. (1985). *Hidden Rhythms: Schedules and Calendars in Social Life.* Berkeley: University of California Press.

17 Organizational Memory as Technology

Mike Zundel, Sam Horner and William M. Foster

Introduction

Conceptions of organizational memory in management studies have evolved from early discussions of technical models, including how information systems designs function, like databases in which information is stored, retrieved or deleted (Brandon & Hollingshead, 2004; Lewis & Herndon, 2011) or, alternatively, how they function like storage-bin-type containers (Walsh & Ungson, 1991) which are navigated through maps that point to the location of distributed bits of knowledge. More recent work, however, has eschewed technological models in favour of the consideration of the human and social aspects involved in remembering. In this, organizational memory studies (Foroughi et al., 2020; Rowlinson et al., 2010) follow sociological approaches, in particular Halbwachs's (1992) conception of collective memory which, *inter alia*, shines a light on the distortive processes that accompany the reconstruction of memory.

Individual (Connerton, 1989) and organizational (Anteby & Molnár, 2012) processes of recollection are influenced by the collective processes that keep particular memories alive *within* groups, families and social classes, while also being coupled with the dialectically oppositional need and drive for unity and cohesion *across* such factions. Halbwachs, who had produced his work against the backdrop of two world wars and the Holocaust, and so having experienced propaganda, lies and demagogy, understood that the past is not a fixed or closed domain. Memory is selected and reconstructed actively, so that even the most intimate and personal recollections are mediated by ongoing and dynamic social processes, inscribed in physical and cultural-historical environments and brought to life through exchanges with others and with groups – each providing and developing frames of reference and interpretation.

Organizational memory studies have similarly begun to study processes of reinterpretation and reframing involved in remembering, and the social mediation and historico-cultural milieu indicated by myths (Sapir, 2020), symbols (Foster et al., 2011) and other collectively shared elements (Zundel et al., 2016), or in terms of the influence of organizations, institutions and ideologies. In this chapter we seek to extend the inquiry into organizational memory by asking about the role of technology, in particular what Mark Hansen (2014) calls '21st century media', which comprises a wide range of sensors, cameras and microphones which automatically capture data to guide (or replace) human decision making. Put differently, twenty-first century media operate at scales and sensory thresholds that are beyond the narrow bandwidth of human conscious grasp – and, yet, they have come to fundamentally shape our sensory experiences.

These technologies unsettle the idea of the predominance of human and social elements involved in memory and remembering as they indicate a growing 'tendency' towards operations that occur at a microtemporal scale without requiring or involving human perception and conscious awareness (Hansen, 2014, p. 37). For example, Hayles (2017, p. 42) compares the near instantaneousness of computational operations with the 'cost' of consciousness, which lags several hundred milliseconds behind perception, followed by processes of reasoning or negotiating, which take seconds, minutes or even longer. In comparison, digital machines operate in their own intrinsic instantaneous temporality, which Ernst (2013, p. 54) calls *Eigenzeit*. Digital media not only outpace human forms of noticing and contemplating, but they also play havoc with the all too human idea of the sequencing of time which, *inter alia*, underpins the possibility of a historical or mnemonic discourse made up of narrative accounts connecting the progression of things and events in more or less linear terms, indicated by the ubiquitous arrow of time. Digital media require neither arrows nor narratives; they do not have a history, nor do they store or preserve information in ways that can be arranged or sequenced – they merely compute, send and receive, instantaneously and infinitely, at least for as long as the apparatuses are switched on and programmes are not idling or, as de Vaujany and Mitev (2017, p. 382) have it, they generate 'a constant [informational] flow that is simultaneously and recursively materialised through media, most of which [is] now global'. In so doing, technical media do not just operate alongside human practices, but actively intervene in them by intersecting cognitive processes. For example, technical media can guide human action through recommender systems through which non-conscious cognitive processes generate outputs that are fed-forward to the 'screen' of consciousness for processing; can supplant human involvement by automatically and often pre-emptively taking action, such as in automatic trading or driving contexts; or can interact with human sense directly when we thumb 'mindlessly' through gamified interfaces.

These changes are profound because human communication is now mediated. It is simultaneously mediated technologically, externally, and through (or rather 'as') computable, networkable, disembodied and infinitely transferrable screen imagery that no longer requires or is capable of 'representing' anything (de Vaujany & Mitev, 2017). Digital technologies are, therefore, implicated in the growing distribution of human cognition and it no longer seems viable to configure technologies as mere supplements to mnemonic processes that are animated by conscious, deliberative social action.

These changes have significant implications for the possibility of memory in the context of organizations, which are by now deeply enmeshed with their technologized environments. Because twenty-first century media are no longer concerned with the storage of human knowledge and experience as was still the case with more traditional archives, libraries or even films, their mode is characterized by recycling and refreshing rather than the preservation of artefacts for the future (Ernst, in Hansen, 2014, p. 41; Kallinikos & Mariategui, 2011). The result is an organizational focus on data processing and the generation of immediate feedback loops. This means that alternative conceptions of organizational memory are required. In this chapter, we attempt to contribute to such a direction by outlining a technologized account of organizational memory first in terms of the influence of analogue and mechanical systems, and then with a view to identifying how these change with the onset of sensor and feedback-driven twenty-first century media.

Technological Memory

To set the scene for an investigation of computing and network-based conditions of organizational memory, we begin by outlining a technology-focussed account of memory involving pre-twenty-first century technologies. The philosopher Bernard Stiegler (1998, 2009, 2011) offers a theorization of the interplay of technology (he speaks of *technics* to refer to what he calls 'organized inorganic matter') and organized human development in which memory takes a central role. Particularly important for our purposes is that in this account memory is no longer purely something inside a person, such as *genetic* memory, which is stored and inherited through DNA, nor is it epigenetic memory, which comprises individually acquired experience stored in the central nervous system (and which cannot be inherited genetically). Stiegler identifies a third kind of memory involved in this human-technology nexus: knowledge inscribed in tools; an *epiphylogenetic* or *tertiary* kind of memory, which is exteriorized into instruments and so can be passed on to the next generation outside, as it were, of the human body. Tertiary memory is not a mere extension of the human body by technical means, and while it bears resemblance to Landsberg's (2004) idea of prosthetic mnemo-techniques by which 'societies, cultures and even individual persons systematically attempt to remember, as well as cultural strategies for passing on memories to future generations', it reverses the emphasis from the purposive or systematic attempts of humans and societies to remember but by stressing the ontologically prior nature of technology: first giving rise to the possibility of the creation, perseverance and development of humanity itself.

Stiegler discusses the importance of technics for human memory in some very dense sections towards the end of his book *Technics and Time, Vol 1* (Stiegler, 1998). From Husserl (1991) he takes the emphasis of the role of a 'big' or 'large' *now* of perception. The temporal object, such as a conscious or mental process such as memory that is extended through time is, for Husserl, constituted in its duration as a flux which is coincident with the flux of consciousness of which it is the object. An example is a melody, which is constituted only in its duration, hanging together with notes preceding and following it (Stiegler, 2009, p. 5). Husserl identifies with every present moment (with each originary impression), an additional element that extends that now; its 'just past' which is constitutive of the present. In the case of the melody, the 'just past' are the already disappeared notes that conjoin the present ones. Immediate perception therefore drags with it a 'comet's tail' of this immediate past, and the ensuing conjoining '*present+immediate past*' construct what Husserl calls '*primary memory*' – memory that constitutes an original impression. Husserl invokes the fading sound of a violin:

> When a tone dies away, it itself is sensed at first with particular fullness (intensity); and then follows a rapid weakening in intensity. The tone is still there, still sensed, but in mere reverberation (Husserl, 1991: 33).

The reverberation is therefore different from the perception itself, but as a memory it is neither 'really' present in retentional consciousness (*retentionales Bewußtsein*), nor is it a different tone in addition to the original one. Instead, the intuition of time, at any point, involves not just what appears to be enduring right now, but also what has just been. 'Primary memory or primary retention' names this immediate form of retention-coupled-with-perception, which differs from what Husserl calls 'secondary memory or secondary retention', which is detached from primary retention, existing only as a memory in the sense of a recollection of a past as a total temporal phenomenon that can come back into presence (*Wiedererinnerung*). Where primary retention names the tail of a reverberating note, secondary retention is like remembering a melody one has heard at a recent concert – it is therefore a selection – as everyone in the audience will retain something different from all the music played in the concert. Secondary memory is somehow *like* the '*perception+primary retention*' couplet, but it differs as it is merely a *represented* past, not a *perceived* past.

Stiegler then directs us to a later passage where Husserl asserts that both primary and secondary retention are also different from a third kind of memory, which is not lived or subject to an individual's own experience but retained through paintings or sculptures (which he refers to as image-consciousness, *Bildbewußtsein*). Primary and secondary retentions share a character of 're-presentation of something itself' – primary retention re-presents perception, while secondary retention re-presents a total temporal phenomenon. Images and sculptures, on the other hand, retain memory in an external (or exteriorized) way and it is precisely this third form of retention – through non-living things – that preoccupies Stiegler's own work.

Husserl directly opposes primary and secondary memory as separate forms of retention – but Stiegler instead argues that primary memory can be influenced by secondary memory. Here, we witness a profound shift in memory with the invention of, first, the analogue phonograph which has transformed the play of memory, imagination and consciousness as, for the first time in human history, the identical repetition of a temporal object became possible (Stiegler, 2011, p. 40). Perception can change, for example, when listening to the same recording of a song over and over again, always hearing new things in the same object (and also changing our anticipation of the next moments); and this is only possible through media (the recording as tertiary memory), where now both secondary and tertiary memories can influence perception in the now.

To understand the far-reaching implications of technical memory and, in particular (following Stiegler), their working as and through temporal objects, we need to follow Stiegler from Husserl to Heidegger – and so from the phenomenological concern for the living present in the former – to the consideration of the role of heritage in the latter.

Dasein (Heidegger's term roughly equating to the human being) comes into a world that is *always-already-there* (*ready-to-hand*); a world that it inherits without having experienced it directly (Stiegler, 1998, p. 140). Heidegger's *always-already-there*, what he calls 'world-historiality' (*Weltgeschichtlichkeit*), names this ghostly presence of the dead who have not entirely vanished because their traces remain for future generations. Rather than beginning afresh with each new generation – that is, beginning just with the genetic predispositions that are germane to the particular evolutionary stage of humanity's development – the *always-already-there* bestows individual humans their identity, their customs and manners, their speech and gestures. Dasein is being-thrown into a world and so inherits its past; it inherits experience in addition to genetic information, which allows it to become a 'who' – a child or grandchild, a member of a family, culture, city and so on, and even though this past is not anything the new earthling has lived, it is still *its* past. Having a past is a facticity, a sense of self and belonging, from out of which the self can project itself forth into its future; to become this or that person, and so to glance at possibilities that are rooted in their heritage: ways of being that arise out of the thrownness into a world that is already brimming with cultural life, recipes, traditions, labels and much more, even if none of these have been experienced by that individual themself. As heritage (past) and possibility (future) hang together so closely, it is therefore possible to say that ' . . . the past is not something which *follows along after* Dasein, but [it is] something which already goes ahead of it' (Heidegger, 1967a, p. 20, in Stiegler, 1998, p. 207).

Exteriorized Memory

Stiegler follows Heidegger in this analysis of heritage but accuses him of shying away from the most radical implication of the *always-already-there*, namely, that at the very ground of human being lie *material elements*, media, which convey traces of the dead:

> It is a memory that is neither primary nor secondary; it is completely ignored in Heidegger's analyses, as it was in those of Husserl, and yet it is immediately there in a tool; indeed it is the very meaning of a tool. (Stiegler, 1998, p. 254)

Like Husserl's pictures and sculptures which he excludes as mere image-consciousness from the conception of retention, Stiegler argues that Heidegger excludes the realm of the technical from the analysis of world-historiality. Instead, Heidegger retreats into a quite human concern of a totality (or finality), in which authentic beings run against the sway of what is already there. Put differently, an authentic life needs to be lived in view of the possibility of the end of that life (its own mortality), rather than in projecting one's future in terms of what has already been there; it is therefore precisely the 'being-having-been' that needs to be forgotten in order to regain a temporally authentic relation to one's own being.

In addition to the comings and goings of humans there is therefore an experiential (*epigenetic*) layer of life that is not lost with the living when they die; this layer conserves *itself* and passes *itself* down to future generations (Stiegler, 1998, p. 140). Stiegler attributes to this layer an active and ontologically prior character; not a biological programme (and not a process attributable to 'pure life', as experience cannot be inherited genetically) but instead:

> . . . a cipher in which the whole of Dasein is caught; this epigenetic sedimentation, a memorization of what has come to pass, is what is called the past, what we shall name the *epiphilogenesis* of man, meaning the conservation, accumulation and sedimentation of successive epigenesis, mutually articulated. (1998)

In identifying the importance of technics as a medium that allows for heritage, Stiegler follows the Heideggerian idea of Dasein being reliant upon a past, and that this past is not just what has been individually experienced. However, unlike Heidegger, Stiegler does not allow for Dasein to have its having-been on its own accord. In being more than its own past, Dasein is always-already technological; being happens amidst and as a result of tools. Any engagement with tools, even in their most basic form such as chipping a flint stone to develop sharp edges that can then be used in the collective organization of work (hunting, preparing food or carpeting), as well as conflict and exchange, involves remembering how the tool was made, how it was deployed and modified, so creating a form of memory that is inscribed in the activity of social life (Stiegler, 1998, 150–4).

We can now also see how Stiegler's account differs from Halbwachs's (1992) which identifies human interchanges as the basis for the development of self and culture (subject to the dialectic struggle between individual and collective forms of memory) and with much of the recent organizational memory literature similarly lacking engagement with the technological foundation of human (organized) memory. Stiegler, instead, locates a much earlier event – earlier even than the development of articulation and language – in the capacity to fashion and use tools. He goes as far as to suggest that it is not the human that invents the tool, but the tool that makes the human (or rather that the development of tools makes it possible for humans to emerge):

> Tertiary retention is in the most general sense the prosthesis of consciousness without which there could be no mind, no recall, no memory of a past that one has not personally lived, no culture. (Stiegler, 2011, p. 39)

It is, therefore, subsequent technological regimes that simultaneously open up new forms of cognition and linguistic expression. *Hominization* is, for Stiegler, inseparable from *technicization*; man is a technical animal. Humans depend on technical objects that preserve *epigenetic* experience outside of the body and so make *experience* available for future generations which is something genetic evolution is unable to do. The task, therefore, is

... to see in the instrument what truly sets in play the temporality of being, what regarding access to the past and, therefore, to the future, is constituted through the instrument techno-logically, what through it constitutes the historical as such. (Stiegler, 1998, p. 245)

Put in terms of our inquiry into organizational memory, the task is to begin to analyze technology no longer in terms of retention bins (i.e. Walsh & Ungson, 1991) or transactive memory systems that function akin to Husserl's secondary retentional systems, storing selective sequences from otherwise continually flowing primary perception. Instead, we are to accord technology a much more fundamental, foundational and transformative role in the organization of human activity – and of human consciousness as such. Put differently: something happens memorially from within the technological elements themselves: a mode of existence that is itself technological. The question of memory is therefore a question of technics.

The Pharmacological Function of Exteriorized Memory

To elaborate the role of exteriorized memory for our understanding of memory in organizations, we need to turn from simple tools (technical elements) to more complex machines, such as integrated information systems (technical ensembles) (see D'Adderio, 2003). A book retains speech in the same way in which the tool retains the gesture of the worker. As simple tools give way to machines and industrial complexes, the knowledge of generations of labourers passes into the machines, so that it is no longer possible to suggest that workers bear tools or operate machines, but rather that workers are now reduced to operating (Stiegler speaks of 'serving') technical ensembles (Stiegler, 2010a, p. 37). As machines and machine complexes get upgraded continually (a process Simondon, a philosopher of technology, calls 'concretization'), the worker does not. What resides in machines is 'human reality, the human gesture set and crystallized into functioning structures' (Simondon, 1958, p. 12, cited in Stiegler, 1998, p. 67).

Günther Anders (2016) even sees the human adopting a shameful position, finding itself falling further and further behind the capacities of technology which are updated continually while the worker is merely reborn, naked and wrinkly, from generation to generation with the same limited set of skills. Put in Stiegler's conceptual framing, the stock of tertiary knowledge, retained in massively growing knowledge and productive facilities comes at the expense of a loss of knowledge in the worker (which Stiegler calls proletarianization), now left merely to operate buttons and computer interfaces, so becoming unable to penetrate these surface-level inputs into otherwise incomprehensible machine operations. Even the engineers and other experts who design, maintain, repair and upgrade technological systems mostly do so by drawing on defined processes, manuals and by installing modular, black box systems (Stiegler, 2010a, p. 47).

All this points to a profound reorientation of memory systems, in particular, in the context of organizations which are replete with such technological ensembles which mimic and therefore retain human knowledge and action. Unlike individual machines which merely repeat tirelessly the gesture of a worker, ensembles are able to be continually upgraded and adjusted. This means that industrial technical objects have a consistency that goes beyond being tools, owing to their capacity to operate at their own accord, harbouring a self-determining logic that belongs to them alone: their own mode of existence (Stiegler, 1998, p. 68). Organizational memory is therefore no longer merely a retainer for selective human memory (such as the secondary kind of memory identified by Husserl, which retains certain elements of a wider flow of primary perceptions). Technical objects are a form of social memory – and they are part and parcel of a transformation from a version of humanness characterized by their bearing of tools towards machines (which are organized inorganic matter), taking the role of tool bearers. Conceptualizing organizational memory in terms of human and social processes or remembering alone therefore misses that humans are increasingly squeezed out of the processes involved in organizing technical knowledge. This is particularly so with digital media which are not only elements of control and surveillance (as, for instance, elaborated by Zuboff, 2018), but also, argues Stiegler (2016b, p. 80), effect the rise of stupidity and madness; a process of proletarianization that indicates the degradation of the reflective and expressive potential in societies.

At this point, it is helpful to turn to Stiegler's analysis of the effects of this industrialization of memory in terms of both its beneficial and negative effects. For this, Stiegler invokes the Greek term *pharmakon*, earlier used by Derrida, naming both a poison and its remedy, to indicate the relation between technology and humans whose duplicity is indicated both by a gain and a loss. Just as the growth of pharmaceutical chemistry brings both relief while turning health into a market, the act of writing exemplifies this pharmacological pattern as it involves a loss since it no longer makes necessary the practice of internal memorization, and a gain because it allows for the storage of information on paper: 'Tertiary retention is . . . what compensates for the default of retention – which is also to say, the loss of both memory and knowledge. But it is also what accentuates this loss (this default): it is a pharmakon' (Stiegler, 2016a, p. 17).

Writing is pharmacological in the sense that it takes something away (the need for, and eventually capacity of short term memory) while giving back something similar but different (long-term memory, exteriorized into a technical support); technics allow for the development and transmission of culture and science, and so for humans to become human; they provide a supplement for a lack (*de-fault*) and so give to humans the capacity to evolve by means other than life. Memory is key in Stiegler's account: 'content' that *could have been lived*, even if it was in fact not experienced (or lived) by consciousness – but which still informs consciousness as it is exteriorized into tools, machines and retentional devices (see Hansen, 2017, p. 170). But the deficit amasses as humans can no longer encompass these exteriorized memories,[1] instead relying on maps, index systems, tables and, increasingly, automated recommender systems as technical developments are unpredictable. There has also been a rise in mental illness, disillusion (owing to the standardization and marketization of belonging and desire) and what Stiegler (2016b, p. 26) calls 'algorithmic ill-being' as a product of large-scale automatization. Each new technology has the potential to bring about a new pharmakon, but what distinguishes the digital era from the book press, the gramophone or even the cinema is, for Stiegler, that the digital harbours a particularly destructive toxicity for social systems and democracy – and so they make it impossible (unlike in earlier technological developments) to find therapies that mitigate against their effects; that is to rewire the short-circuiting. Where the Industrial Revolution, for example, spawned debate about the tempering of profit, environmental deprivation and exploitation through tax systems, laws and social welfare programmes, an epoch of real-time adaptation and light-speed feed-forward processes – that is of full automation – obviates the deliberative and reflective processes required to develop and cultivate such slow human remedies. Knowledge, he says, takes time: time to think, to sleep and to dream (Stiegler, 2016a, pp. 50, 84).

Temporal Objects

To understand why Stiegler attributes such destructive power (or rather pharmacological toxicity) to digital media, it is necessary to briefly return to the question of memory as primary and secondary retentions as in

---

[1] Stiegler (1998, p. 68) makes the more radical claim that it is the human that supplements the absence of machines, up to the Industrial Revolution, by being a technical individual, right up to the point where the tool-equipped machine is no longer in need of such supplementation.

Husserl's experience and recollection of a concert, and Stiegler's tertiary extension through a phonographic repetition of the *same* temporal object. Perception, we recall, can change when exteriorized memory is presented again (even over and over). Stiegler calls the work of the phonograph a prosthesis of a 'singular type', one 'making it obvious' that it produces the recording of a track on a material object (Stiegler, 2011, p. 39). However, the matter gets more complicated when we turn from the simple and analogue phonograph to the cinema. Unlike the exteriorization of memory in music, the cinema brings a shift in the relationship between the three types of memory, as it connects disparate elements into a single temporal flux (Stiegler, 2011, p. 15). It does so by working with all three elements of memory whereby tertiary memory first roots secondary and primary memory in one another. The cinematic is so profoundly influential because it works precisely at the level of tertiary memory: a temporal object that coincides with consciousness which, in turn, is 'intimately penetrated and controlled by cinematic sequences' (Stiegler, 2011, p. 38). Put differently, for Stiegler, the temporal flux of cinema coincides with the spectator's consciousness – not, however, because cinema has adapted human memory, but because the work of consciousness 'is already somehow cinemato-graphic' (Stiegler, 2011, p. 87). This is so because any sense of '*We*', that is of a social body, of belonging, culture, history and scientific progress (but also Halbwachs's collective memory) is only possible because *epiphylogenetic*, technical memory provides access to a past that was never lived:

The process requires access to a false past, but one whose very falsity is the basis of an 'already-there' out of which the phantasmagorical inheritor can desire a common future with those who share this (false) past by adoption, phantasmagorically. (Stiegler, 2011, p. 90)

The trick performed by the cinema is to replace the source of the past that was not lived. Unlike earlier technologies like the phonogram, which for Stiegler, still worked as a prosthesis of a 'singular type' by 'making it obvious' that it produces the recording of a track on a material object (Stiegler, 2011, p. 39), the cinema does no such thing as the technology of the moving image now *coincides with consciousness* (with primary retention) which is equally, at its base, fundamentally artificial; that is, it is always-already modified and constituted through secondary and tertiary memory (i.e. it is always-already 'somehow' cinematographic).

The effects of this change are far-reaching. The formation of a self is, as we have seen, subject to engagement with tertiary memory – with the continually growing masses of things that are made available for experience through mnemonic devices – Heidegger's *always-already-there*.

Libraries, rituals, cultural practices, songs and stories preserve the collective memory of a '*We*' as a shared, common past which allows for the development of a shared desire of a common future (Stiegler, 2011, p. 88). Any self (the '*I*') is continually formed in relation to this *We* through processes of synchronization (Stiegler, 2011, p. 102) by which a self experiences these rituals, reads books or engages in social practices, but never totally fuses with the remnants of the old. And just like the *I* must remain partially undetermined to be part of a group, so the collective *We* also retains an open and developing character (Stiegler, 2011, p. 97). The collective *We* relates to a conforming *I* that is never fully formed and so capable of both continuation and novelty in a process of co-individuation – something Halbwachs had well recognized and precisely what Stiegler now sees as endangered with the cinema and the culture industries writ large, and with more recent digital media. The cinema (and as we will see, more recent digital developments) destroys these processes of self- and society-making (Simondon's 'co-individuation') as the cinema provides scripted and standardized versions of non-lived pasts – and of desired futures without requiring the deliberative, reflective and self-forming processes of synchronizing self and other. Retentions (tertiary memories) but also protentions (desires for futures) become standardized and, in Stiegler's analysis, fall under the control of marketing (Stiegler, 2020, p. 172). The cinema begins a process of confusion of primary and secondary retentions with tertiary ones – it is as if one has lived through the film; as if these memories are not just those of a collective *We* – from which every developing self has to choose elements, modify what does not fit, and so engage in a process of synchronization, but precisely this process is now short-circuited:

> ... just as the worker has been deprived of individual technical potential by machine tools, the subject-conscious-of-objects has become a consumer of products deprived of all possibilities of participating in the process of defining, constructing, and implementing the retentional criteria for a life of the mind. (Stiegler, 2011, p. 103)

Digital Memory Technologies

The structural workings of the cinema are now exacerbated by digital technologies and, in particular, social media, which equally bypasses the individuation processes that allow for the synchronized development of self and community (*I* and *We*) and instead short-circuit a pathway from commercial and political interests to the very process that produces the self. In addition to its implication on the formation of selves, digital media also impact the formation of democratic social bodies which, in mandating decision-making powers to elected representatives, require the possibility for participation through debate and reflection, which can only happen in the slow processes that mark political and social institutions and organizations (Stiegler, 2010b). Precisely this 'time delayed' mode, however, is now destroyed by the real-time workings of digital media, both in terms of the direct effects of memory systems that no longer merely store information but actively feed forward and so affect decisions through recommender systems (e.g. TripAdvisor, see Orlikowski & Scott, 2015), or directly (e.g. in automated trading, see Beverungen & Lange, 2018) and the real-time adaptation of politics to public opinion (e.g. whipped up on Facebook or Twitter).

Even darker than Stiegler's identification of the workings of digital media on consciousness are Mark Hansen's (2014) elaborations of the effects of what he calls twenty-first century media, a term comprising a vast array of digital developments from social media to the internet of things, sensors, platform ecologies and so on, on pre-, sub- or non-conscious processes. Twenty-first century media, for Hansen, represent a form of retention that is radically different from previous technologies. Not only due to their miniaturization, portability and the ubiquity of sensors that automatically gather, process and propagate data – making human behaviour itself a kind of archive (Hui, 2016, p. 316), but because – for the first time in human history – such processes unfold largely without humans having direct experience, awareness or even potential access to what is processed and computed. Galloway and Thacker (2007, p. 155) speak of the 'unhuman' qualities of networks which nevertheless do not exclude human decision and commonality:

Networks are elemental, in the sense that their dynamics operate at levels 'above' and 'below' that of the human subject. The elemental is this ambient aspect of networks, this environmental aspect – all the things that we as individuated human subjects or groups do not directly control or manipulate. (Galloway & Thacker, 2007, p. 157)

However, this unhuman element of networks does not mean that there is no connection to humans on the very elemental level. N. Katherine Hayles (2017, p. 10) – following the work of Andy Clark (2008) – argues that large parts of human awareness happen not on the conscious level, but as non-conscious operations at a level of neuronal processing which recognize patterns too complex, subtle and fast for consciousness to discern. These operations are crucial for the functioning of consciousness as such but not accessible to awareness. It is precisely here that Hansen diverges from Stiegler, suggesting that twenty-first century media directly mediate mediation itself (Hansen, 2014, p. 43). Put differently: while higher-level human processes associated with cognition, awareness or sensemaking are still involved, they are now intricately linked with immensely fast, distributed, parallel and now decentred processes:

> ... today's ubiquitous computational environments and bionic bodily supplementations operate more by fundamentally reconfiguring the very sensory field within which our experience occurs than by offering new contents for our consciousness to process or new sensory affordances for us to enframe through our embodiment. (Hansen, 2014, p. 45)

Only infrequently so far does organizational research probe into the material aspects involved in relaying information (de Vaujany & Mitev, 2017, p. 385), and yet the ubiquity of computational environments, particularly in organizational contexts which are replete with technological structures, has already given rise to a form of *experiential* computing, whereby embodied experiences are digitally mediated by everyday artefacts with embedded computing capabilities (Yoo, 2010, p. 215). More specifically, the ubiquity of everyday objects with embedded computing capabilities now facilitates a condition in which embodied human experience, manifest in relations between the body and 'the world' (e.g. relations between the body, time, space, others and things) is fully or partially mediated by digital technologies (Yoo, 2010). 'Computers' lurk in cars, televisions, watches, phones, doorways and traffic lights, and the process of computation is implicated (although often concealed) as we choose where to go, what to do, how to do it and when to do it (Hayles, 2017; Yoo, 2010). Therefore, in this mode of computing, technology is no longer an object of interpretation (Blagoev et al., 2018; Humphries & Smith 2014), nor is the experience of technology an end in and of itself; rather technology intervenes in, configures and shapes conscious experience (Yoo, 2010, p. 218).

Organizational scholars, echoing Stiegler's assertion that technics lie at the core of being, have suggested that the emergence of experiential computing constitutes an 'ontological reversal' insofar as information systems no longer function to represent preceding physical realities, but instead construct the physical environs in which humans act and experience (Baskerville et al., 2020). For example, new buildings or structures are typically rendered digitally through computer-aided design, their integrity and behaviour under different environmental conditions are tested through in-silico modelling, physical models which inform the discussions of designers and architects are produced by 3D printers: the building or structure is 'digital first'. Similarly, airline tickets are continually modified after they are 'issued' in connection with airlines' booking systems to reflect changes or cancellations, and despite their on-material and flexible nature, are translated into images on smartphone screens that open barriers at gates or transfer vaccination information (Baskerville et al., 2020; Boland et al., 2007). All this happens outside of and in excess of human perception and noticing, involving networks, data processing and a multitude of devices.

Despite this apparent ontological reversal, twenty-first century media equally offer a supplementation. These media have become unavoidable in many sensory engagements with the world – from finding one's way through maps on smartphones, trackers eliciting biometric data, media feeds purveying news or communication; to the many invisible assistants that keep cars on track, and recommender systems calculating ideal places to eat, sleep or live. These media therefore provide massively enlarged and microtemporally speeded-up access to the world but the pharmacological recompense is that these newly expanded sensory data can no longer be experienced directly and slowly through the human senses and so we require devices and interfaces to translate the sensory expansion so it can once again be experienced (retrospectively) by human senses.

Twenty-first century media therefore appear to offer a similar supplementary (exosomatizing) function to that of writing – by providing access to the very experiences that have been removed from human control and relegated to technology. But Hansen (2014, p. 50) identifies a crucial change in the supplementary pattern: while writing directly gives back what it takes away (a source of memory: first, natural and short term become artificial and long term), twenty-first century media constitute an indirect recompense: the waning powers of perception and the loss of control over one's non-conscious processes is not restored artificially but rather develops a *different* capability in its stead, one that is neither entirely human nor purely machinic. There simply is no perceptual access to these enlarged sensibilities – only their 'presentification' in humanly accessible form (heartbeats shown retrospectively as graphs or numbers; recommendations as rankings, and so on), but that is not even their point or purpose. Twenty-first century media no longer merely store memory, but are geared towards gathering microsensory data directly (bypassing consciousness) and then processing these to influence action and emotion (the re-engineered sensibility again bypassing consciousness) in real time:

... the technical sensors now ubiquitous in our lived environments are able to capture experiential events directly at the microtemporal level of heir operationality and – independently of consciousness's mediations – 'feed them forward' into (future or 'just-to-come') consciousness in ways that can influence consciousness's own future agency in the world. (Hansen, 2014, p. 52)

In distinction to Stiegler (and Heidegger's) notion of the 'already there', which forms one's tertiarily retained past but which the individual need not have experienced themself, Hansen (2014, p. 53) argues that it is now 'contemporary data of sensibility [which] can be defined as data that *cannot be directly lived* by consciousness' – nor *can* they ever be experienced or lived directly by consciousness. They simply fall outside of the realm of human consciousness.

Challenges for the Study of Organizational Memory

In the above sections we have elaborated a technical conception of memory. Stiegler's outline of tertiary retention has allowed us to shift the focus from primary streams of perception (experiencing a piece of music) and secondary retentive selections (remembering some elements from the experience) as the key aspects of human memory towards tertiary forms of retention. Tertiary memory is retained in elements other than life, be that tools or machines, or more direct technologies that memorize experience, such as the phonograph. Via Heidegger, we have elaborated the importance of the *always-already-there* – that is, the entirety of memories that allow for the formation of selves and societies (the co-individuation that synchronizes the *I* and the *We*). Stiegler's correction of Heidegger connects the *always-already-there* with tertiary memory: only what is retained outside of the human body can be conveyed from generation to generation, and this *epiphylogenetic* pattern of inheritance first affords the rise of the human as a bearer of tools. The onset of machines, however, adds a further twist, and via Simondon's 'concretization' we have seen how knowledge passes into machines which, as bearers of tools, engender their own modes of existence, leaving the human being to merely operate on the surface of complex technical ensembles, pressing buttons, turning levers or typing commands without, however, being able to penetrate, oversee or control the complexities of these new complexes. For Stiegler, a bleak picture emerges of humans bereft of control and sense of self, lagging behind autonomously improving technological apparatuses; idiocy growing from generation to generation. Finally, we turned to the influence of computing and digital media on memory. Via Stiegler's outline of the workings of the cinema, populating the *always-already-there* of a non-lived past with scripted and standardized memories, we arrived at Hansen's outline of twenty-first century media which are no longer geared towards storage of memory, but to collecting, processing and feeding back sensory data below and above conscious awareness.

The above sections no doubt represent a wild ride through a complex territory, but at the centre of all concerns is the question of memory –

exteriorized as consciousness or as raw sensations into technical media. To return to our concern with organizational memory, we therefore suggest that while the (re)current focus on human and social elements which we indicated via Halbwachs is interesting, it nonetheless merely covers a small aspect of what happens with and to memory in and through organizations, leaving the question of technology unanswered. In closing, we therefore want to outline a series of challenges for organizational memory studies, if this field is to attend seriously to *mnemotechnics*.

Reconfiguring Mnemonic Processes

The most significant implication for the concept of memory advanced here is that technics can no longer be configured as supplementary to mnemonic processes that are fundamentally social, but rather these social mnemonic processes are conditional upon technics. This claim requires a theoretical recalibration in the relation between the technological and the social in organizational memory studies. For example, the retention-bin analogy that lies at the core of functionalist memory studies (D'Adderio, 2003; Fiedler & Welpe, 2010; Walsh & Ungson, 1991) attends to the notion that memory may be exteriorized. However, mnemonic processes (e.g. acquisition and retrieval) are configured as conscious, deliberative processes undertaken exclusively by individuals or groups of individuals (Walsh & Ungson, 1991, p. 70). Similarly, interpretive organizational memory studies highlight the exteriorized aspects of memory through the notion of *mnemonic traces*, which may be 'maintained in objects of the world' such as archival documents, monuments and museums (Mena et al., 2016, p. 723). Within interpretive approaches, these material or objectivized mnemonic traces feature in the strategic and rhetorical work of managers, who might corral or discard these objects in the creation of social memory assets (Foster et al., 2011, 2017), or in the development of collective memory (Mena et al., 2016). More recently, organizational memory studies have sought to elucidate the active functions of technology in mnemonic processes, highlighting how technological affordances facilitate and constrain the process of organizational remembering (Humphries & Smith, 2014). While these developments move organizational memory studies towards a more symmetrical configuration of the social and the technical in mnemonic processes, the human and the organization remain the authors of memory, responsible for and capable of reconstructing the past *with* material rather than *from* material (Blagoev et al., 2018, p. 1761).

Here, we propose that materialist treatments of technology in organizational memory studies are challenged by twenty-first century media, which are computationally contingent and non-material, and therefore increasingly inaccessible to conscious perception (Faulkner & Runde, 2019). The ubiquity of these imperceptible, open, flexible, editable and communicative objects, present a condition in which human (and thus organizational) experience is always technologically mediated (Baskerville et al., 2020; Yoo, 2010). The Stieglerian notion of tertiary retention, in light of the features of digital objects, suggests that mnemonic processes are not accomplished *with* technology, but rather *through* technology. This configuration of memory as technologically contingent has implications for future research in organizational memory studies, across functionalist, interpretive, critical and performative traditions (Coraiola & Murcia, 2019; Foroughi et al., 2020) at the cognitive, organizational and environmental levels of analysis.

Future Research

First, at the cognitive level, organizational memory studies might take up a concern for the co-relation of humans and non-human media in ways that avoid privileging the human. One approach might be to conceptualize individuals and organizations as *exosomatic organisms*, that is, 'organisms whose survival depends on equipping itself with technical or prosthetic organs external to its own body' (Alombert & Krzykawski, 2021, p. 306). In configuring organizations as exosomatic organisms, it becomes possible to overcome the dualism that distinguishes organization from technology, and we are instead encouraged to adopt a relational unit of analysis that foregrounds the coupling of the organization and its technical organs. Research on organizational memory might ask how technical organs construct, influence and direct contexts of human reflection and deliberation. Future research might also attend more directly to the role of consciousness in mnemonic processes, which are typically assumed to be purposive, deliberative and strategic. For example, research might draw on Hayles's (2017) notion of cognitive assemblages to explore how non-conscious cognition, externalized in technological infrastructures, functions to guide and direct attention, and the implications of this for the strategic, rhetorical construction of collective memory. Others might focus on the processes of *exosomatization*, that is, 'the production of technical organs by living organisms' and the role humans play in setting up and maintaining technological systems (Beverungen & Lange, 2018). In the context of organizational memory studies, this would entail a focus on the ways in which memory is embedded in (intentionally or unintentionally) technological infrastructures and shed light on how memory embedded in technological contexts interacts with somatic memory in embodied contexts.

Second, at the organizational level, the idea of technology-as-memory might prompt consideration of the ways in which collective identities are technologically curated. Existing organizational memory research has identified how organizational actors engage in rhetorical mnemonic processes to construct, reconstruct and preserve organizational identity, and the implications for legitimacy (Zundel et al., 2016). However, the ideas we have advanced here suggest that the capacity to 'remember' strategically to affect identity may be problematic, since these processes themselves are conditioned by technology. Future research might explore how the capacity to establish identity claims is influenced by the degree of externalization of organizational memory. For example, research has indicated that material forms of memory are particularly important in identity (re)construction (Hatch & Schultz, 2017) and maintenance (Anteby & Molnár, 2012), but future research might go further in elaborating the notion of materiality, unpacking how the materiality of particular tools influences constructions of self and organization.

The notion of technical memory also has implications for research that has examined the role of mnemonic processes in the propagation of exploitative power dynamics (Anteby & Molnár, 2012). Specifically, if mnemonic processes can no longer be fully controlled or directed by human agents, then is the capacity to mobilize these processes for preserving unequal power arrangements undermined? With what implications for entrenched power arrangements? Alternatively, future research might build on the notion of proletarianization described above; that is, 'the process that deprives individuals and communities of their knowledge ... that occurs when the re-interiorization of knowledge externalized in technical supports is made impossible' (Alombert & Krzykawski, 2021, p. 320). In contemporary organizational settings, characterized by algorithmic management, particular rationalities and modes of ordering may be concealed from, imposed upon and internalized by workers. Research on organizational memory studies might explore the dynamics of this proletarianization, eliciting insights on how this insidious form of alienation might be resisted.

Finally, at the environmental level, it might be argued that exteriorized technical memory plays an active role in the collective memory-making process that drives the formation of societal logics (Ocasio et al., 2016). In light of this, future organizational memory research might explore the role of technology in shaping representations of the past. It might look at how technologically constructed representations are propagated, and (re)presented to social actors, and the impact this has in the construction of meta-narratives and the emergence of societal logics. As highlighted above, technological construction and propagation of representations of events increasingly unfold in temporal regimes that render conscious participation impossible – for example, the flash crash of 6 May 2010 (Lange et al., 2018). Future organizational memory research might consider how such novel temporal regimes function to undermine conscious reflection, deliberation and judgement which are central to strategic uses of the past. A key challenge for organizational memory studies, in light of technology-as-memory, concerns its role in cultivating wider reflection on the exteriorization of memory, the exclusion of the human from memorializing and the diminishing role of the social in the creation, maintenance and use of organizational memory.

References

Alombert, A. & Krzykawski, M. (2021). Lexicon of Internation: Introduction to the Concepts of Bernard Stiegler and the Internation Collective. In B. Stiegler (ed.), *Bifurcate: There Is No Alternative* (pp. 305–30). London: Open Humanities Press.

Anders, G. (2016). On Promethean Shame. In C. J. Müller (ed.), *Prometheanism. Technology, Digital Culture and Human Obsolescence* (pp. 29–96). London: Rowman & Littlefield.

Anteby, M. & Molnár, V. (2012). Collective memory meets organizational identity: Remembering to forget in a firm's rhetorical history. *Academy of Management Journal*, *55*(3), 515–40.

Baskerville, R. L., Myers, M. D. & Yoo, Y. (2020). Digital first: The ontological reversal and new challenges for information systems research. *MIS Quarterly: Management Information Systems*, *44*(2), 509–23.

Beverungen, A. & Lange, A. C. (2018). Cognition in high-frequency trading: The costs of consciousness and the limits of automation. *Theory, Culture and Society*, 35, 75–95.

Blagoev, B., Felten, S. & Kahn, R. (2018). The career of a catalogue: Organizational memory, materiality and the dual nature of the past at the British Museum (1970–Today). *Organization Studies*, *39*(12), 1757–83.

Boland, R. J., Lyytinen, K. & Yoo, Y. (2007). Wakes of innovation in project networks: The case of digital 3-D representations in architecture, engineering, and construction. *Organization Science*, *18*(4), 631–47.

Brandon, D. P. & Hollingshead, A. B. (2004). Transactive memory systems in organizations: Matching tasks, expertise, and people. *Organization Science*, *15*(6), 633–44.

Clark, A. (2008). *Supersizing the Mind: Embodiment, Action, and Cognitive Extension*. Oxford: Oxford University Press.

Connerton, P. (1989). *How Societies Remember*. Cambridge, UK & New York: Cambridge University Press.

Coraiola, D. M. & Murcia, M. J. (2019). From organizational learning to organizational mnemonics: Redrawing the boundaries of the field. *Management Learning*, *51*(2), 227–40.

D'Adderio, L. (2003). Configuring software, reconfiguring memories: The influence of integrated systems on the reproduction of knowledge and routines. *Industrial and Corporate Change*, *12*(2), 321–50.

De Vaujany, F-X. & Mitev, N. (2017). The post-Macy paradox, information management and organising: Good intentions and a road to hell? *Culture and Organization*, *23*(5), 379–407.

Ernst, W. (2013). From media history to Zeitkritik. *Theory, Culture & Society*, *30* (6), 132–46.

Faulkner, P. & Runde, J. (2019). Theorizing the digital object. *MIS Quarterly: Management Information Systems*, *43*(4), 1278–302.

Fiedler, M. & Welpe, I. (2010). How do organizations remember? The influence of organizational structure on organizational memory. *Organization Studies*, *31* (4), 381–407.

Foroughi, H., Coraiola, D. M., Rintamäki, J., Mena, S. & Foster, W. M. (2020). Organizational Memory Studies. *Organization Studies*, *41*(12), 1725–48.

Foster, W. M., Coraiola, D. M., Suddaby, R., Kroezen, J. & Chandler, D. (2017). The strategic use of historical narratives: A theoretical framework. *Business History*, *59*(8), 1176–1200.

Foster, W. M., Suddaby, R., Minkus, A. & Wiebe, E. (2011). History as social memory assets: The example of Tim Hortons. *Management & Organizational History*, *6*(1), 101–20.

Galloway, A. A. & Thacker, E. (2007). *The Exploit: A Theory of Networks*. London: University of Minnesota Press.

Halbwachs, M. (1992). *On Collective Memory*. Trans. L. Coser. Chicago: University of Chicago Press.

Hansen, M. B. (2014). *Feed-Forward: On the Future of Twenty-First-Century Media*. Chicago: University of Chicago Press.

Hansen, M. B. (2017). Bernard Stiegler, philosopher of desire? *Boundary 2*, *44*(1), 167–91.

Hatch, M. J. & Schultz, M. (2017). Toward a theory of using history authentically: Historicizing in the Carlsberg Group. *Administrative Science Quarterly*, *62*(4), 657–97.

Hayles, N. K. (2017). *Unthought: The Power of the Cognitive Nonconscious*. Chicago: University of Chicago Press.

Hui, Y. (2016). On the Synthesis of Social Memories. In I. Blom, T. Lundemo & E. Røssaak (eds), *Memory in Motion: Archives, Technology, and the Social* (pp. 307–27). Amsterdam: Amsterdam University Press.

Humphries, C. & Smith, A. C. T. (2014). Talking objects: Towards a post-social research framework for exploring object narratives. *Organization*, *21*(4), 477–94.

Husserl, E. (1991). *On the Phenomenology of the Consciousness of Internal Time (1893–1917)*. Trans. J. B. Brough. London: Kluwer.

Kallinikos, J. & Mariategui, J-C. (2011). Video as digital object: Production and distribution of video content in the internet media ecosystem. *The Information Society*, *27*(5), 281–94.

Landsberg, A. (2004). *Prosthetic Memory: The Transformation of American Remembrance in the Age of Mass Culture*. New York: Columbia University Press.

Lange, A.-C., Lenglet, M. & Seyfert, R. (2018). On studying algorithms ethnographically: Making sense of objects of ignorance. *Organization*, *26*(4), 598–617.

Lewis, K. & Herndon, B. (2011). Transactive memory systems: Current issues and future research directions. *Organization Science*, *22*(5), 1254–65.

Mena, S., Rintamaki, J., Fleming, P. & Spicer, A. (2016). On the forgetting of corporate irresponsibility. *Academy of Management Review*, *41*(4), 720–38.

Ocasio, W., Mauskapf, M. & Steele, C. W. (2016). History, society, and institutions: The role of collective memory in the emergence and evolution of societal logics. *Academy of Management Review*, *41*(4), 676–99.

Orlikowski, W. J. & Scott, S. V. (2015). The algorithm and the crowd: Considering the materiality of service innovation. *MIS Quarterly*, 39, 201–16.

Rowlinson, M., Booth, C., Clark, P., Delahaye, A. & Procter, S. (2010). Social remembering and organizational memory. *Organization Studies*, *31*(1), 69–87.

Sapir, A. (2020). Mythologizing the story of a scientific invention: Constructing the legitimacy of research commercialization. *Organization Studies*, *41*(6), 799–820. doi:10.1177/0170840618814575

Stiegler, B. (1998). *Technics and Time, 1: The Fault of Epimetheus*. Trans. R. Beardsworth & G. Collins. Stanford: Stanford University Press.

Stiegler, B. (2009). *Technics and Time, 2: Disorientation*. Trans. S. Barker. Stanford: Stanford University Press.

Stiegler, B. (2010a). *For a New Critique of Political Economy*. Trans. D. Ross. Cambridge: Polity.

Stiegler, B. (2010b). Telecracy against democracy. *Cultural Politics*, *6*(2), 171–80.

Stiegler, B. (2011). *Technics and Time, 3: Cinematic Time and the Question of Malaise*. Trans. S. Barker. Stanford: Stanford University Press.

Stiegler, B. (2016a). *The Age of Disruption: Technology and Madness in Computational Capitalism*. Trans. D. Ross. Cambridge: Polity.

Stiegler, B. (2016b). *Automatic Society, Vol. 1: The Future of Work*. Trans. D. Ross. Cambridge: Polity.

Stiegler, B. (2020). *The Nanjing Lectures 2016–2019*. Trans. D. Ross. London: Open Humanities Press.

Walsh, J. P. & Ungson, G. R. (1991). Organizational memory. *Academy of Management Review*, *16*(1), 57–91.

Yoo, Y. (2010). Computing in everyday life: A call for research on experiential computing. *MIS Quarterly*, *34*(2), 213–31.

Zuboff, S. (2018). *The Age of Surveillance Capitalism: The Fight for a Human Future at the New Frontier of Power*. New York: Public Affairs.

Zundel, M., Holt, R. & Popp, A. (2016). Using history in the creation of organizational identity. *Management & Organizational History*, *11*(2), 211–35.

Conclusion: Time and Political Organizing
Five Avenues for Further Research on the Way to Power and Emancipation

François-Xavier de Vaujany, Robin Holt and Albane Grandazzi

As we have seen in the context of this rich, edited volume, numerous ways are possible for the exploration of organization as time and the political description of this process as power, emancipation or ethics. A politics of time, at the intersection of critical management studies and process studies, is particularly promising. In this short conclusion, we would like to invite Management and Organization Studies (MOS) researchers to explore five continents: digitality, narrativity, materiality, time-space and subjectivity as five promising ways to think of a politics of organization as time.

Firstly, digitality, in particular digital images (see Barker, 2012 and Chapter 1, this volume, or de Vaujany, 2022a), are more and more central to our ways of working and organizing. Beyond a new visuality, they often settle new temporalities for what is produced through their happening, and these new temporalities also correspond to new forms of power, of agencement, of violences, of state domination. Images, their holes, folds or differential intensities, lines, speeds and rhythms, discipline and organize our lives in new ways (de Vaujany, 2022a). What happens in the world is the event of these images and their modes of existence. More work needs to be done by MOS scholars to understand the politics of images, their role and their possible domination of organizations and in organizing. What is decentered and how? In which way do our new Zoom-based remote ways of working become gradually image-based? With what consequences for ways of working and organizing? How do images (in particular digital images) observe and surveil each other? What are the new modes of legitimacy or alegitimacy at stake for management and managers? What is the temporal panoptic of our time, and with what role for digital images? More specifically, our selves are more and more quantified and produced by digitality and digital images. What is the importance of speed, rhythms and intensity in this process? In contrast, in what way do digital images contribute to new modes of indistinguishability of subjects and objects and of an atmopshericity of being(s)?

Narrativity is also another important issue when thinking about a politics of organization as time. If calculus has been and remains an important part of the *techne* of our time (see Heidegger, 1977; Ciborra & Hanseth, 1998; Ciborra, 2004, 2006), if technique sets forward and unveils the world in its punctual mobilization, digital technique is more and more a continuous narrative process, unveiling and revealing the world with a decentered set of narratives and images combined by digital infrastructures (de Vaujany, 2022b). Technique itself disappears, is miniaturized, grounded directly in bodies and gestures, invisible and folded in movements. Cognition is outsourced to it. Individuality becomes a digital event, or rather, the mattering of this digital event giving a sense, logic and narrativity to being. The world is told in a decentered way at least as much as it is calculated. The 'managerial apocalypse'[1] of our time is told and materialized in the same movement, narrated and visualized simultaneously. Managers and management continue territorializing and possessing this strategic futurity. This opening settles ephemeral pockets of time that are likely to be commodified and provides strategic directions for collective activity. But today's *One Thousand and One Nights* are not told any more by a clear, identifiable, unique Scheherazade. A multiplicity of people tells the story, and 'it' tells as much as 's/he' or 'they' tell and gives a sense to the world. How to explore these new strategic temporalities of management grounded in a new narrativity? What are the relevant methods? How are emancipations and subjectivations cultivated from within this movement of narration and non-narration (visuality being part of it and beyond narration)? How does the digital management of our present make the world ever more incomplete? How is our Anthropocene a temporal product of this new narrativity and futurist visuality? How to better inhabit our present and dwell in it?

Materiality is the third continent we invite MOS scholars interested in organization as time to explore. If being is a material present interwoven with the becoming of the world (Bergson, 1896; de Vaujany, 2022a), if events are concrete or material happenings (Whitehead, 1929; Wahl, 1932; Hernes et al., 2021), if in everyday organizationality time is materialized and performed as much as materialization is time[2] (de Vaujany et al.,

---

[1] From the Greek *Apocalupsis* (ἀποκάλυψις): revelation, disclosure, revelation.
[2] Parts of the literature deal with time as something performed by managerial techniques and devices (time as organization), and other parts of the literature adopt a more metaphysical approach of becoming and events as mattering (organization as time). If the former is rather constructionist, the latter is more processual. Both can result in very interesting discussions for a politics of time. Nonetheless, the former approach has been more implemented in MOS than the latter, and the chapters selected for this book were thus mainly focussed on organization as time.

2014), what is the power of these processes? What is the agency of this emergent materialization? How can emancipation happen from the within of the time-space mattering of the world (Barad, 2007)? How can it also happen in absence and silence, in the non-mattering of organizing (de Vaujany & Aroles, 2019)? If experience is propositional, made both of events and non-events proposing the world (Whitehead, 1938), how can emancipation occur from this paradoxical combination of emptiness and fullness? How can the re-exploration of the unaccomplished or unfulfilled events of the past (Ricoeur, 2000) help to cultivate emancipation and freedom in organizations? How can we renew our relationships with the future and its resonance with the past to space and express more emancipated selves?

Time-space is also a key dimension for further research interested in a politics of organization as time. Events and durations open sites, expand volumes, space experience and emplace people and things (Alexander, 1920; Whitehead, 1929; Czarniawska, 2004; Jones et al., 2004; Seamon, 2012, 2018; de Vaujany, 2022a). If temporality is primordial for the process of metaphysics and the phenomenologies mobilized in this book, flows and temporal trajectories are interwoven with spatial ontologies. On the way to a politics of organization as time, it is important to keep in mind that resistance often involves a spatial subjectivation (Revel, 2015). In this vein, how can happening, spacing and emplacing be jointly explored in the description of emancipation and freedom at stake in organizing processes? How to integrate time and space in the elaboration of a politics of digital organizing? What are the concepts likely to illuminate the time-space of collective activity?

Lastly (and we see our five avenues as deeply interrelated), subjectivity, subjectivation and ethics are another very important avenue for further political research about organization as time. As defended by Foucault, an important way towards a better world lies in 'acts of courage' and a 'work of the self on the self'. Subjectivation is a process from within (see Revel, 2015). But our digital or post-digital presents are obviously a new temporal order for such a work. What are the new attitudes, historicity regimes and eventalization at stake in this new present (de Vaujany, 2022b)? What are the new processes of organizing and modes of (self)management at stake? How can we imagine and create an 'ethic of the self'? How can MOS contribute to this movement? How can new ways of teaching and learning be settled in business school? New pedagogies focussed on this necessary ethics of care need to be experienced collectively.

The five aforementioned avenues for further research are particularly exciting tasks for MOS scholars. Beyond new theories and concepts, beyond more qualitative and ethnographic explorations of our digital world, they likely require a sense of experimentation. We need to experiment further with our colleagues, respective departments, techniques and narratives. We need a more playful relationship with time. A new sense of adventure.

References

Alexander, S. (1920). *Space, Time, and Deity*. London: Macmillan.
Barad, K. (2007). *Meeting the Universe Halfway*. Durham, NC: Duke University Press.
Barker, T. S. (2012). *Time and the Digital: Connecting Technology, Aesthetics, and a Process Philosophy of Time*. London: UPNE.
Bergson, H. (1896, 2020). *Matière et mémoire*. Paris: PUF.
Ciborra, C. (2004). Encountering Information Systems as a Phenomenon. In C. Avgerou, C. Ciborra & F. Land (eds), *The Social Study of Information and Communication Technology* (pp. 17–37). Oxford: Oxford University Press.
Ciborra, C. (2006). Imbrication of representations: Risk and digital technologies. *Journal of Management Studies*, *43*(6), 1339–56.
Ciborra, C. U. & Hanseth, O. (1998). From tool to Gestell: Agendas for managing the information infrastructure. *Information Technology & People*. *11*(4), 305–27.
Czarniawska, B. (2004). On time, space, and action nets. *Organization*, *11*(6), 773–91.
de Vaujany, F-X. (2022a). Imagining the name of the rose with Deleuze: Organizational and self world-making on the screen. *Culture and Organization*. https://doi.org/10.1080/14759551.2022.2105338.
de Vaujany, F-X. (2022b). *Apocalypse managériale*. Paris: Editions Les Belles Lettres.
de Vaujany, F-X. & Aroles, J. (2019). Nothing happened, something happened: Silence in a makerspace. *Management Learning*, *50*(2), 208–25.
de Vaujany, F-X., Mitev, N., Laniray, P. & Vaast, E. (2014). Introduction: Time and Materiality: What Is at Stake in the Materialization of Time and Time as a Materialization? In F-X. du Vaujany, N. Mitev, P. Laniray & E. Vaast (eds), *Materiality and Time* (pp. 1–13). London: Palgrave Macmillan.
Heidegger, M. (1977). *The Question Concerning Technology*. New York: Harper Perennial.
Hernes, T., Feddersen, J. & Schultz, M. (2021). Material temporality: How materiality 'does' time in food organizing. *Organization Studies*, *42*(2), 351–71.
Jones, G., McLean, C. & Quattrone, P. (2004). Spacing and timing. *Organization*, *11*(6), 723–41.
Revel, J. (2015). *Foucault avec Merleau-Ponty: Ontologie Politique, Présentisme et Histoire*. Paris: Vrin.
Ricoeur, P. (2000). L'écriture de l'histoire et la représentation du passé. *Annales. Histoire, sciences sociales*, *55*(4), 731–47.
Seamon, D. (2012). Place, Place Identity, and Phenomenology: A Triadic Interpretation based on J. G. Bennett's Systematics. In H. C. Israel & F. B. Portugal (eds), *The Role of Place Identity in the Perception, Understanding,*

and Design of Built Environments (pp. 3–21). London: Bentham Science Publishers.

Seamon, D. (2018). *Life Takes Place: Phenomenology, Lifeworlds, and Place Making.* London: Routledge.

Wahl, J. (1932, 2004). *Vers le concret: études d'histoire de la philosophie contemporaine: William James, Whitehead, Gabriel Marcel.* Paris: Vrin.

Whitehead, A. N. (1929, 2010). *Process and Reality.* New York: Free Press.

Whitehead, A. N. (1938, 1968). *Modes of Thought.* London: Simon and Schuster.

Index